NATURALIZING POWER

Naturalizing Power

ESSAYS IN FEMINIST CULTURAL ANALYSIS

Edited by

Sylvia Yanagisako *and* Carol Delaney

ROUTLEDGE

NEW YORK LONDON

Published in 1995 by

Routledge
29 West 35th Street
New York, NY 10001-2299

Published in Great Britain by

Routledge
11 New Fetter Lane
London EC4P 4EE

Library of Congress Cataloging-in-Publication Data

Naturalizing power : essays in feminist cultural analysis / edited by
  Sylvia Yanagisako and Carol Delaney.
      p.   cm.
  Includes bibliographical references and index.
  ISBN 0-415-90884-1 (pbk.) — ISBN 0-415-90883-3 (cloth).
  1. Feminist theory—Congresses.   2. Power (Social sciences)—
Congresses.   3. Kinship—Congresses.   I. Yanagisako, Sylvia Junko,
1945- . II. Delaney, Carol Lowery, 1940-   .
HQ1190.N37   1994
303.3—dc20   94-3573
                                             CIP

To David Schneider

In Diffuse, Enduring Solidarity

Contents

The American Dream: Gender, Class and Ethnicity

Preface

This volume grows out of a symposium, "Naturalizing Power: Conversations with David Schneider," that was held at the 1992 American Anthropological Association meeting in San Francisco. The essays by Phyllis Chock, Carol Delaney, Susan McKinnon, Rayna Rapp and Sylvia Yanagisako were given as papers there. The papers by Janet Dolgin, Sherry Ortner, Anna Tsing, Kath Weston and Brackette Williams have been added. One paper, by Esther Newton, which was a tribute to David Schneider's early encouragement for gay and lesbian studies, is not included here. As with those who presented papers on the panel, some of the contributors to this volume were students of his, others were not, but all of us have been influenced by his work.

Just as David Schneider's questioning of the universal, genealogical basis of kinship denaturalized kinship and displayed its cultural foundations, these papers scrutinize a number of seemingly natural identities and institutions—including gender, kinship, nationality, ethnicity, religion and sexuality.

In his cultural analysis of American kinship, Schneider demonstrated that a particular folk model of heterosexual reproduction lies behind assumptions of the genealogical grid. In a more graphic vein, he tried to explain that the thin red fluid we call blood does not make ties strong; the ties that bind are in culture, not nature. That is, blood *symbolizes* kinship rather than constitutes it. By explicating the symbolic system through which Americans construct seemingly natural relationships of shared bio-genetic substance, Schneider opened up the possibility for anthropologists to explore other areas in which social relations are naturalized.

Schneider did not address the question of how inequality is embedded in the cultural system of American kinship. Yet his explication of the folk model of biology underlying both anthropological and American cultural models of kinship laid the groundwork for analyses that link ideologies of biology and nature to systems of inequality.

Feminist anthropologists have been at the forefront of this analytic venture, initially because of our interest in gender inequality. We have added to Schneider's analysis the insight that inequality and hierarchy come already embedded in symbolic systems as well as elaborated through contextualized, material practices. Because of our interest in understanding the relation between gender and other forms of inequality, feminist anthropologists have begun to explore the ways in which other relations of inequality are naturalized.

The papers in this volume analyze a variety of cultural practices in which inequality and hierarchy appear to be logical consequences of people's identities and the order of things. The natural order that people and institutions are perceived to reflect is sometimes construed as rooted in biology, sometimes as functional and rational, and sometimes as god-given.

The American kinship project was launched at the University of Chicago in the 1960s—a time thought to be pretty radical. Neither David Schneider nor his colleagues could ever have foreseen that the truly radical implications of his cultural analysis would be picked up by feminist anthropologists; even less could they have imagined that thirty years later a group of feminist anthropologists would form a panel at the AAA meetings and publish a volume to tell him where their conversations with him are taking them.

Naturalizing Power

Sylvia Yanagisako and Carol Delaney

The essays in this volume explore ways in which differentials of power come already embedded in culture. That is what we mean by *naturalizing power,* for power appears natural, inevitable, even god-given. The focus of these essays is those domains in our society that are crucial for people's identity—family, sexuality, race, nation, religion.

The question of identity has always been important, and in the past few years it has come to the forefront of academic and popular discourse in our society. A good deal of the concern with identity obscures the fact that the question "Who are we?" entails the questions of origin, "Where did we come from?" This in turn implies a question of orientation: "Where are we going?" The concern today is an indication that we have lost our way; we don't know where we've come from or where we are going, and thus we do not know who we are. The problem is ontological as well as social—just who is the "we," anyway? Not only has it seemingly become problematic to assume a "we," but many people appear to have lost ways of knowing how to think about who the "we" is—that is, of forming bases of community and solidarity—except in the most narrow and constricting of essentialisms.

Answers to each of these questions involve biological, social, and ontological dimensions which, in any one person, were once assumed to be coterminous even though they could be separated analytically. Today, however, with the increasing circulation of peoples globally, identities are being fragmented, hyphenated and in conflict, and can no longer be put back together in the same old way. The verities on which identity—whether of gender, sexual orientation, nationality, ethnicity, or religion—have traditionally been based no longer provide the answers, in part because of the contact and conflict between peoples and in part because the explanatory schemes upon which identity was based have been shown to rest not on the bedrock of fact but suspended in narratives of origin.

Narratives of origin tell people what kind of world it is, what it consists of, and where they stand in it; they make it seem natural to them. By anchoring individual lives to some kind of larger, cosmic order, identities are secured (Geertz, 1973:90). Within the context of origin stories, people spin meaningful lives. Narratives of origin incorporate classificatory schemes that describe the order of things, as well as the relations between things and between different kinds of people. For people whose origin story it is, these schemes take on aura of the sacred. As Mary Douglas pointed out some time ago: "holiness consists in keeping distinct the categories of creation" (1966:53).

When the order is disrupted or when people are uprooted from the sites where these stories and identities make sense (such as is occurring with the contemporary movement of peoples on a world-wide scale), then not only are identities challenged but so too the hegemonic order. For some people this situation contributes to an erosion of faith in the explanatory schemes, while for others it leads to championing their own particular visions more emphatically—as, for example, in the reinvigorated debate between creationists and evolutionists.

Origin Stories

Origin stories are a prime locus for a society's notion of itself—its identity, its worldview, and social organization. Anthropologists often include origin stories of the peoples they study, recognizing, after Malinowski, that "an intimate connection exits between the word, mythos, the sacred tales of a tribe, on the one hand, and their ritual acts, their moral deeds, their social organization, and even their practical activities, on the other" (1954:96). Yet these same anthropologists hesitate at the threshold of their own society, reluctant to explore their own origin myths (whether religious or scientific), as these have naturalized their own world view. They have treated their own origin myths as taboo—set apart and sacred—under the notion that their stories of origin are, in some sense, real and true while those of others, especially primitive others, are myth and superstition. This view is, itself, embedded in an evolutionary paradigm—first there were myths, then religion, and finally science. Myths are something relegated to the dim past, something we have outgrown. Because of the lingering view of myth as false stories, we have ignored the extraordinary power of myth to provide identity to a community and meaning to individual lives.

We propose to treat origin stories neither as false tales nor as possible windows into real true origins, but as *representations* of origins. Stories of origin are told to every generation and thus affect how people imagine themselves to be. New contexts and changed circumstances can imbue the stories with new meanings and generate new interpretative challenges; in the process both the understandings and the stories can be transformed.

Stories of origin have to do with notions of "coming-into-being," simultaneously physiological, social, and ontological. Yet while all peoples have origin stories, origin stories are hardly the same world-wide. Not only do the specifics vary by culture but so too the form; for example, not all origin myths are myths of creation. Anthropologists and others have often carelessly elided these two ideas—origin and creation—without realizing that the different assumptions and trajectories inherent in each type have different implications (for example, for notions of time and history). In other words, the assumptions embedded in the origin stories have wider ontological meaning that affects the way the world is conceived. Rather than a story of creation, for example, some stories of origin imagine emergence from underground, others the perpetual transformation of one thing into another. A monistic or pantheistic system has quite different implications from one in which a Creator creates a world which is not only different from but dependent on that Creator.

The notion of Creation is part of the dominant origin narrative in the West—the story is told in Genesis, common to both Jews and Christians, and in a slightly different way to Muslims. It is unlikely that devout Jews and Christians would accept a Hopi or Australian aboriginal origin myth as a replacement for Genesis. Because of our embeddedness in a monotheistic system, we often assume there must be one origin myth, yet a number of cultures have a variety of origin stories to describe the origin of a variety of things. Origin myths, precisely because they hook individual identities to ontological realities, are not substitutable; they describe the natural and supernatural orders that people often fight over and are willing to die for.

In the story told in Genesis, God created the world and everything in it. He did it by himself; he had no partner. Nor did he create it out of himself, but by fiat, by his word. The world (nature) was created material, dependant for its existence upon the Creator and subordinate to Him. In the biblical story, God is symbolically masculine while nature becomes symbolically feminine, and these symbolic associations have implications for the way men and women are imagined to be. In this origin myth, Man was the epitome of creation and often imagined as the mediator between God and nature; Man was given dominion over nature and ordered to increase and multiply. Yet the *power* to procreate was given to the male of the species.

Nature, in this cosmological picture, has a very specific meaning and place—a place and meaning it could not possibly have in a dualistic or pantheistic worldview. In the biblical world view, God's order and plan were imposed or implanted in the world, and the world of nature obeyed God's commands. What was "natural" was god-given. Early modern scientists such as Bacon, Copernicus and Galileo assumed they were discovering God's order when they explored nature. That is to say that the nature they were exploring was already of a specific kind, and imbued with a specific form.

From the Order of Creation to the Natural Order

In the nineteenth century the Biblical worldview began to collapse and God began to drop out of the picture—at least among certain members of the intellectual elite—and what was left was a rule-governed Nature, Nature stripped of its cosmological moorings and therefore presumably generalizable to all peoples. Rather than the dichotomy between the natural and supernatural, what was left was "nature" vs. what man did with it—namely, "culture." This move obscured the specificity of the concept of "nature." It precluded an awareness that it could not possibly have the same meaning everywhere. But without a similar notion of nature, could "culture" have the same meaning? Culture, for us, is after all dependent on this concept of nature. What is considered "natural" cannot be assumed *a priori*, as Strathern (1980) has so convincingly argued in "No Nature, No Culture." Indeed, how could nature and culture be considered universal categories in vastly different world views? The fact that the opposition nature-culture derived from and related to a very specific world view at a specific historical moment went unnoticed, and instead its supposed universal character became part of the assumptions and project of anthropology.

The nature-culture dichotomy, we suggest, was a precipitate of the upheavals in 19th century European and American society. The turmoil within these societies—due to industrialization, questions about slavery and women's rights as well as increased contact with other peoples and other classificatory schemes—all worked to call into question the basis of their own. The biblical world view that had provided the master narrative within which individual lives were placed and found meaningful was being undermined from within and without. Biblical scholars began to question the origin and composition of the text and suggested that, rather than the Word of God transmitted directly to Moses, it was composed from fragments of different provenance. Discoveries of ancient, sophisticated and literate cultures in the ancient near east challenged the biblical view of ancient society and, especially as a number of parallels to the stories in Genesis began to emerge, the Bible's claim to uniqueness was severely undermined. As the foundations of the 19th-century Euro-American world were crumbling, social philosophers—Bachofen, Darwin, Maine, Morgan, and others—scrambled for more solid ground, which they felt would be provided by science. They sought scientific explanations for origins. The extent of their anxiety can, perhaps, be gleaned from the number of titles directly related to origins—of society, of species, of institutions such as marriage and the family, and of the world itself. Determined to get to the bottom, they searched for scientific bedrock on which to build a more secure order. In the process, however, many assumptions and categories of the biblical order were unwittingly built right back into the foundation. Rather than being spurred to question their own schemes they anxiously responded to the disruptions "by constructing *evolutionary* accounts of 'how it all began' " (Collier, Rosaldo, and Yanagisako, 1982:6), both at the human and non-human levels. But in the shift from the biblical account to an evolutionary one, something of the god-given quality remained—that is, the accounts appeared to *naturalize* the orders of creation.

The social was embedded in the natural, but in a particular version of it. The vision of nature that permeates both the social and the natural accounts is of the Hobbesian variety—the struggle for survival in a situation of scarce resources, with self-interest as a motivating force. This vision of the socioeconomic order was then read into the natural world. Marx, the first to point this out, noted: "It is remarkable how Darwin recognizes among beasts and plants his English society with its divisions of labor, competition, opening of new markets, 'inventions' and the Malthusian 'struggle for existence'. It is Hobbes 'bellum comnium contra omnes' " (quoted in Sahlins, 1976:53). But in this struggle, not only did Man just naturally arrive at the top of the "tree of life," but so too did the white Euro-American represent the epitome of civilized Nature.

"We are the only people who think themselves risen from savages; everyone else believes they descend from the gods" (Sahlins, 1976:52–53). Yet, ironically, the title of Darwin's book on human origins was *Descent of Man*, rather than *Ascent of Man*. In Darwinian theory the natural order retained both the hierarchical order of Creation and its god-given quality; the difference is that the power no longer came from God, it came from Nature. No longer did the principle of "divine election" determine who would be saved; instead "natural selection" determined who would survive.

The secularization of the hierarchical order of Creation was exemplified in social evolutionary models such as that constructed by Morgan. Morgan's goal was to find the origin of the American Indians and through them, perhaps, the origin of and the relationship between all the races of mankind. When he realized that the Iroquois system of relationship differed in important respects from the system with which he was familiar—the European system of kinship—he thought he had discovered the method of arriving at an answer to his questions. Morgan made several crucial assumptions. First, he assumed that in kinship terminology systems the oldest memorials of human history were deposited and one needed only to find the key to tap this vein. Second, and like many others at that time and since, he assumed that kinship was a matter of blood and sex, and therefore he reasoned that different systems reflected different forms of marriage—forms that would obscure the "real, true" blood relations. These, of course, were known to the Euro-Americans, and the acquisition of that knowledge was felt to constitute one of the great achievements of humankind. Finally, he assumed that even though the vocabulary might change, the *structure* of the various systems might provide a means to trace the ancient divergence of nations from least complexity to the most. At a later date, he construed these differences in evolutionary sequence and ranked the peoples of the world in hierarchical order. Not surprisingly, the Australian aborigines came to occupy the lowest rung, as they did in numerous other studies of the time, whereas the Euro-Americans were at the summit. Kinship, which has been at the core of anthropology since the nineteenth century, has been a primary site for the development of a natural progression that echoes the hierarchical order inherent in the Great Chain of Being.

What is More Natural than Sex?

Evolutionary theory or ideas have so permeated human consciousness in the West that it has seemed "natural" to compare human society and behavior to that of animals. Once this projection has been effected "the same theories are transferred back again from organic nature into history and it is claimed that their validity as eternal laws of human society has been proved" (Engels quoted in Sahlins, 1976:54).

Especially are sex and reproduction held to be quintessentially natural activities; indeed they are considered our "animal" behavior. And when we attempt to answer the child's perennial question "Where did I come from?" we often employ metaphors that claim parallels between humans and the animal kingdom such as "the birds and bees." Knowing that this was the cultural euphemism for "sex education," Sylvia Yanagisako and her sister, as teenagers, jokingly berated their father for his failure to tell them about "the birds and the bees." They were surprised when their usually untalkative father agreed that he had been remiss and decided that it was time to do so. They became even more incredulous as he proceeded in a very serious and ponderous tone and were totally unprepared for his concise summation of the "facts of life." "The average bird," he said, "is bigger than the average bee!" Although he was making fun of the association, this joke would totally backfire in cultures where the association between animal reproduction and human "coming-into-being" is not made. This has been humorously recounted by David Schneider in describing his perplexity when confronted by 'obviously' contradictory statements of the Yap about procreation.[1]

First, Schneider said, there is "the *simple* question of whether coitus did or did not result in pregnancy" (1968:127, emphasis added). The Yap (a group of people living on an island in the Pacific) told him of all the promiscuous women who nevertheless remained childless "and, they added, quite properly too, for women as promiscuous as they could never be rewarded for such behavior." To prove their point that the connection (between coitus and pregnancy) is not necessary, they went on to point out a very ugly woman with whom no man would think of engaging in sexual relations, yet there she was with two children. What complicated the problem, however, was when he came upon several men removing the testicles of a pig.

> "Always the anthropologist, I did not assume that I knew why; I asked. Makes the pig grow much bigger, they said. But, said I slyly, could a sow ever get pregnant from such a boar? Not from that one! they affirmed. It needed a boar whose testicles had not been removed. I was unnerved, I admit. So I went back over the whole matter slowly and carefully. Castrate the pig and he grows larger than if he not castrated. Right! But a castrated pig cannot get a sow pregnant. Right! And then they added once again, if you want a sow pregnant you must get her to a boar which has not been castrated. They copulate, the sow gets pregnant, the pigs are born.
>
> But, I protested, everyone has been telling me that coitus does not make women pregnant. That is correct they said. But they were puzzled and so was I . . . I had presented them, I felt, with logically inconsistent statements that fairly cried out for explanation. They could not see what my problem was since they had provided me with the full array of necessary, correct facts and to them there was no problem. So we kept at it until I again put the contradiction to them. . . . suddenly one man saw what my problem was, for he put it plainly and emphatically: *'But people are not pigs!'* (Schneider, 1968:127–28, emphasis added)

Schneider goes on to say that "once that point was made, the rest followed in happy, logical order. I had obviously assumed that biological processes operate for all animals and had included man among them. But they had assumed that no one but a fool would equate people and pigs" (ibid. 128).

So thoroughly has the process of naturalizing sex and reproduction been accomplished that it is difficult for a Westerner to realize this has not always been the case. "Reproduction" as the term to refer to the process of coming into being came into use in the 19th century and was at first considered a quaint *metaphor,* hardly a description of fact. The metaphor consisted of analogizing human procreation to that of animals and plants. Previously the process was discussed in one of three ways: in terms of procreation, with clear allusion to Creation; in terms of generation, with the stress on generativity; or, more simply, the biblical "begetting and bearing," highlighting what were conceived to be the male and female roles in the process. These roles clearly had very different meaning and value. In Genesis only males beget, and there are long chapters of who begat whom as the basis of the patrilineage. Women, in contrast, were those who bear; they were conceptualized as the *means* through which what was begotten comes to be.

This is not unlike the Aristotelian explanation of human procreation in *Generation of Animals* (1979), another extraordinarily influential text that naturalized male power as it constructed notions of gender that have persisted, in one form or another, to this day. Supposedly a work that was empirical and biological, *Generation of Animals* incorporated a number of prior assumptions that framed the evidence. By virtue of their power, men were thought able to heat the blood so that it would become more concentrated (concocted) as it evolved into the essence of semen. The female analog, menstrual blood, remained in an undifferentiated state and was the matter that semen in-formed. Semen was imagined to impart the form as a carpenter or artist gives form to a block of wood (Aristotle, 1979:113). Nothing physical or material passes between one and the other. While menstrual blood was the source of the "nutritive soul" (that which distinguishes the living from the non-living), semen was the vehicle through which the sentient soul (that which distinguishes animals from plants) and the rational soul (that which distinguishes humans from animals) were allegedly transmitted.

Although all women have sentient and rational souls, according to Aristotle, they receive them from their fathers; women, therefore, depend on men for their full humanity. Because the rational soul was free of its physical element (transmitted through the semen but not of it) Aristotle imagined that it was related to the eternal and divine; it was seen as analogous to an element belonging to the stars, "ungenerated, indestructible and divine" (Aristotle, 1979:171).

> "That is why in cosmology they speak of the nature of the earth as something female and call it mother while they give to the heaven and the sun and anything else of that kind the title of generator and father." (ibid. 11)

This is not so different from Bachofen's statement in the 19th century: "Triumphant paternity partakes of the heavenly light, while childbearing maternity is bound up with the earth that bears all things" ([1861] 1973:110).

Aristotle's views were reintroduced to the West by Muslims in the Medieval period. A number of eminent Christian, Jewish and Muslim theologians—Aquinas, Albertus Magnus, Giles of Rome, Maimonides and Ibn Sina, Averroes—utilized his theories not just to systematize theology, but to rationalize the social implications of these patriarchal religious traditions. This included rationalizations of notions of gender, including that of God. Aquinas, for example, argued that the attribute of "Father" was not symbolic but represented a real quality: "for we can say that paternity is God, and that paternity is the Father" (*Summa Theologica*, I, q.32, a. 2).[2]

Men and women became defined by and identified with what they contributed to procreation. In contemporary Euro-American belief, "reproduction" has been reduced to its natural character and is associated with women; women have been defined by and confined to their reproductive role. Men, on the other hand, have not been so confined because a man need not become a father to partake of the power assigned to the male role in procreation; instead that power is abstracted and generalized as creativity, productivity, genius.

Gender definition and value have been inherent in the Western theory of procreation, but procreation is not just about the natural; it includes an ontological dimension. Because gender is at the heart of these socio-religious systems it is not surprising that issues of gender and procreation—marriage, family, birth control, abortion, sexuality, homosexuality, new reproductive technology—are at center of contemporary debates in our society, for new beliefs and practices are not just about the private, domestic domain, but challenge the entire cosmological order.

Blurred Boundaries

By bringing to light the gender definitions and values inherent in theories of procreation—both ours and those of others—feminist cultural analysis challenges the assignment of sex and reproduction to the category of "biology." As with our rejection of the assignment of women and families to a "domestic" domain that stands in opposition to a "politico-jural" or "public" domain (Yanagisako 1979, Yanagisako and Collier 1987), this calls into question the analytic domains conventionally used by social scientists as well as by those they study. We argue instead that cultural domains, like social institutions, are human-made and only appear to be natural.

Our challenge to conventional distinctions among analytic domains has been incited, in good part, by David M. Schneider's denaturalizing of kinship through his questioning of its supposed universal, genealogical basis (1964, 1968, 1972, 1984). Until Schneider demonstrated that anthropological kinship theory was rooted in the cultural system of symbols and meanings to which most North Americans ascribe, anthropologists assumed that all people who knew the "facts of life" reckoned their kinship relationships using a genealogical grid in which relations of blood (consanguinity) and marriage (affinity) were mapped. The genealogical relation between any two individuals could be determined using combinations of the basic units of father, mother, husband, wife, son and daughter (Schneider 1984). Any particular kinship system was thought to be a cultural elaboration of the biological facts of human reproduction, and anthropologists recognized that there were significant differences in how far out these genealogical maps extended and how the relations in them were classified. But these differences, which constituted the basis of anthropologists' classifications of "kinship terminological systems," were considered variations of "The Genealogical Unity of Mankind" (Schneider 1984).

In contrast to other people's "classificatory" systems of kinship terminology, which lumped together categories of kin that we would keep separate, our "descriptive" system of kinship terminology was viewed as accurately representing natural categories.

> "As a system it is based upon a true and logical appreciation of the natural outflow of the streams of blood, of the distinctiveness and perpetual divergence of these several streams, and of the difference in degree, numerically, and by line of descent, of the relationship of each and every person to the central Ego. It is therefore a natural system, founded upon the nature of descents and may be supposed to have been of spontaneous growth. (Morgan 1870:468)

The "natural system" to which Morgan referred was, we now recognize, a cultural system of symbols and meanings which attributed to "the streams of blood" connections of diffuse, enduring solidarity.

Schneider's argument that kinship theory in anthropology is rooted in the beliefs of our own cultural system has led feminist anthropologists to recognize that similar assumptions pervade anthropological analyses of a number of other institutions and cultural domains. Like other symbolic anthropologists of the 1960s and 1970s, Schneider did not address the question of how inequality is embedded in cultural systems—including its categories of persons and domains—in part because he did not follow out the logic of the specificity of symbols, but instead made abstractions of them. He failed to explicate the meanings of other crucial elements besides "blood" in the "facts of life" out of which American kinship is constructed, such as the different and differentially-valued contributions of fathers (generative seed) and mothers (nurturant soil) in the creation of babies (Delaney 1986; 1991). Likewise, though he recognized that coitus is a key symbol of American kinship, he overlooked the gender hierarchy entailed in most Americans' expectations about who should be "on top" in sexual intercourse. Yet Schneider's explication of the folk model of biology underlying both anthropological and American cultural models of kinship laid the groundwork for analyses which link ideologies of the "natural" to systems of inequality.

Because of our commitment to challenging the gender status quo, feminist anthropologists have been at the forefront of these attempts to situate ideologies of natural identities within structures of inequality. We have brought to cultural analysis the insight that hierarchies of status and power come already embedded in symbolic systems which, however, can be known only through contextually specific cultural practices. This has proven a crucial step in the development of critical analyses of ideologies of character, power, and substance, especially in the realm of kinship and gender (see for example Delaney 1986 and 1991; Strathern 1988 and 1992; Yanagisako and Collier 1987).

If the meanings of "male" and "female" are not, as we have shown, just about natural differences, this prompts us to explore the ways in which these meanings articulate with other inequalities which are supposedly structured by other differences. We need to ask not only how these other inequalities are themselves naturalized—i.e, made to appear the logical outgrowths of other "facts of life"—but how their distinctiveness from gender is naturalized. This has led us to critically examine the boundaries between gender and other categories of difference. Among these are sexuality, race, nation, ethnicity, and religion. As Schneider has noted, since the mid-nineteenth century anthropologists have viewed institutions and cultural domains as the basic building blocks of society. The "quartet of kinship, economics, politics, and religion" (Schneider 1984:181) was purported to fulfill functions considered indispensable to the orderly reproduction of society. Despite the shifts in anthropological theory in the nineteenth and twentieth centuries, this traditional quartet has proven resilient. Yet, it has never been clear where one cultural domain ends and another begins. In our own society, for example, rules and practices of property inheritance blur the boundaries of the domains of kinship and economics. "Ancestor worship"—a term formerly popular in the comparative study of religion—challenges the distinction between kinship and religion.

Previous works, including those by some of the authors in this volume, have demonstrated the benefits of investigating the permeability of cultural domains and their mutual structuring (see Strathern 1981 on kinship and social class; Yanagisako 1985 on kinship and ethnicity; Yanagisako and Collier 1987 on kinship and gender; Delaney 1991 on kinship, gender, and religion). A productive question is to ask how culturally-specific domains have been dialectically formed and transformed in relation with other cultural domains, how meanings migrate across domain boundaries, and how specific actions are multiply constituted. In other words, we need to historicize our domains and trace their effects.

Abandoning the *assumptions* that have defined the analytic domains of "kinship," "gender," "politics," and "religion," however, is not the same as abandoning the *study* of the meanings and relations previously confined to those domains. The notion that the members of the "social constructivist school" who have purportedly "deconstructed kinship" are calling for the end to kinship studies is an unfortunate misunderstanding (di Leonardo 1991; Scheffler 1991). This misunderstanding appears to stem from an inability to differentiate those relations and institutions conventionally included in the domain of kinship from assumptions about their basis in the "facts of life." When, for example, we call into question the assignment of "motherhood" to the domain of "kinship" defined as rooted in sexual reproduction, we deny neither the existence of physiological processes of human reproduction nor the importance of studying ideas and practices of motherhood. Rather, by questioning the assumption that motherhood in our society as well as in others is fundamentally structured by these physiological processes, we suggest paths of inquiry that will lead us to the productive analysis of other social processes and cultural meanings that are inscribed in motherhood. In other words, we argue that we should discard the assumptions that have defined kinship as a domain of study, but not the study of those relations previously located in that domain.

Our argument that "kinship" and "gender," like "race" and "religion," are not rooted in a universal set of facts is not an expression of an "idealist" position that denies the existence or significance of material and bodily realities. We accept the existence and salience of physiological processes, but we reject the idea that they are the same, immutable "facts of biology" that form the core of the domain of kinship and gender everywhere. As Marilyn Strathern (1992) acutely notes, it is a misnomer to call those who argue this point *social constructivists,* because this implies that gender (and kinship) is constructed on certain stable, essential facts of life and nature. Like Schneider, we think that what constitutes kinship and any other cultural domain must be discovered rather than assumed (Schneider 1972).

Cultural domains are culturally specific, but they usually come with claims of universality, which are part and parcel of their seeming to be given-in-nature and/or god-given. The apparent logic and naturalness of these domains is a consequence of the way they are made real through the institutional arrangements and discourses people encounter in everyday life. Unlike explicit ideologies that can be traced to people with particular social positions and interests, hegemonic understandings are more difficult to trace to human agents (Comaroff & Comaroff 1991). Instead, they seem to emerge from each person's own experiences. The discreetness of domains is encountered directly by people whose lives are organized along institutional fault lines that are themselves the products of hegemonic cultural distinctions. As a consequence, religion seems to be about god rather than about gender; the family seems to be about reproduction and childrearing rather than about gender and religion.

In addition, cultural domains usually come with prohibitions against reading across them. The confinement of cultural exegesis to the space inside domains is especially rigid when it comes to the sacred. Sacred meanings may be read into other domains, but the reverse is not acceptable. Indeed, what defines the sacred is that which is sealed off from readings emanating from other cultural domains. The meaning of the sacred can only be revealed by those with cultural authority to interpret it. If the sacred is open to divergent readings by people who bring with them ideas associated with human social life, the claim that it is "god-given" is undermined.

What constitutes the sacred, of course, differs from one instance to another. For anthropologists, the sacred has generally been coterminous with religion. "Primitive" religion, with its myths of origin and ritual practices, constituted the sacred in comparative ethnology. As social scientists working in a discipline rooted in liberal humanism, anthropologists have felt we can look critically and dispassionately at *other* people's religion, but not our own. This is in part because *our* religion generally has been construed as "real" religion, whereas those of others have been construed as myth and fantasy. It is also in part because liberal humanists tend to be distanced from religion, which they view as an archaic "survival" of the pre-modern past in the modern world. In the implicit social evolutionary scheme to which most anthropologists have subscribed, the rationalism of science was expected to displace the mysticism of religion, rendering it inconsequential, if not non-existent. At most, religion would become a matter of sentiment and individual choice rather than continue to be a generative force in cultural production. Embedded in this social evolutionary scheme is an implicit progression of human understanding: from myth to religion to science.

This formulation is self-serving rather than self-reflexive, and misses the fact that for liberal humanists the sacred is not religion, but science. For us, science is the sacred domain we are prohibited from reading across, because the truths claimed by science supposedly transcend human agency. These truths, it is argued, reside in the natural world and are only *discovered* by humans. The claim that science is separate from culture naturalizes a hierarchy of knowledge, much as does the claim that religion is separate from culture. It entails a prohibition against reading across the boundaries of the sacred whose truths are said to exist apart from human subjectivity and agency.

Reading across domains, including the sacred, is by no means new to our discipline. It has been a standard analytic strategy of cultural anthropologists, who have happily read across other people's cultural domains. Indeed, the holistic analysis of culture, the dominant paradigm of North American ethnography, is rooted in the practice of reading across the domains of other people, especially those in so-called "simple" societies that are not characterized by formal social institutions like our own and so are deemed to be "less-differentiated." Among these other societies, the intermingling of the sacred and the political (e.g., African kingship), of ritual and economy (the potlatch), and of religion and kinship (ancestor worship) rendered necessary reading across cultural domains, however sacrilegious or foolish this might seem to the natives.

Cultural domains in our supposedly more functionally and institutionally differentiated society, on the other hand, could not be read across so cavalierly. In particular, our sacred domain of science, which includes the "scientific study of cultures," could not be read across. The topics we chose to study, the human dilemmas and puzzles we chose to investigate, and the analytic categories and methods we found to be most useful could be traced neither to our economic system nor to our political hierarchy. It certainly could not be thought of in relation to our gender hierarchy. After over a decade of work by feminist scholars of science (Haraway 1989; Martin 1987; Traweek 1988), however, it has become apparent that studies of primate behavior, immunology, and particle physics are not quite so independent of our cultural vision of gender and our cultural concerns and predicaments.

The purpose of this volume is to reverse the conventions of anthropological reading rules concerning cultural domains and cultural others. Ten of the eleven essays in this volume read across cultural domains in ways that breach the reading rules of anthropology as well as of the natives studied. In all of these cases, the natives are members of our own society or a society whose cultural system shares much with our own (members of the Turkish nation-state). These ten essays constitute a genre of reading across cultural domains that are defined as separate, isolated, and constituted by different rules. It is a critical genre of reading across genres, especially those which are supposedly independent of social life and whose truths are said to be rooted in nature. What makes it a genre of feminist cultural analysis is that the incitement to challenge the boundaries of the domains and their knowledge claims has emerged from a feminist critique of the fixed truths of gender.

In her discussion of genres among the Mountain Ok of New Guinea, Harriet Whitehead cautions against cavalier readings across meaning domains in other societies. Whitehead argues that we may be doing interpretive violence to other cultures when we disregard their reading rules in ways that we find useful in critically analyzing our own culture. Just as we cannot assume that others' cultural domains are organized like ours, we cannot read across these domains as we would ours and expect the same analytic benefits. Rather, we need to pay careful attention to local patterns of meanings-in-practice,[3] figure out what constitutes particular cultural domains, and find ways to appropriately and productively read across them. We then need to proceed carefully to construct a compelling reading across domains, considering the culturally specific evidence required to make such a reading convincing. This is not to say that breaking other people's hegemonic reading rules is taboo, for complying with such a proscription would make cultural analysis very dull indeed. Rather, such breaches must themselves emerge from a cultural analysis that is grounded in the meaningful practices—including contestations over meanings—of the people studied.

Feminism and Culture

An argument for feminist cultural analysis cannot escape confronting the issue of the usefulness of the concept of culture for feminist theory. Perhaps no other concept in the social sciences and humanities has been subjected to as unrelenting a critique over the past decade as that of culture. The combination of post-structuralist, post-colonial and postmodernist critiques has laid bare the totalizing, homogenizing, essentializing, and orientalizing modes in which the culture concept has been deployed. While most anthropologists today acknowledge these abuses of the culture concept—and many were aware of them before the recent round of criticisms—there is considerably less agreement as to whether these failings are inherent in the concept or a result of its reductionist misuse. Anthropologists, after all, have never agreed on a single concept of culture.

A good deal of the recent critique of the concept of culture has focused on its role in regimes of power and knowledge that have legitimated the political and economic domination of those studied by those who have studied them. Out of the political project of dismantling hierarchies of "cultures" has emerged a broader epistemological critique of an objectified notion of culture as something which exists apart from the representational politics of those who employ the concept. Some critics have argued that the idea of cultural "difference" is what makes possible distinctions between groups of "natives" (conceptualized in primordial, essentialist, static, and ahistorical terms) and "us" (metropolitan Western society conceived in just the opposite terms). Abu-Lughod, for one, suggests that

> ". . . 'culture' operates in anthropological discourse to enforce separations that inevitably carry a sense of hierarchy. Therefore, anthropologists should now pursue, without exaggerated hopes for the power of their texts to change the world, a variety of strategies for writing *against* culture." (1991:138)

A promising theoretical strategy for "writing against culture," according to Abu-Lughod, lies in shifting to the increasingly popular terms "practice" and "discourse." Drawing on Bourdieu (1977), Abu-Lughod claims for "practice" a focus on "strategies, interests, and improvisations over the more static and homogenizing cultural tropes of rules, models, and texts" (1991:147). Discourse, on the other hand, derives from Foucauldian "notions of discursive formations, apparatuses, and technologies . . . [and] is meant to refuse the distinction between ideas and practices or text and world that the culture concept too readily encourages" (1991:147). Abu-Lughod's research on an Egyptian Bedouin community led her to think in terms of discourses rather than culture as she grappled to make sense of what appeared to be

> ". . . two contradictory discourses on interpersonal relations—the discourse of honor and modesty and the poetic discourse of vulnerability and attachment—which informed and were used by the same individuals in different contexts." (Abu-Lughod 1991:162)

These terms, Abu-Lughod suggests, might "enable us to analyze social life without presuming the degree of coherence that the culture concept has come to carry" (1991:147). When combined with self-reflexive attention to the historical connections between the community of the anthropologist and those studied and an ethnography of the particular that avoids the generalizations inscribed in terms such as "Bedouin culture," such a theoretical shift would enable anthropology to avoid its past tendency towards "othering" and instead bring out the "similarities in all our lives" (Abu-Lughod 1991:157).

Ethnographic representations of *cultural difference* are certainly produced by people placed in historically specific relation to those they represent. These representations, as feminist critics of colonial discourse (Mohanty 1989; Trinh 1989; Mani 1987) have shown, can legitimate colonial domination when they are part of an orientalizing discourse. But ethnographic representations of *cultural similarities* are no less the products of people placed in historically specific relation to those they represent. Assimilating "them" to "us" can do violence to what people cherish that is distinct about themselves. And, claims of cultural similarity can also justify forms of social domination. The naturalizing of gender inequality, for example, is commonly based on observing "similarities" in the relations between women and men in different societies. These "similarities" are adduced as evidence of a common "human condition" that makes gender hierarchy inevitable. Likewise, superficial assessments of similarities in the roles and sentiments of women in different societies can lead to the naive conclusion—rampant in U.S. white feminist scholarship in the 1970s—that all women can readily comprehend each other's suffering, sorrows, and joys. In short, they can lead to patronizing representations of other women as "ourselves unclothed" (Rosaldo 1980).

The attention to discursive formations inspired by Foucault has the advantage of forging connections between forms of knowledge, institutional structures, and regimes of power. Cultural analysis of the 1960s and 1970s tended to overlook these connections, even while noting the cultural and historical specificity of systems of meaning. The insights of Foucauldian discourse analysis have contributed to feminist cultural analysis an awareness of the connections between gender meanings and structures of inequality. However, discourse has not proven to be an adequate replacement of the culture concept.

The analysis of discourse in our own society tends to follow institutional divisions or other social divisions: we have medical discourse, legal discourse, minority discourse, feminist discourse, and so on. An example of this tendency is Martin's (1986) analysis of the metaphors of biological reproduction in contemporary North American medical textbooks which reveal a dominant image of the body as an information transmitting mechanism, managed by an organic structure of authority with obvious parallels to institutional forms of authority in our own society. Martin argues that the metaphors used in medical texts to describe physiological processes have profound implications for the way in which a change in the basic organization of the system (for example, menopause) is perceived. For example, our negative view of menopause derives not only from the devaluation of aging women by American culture, but is a logical outgrowth of a model of the body as a hierarchical information-processing system (Martin 1987:42). Menopause is described in medical textbooks as a breakdown of a system of authority, a breakdown in communicative function that resonates with cultural assumptions about the relations between authority and order and between hierarchy and function in society.

Given this cultural model, it is not surprising that the upper-middle and middle-class white women among Martin's informants speak of the body as separate from the self. In terms consistent with dominant medical metaphors, these women describe the body as sending signals to the self, as needing to be controlled by the self, and—as Martin concludes—as aspects of a fragmented self. In contrast, the black and white working-class women in Martin's study were reluctant "to give the medical view of menstruation" (Martin 1990: 78). Rather than attribute this reluctance to a "radical polyphony" or "heteroglossia," Martin proposes that

> "working-class women have simply been more able to resist one aspect of the scientific view of women's bodies, either because it is not meaningful to them or because it is downright offensive, phrased as it is in the negative terms we have seen. The ironies here are multiple: middle-class women, much more likely to benefit from investment in the productive system, have swallowed a view of their reproductive systems which sees menstruation as failed production, and which is divorced from women's own experience. Working class women, perhaps because they have less to gain from productive labor in the society, have rejected the application of models of production to their bodies." (1990:78)

On the one hand, Martin appears committed to a theory of discursive practices in which people internalize and voice discourses which serve their class interests. On the other hand, she treats the working-class women's accounts as if they were direct readings of bodily experience and not, like the middle-class women's accounts, discursively constructed. Because Martin is intent on demonstrating that working-class women's representations do not conform to the middle-class discourse of failed production, she characterizes the former merely as a discourse of resistance. She does not go on to scrutinize the other ideas that seem to pervade working-class women's accounts—ideas about woman's essential nature, the inevitability of childbirth, and the natural link between gender and reproduction.

Martin's exclusive focus on medical discourse leads her to ignore the multiplicity of non-medical, but equally, if not more, pervasive discourses which shape women's bodily subjectivity in the U.S. There are, after all, other popular discourses at play here, both generalized public, mass-media and more class and ethnically specific folk discourses on natural bodily functions, pornographic discourse, advertising representations of women's bodies, fundamentalist Christian discourse on sex, sin, and abortion, and racist discourse on race and sexuality. It is not just among the working class, but among the upper-middle and middle classes as well, that other discourses about women's bodies circulate. The model of fragmentation Martin distills might be traced to these other discourses, as well as to medical discourse affirming the production hierarchy of capitalist society.

When anthropologists study societies such as the Egyptian Bedouin that appear not to have formal institutional domains like our society, they tend to construct discourses into broad cultural domains or "interpersonal relations," which they further subdivide into coherent systems of meaning such as "the discourse of honor and modesty" and "the poetic discourse of vulnerability and attachment" (Abu-Lughod 1991:162). An overarching cultural coherence connecting these discourses is not claimed—indeed, they may be deemed to be contradictory, as in the case just cited. Instead, coherence is located within each discourse.

In addition to having simply relocated claims for coherence, these analyses of discourses too readily grant the ethnographer's analytic units an ethno-epistemological status, without adequate ethnographic evidence as to whether and how people actually organize their thinking and acting. While institutions and cultural domains of meaning have a profound impact on shaping ideas and practices, people do not necessarily organize their everyday actions according to these divisions. Rather, people think and act at the *intersections* of discourses.

All social action is constituted and interpreted by a multiplicity of discourses. Monodiscursive analysis is limited by a rather stodgy notion of the relationship between discourse and social action, which is in turn rooted in a social cosmology that is a surprisingly conventional one. To assume that "medical discourse" is what shapes "medical practice," discourse on "interpersonal relations" is what shapes "interpersonal relations," and "family discourse" is what shapes "family relations" is to accept these discursive domains as given, rather than analyze them as the products of historically specific social institutions—thus losing the key Foucauldian insight regarding the historicity of domains. This reinforces the boundaries between cultural domains, which is counter to our argument that it is productive to read across them.

An understanding of discourses and practices requires an understanding of the broader frames through which people connect them. We agree with Strathern that

> ". . . culture consists in established ways of bringing ideas from different domains together." (1992:3)

Culture is what makes the boundaries of domains seem natural, what gives ideologies power, and what makes hegemonies appear seamless. At the same time, it is what enables us to make compelling claims for connections between supposedly distinct discourses. In other words, it is both what makes jokes funny and what makes possible our reading across domains in prohibited ways.

We do not intend to defend holism and retreat to an indefensible concept of culture as an isolated, discrete system of symbols, meanings, and practices which are soldered together into a seamless whole. Neither do we want to celebrate a postmodernist dissolution of culture as fragments of meaning which take on the biogenetic aura of a recombinant system of information—as if people can chose bits and pieces and put them together as bricoleurs into whatever meaningful arrangement they like. These "bits and pieces" come not just with histories of embedded meanings which do not allow for the free play of signification; most of them also come through institutional structures which do not allow individuals to freely reinterpret them. Catholicism, for example, is not just what individual people say it is. There is a pope, an institutional apparatus, and structures of power quite removed from what any individual thinks.

The concept of culture has been, in spite of some lapses, a productive site for discussion and debate about difference and similarity. It has also been a productive site for continual assessment of the coherence among a society's discourses and practices. This creative dialectic of the culture concept is lost when it is reduced to one of its poles. The productiveness of the concept depends on our commitment to use it as an incitement to continually rethink what is same and what is different, how they are so and what this means; and to continually reassess the fragmentation or coherence of discourses, domains, and institutions—whether they hold together and how. Once this heuristic tension is resolved in favor of either side of the opposition, culture is no longer good to think with.

Feminist Cultural Analysis

The essays in this volume focus on cultural processes of identity-making and social group formation that naturalize identities and social bonds by claiming for them an autonomy from human social agency. All these identities and bonds are ascribed a nonhuman basis, whether in nature, biology, or god. All legitimize hierarchies of difference in which power relations are embedded. In short, all naturalize power.

Anthropologists have been perhaps most conscious of these processes of naturalizing power in their studies of race. The argument that race is not a system of biological differences but rather a system of social categories constructed *in terms of biological difference* has been a central tenet of cultural anthropology in the twentieth century. The essays in this volume demonstrate that ideologies of ethnicity, sexuality, nation, and religion are also hierarchies of difference in which power relations are embedded. All draw on notions of gender, sex, reproduction and descent. It is the common basis of these processes of identity-making which makes it highly productive to read across them, to understand each in relation to the others.

Unlike race, ethnicity, nation, or religion, gender is not a domain. It is a system of difference that has not been the basis of social groupings of likeness.[4] Yet, gender pervades all these domains, and this is why we think feminist cultural analysis is especially crucial for rethinking them. If holiness is about keeping categories separate, then feminist cultural analysis could be considered sacrilegious, because we are breaking a taboo by reading across culture.

The essays by Susan McKinnon, Janet Dolgin, Rayna Rapp and Kath Weston in the first section, "American Kinship and the Facts of Life," question the taken-for-granted quality of the facts of life which are assumed to be the basis of sex, reproduction, and the family. The family, construed as a natural unit of diffuse, enduring solidarity, takes on an aura of the sacred in social discourse. However, even the biological facts of the family are judged differently depending on class, sexual, or marital status. Taken together these essays ask if, even in the families we choose—whether through gay and lesbian unions, new reproductive technologies, or genetic screening—much of the same ideologies of gender and biogenetic kinship are reinscribed. They also reveal how cultural notions of kinship in the U.S. are increasingly articulated and authenticated through scientific discourse without scientists or the general public being aware of the role of culture.

The essays by Anna Tsing and Harriet Whitehead in the second section speak to the question of what birds and bees have to do with each other, not to mention what they have to do with human sex and reproduction. Even when we are more aware of cultural mediation, as when we talk about "the birds and the bees," we need to be mindful of the comparisons we make. Modes of reading and comparison cannot be generalized across cultures; they must take into account specific systems of classification and meaning.

As Carol Delaney and Brackette Williams argue in the third section, "The Origin of Nations," other forms of diffuse, enduring solidarity—including the nation and race—are also rooted in systems of classification and meaning. The enduring bonds which constitute the nation and its citizens are predicated on naturalized notions of sex, reproduction, and the family. The title of this section is a clear allusion to Darwin's *The Origin of Species* which both offended people and provoked new ways of thinking because it muddied the categories of human and animal.

The final group of essays (by Phyllis Chock, Sherry Ortner, and Sylvia Yanagisako) are all about the American dream of moving up the social hierarchy through making one's self. They show how celebrations of social mobility can simultaneously naturalize inequality—leading to the conclusion that it is your own fault if you did not succeed. The class position of individuals and ethnic groups change and even ethnic categories change, but ideas about the origin of these distinctions in sex and reproduction and their transmission through the family remain.

Notes

1. Anna Tsing also recounts this story in her essay in this volume.
2. Carol Delaney wishes to thank Louise Doire, a graduate student at Harvard Divinity School, for calling her attention to this statement of Thomas Aquinas.
3. We thank Harriet Whitehead for suggesting this phrase.
4. When women have attempted to make it so—as in the recent second wave women's movement in the West—it has provoked fierce resistance.

References

Abu-Luhod, Lila. 1991. "Writing against Culture." In *Recapturing Anthropology: Working in the Present*, edited by Richard G. Fox. 137–162. Santa Fe: School of American Research Press.

Aquinas, Saint Thomas. 1952. *Summa Theologica* Trans. Fathers of the Dominican Province, edited by Robert Maynard Hutchins. Chicago: Univ. of Chicago Press.

Aristotle. 1979. *Generation of Animals*. Trans. A. L. Peck. Loeb Classical Library, Cambridge: Harvard University Press. [1942].

Bourdieu, Pierre. 1977. *Outline of a Theory of Practice*. Trans. Richard Nice. Cambridge: Cambridge Univ. Press.

Collier, Jane, Michelle Z. Rosaldo and Sylvia Yanagisako. 1992. "Is There a Family? New Anthropological Views." In *Rethinking the Family: Some Feminist Questions*, edited by Barrie Thorne with Marilyn Yaom, 31–48. Boston: Northeastern Univ. Press, [Originally published 1982. New York: Longman].

Comaroff, Jean, and John Comaroff. 1991. *On Revelation and Revolution*. Cambridge: Cambridge Univ. Press.

Delaney, Carol. 1986. "The Meaning of Paternity and the Virgin Birth Debate." *Man* 21(3):494–513.

———. 1991. *Seed and Soil*. Berkeley: Univ. of California Press.

di Leonardo, Micaela. 1991. "Introduction." In *Gender at the Crossroads of Knowledge: Feminist Anthropology in the Postmodern Era*, edited by Micaela di Leonardo, 1–48. Berkeley: Univ. of California Press.

Doire, Louise. 1992. "The Influence of Aristotle's *Generation of Animals* on Thomas Aquinas' *Summa Theologica*." unpublished paper. Harvard Divinity School.

Douglas, Mary. 1966. *Purity and Danger*. London: Routledge and Kegan Paul.

Geertz, Clifford. 1973. "Religion as a Cultural System." In *The Interpretation of Cultures.* 87–125. New York: Basic Books.

Haraway, Donna. 1989. *Primate Visions: Gender, Race and Nature in the World of Modern Science.* New York: Routledge.

Malinowski, Bronislaw. 1954. *Magic, Science and Religion and Other Essays.* New York: Doubleday.

Mani, Lata. 1987. "The Construction of Women as Tradition in Early Nineteenth-century Bengal." *Cultural Critique* 7:119–56.

Martin, Emily. 1987. *The Woman in the Body: A Cultural Analysis of Reproduction.* Boston: Beacon Press.

———. 1990. "Science and Women's Bodies: Forms of Anthropological Knowledge." In *Body/ Politics: Women and the Discourses of Science*, edited by Mary Jacobus, et al. 69–82. New York: Routledge.

Mohanty, Chandra Talpade. 1984. "Under western eyes: Feminist scholarship and colonial discourse." *Boundary* 2/3(12&13): 333–358.

Morgan, Lewis Henry. 1870. *Systems of Consanguinity and Affinity of the Human Family.* Smithsonian Contributions to Knowledge, No. 17. Washington, D.C.: Smithsonian Institution.

Rosaldo, Michelle Z. 1980. "The use and abuse of anthropology: Reflections on feminism anad cross-cultural understandings." *Signs* 5(3):389–417.

Sahlins, Marshall. 1976. *Culture and Practical Reason.* Chicago: Univ. of Chicago Press.

Scheffler, Harold W. 1991. "Sexism and Naturalism in the Study of Kinship." In *Gender at the Crossroads of Knowledge*, edited by Micaela di Leonardo, 361–382. Berkeley: Univ. of California Press.

Schneider, David. 1964. "The Nature of Kinship." *Man* 217:180–181.

———. 1968a. *American Kinship: A Cultural Account.* Englewood Cliffs: Prentice-Hall.

———. 1968b. "Virgin Birth." *Man* 3(1):126–128.

———. 1972. "What is Kinship All About?" In *Kinship Studies in the Morgan Centennial Year*, edited by P. Reining, 32–63. Washington, D.C.: Anthropological Society of Washington.

———. 1984. *A Critique of the Study of Kinship.* Ann Arbor: Univ. of Michigan Press.

Strathern, Marilyn. 1980. "No Nature, No Culture: the Hagen case." In *Nature, Culture and Gender*, edited by Carol MacCormack and Marilyn Strathern 174–222. Cambridge: Cambridge Univ. Press.

———. 1981. *Kinship at the Core: An Anthropoplogy of Elmdon, a village in north-west Essex in the nineteen-sixties.* Cambridge: Cambridge Univ. Press.

———. 1988. *The Gender of the Gift: Problems with Women and Problems with Society in Melanesia.* Berkeley: Univ. of California Press.

———. 1992. *Reproducing the Future: Essays on anthropology, kinship and the new reproductive technologies.* New York: Routledge.

Traweek, Sharon. 1988. *Beamtimes and Lifetimes: The World of High Energy Physicists.* Cambridge: Harvard Univ. Press.

Trinh, T. Minh-ha. 1989. *Woman, Native, Other: Writing Postcoloniality and Feminism.* Bloomington: Indiana Univ. Press.

Yanagisako, Sylvia J. 1979. "Family and Household: The Analysis of Domestic Groups," *Annual Review of Anthropology* 8:161–205.

———. 1985. *Transoforming the Past: Kinship and Tradition among Japanese Americans.* Stanford: Stanford Univ. Press.

Yanagisako, Sylvia J. and Jane Fishburne Collier. 1987. "Toward a Unified Analysis of Gender and Kinship." In *Gender and Kinship: Essays Toward a Unified Analysis*, edited by Jane Collier and Sylvia Yanagisako, 14–50. Stanford: Stanford Univ. Press.

American Kinship and the Facts of Life

1

American Kinship/American Incest: Asymmetries in a Scientific Discourse

Susan McKinnon

The family, then, as a paradigm for how kinship relations are to be conducted and to what end, specifies that relations between members of the family are those of love. One can speak of the family as "the loved ones." Love can be translated freely as *enduring diffuse solidarity*. The end to which family relations are conducted is the well-being of the family as a whole and of each of its members.—David Schneider, *American Kinship*

The most dangerous place for children is the home, the most likely assailant their father.—Linda Gordon, *The Politics of Child Sexual Abuse*

When David Schneider undertook to analyze American kinship as a cultural system, he did so by reference to the "distinctive features" of nature, blood, and law, and to the "core symbols" of sexual intercourse, love, and enduring diffuse solidarity (Schneider 1980). The terms of his analysis became central to the work of many who subsequently investigated the intricacies of American kinship and culture.

In the wake of two decades of feminist writings and gender studies, however, one is puzzled by Schneider's insistence that the core symbols of American kinship should be (indeed could be) considered separate from cultural ideas of gender and sexuality (Collier and Yanagisako 1987). Yet the distinction Schneider draws between the "pure" and the "conglomerate" levels of cultural analysis, between the person as a relative and the relative as a person, forces him to neutralize these core symbols in their "pure" form. Stripped of the specificity of cultural understandings of gender and sexuality, sexual intercourse (in both its permitted and prohibited forms) becomes an abstract articulator of the structures of relation within the family:

The distinctive features which define the members of the family and differentiate them from each other and which at the same time define the family as a unit and distinguish it from all other cultural units are those which are contained in the symbol sexual intercourse. Father is the genitor, mother the genetrix of the child which is their offspring. Husband and wife are in sexual relationship and theirs is the only legitimate and proper sexual relationship. Husband and wife are lovers and the child is the product of their love as well as the object of their love; it is in this sense that there are two kinds of love which define family relationships, one conjugal and the other cognatic, and it is in this sense that love is a synonym for sexual intercourse. (Schneider 1980:43)

Sexual intercourse, in its abstracted form at the "pure" level of cultural analysis, defines the "person as a relative." It is only at the "conglomerate" level of cultural analysis that "the relative as a person" is given flesh as other "components" of the person—sex role, age, class, occupation—are rejoined to the kinship "component" (Schneider and Smith 1973; Schneider 1980). Such factors are deemed irrelevant to the definition of a person as a relative and to the core symbols of American kinship relations.[1] Logical rigor more than cultural logic (and the Parsonian theoretical framework more than informants' statements) compel Schneider to exclude gender, age, and other "components" from the core symbols of American kinship at the "pure" level.

While it is still provocative to think about American kinship in terms of Schneider's core symbols, it is no longer possible to think about these symbols in the abstracted framework in which they were first conceived or to neglect the ways in which Americans understand them as "naturally" gendered configurations.[2] Indeed, it would be hard to imagine what could be more saturated with ideas about gender and sexuality than the symbols of sexual intercourse, love (vs. money, home vs. work), and, even, enduring diffuse solidarity.

Moreover, by abstracting the core symbol of sexual intercourse from cultural understandings of gender and sexuality, Schneider has been able to defer a consideration of relations of hierarchy and power that are central to the symbolic meaning of (hetero)sexual intercourse.[3] It is, however, important to see sexual intercourse not as an abstraction, but rather as a set of culturally constituted practices that have different meanings and entailments for men, women, and children, depending upon the context and the combination of players. These differences flow from the structures of power and the hierarchy of values that define the relations of gender and sexuality central to cultural ideas of American kinship.

The purpose of this paper is to explore the asymmetries of hierarchy and power that shape American understandings of gender and sexuality with regard to the symbol of sexual intercourse in American kinship. I do this by looking not at the "grammatical" forms of sexual intercourse but at the "ungrammatical" forms that are manifest in relations of incest.

Regardless of the presumed universality of the incest taboo, it is necessary, Schneider has suggested, to look at incest as it is differentially constituted in different cultures (1976:160). Indeed, an examination of the cultural discourse on incest reveals much about the manner in which ideas about American kinship and the symbols of sexual intercourse, love, and enduring diffuse solidarity are structured in terms of a hierarchy of cultural values and along the power lines of gender.

Schneider conjectured that incest would be conceptualized as an inverse and opposite of "normative" behavior:

> "Incest" is symbolic of the special way in which the pattern of social relationships, as they are normatively defined, can be broken. "Incest" stands for the transgression of certain major cultural values, the values of a particular pattern of relations among persons. . . . "Incest" means the wrong way to act in a relationship. . . . To act not merely wrong, but to act in a manner *opposite* to that which is proper. It is to "desecrate" relationships. It is to act "ungrammatically." (1976:166)

Yet, at least in American kinship, this is only partially true. Because Schneider did not see (en)gendered relations of power and hierarchy as integral to the "grammatical" forms of American kinship, he could not anticipate the manner in which they would be asymmetrically skewed in their "ungrammatical" forms. A reversal of hierarchically related opposites does not simply carry over the same oppositional values but, rather, transforms them in asymmetrical ways.

The "grammatical" forms of (hetero)sexual intercourse, love, and solidarity do not bear the same meanings for men and women. The difference in meanings derives from the difference in the positional values that gender gives to "traditional family" kinship configurations. That is, men (fathers and husbands) are seen as the "naturally" active (even aggressive) agents of sexuality and the possessors of power and authority over women and children; women (mothers and daughters) are seen as the acquiescent objects of sexuality and the sole possessors of "naturally" nurturant qualities.

Because ideas of gender refract asymmetrically through the "grammatical" forms of (hetero)sexual intercourse, love, and kinship, it should be no surprise that the "ungrammatical" forms are not simply a mirror-image reversal but instead, become more deeply skewed. That is, given the asymmetries in the conventional understandings of the nature of fathers and mothers, it is not surprising that the behavior of incestuous mothers is "pathologized," whereas that of incestuous fathers is, as it were, "normalized" (Tavris 1992).

The interpretations of incest[4] that I have chosen to focus on in this paper are limited in certain ways. First of all, they comprise those developed in the "scientific" literature by (primarily nonfeminist) clinical psychologists, psychoanalysts, and social workers up to the early 1980s, when the feminist critique began to revolutionize the ways in which incest is viewed in America. Mapping that critical transformation is, unfortunately, beyond the scope of this paper. Second, they concern heterosexual but not homosexual incest and parent-child but not sibling incest. For most commentators during the 1980s, incest was, by definition, not only heterosexual but also predominantly paternal (father-daughter). This paper traces, in part, the difficulties with which analysts began to conceptualize the possibility of heterosexual maternal (mother-son) incest. Although father-son incest also began to be conceptualized during this period by a few writers, mother-daughter incest remained a noncategory altogether. In future work, I hope to address the invisibility of homosexual incest as well as the very different configurations of sibling incest.

Decent Men and Model Citizens

In discussions of father-daughter incest, what is remarkable is the repeated refrain of normalcy. The families are "intact"[5] or, at least, they present a conventional appearance (Justice and Justice 1979:59–61; Herman and Hirschman 1981a:968). The incestuous father is virtually indistinguishable from any other man in American culture, "at least in regard to any major demographic characteristics. Such offenders do not differ significantly from the rest of the population in regard to level of education, occupation, race, religion, intelligence, mental status, or the like. They are found within all socioeconomic classes" (Groth 1982:215). Rist reports that the incestuous father is "both more intelligent and better educated than the criminal population. In fact, these men are often considered outstanding citizens: their only 'crime' is the hidden one of incest" (1979:686; see also Cavallin 1966:1133–34; Forward and Buck 1978:31; cf. Weinberg 1955:46–47). As one bewildered man himself put it, " 'I am a decent man. I provide for my family. I don't run around on my wife, and I've never slept with anyone except my wife and my daughters' " (MacFarlane 1978:89).

Many analysts maintain that fathers who assault their daughters are often patriarchal, authoritarian, and conservative—both religiously and sexually (Cormier, Kennedy, and Sangowicz 1962:212; Lustig et al. 1966:33; Dietz and Craft 1980:603; Gordon 1986:256). The high moral and religious profile of incestuous fathers is repeatedly mentioned. As Westermeyer remarks, "Some of these fathers maintained a righteous or religious social image: one father was a clergyman, another a church elder, and a third led his church choir" (1978:645). The religious conservatism of these men also extends to a conservativism with regard to sexual practices and extramarital sexuality (MacFarlane 1978:89). Adultery is not, on the whole, considered an option, or, if an option, it is considered worse than incest. "One Catholic aggressor, when asked by the police why he had seduced his daughter instead of having an affair or hiring a prostitute, replied incredulously, 'What? And cheat on my wife?' " (Forward and Buck 1978:32).

The outward picture of incestuous fathers as patriarchal, authoritarian, moralistic, and both sexually and religiously conservative may perhaps exaggerate the cultural norm, but it is hardly at odds with it (Gordon 1986:260).[6] So too, turning inward, the psychological profile of incestuous fathers is also hardly exceptional (Herman 1988:701–702). Serious psychic disorders such as psychosis and schizophrenia are almost never mentioned in relation to paternal incest (Weinberg 1955:51–52; Weiner 1962:621–24; Finkelhor 1979:21; Justice and Justice 1979:87). Rather, various personality disorders—ones that might afflict any otherwise functional person—are often discussed. Cavallin (1966:1134) reports that the incestuous fathers in his study had no previous psychosis, but displayed "1) inadequate or weak object relations, 2) weak psychosexual identity, 3) signs of unconscious homosexual strivings and 4) projection as a major defense." In describing such fathers, Rist (1979:686) outlines three personality types: introversive personality (socially isolated and highly dependent emotionally upon his family), psychopathetic personality (indiscriminate promiscuity), and psychosexual immaturity (pedophilia)—of which the first is most predominant in clinical studies.

Groth discusses two forms of personality disorder that he sees as characteristic of the incestuous father: passive-dependent and aggressive-dominant. Yet each is characterized by a

> deep-seated, core feeling of helplessness, vulnerability, and dependency. As he experiences the stresses of the adult life-demands of marriage and parenthood, his underlying insecurities and feelings of inadequacy become activated and increasingly prominent. He feels overwhelmed and not able to control or manage these life-demands. As a result he may exhibit one of two basic responses in an effort to cope with his crisis. He may either withdraw from adult responsibilities and adopt a passive-dependent role as a quasi child with respect to his family. Or he may overcompensate by adopting an excessively rigid, controlling, authoritarian position as the "boss in the family." (1982:225)

In the end, the incest offender is just like the rest of us: a little guy overwhelmed by the stresses of a complex adult world. The man who would molest his daughter is, at heart, a helpless, vulnerable, and pitiful victim himself. "The more common type of aggressor . . . ," according to Forward and Buck (1978:34), "turns to incest as a response to loneliness and emotional neglect. Although he may be a good father in every other respect, he loses control at some point and is virtually victimized by his own impulses."

While Groth asserts that the assault is a "sexual misuse of power" (1982:227), he short-circuits this line of argument when he claims that it is motivated by common "issues surrounding competency, adequacy, worth, recognition, validation, status, affiliation, and identity" (1982:227). In a similar vein, MacFarlane suggests that the offenders' "negative self-concepts and low personal esteem make them prime targets for the adoption of behavior that is destructive to themselves and to others" (1978:89). In the end, Herman maintains, such accounts see sexual assault as "an ineffectual attempt to meet ordinary human needs" (1988:708).

Paternal Love and Protection

It is not only the analysts who view the sexual assault of a daughter by her father in terms that stress the relative "normalcy" of the motivations. The fathers, themselves, have a battery of rationalizations that interpret their actions in light of their protective, caring role as a good parent (Cormier, Kennedy, and Sangowicz 1962:206). Some claim that "this is the way love and affection are expressed in their family" (MacFarlane 1978:90; see also Groth 1982:234). Others stress their educational role in their daughter's upbringing (Lustig et al. 1966:36; MacFarlane 1978:89; Meiselman 1978:155; Rist 1979:686; Groth 1982:234; La Fontaine 1988:12): it is the father's duty to teach his daughter the "facts of life," one father adding "that his sex education program for his daughter would prevent her from becoming frigid, like his wife, when she grew up" (Meiselman 1978:155). By a particularly twisted bit of logic, certain fathers assert their paternalistic protective role: one suggested that his assaults were a means of "protecting the child's physical health by preventing the contraction of venereal disease from other men" (MacFarlane 1978:89); another, "that his daughter was not a virgin anyway and this way he could keep her off the streets" (Rist 1979:686; see also Cormier, Kennedy, and Sangowicz 1962:208); and yet another that "he believed that the daughter would get pregnant very soon anyway so she might as well have his child since he would have to support it" (Meiselman 1978:155).

Contravening the logic of the incest taboo, entirely, and expressing the longing with which Levi-Strauss ends *The Elementary Structures of Kinship*—"of a world in which one might *keep to oneself*" (1969:497), "[t]wo fathers volunteered that they thought it was better 'to keep it in the family' rather than seek 'outside sex' " (Westermeyer 1978:645) or engage in adultery (Cormier, Kennedy, and Sangowicz 1962:211; Meiselman 1978:155; Groth 1982:234). Another expressed the same sentiment, but with a negative inflection, saying "he was 'afraid of disease' from partners outside the family" (Westermeyer 1978:645).

With the "combined power of men, parents, and adults" (Gordon 1986:254), incestuous fathers assert, in these statements, their "normative" authoritarian, paternalistic, protective, and educational role in relation to their daughters. The "ungrammatical" version of sexual intercourse, love, and enduring diffuse solidarity is transformed, through the asymmetric refraction of power through the relations of gender and age, into a "grammatical" version of "traditional family values."

Seductive Daughters

Groth (rather uncritically) gives an account of the logic of the father's choice of his daughter over a woman from outside the family:

> His daughter is more readily accessible, less demanding, more compliant. She is part of him, related, part of the family and therefore someone he feels closer to than an outsider. She is sexually inexperienced and if prepubertal, doesn't pose the risk of pregnancy. She can fulfill his sexual fantasies: the undemanding female who will be eagerly responsive to his every whim. (Groth 1982:229)

Such justifications and fantasies are, of course, revealing of the relations of power and dependency that characterize paternal incest. Yet, in many accounts, these power relations are reversed and the incestuous situation is accounted for by the daughter's seduction of a father who is "naturally" helpless to do anything other than respond.

Although the evocation of the "seductive daughter" is a common rationalization among the fathers (Forward and Buck 1978:35–41; Meiselman 1978:156), the "myth of the 'seductive' child is one fostered by psychoanalytic practitioners as well as child molesters" (Groth 1982:234; see also Breines and Gordon 1983:523–24). In an early account, Bender and Blau state:

> The history of the relationship in our cases usually suggested at least some cooperation of the child in the activity, and in some cases the child assumed an active role in initiating the relationship. . . . [A] most striking feature was that these children were distinguished as unusually charming and attractive in their outward personalities. Thus, it is not remarkable that frequently we considered the possibility that the child might have been the actual seducer rather than the one innocently seduced. (1937:514)

The image of the seductive child continues to manifest itself over the years up until quite recently (Weinberg 1955:115–16; Cormier, Kennedy, and Sangowicz 1962:204–209; Weiner 1962:613; Cavallin 1966:137; Poznanski and Blos 1975:59; Forward and Buck 1978:42; Justice and Justice 1979:94–95).

If the daughter is not presumed to initiate actively the incestuous relationship, she may be seen as receptive and secretly enjoying it. Westermeyer, using the terms "initiating partner" and "receptive partner" to refer to the offender and the victim,[7] respectively, makes the common assertion that "the daughters usually obtained gratification from the relationship during the time it was active. It was a means of obtaining affection in families where affection was scarce" (1978:645). In a curiously involuted argument, Rist suggests that the daughter's "guilt feelings are avoided by denying enjoyment from the sexual activity and behaving in an outwardly passive manner" (1979:688). Statements like this presuppose that the daughter's (not the father's) guilt feelings are justified by an active sexual desire that she disguises.

Such representations follow from Freudian assumptions concerning the incestuous desires and "fantasies" of children (Wahl 1960:188–89; Cavallin 1966:1132; but cf. Peters 1976:399–401). A flood of literature has critiqued Freud's denial of his female patients' reports of sexual abuse by their fathers and his reformulation of their reports as incestuous fantasies (e.g., Masson 1984; Westerlund 1986). In addition, a number of critics have pointed to a general tendency among psychoanalysts to concentrate on the child's desires, while the "adult's desire (and capacity for action) were forgotten" (Herman and Hirschman 1977:737; see also Rist 1979:684; Breines and Gordon 1983:523–24).

Whether it is in the accounts by fathers or those by psychoanalysts, one is struck by the conjuring act through which the sexual agency of the father is displaced onto the daughter. In the process, the daughter's presumed sexual agency is pathologized, while the "natural" and uncontrollable "response" of the father becomes "normalized."

Collusive Mothers

Regardless of how the daughter is viewed, the major blame for the father's incestuous acts is reserved for the mother. When the "dysfunctional family" is evoked as the cause of incest, the real culprit is a "dysfunctional" mother. In the numerous accounts of father-daughter incest, the father quickly disappears from the analysis and it is the mother who becomes the central figure (Herman and Hirschman 1977, 1981b; Jacobs 1990). Indeed, by the tortured logic of both the father/husband and analysts, she becomes the perpetrator of the incest—"the sine qua non for the existence of incest" (Poznanski and Blos 1975:57). Jacobs classifies the "mother blame" theories into three categories: "the mother as colluder; the mother as helpless dependent; and the mother as victim herself" (1990:502). The mother as colluder is predominant in nonfeminist accounts, where she is most often seen as " 'the family member who 'sets up' the father and daughter for the incest relationship, usually by withdrawing from her sexual role in the marriage and ignoring the special relationship that may then develop between husband and daughter' " (Jacobs 1990:502). It is the mother's withdrawal from her husband (and her daughter) that directly "leads to" or "results in" the father's incestuous attentions to his daughter.

In this scenario, the mother is (for any number of reasons) absent, withdrawn, and incompetent, "unable to fulfill even the traditional female familial role—that of housekeeper and nurturer of children" (Gordon 1986:256). She is described, variously, as "rejecting," "threatening," "unloving," "cold," "hostile," "selfish," and "irresponsible" by both her husband and her daughter (Kaufman, Peck, and Tagiuri 1954:269; Cavallin 1966:1134; Machotka, Pittman, and Flomenhatt 1967:100–101, 110–11; Poznanski and Blos 1975:57; Justice and Justice 1979:99; cf. Herman and Hirschman 1977, 1981a, 1981b; Dietz and Craft 1980:603; Jacobs 1990:502). The generally unspoken accusation beneath all of these charges is that, as both a wife and a mother, she is "unnaturally" unnurturant—a monstrous perversion of nature.

The mother may also be absent or withdrawn because she is physically disabled, ill, or (more often) mentally disabled—depressed, alcoholic, psychotic, or infantile (Cavallin 1966:1134; Browning and Boatman 1977:71; Herman and Hirschman 1977:745, 1981a:968, 1981b:44–49; Rist 1979:687). Or she may be burdened with repeated pregnancies and large families (Herman and Hirschman 1981a:968). She may also be viewed as inordinately "passive," "dependent," "submissive," "helpless," "masochistic," or "victimized" (Herman and Hirschman 1977:745–46, 1981a:968–69, 1981b:47–49; MacFarlane 1978:91; Justice and Justice 1979:98; Dietz and Craft 1980:603; Jacobs 1990:502–503). That her varying afflictions and resulting incompetencies as a mother and a wife might "push" her husband and daughter into an incestuous relationship is deemed self-evident. Rarely is the husband's role in precipitating his wife's afflictions or withdrawal ever contemplated.

The crucial absence, however, is a sexual one. The wife is "frigid" or sexually rejects her husband (Cormier, Kennedy, and Sangowicz 1962:207–208; Weiner 1962:612, 627; Lustig et al. 1966:34; Herman and Hirschman 1981b:42–44; MacFarlane 1978:89; Westermeyer 1978:645; Justice and Justice 1979:97–98; Dietz and Craft 1980:603). The refrain is repeated by both the husbands and the analysts, although, again, the question never arises as to why the wife has sexually withdrawn from her husband. It is always assumed to be her fault; her frigidity and rejection are to blame. The unspoken assumption, here, is that sexual relations are "naturally" asymmetric and hierarchical: the husband rightfully demands, the wife dutifully acquiesces; the man is the active agent, the woman the passive object; the man has needs that must be satisfied, the woman has the duty to satisfy his (but not her own) needs. When the wife chooses not to participate in sexual relations with her husband, for whatever reasons, it is assumed that her sexuality (but not her husband's) is pathological and it follows that she is to blame for the resulting marital problems between her husband and herself (see, for instance, Kaufman, Peck, and Tagiuri 1954:270–71).

The wife/mother is not only seen as refusing to fulfill her sexual duties toward her husband but also seen as actively forcing these, as well as her maternal duties, onto her daughter.

> Typically the silent partner is unable to maintain any sort of nurturing, affectionate relationship with either her husband or her daughter. This emotional abandonment of the family often *causes* the husband and the daughter to seek emotional refuge with each other. (Forward and Buck 1978:45) (emphasis added)

The mother "abdicates" her role as wife and mother to her daughter (Kaufman, Peck, and Tagiuri 1954:269; Weiner 1962:612; MacFarlane 1978:89; Justice and Justice 1979:97) "in a gradual transfer of duties that have become unpleasant to her, ranging from housekeeping to sex" (Forward and Buck 1978:46); is (in the words of a medical journal) " 'only too happy to turn over the burdensome sexual role to the daughters' " (quoted in Dietz and Craft 1980:607); or (in the words of a 1976 psychology textbook) " 'forces a heavy burden onto her daughter by causing her to assume the role of the wife and lover of her own father, thus absolving the mother of this unwanted role' " (quoted in Rush 1980:140; see also Machotka, Pittman and Flomenhaft 1967:110; Justice and Justice 1979:147–48). Again, there is no critique as to why sexual relations with her husband, or housekeeping and parental chores, might have become "burdensome" to a wife and mother. Rather, a woman's normative roles as wife and mother are seen as "natural," and father-daughter incest is considered the logical consequence of her "unnatural" abandonment of these roles.

This is true not only when she remains in the home (but does not carry out her sexual and maternal duties) but also when she leaves the (traditionally, white middle-class) female sphere of the home and enters the (traditionally, white middle-class) male sphere of work. Such a move is often interpreted as a causative factor in promoting incest. "Finding no fulfillment at home she may turn her attention elsewhere, developing new interests— volunteer work, school, a job, social commitments—as a means of escape" (Forward and Buck 1978:46). This is regarded less as a flight to fulfillment than as an escape from her proper maternal and sexual duties. The medical journal quoted above, which suggested that mothers are "only too happy to turn over the burdensome sexual role to the daughters," goes on to say "and to this end mothers take jobs that require them to be absent from the home in the late afternoon and evening hours" (quoted in Dietz and Craft 1980:607). Unlike a husband's work outside the home, a wife's work outside the home can be interpreted as "emotional neglect of her family" (Forward and Buck 1978:46; see also Machotka, Pittman, and Flomenhaft 1967:111; Justice and Justice 1979:98; Finkelhor 1980:268). The inversion of the conventional roles of husband and wife is thought to subordinate the husband to a secondary role. Cavallin can barely contain his discomfort when he reports that, in one case, "incest took place when the patient was unable to be gainfully employed and the wife, who had to support the family, had relegated the husband to the role of a babysitter" (1966:1134). The same theorists who fault a woman for withdrawing from the exalted role of "mothering" consider a man's humiliation in being relegated to such a role to be a cause of incest.

In Groth's account of the "passive-dependent" type of incest offender (see also Peters 1976:411), the self-sufficiency of the offender's wife is viewed as a causative factor:

> Over time she comes to feel emotionally unsupported, neglected, or even deserted by her husband and may turn elsewhere for emotional support and fulfillment. As she becomes increasingly self-sufficient and no longer is constantly attentive to his needs he turns to his daughter as a substitute or surrogate companion-wife-mother, who is then expected to take care of him, prepare his meals, do his laundry, get him up for work, spend leisure time with him. Eventually his emotional dependency and intimacy with her evolves into a sexual relationship. (Groth 1982:218)

In Groth's mind, the cure for incest in such cases depends not on the husband/father assuming an adult role but upon his finding a wife who will fulfill her "duties" and be "constantly attentive to his needs":

> To some extent his likelihood of recidivism may depend on how successful he is in establishing a relationship with a woman whose needs are congruent with his, a relationship in which his passive-dependent longings will be fulfilled, and one which does not make demands on him he cannot meet. He needs to feel he is cared for and needs to be given to as evidence of this caring. (Groth 1982:222)

It is the father, not the daughter, who needs and has a right to be "mothered." It is the mother, not the father, who threatens her daughter by having needs other than those defined by "traditional" social norms. Nurturance is not the natural domain of the father, nor is the lack of nurturance in the father considered to be a cause of incest. Indeed, the opposite is the case, as MacLeod and Saraga point out: "The assumption that families exist to satisfy men's emotional and sexual needs is never explicitly stated. But scrutinise the arguments, their descriptions of 'what has led up to abuse' and this is what you find" (1988:17). It is no surprise, then, that the cause of incest is so often presumed to be the neglect of the father by his wife rather than the father's neglect of his daughter as a daughter.

In these arguments, then, the role of the father in paternal incest is "normalized" to the extent that paternal authority and sexual agency and female nurturance and sexual acquiescence are, themselves, considered to be "natural" and, therefore, normative. It follows that the "underlying" cause of paternal incest is not to be found in the father's behavior, which, after all, is only an exaggeration of the "norm," but rather in the mother's behavior, which, as a negation of conventional norms, is "pathologized."

The Rarity of Maternal Incest

The peculiarities of these "scientific" conceptualizations of incest become evident when the characterization of father-daughter incest is contrasted with that of mother-son. The same cultural logic of gender asymmetries underlies interpretations of both forms of incest, but, given these asymmetries, maternal incest is appraised in an entirely different manner from paternal incest.

Most commentators agree upon the prevalence of paternal incest at the same time that they remark upon the absolute, or at least comparative, rarity of maternal incest (Herman and Hirschman 1977:741; Meiselman 1978:298; Finkelhor 1979:75; Rist 1979:688; McCarty 1986:447). Even in a recent college textbook on abnormal psychology, the one sentence that refers to maternal incest reads: "Very few instances of mother-son incest are reported" (Davidson and Neale 1990:332).

Indeed, there is a tendency to view maternal incest as a contradiction in terms, a logical impossibility:

> In the rare cases where women seek help for unnatural feelings towards their children, they tend to be fobbed off with assurances that all mothers feel physical tenderness. Welldon finds that, in the sex-offender groups she runs, incestuous mothers are seldom taken seriously. (O'Grady 1988:29)

Where fathers might be considered "naturally" to develop a sexual attraction for their daughters and "find" themselves compelled to act upon it, any sexual attraction of mothers toward their sons is perceived to be so "unnatural" and in such conflict with their nurturant roles that they should be compelled to react against it. There is, however, no end of speculation upon the reasons for the relative absence of maternal incest. The reasons advanced generally concern, once again, conceptualizations of female nurturance, female sexuality, and male authority and control.

The "naturalness," and therefore incontrovertability, of female nurturance that is thought to account for the rarity of maternal incest is represented in various arguments about the incest taboo in relation to the propinquity of the mother and child (Weinberg 1955:216–18; Wahl 1960:191; Rist 1979:682–83; Rush 1980:140). Whether propinquity is presumed to foster incestuous attraction (and therefore must be strongly tabooed) or to inhibit attraction (and therefore forms the basis of the taboo), both arguments assume that the rarity of maternal incest, and the "horror" with which women contemplate its possibility (Rush 1980:140), is due to the "naturally" nurturant role of women as mothers (Weinberg 1955:216–18).

Mothers are also thought incapable of the sexual assault of their sons because they lack the sexual equipment necessary for direct sexual agency or assault (see Finkelhor 1979:76–77). Without a penis, women are assumed to be the acquiescent objects, not the active agents, of sexual acts. Conceptualizing how a mother might force a sexual assault on her son therefore tries the imagination of some analysts:

> Where an incestuous father can force himself on his daughter, an incestuous mother must seduce (or allow herself to be seduced by) her son, for if he is not sensually aroused he cannot maintain an erection. This *mandatory tenderness* makes it difficult to comprehend the emotional pain and unconscious conflicts that both lead to and result from the incest. (Forward and Buck 1978:73) (emphasis added)

Female sexual assault (as opposed to seduction) is a noncategory, since both sexual agency and assault are, in general, presumed to be "naturally" male in character (O'Grady 1988:29).[8]

It is, finally, the presence of a strong husband/father, a dominant male, that makes mother-son incest a virtual impossibility. Arguing from a Freudian perspective, Rist notes: "It is speculated that this [maternal] incest may be so rare because it engenders in the child a fear of both parents—the castrating father and the all-encompassing mother—that seems practically intolerable" (Rist 1979:688). The power of the father's authority and the strength of his defense of "his women" (Wahl 1960:191) makes maternal incest inconceivable for these analysts.

Maternal incest is seen as a logical impossibility to the extent that it inverts the most fundamental assumptions upon which the "traditional" gender hierarchy in American culture has been based. The existence of maternal incest would intimate that women might have sexual agency, that mothers might not be naturally nurturant, and that fathers might not have ultimate power, authority, and control over women and children.[9]

Psychotic Mothers and Schizophrenic Sons

As cases of maternal incest began to come to light, authors struggled to devise theories that would account for the contravention of what was otherwise deemed the natural capacity of maternal nurturance. Unlike interpretations of paternal incest, however, maternal incest was not, on the whole, seen to involve an exaggeration of the conventional attributes of mothers but rather to involve a complete inversion or negation of these attributes.

The nurturant bond between mother and child is assumed to be so strong that something must be severely wrong with the mother for her to be able sexually to assault her child. In early accounts, the mother was often characterized as either somewhat retarded or extremely disturbed psychologically. In a particularly obtuse statement concerning the intelligence of incestuous mothers, Wahl suggested that "maternal incest may be associated with low intelligence. Persons of higher intelligence presumably can find more effective symbolic substitutes and sublimations or utilize other neurotic defenses" (1960:192). Whereas the often noted (above)-average intelligence of incestuous fathers contributed to the perception of the normalcy of the paternal offender, the assumed subaverage intelligence of incestuous mothers supported the impression of deviance and pathology thought to characterize the maternal offender. Later analysts, however, questioned the assumption about the low intelligence of incestuous mothers (Groth 1982:230).

Although the argument concerning intelligence receded, the question of the psychological status of the maternal offender persisted:

> In 1886 Richard von Krafft-Ebing asserted that sexual desire in the female "arouses suspicion of its pathological significance." And less than 100 years later, a psychiatric text [published in 1976] used by medical students informed that "the occurrence of mother-son incest bespeaks more severe pathology than does father-daughter incest." (Rush 1980:139)

Rist reiterated the common perception: "Mother-son incest seems to be extremely rare. It appears to occur only under extremely pathological conditions, generally where there has been an absence of early closeness between mother and son" (1979:688). Clearly, underlying these assumptions was the presupposition that only a woman who is deeply disturbed could neglect her "natural" role as a nurturant mother of her children. The contrast with offenders in father-daughter incest is extreme. Fathers may have personality disorders, but they remain more or less within the boundaries of what is considered "normal." Mothers are fully psychotic and have exceeded the bounds of normalcy (Shengold 1980:470).[10]

Interpretations of the pathology of maternal incest are linked to ideas about sexual agency; the instigator is the one who is seen as most pathologically disturbed:

> In the great majority of reported cases in which the son initiates incest with his mother, the son is schizophrenic or severely disturbed in some other way prior to incest (Meiselman 1978:299–300).
>
> Mother-initiated incest presents a slightly different picture, in that there seems to be somewhat less psychopathology in the son and more in the mother. (Meiselman 1978:302)

It is as if the only way to conceive of the possibility of maternal incest is to posit the extreme psychological disorganization of the one who initiates it.

The link between maternal incest and severe psychiatric conditions is also evident in the assumption that the effects upon the victim of maternal incest are far more catastrophic than those upon the victim of paternal incest (Masters and Johnson 1976:58).

> Perhaps because of the central role of the oedipal situation in personality development, theorists and researchers alike have made clear-cut pronouncements about the relationship between mother-son incest and serious psychopathology. For instance, Barry (1965) asserted that the son subsequently became psychotic in almost all cases of mother-son incest; Parsons (1954) believed that an obvious corollary of his theory of personality development was that mother-son incest would constitute a severe regression and would thus be associated with serious psychopathology, especially in the son; and Frances and Frances (1976, 242) concluded that "in those rare families where mother-son incest is actually consummated, either or both partners are almost always psychotic, with clear evidence of lack of psychic differentiation." No such dire predictions are made for father-daughter or sibling incest. (Meiselman 1978:299)

But the linkage between maternal incest and psychiatric disorders extends not only to psychosis but further, to schizophrenia. Rist, for instance, asserts that "most reported cases have occurred between adult schizophrenic sons and their domineering mothers" (1979:688; see also Weinberg 1955:90). Wahl notes that

> in a recent study by Fleck et al. of Yale on the intrafamilial environment of the schizophrenic patient, it was found that incestuous problems in schizophrenic patients play a much larger role in the development of schizophrenia than had hitherto been supposed. My own experience abundantly supports this view. (1960:192)

Given the seriousness with which Americans take the "natural" bonds of motherhood, the only way to account for the contravention of the "natural" is by conjuring the "unnatural"—a woman whose intellectual deficiency or psychological pathology completely undermines her maternal nature.[11]

Promiscuous Mothers and Female Perversions

Interpretations of maternal incest also rest upon conventional assumptions about female sexuality. Incestuous mothers either invert the normative female sexual submissiveness, passivity, and acquiescence, or they fulfill these normative expectations in an exaggerated expression of maternal nurturance.

Descriptions of maternal incest offenders often stress that these women engage in various forms of sexual excess. They are highly promiscuous; they are (or act like) prostitutes; and they are sexually compulsive, indiscriminate, and conspicuous (Weinberg 1955:85–93; Wahl 1960:192; Meiselman 1978:301; Groth 1982:230–31). The sexuality of incestuous mothers is represented as more "male" than "female": they display a sexual agency that is fully active and aggressive, one that does not display "proper" female reserve, control, and modesty.

When incestuous mothers are not considered sexually aggressive, they are occasionally described as sexually acquiescent, in a maternally protective manner, to a schizophrenic, or otherwise psychologically disturbed, son.

> Shelton (1975) . . . described a young man who suffered a schizophrenic breakdown at age twenty-one, shortly after his father's death. He had entered his mother's bedroom in the middle of the night and had intercourse with her on just one occasion. The mother was extremely disturbed by this incident and remorsefully admitted to a court psychiatrist that she had not resisted her son's advances because she thought he was "sick." (Meiselman 1978:301)

Sexual agency has been returned, here, to the (sick, retarded) male, and the mother displays a combination of conventional (although inappropriately directed) sexual submissiveness and maternal nurturance, compassion, and protectiveness. Like the interpretations of paternal incest that stress the exaggeration of male dominance, authority, and control, these interpretations of maternal incest stress the exaggeration of a long-suffering, self-sacrificing maternal nurturance in the face of extreme psychopathology.

It is only later that various analysts begin to conceptualize the possibility of particularly female forms of sexual assault. After the initial categorical contradictions of the female sexual assault of males is overcome, various acts such as genital manipulation and obsessive concern with hygiene come to be seen as forms of sexual assault (Masters and Johnson 1976:58; Meiselman 1978:302–303; Shengold 1980:465; O'Grady 1988:29; Dolan 1991:47). Yet such assaults are not so much conceptualized in terms of aggressive female sexual agency as they are understood in terms of an exaggeration and extension of the daily acts of maternal nurturance and care.

In the end, female sexual agency and maternal nurturance remain mutually exclusive categories. Incestuous mothers either invert the norms of female sexuality, assuming a more "male" form of aggressive sexual agency and, in the process, fully negating their maternal, nurturant, protective, and caring nature; or they retain the norms of female sexual submissiveness and exaggerate their nurturant activities in an obsessive fashion.

Absent and Passive Fathers

In maternal incest, the father's absence, or his "unnaturally" passive character, is perceived to be at least part of the problem (Justice and Justice 1979:102). Yet, in literature on maternal incest, there is no proliferation of accounts of the "collusive father" to match that of the "collusive mother" in the literature on paternal incest.

The father's absolute absence is often remarked upon in cases of mother-son incest:

> Instead of a silent partner there is usually an absent partner. In probably 95 percent of all mother-son cases the father is either no longer part of the nuclear family or is frequently away from the home. This makes mother-son incest much more of a direct relationship between aggressor and victim than father-daughter incest is. There is no third party. (Forward and Buck 1978:74)

The possible reasons for this absence are not commented upon. But, following from this absence, analysts note that either the son "assumes" the role of the father, sometimes both economically and sexually (Wahl 1960:191; Rist 1979:688; Groth 1982:230–31; McCarty 1986:455) or the "mother seeks substitute gratification with her son" (Forward and Buck 1978:74; Meiselman 1978:305; Chasnoff et al. 1986:579; McCarty 1986:455; Lawson 1991:397).

One senses, however, that the "real" problem is not simply the absence of the father (sexually or otherwise) but rather the absence of a "strong" father. For example, Wahl suggests that the "absence of a strong parent of the same sex or a weak, passive father would seem to conduce to overt incest. The child feels a sense of comfort and security in knowing that father is strong enough to guard against encroachments against his own woman (1960:191). Rist notes that the rarity of maternal incest is due to the fear of a castrating father; at the same time, she claims that, in cases where maternal incest does occur, there is usually a domineering mother (1979:688). The father is faulted not for a lack of nurturance toward his children (or his wife) but rather for his passivity—his lack of authority and control. The father poses an inadequate threat to his son, and is incapable of adequately "protecting his women"; the mother is faulted for her excessive dominance. It is this inversion of the "traditional family values"—of the conventional gender hierarchy—that is generally thought to provoke the incestuous relation between mother and son. The obvious implication is that a reversal of conventional gender roles is conducive to maternal incest (Weinberg 1955:85–86), which is otherwise averted where there is an author-itative father and a (sexually) unassertive mother (see Lawson 1991:397).

Asymmetries at the Core of American Kinship

Perhaps there is an abstract world in which sexual intercourse, love, and enduring diffuse solidarity exist in some "pure" cultural form, unadorned by considerations of gender and sexuality. But such a world is not revealed in the "scientific" accounts of incest in America. Here, conceptualizations of sexual intercourse (in both its "grammatical" and "ungrammatical" forms) are shaped by fundamental asymmetries in the gendered hierarchy of values and structure of power that inform "traditional" American kinship. These asymmetries are manifest in the different meanings and entailments that sexual intercourse has in relation to husbands and wives, fathers and mothers, sons and daughters. And they are reflected in cultural presupposi-tions concerning the "nature" of both "conventional" and "deviant" behavior.

Where sexual intercourse is thought to involve the "naturally" assertive, even aggressive, agency of men and the equally "naturally" passive acquies-cence and "mandatory tenderness" of women, it follows that paternal incest would be viewed in terms that stress its relative "normalcy" at the same time that maternal incest would be viewed in pathological terms. This asym-metry in interpretations of paternal and maternal incest also follows from cultural understandings about the "natural," and therefore "normative," apportionment of gendered attributes within the framework of the family: whereas authority and control ought to inhere in fathers and husbands, responsibility for nurturance properly belongs to mothers and wives. Because paternal incest is perceived to involve only an exaggeration of "normative" expectations about what it means to be a man, a father, and a husband, the location of cause is shifted: the cause of paternal incest becomes the negation of "normative" expectations of what it means to be a woman, a mother, and a wife. Maternal incest, by contrast, is seen as a double negation of convention: cultural presuppositions concerning the "nature" of both men and women, fathers and mothers, husbands and wives, are wholly negated. It is this doubly unnatural nature of maternal incest that renders it particularly "pathological."

Notes

1. Yet Schneider's account of the American family does presuppose specific relations of gender and sexuality: the family he analyzes is heterosexual, not gay or lesbian. Gay and lesbian families may play upon the symbolic coordinates of American kinship, but they also significantly alter their meanings (Hayden 1992).

2. Although the same argument can be (and has been) made for other "components" of American kinship (such as age, sexuality, class, and race), this paper focuses primarily on gender.

3. Schneider explicitly addresses issues of gender inequality only in a later book (Schneider and Smith 1973:75–77).

4. For definitions of incest, see Herman and Hirschman (1977:742; 1981a:967), MacFarlane (1978:85), Russell (1983:135–36 and 1984:17). Both Schneider (1976) and La Fontaine (1988) discuss the definitional problems encountered in considerations of incest.

5. Occasionally, and mostly in earlier works, the families are represented as not intact: fathers are alcoholic, violent, unemployed, and often desert their children (Kaufman, Peck, and Tagiuri 1954; Weiner 1962:610–11; Browning and Boatman 1977).

6. As Finkelhor notes, however, "not all incestuous fathers are such tyrants. A second group, probably a minority to judge by its visibility in the literature, appears to be quite a bit more restrained, in fact inhibited. These men are described as shy, ineffectual types, who had difficulty in their social relations prior to marriage. They are often quite dependent on their wives for emotional and even financial support" (1980:265; see also Cormier, Kennedy, and Sangowicz 1962).

7. Landis, who questions the accuracy of the "emphasis upon the victim as a co-operating participant" (1956:91), nevertheless identifies two categories of victims: "those whose experiences were clearly accidental, and those whose experiences might possibly include cases of co-operative participation" (1956:104–105). Gagnon classifies "non-accidental victims" into "collaborative victims" and "coerced victims" (1965:180–86). Even Finkelhor, whose 1979 article critiques the myth of the "seductive child," continues to use the term "partner" for both the offender and the victim.

8. The possibility of a truly violent female sexual assault was documented in a paper by Sarrel and Masters (1982) but was not taken up again until the late 1980s and 1990s (see Bolton 1989, Lawson 1991, and Macchietto 1992).

9. Maternal incest becomes a logical impossibility for some feminists, too, but for different reasons. For example, because Herman and Hirschman's argument rests so strongly upon the entailments of patriarchy, they are, perhaps, too quick to assume that maternal incest is scrupulously avoided by women who, as a class, are perceived to have a critical and reflexive awareness of the implications of subordination and dependency (Herman and Hirschman 1981b:20–21, 54–58).

10. Later in the 1980s, the correlation between severe psychological disturbance and maternal incest was called into question and found not to hold in all cases (McCarty 1986:453; Marvasti 1986:68).

11. Other reasons postulated for the "unnaturally" unnurturant behavior of mothers is their absence in the early years of their sons' lives and their loss of "maternal control" due to the abuse of alcohol (Wahl 1960:191–192; Meiselman 1978:301; Rist 1979:688; Groth 1982:230–31).

References

Barry, M.J. 1965. Incest. In *Sexual Behavior and the Law,* edited by R. Slovenko, Springfield, IL: Thomas.

Bender, Lauretta, and Abram Blau. 1937. "The Reaction of Children to Sexual Relations with Adults." *American Journal of Orthopsychiatry* 7: 500–518.

Bolton, Frank G., Larry A. Morris, and Ann E. MacEachron. 1989. *Males at Risk: The Other Side of Child Sexual Abuse.* London: Sage.

Breines, Wini, and Linda Gordon. 1983. "The New Scholarship on Family Violence." *Signs* 8(3): 490–531.

Browning, Diane H., and Bonny Boatman. 1977. "Incest: Children at Risk." *American Journal of Psychiatry* 134(1): 69–72.

Cavallin, Hector. 1966. "Incestuous Fathers: A Clinical Report." *American Journal of Psychiatry* 122(10): 1132–1138.

Chasnoff, Ira J., William J. Burns, Sidney H. Schnoll, Kayreen Burns, Gay Chisum, and Linda Kyle-Spore. 1986. "Maternal-Neonatal Incest." *American Journal of Orthopsychiatry* 56(4): 577–580.

Collier, Jane Fishburne, and Sylvia Junko Yanagisako, eds. 1987. *Gender and Kinship: Essays Toward a Unified Analysis.* Stanford: Stanford Univ. Press.

Cormier, Bruno M., Miriam Kennedy, and Jadwiga Sangowicz. 1962. "Psychodynamics of Father Daughter Incest." *Canadian Psychiatric Association Journal* 7(5): 203–217.

Davidson, Gerald C., and John M. Neale. 1990. *Abnormal Psychology.* 5th ed. New York: Wiley.

Dietz, Christine A., and John L. Craft. 1980. "Family Dynamics of Incest: A New Perspective." *Social Casework* 61(10): 602–609.

Dolan, Barbara. 1991. "My Own Story." *Time* 138 (October 7): 47.

Finkelhor, David. 1979. *Sexually Victimized Children.* New York: Free Press.

———. 1980. "Psychological, Cultural and Family Factors in Incest and Family Sexual Abuse." In *Child Abuse: Commission and Omission,* edited by Joanne Valiant Cook and Roy Tyler Bowles, 263–69. Toronto: Butterworths.

Fleck, S., T. Lidz, A. Cornelison, S. Schafer, and D. Terry. 1959. "The Intrafamilial Environment of the Schizophrenic Patient." In Individual and Family Dynamics, edited by Jules H. Masserman, 132–39. New York: Grune & Stratton.

Forward, Susan, and Craig Buck. 1978. *Betrayal of Innocence: Incest and Its Devastation.* New York: Penguin.

Frances, Vera, and Allen Frances. 1976. "The Incest Taboo and Family Structure." *Family Process* 15(2): 235–44.

Gagnon, John H. 1965. "Female Child Victims of Sex Offenses." *Social Problems* 13(2): 176–92.

Gordon, Linda. 1986. "Incest and Resistance: Patterns of Father-Daughter Incest, 1880–1930." *Social Problems* 33(4): 253–67.

———. 1988. "The Politics of Child Sexual Abuse: Notes from American History." *Feminist Review* 28: 56–64.

Groth, A. Nicholas. 1982. "The Incest Offender." In *Handbook of Clinical Intervention in Child Sexual Abuse,* edited by Suzanne M. Sgroi, 215–39. Lexington, MA: Lexington Books.

Hayden, Corinne P. 1992. "Making Kinship Trouble: Lesbian Motherhood and the Dynamics of Choice in American Kinship." Senior honors thesis, University of Virginia.

Herman, Judith Lewis. 1988. "Considering Sex Offenders: A Model of Addiction." *Signs* 13(4): 695–724.

Herman, Judith, and Lisa Hirschman. 1977. "Father-Daughter Incest." *Signs* 2(4): 735–56.

———. 1981a. "Families at Risk for Father-Daughter Incest." *American Journal of Psychiatry* 138(7): 967–70.

———. 1981b. *Father-Daughter Incest.* Cambridge, MA: Harvard Univ. Press.

Jacobs, Janet Liebman. 1990. "Reassessing Mother Blame in Incest." *Signs* 15(3): 500–514.

Justice, Blair, and Rita Justice. 1979. *The Broken Taboo: Sex in the Family.* New York: Human Sciences.

Kaufman, Irving, Alice L. Peck, and Consuelo K. Tagiuri. 1954. "The Family Constellation and Overt Incestuous Relations between Father and Daughter." *American Journal of Orthopsychiatry* 24: 266–79.

La Fontaine, Jean S. 1988. "Child Sexual Abuse and the Incest Taboo: Practical Problems and Theoretical Issues." *Man* 23(1): 1–18.

Landis, Judson T. 1956. "Experiences of 500 Children with Adult Sexual Deviation." *Psychiatric Quarterly Supplement* 30(1): 91–109.

Lawson, Christine. 1991. "Clinical Assessment of Mother-Son Sexual Abuse." *Clinical Social Work Journal* 19(4): 391–403.

Levi-Strauss, Claude. 1969. *The Elementary Structures of Kinship.* Boston: Beacon.

Lustig, Noel, John W. Dresser, Seth W. Spellman, and Thomas B. Murray. 1966. "Incest." *Archives of General Psychiatry* 14(1): 31–40.

McCarty, Loretta M. 1986. "Mother-Child Incest: Characteristics of the Offender." *Child Welfare* 65(5): 447–58.

Macchietto, John G. 1992. "Aspects of Male Victimization and Female Aggression: Implications for Counseling Men." *Mental Health Counseling* 14(3): 375–92.

MacFarlane, Kee. 1978. "Sexual Abuse of Children." In *The Victimization of Women,* edited by Jane Roberts Chapman and Margaret Gates, 81–109. Beverly Hills, CA: Sage.

Machotka, Pavel, Frank S. Pittman, and Kalman Flomenhaft. 1967. "Incest as a Family Affair." *Family Process* 6(1): 98–116.

MacLeod, Mary, and Esther Saraga. 1988. "Against Orthodoxy." *New Statesman and Society* 1(4): 15–19.

Marvasti, Jamshid. 1986. "Incestuous Mothers." *American Journal of Forensic Psychiatry* 7(4): 63–69.

Masson, Jeffrey Moussaieff. 1984. *The Assault on Truth: Freud's Suppression of the Seduction Theory*. New York: Farrar, Straus and Giroux.

Masters, William H., and Virginia E. Johnson. 1976. "Incest: The Ultimate Sexual Taboo." *Redbook* (April): 54, 57–58.

Meiselman, Karin C. 1978. *Incest: A Psychological Study of Causes and Effects with Treatment Recommendations*. San Francisco: Jossey-Bass.

O'Grady, Jane. 1988. "Mother Knows Best." *New Statesman and Society* 1(29/30): 29.

Parsons, Talcott. 1954. "The Incest Taboo in Relation to Social Structure and the Socialization of the Child." *British Journal of Sociology* 5(2): 101–117.

Peters, Joseph J. 1976. "Children Who Are Victims of Sexual Assault and the Psychology of Offenders." *American Journal of Psychotherapy* 30(3): 398–421.

Poznanski, Elva, and Peter Blos. 1975. "Incest." *Medical Aspects of Human Sexuality* (October): 46–76.

Rist, Kate. 1979. "Incest: Theoretical and Clinical Views." *American Journal of Orthopsychiatry* 49(4): 680–91.

Rush, Florence. 1980. *The Best Kept Secret: Sexual Abuse of Children*. New York: McGraw-Hill.

Russell, Diana E.H. 1983. "The Incidence and Prevalence of Intrafamilial and Extrafamilial Sexual Abuse of Female Children." *Child Abuse and Neglect* 7(2): 133–46.

———. 1984. "The Prevalence and Seriousness of Incestuous Abuse: Stepfathers vs. Biological Fathers." *Child Abuse and Neglect* 8(1): 15–22.

Sarrel, Philip M., and William H. Masters. 1982. "Sexual Molestation of Men by Women." *Archives of Sexual Behavior* 11(2): 117–31.

Schneider, David M. 1976. "The Meaning of Incest." *Journal of the Polynesian Society* 85(2): 149–169.

———. 1980. *American Kinship: A Cultural Account* 2d ed. Chicago: Univ. of Chicago Press.

Schneider, David M., and Raymond T. Smith. 1973. *Class Differences and Sex Roles in American Kinship and Family Structure*. Englewood Cliffs, NJ: Prentice-Hall.

Shelton, W.R. 1975. "A Study of Incest." *International Journal of Offender Therapy and Comparative Criminology* 19(1): 139–53.

Shengold, Leonard. 1980. "Some Reflections on a Case of Mother/Adolescent Son Incest." *International Journal of Psychoanalysis* 61(4): 461–76.

Tavris, Carol. 1992. *The Mismeasure of Woman*. New York: Simon and Schuster.

Wahl, Charles William. 1960. "The Psychodynamics of Consummated Maternal Incest: A Report of Two Cases." *Archives of General Psychiatry* 3: 188–93.

Weinberg, S. Kirson. 1955. *Incest Behavior*. New York: Citadel.

Weiner, Irving B. 1962. "Father-Daughter Incest: A Clinical Report." *Psychiatric Quarterly* 36(3): 607–632.

Westerlund, Elaine. 1986. "Freud on Sexual Trauma: An Historical Review of Seduction and Betrayal." *Psychology of Women Quarterly* 10(4): 297–310.

Westermeyer, Joseph. 1978. "Incest in Psychiatric Practice: A Description of Patients and Incestuous Relationships." *Journal of Clinical Psychiatry* 39(8): 643–48.

2

Family Law and the Facts of Family

Janet L. Dolgin

Introduction

"What is problematic in the definitions of kinship," wrote David Schneider, "is whether the sociocultural aspects can be set apart entirely from the biological aspects or whether any concern for the sociocultural aspects necessarily implicates the biological aspects" (1984:97).

At present, that issue is reflected directly and clearly in decisions rendered by U.S. courts that concern the definition and regulation of family matters. Within the last two decades, courts deciding family-law have been faced repeatedly with cases calling traditional definitions of the family into question. Generally conservative, especially in family-law matters, the judiciary tends to preserve old patterns when faced with new possibilities for organizing or defining families.

Yet in the last two decades, courts have increasingly permitted adult family members to define their relationships in contractual terms. In consequence, the contrast between home and work blurs (Barnett and Silverman 1979:46–48; Schneider 1968:50). Especially where the rights of, or relationships with, children are not involved, U.S. law has widely accepted the possibility that adults can negotiate the terms of relationships previously defined as nonnegotiable and has begun to recognize family members as fungible.

In cases in which children are concerned, the law has been slower to approve the amalgamation of family law with contract law. Courts struggle to safeguard the family by preserving the parent-child relationship in traditional terms or by protecting particular parent-child relationships as instances of what the family should be. Thus, some courts hearing family-law cases, particularly cases that involve children, approve change but deny they are doing so; while others, attempting to preserve an older conception of the family, reject change but do so in terms that empower the very changes opposed. In the process, courts begin explicitly to reconsider the basic symbols (the "biological facts," as Schneider put it) through which the family and its component actors are understood. At the same time, courts prove ready to ignore the "biological facts" altogether when that serves their ends.

Currently, two sets of cases particularly pressure courts to establish the dimensions of biological parenthood and to clarify the relation between biological and legal parenthood. One set involves the paternal rights of unwed "putative" fathers. The second set involves the rights of parties to surrogacy and gestational surrogacy agreements. All of these cases call upon the legal system to acknowledge family patterns that welcome choice and individuality in the parent-child relationship. On the whole, the judiciary has been reluctant to answer this call. But ironically, the judiciary's essentially conservative response, concerned to safeguard decent parents in proper families, itself contains the seeds of change.

Cases Involving Unwed Fathers

Between the early 1970s and the late 1980s, five cases involving the paternal rights of men not married to the mothers of their biological children reached the United States Supreme Court. Until that time, state law provided little or no protection for such men. In the first four cases, beginning with *Stanley v. Illinois* in 1972 and including *Quilloin v. Walcott* (1978), *Caban v. Mohammed* (1979), and *Lehr v. Robertson* (1983), the Court was indecisive, holding twice for the fathers and twice against them.

The facts of *Stanley v. Illinois* differed somewhat from those in the other three cases. Stanley and the mother of his children lived together intermittently for eighteen years, during which time three children were born to them. When the children's mother died, the state, as required by an Illinois statute, took the children from Stanley and declared them wards of the state. Reversing the decision of Illinois's highest court, the U.S. Supreme Court declared the statute unconstitutional in discriminating against men like Stanley. The Court's opinion failed to make clear whether the protection afforded Stanley reached all unwed fathers, or only those who had established homes with their children, or with their children and the mothers of those children.

Although the subsequent three unwed-father cases seemed to require the Court to face this question, the answer remained opaque. *Quilloin v. Walcott,* decided six years after *Stanley,* involved a father who was precluded by a Georgia statute from vetoing the adoption of his child by the mother's new husband. Declaring the statute constitutional, the Supreme Court explained that the case was not one in which "the unwed father at any time had, or sought, actual or legal custody of his child" (*Quilloin v. Walcott,* 434 U.S. 555 [1978]). The Court continued:

Nor is this a case in which the proposed adoption would place the child with a new set of parents with whom the child had never before lived. Rather, the result of the adoption in this case is to give full recognition to a family unit already in existence, a result desired by all concerned, except appellant. (*Id.*, 555)

The next case, *Caban v. Mohammed,* was similar to *Quilloin* (the father contested the adoption of his children by the mother's new husband), but in *Caban* the Court declared unconstitutional a New York statute that gave unwed biological fathers little or no opportunity to veto adoptions of their children by other men. In the fourth case, *Lehr v. Robertson,* decided in 1983, the Court again faced a similar set of facts and laws, and decided, as in *Quilloin,* that the Constitution did not protect the paternity of the unwed father involved.

The Court and legal commentators have attempted to interpret and harmonize the four cases. In almost every such attempt, the analyst has distinguished *Stanley* and *Caban,* cases in which the biological fathers' paternal rights were protected, from *Quilloin* and *Lehr,* cases in which the fathers' rights were not so protected, by asserting that the fathers in the first two cases acted as fathers should, and that the fathers in the second two cases failed adequately to establish relationships with their biological children.

In this regard, the Court explained that fathers differ from mothers. Biological maternity, it argued, entails and ensures social maternity. In contrast, biological paternity carries no social (and thus, no legal) implications for the development of a parent-child relationship.

Justice Stewart, in a dissenting opinion in *Caban* (quoted approvingly by Justice Stevens in his opinion for the Court in *Lehr*) declared:

> Parental rights do not spring full-blown from the biological connection between parent and child. They require relationships more enduring. The mother carries and bears the child, and in this sense her parental relationship is clear. The validity of the father's parental claims must be gauged by other measures. *Caban v. Mohammed,* (441 U.S. at 397)

Justice Stevens elaborated in *Lehr:*

> The significance of the biological connection [between men and their children] is that it offers the natural father an opportunity that no other male possesses to develop a relationship with his offspring. If he grasps that opportunity and accepts some measure of responsibility for the child's future, he may enjoy the blessings of the parent-child relationship. *Lehr v. Robertson,* (463 U.S. at 262)

The Court assumed that biological paternity provided an "opportunity" for asserting social paternity, but did not necessitate that response, whereas biological maternity, especially in its gestational aspect, conditioned and necessitated social maternity.

Thus, the premise of the Court's position that paternity, even when proved as a biological "fact," had to be established socially was that, for men, biology does not constitute automatically a parent-child relationship. Men are free to choose whether or not to develop such a relationship. Each of the first four unwed-father cases suggested the necessity of demonstrating something beyond the mere fact of a biological link before a man's paternity would receive constitutional protection.

In *Lehr,* the Court asserted clearly that the Constitution protects the paternity of certain, but not all, unwed biological fathers. Those fathers whose paternity deserves protection were defined to include men who "demonstrate a full commitment to the responsibilities of parenthood by 'com[ing] forward to participate in the rearing of [their] child[ren]' " (*Lehr v. Robertson,* at 361). The case involved the paternal claims of Jonathan Lehr to his biological child, Jessica M., born in 1976. After the child's birth, her mother, Lorraine Robertson, married Richard Robertson. Two years later Richard petitioned a New York state family court to adopt his wife's child. Jonathan Lehr contested the adoption, yet he had done none of the things that the applicable state law required unwed fathers seeking paternal rights to do.[1] Because Lehr had not adequately "acted as a father" to his biological child, the Court upheld the statute that denied him paternal rights. Lehr had failed to make use of the "opportunity" extended by his biological connection to Jessica.

However, the Court's opinion is called into question by facts presented in Justice White's dissent. According to Justice White's account (never denied by the majority), after Jessica's birth her mother hid the child from Lehr, who ceaselessly searched for Jessica and her mother. In 1978, Lehr found Lorraine already married to Richard Robertson. Lehr's offer to provide financial support and create a trust fund for the child was turned down. This information demands that an explanation be sought for the *Lehr* decision other than that usually offered: that Lehr had simply not been a good enough father to Jessica. That alternative explanation is suggested by the fifth of the unwed father cases, *Michael H. v. Gerald D.,* decided in 1989.

Michael H. involved a situation defined as factually different—indeed, as the Court saw it, conclusively different—from that found in any of the four earlier cases. The mother in *Michael H.,* unlike the mothers in any of the other unwed-father cases, was married to another man at the time that the child involved was conceived and born, as well as thereafter. At issue in *Michael H.* was a California statute presuming a child's mother's husband to be the father. The presumption was irrebuttable.[2]

Michael H. contested the constitutionality of the statute as it applied to him. Michael, the biological father of Victoria D., had lived with his child and her mother for two periods during the child's early years, and had continually offered financial and emotional support to Victoria, who called him "Daddy." Under the usual reading of the earlier unwed-father cases, Michael, who was almost certainly the child's biological father according to blood-test results, had established exactly the sort of relationship with the child that would assure him constitutional protection in asserting his paternal rights. Michael, however, was not the only "father" involved. Victoria's mother, Carole, was married to Gerald, and the state presumed him to be Victoria's father.

The Supreme Court, in an opinion written by Justice Scalia,[3] labeled Michael the "adulterous natural father,"[4] treated his claim as preposterous, and, in effect, decided that Carole's marriage to Gerald definitively precluded Michael from establishing a paternal relationship to Victoria. Thus, *Michael H.* suggested that a biological father demonstrates the appropriate social relationship with his child only when that relationship occurs in the context of a relationship between the father and the child's mother. In Justice Scalia's view, such a relationship was precluded for Michael by Carole's marriage to another man.

The Court clearly recognized Michael as Victoria's "natural" father and held that "fact" of no relevance to his paternity. In the Court's accounting, the circumstances of Michael's biological paternity (making him the "adulterous natural father") vitiated the "opportunity" biological fatherhood provides other men, in other circumstances, to claim social paternity. In response to the argument presented to the Court by the child's guardian *ad litem*—that failing to protect Michael's paternity would deprive the child, as compared with legitimate children, of equal protection under the law—Justice Scalia responded: "Under California law, Victoria is not illegitimate, and she is treated in the same manner as all other legitimate children: she is entitled to maintain a filial relationship with her legal parents." (*Michael H. v. Gerald D.*, 491 U.S. 131). Those legal parents were Carole and her husband Gerald.

Thus, the message of *Michael H.* was clear. Biological paternity alone does not create the kind of connection between a father and a child that the state must protect.[5] If a state chooses, as did California, to protect and preserve what Justice Scalia called the "unitary family" (consisting, in this case of Carole, Gerald, and Victoria) over the claims of the "natural" father, so much the better.

Nothing in *Michael H.* conflicted with the presumption, clearly articulated in the earlier unwed-father cases, that women become mothers naturally while men become fathers by choice. However, *Michael H.* refined the meaning of paternal choice. In *Michael H.*, the importance of protecting traditional families was clear. In the earlier cases, that purpose, though present, was less consistently and obviously served. But to protect its notion of traditional families (well defined by David Schneider's characterization of family relations as relations of "diffuse enduring solidarity"), the Court had to restrict the meaning of the choice involved. Appropriation of the opportunity extended by biological fatherhood would not do. Were that possible, a biological father's decision to chose paternity might not be a *family* choice. In order to protect the family in its traditional form, a father's decision to choose paternity had to be distinguished from other decisions he might make. The *choices*, that Marilyn Strathern so provocatively analyzes, of whether to be a parent, when to be a parent, how to have children, and what kind of children to have (Strathern 1988, 1992), must be limited and cordoned off if men *and women* are to continue to reproduce the family "as it always was." For the Court, this should not be a choice like any market choice. The choice to be a father is the choice a man makes to establish a family with the mother of his children. That choice, not the biological facts alone or the biological facts in concert with a father-child relationship that excludes the mother, embodies the sort of paternity deserving constitutional protection.

Thus, *Michael H.* framed the theme that runs, though not entirely consistently, through the earlier unwed-father cases, and that makes sense of those cases: biological paternity alone cannot establish legal paternity; biological paternity, along with other things, has a place in a court's consideration of a man's legal paternity, but is neither a necessary nor a sufficient ground for recognition of the biological father as a legal father. That recognition depends, primarily, on evidence that the man is part of a family; and, at least in most cases, being part of a family entails establishing a home with the child's mother.

The unwed father cases decided before *Michael H.* seemed to acknowledge that a biological father's choice to relate to his child constituted his parenthood. However, the fathers to whom constitutional protection was extended in those cases were men who had, in fact, established homes with their children and *with those children's mothers.* When the cases came to court, those homes had been disbanded, but, in this regard, such fathers were like divorced fathers. The two fathers who had not established homes with their children and those children's mother, in one case because the couple separated before the child's birth and in the other because the mother refused to participate, were not recognized as legal fathers.

Surrogacy and Gestational Surrogacy Cases

The law has presumed that biological maternity *is* maternity. As Justice Stewart's language put it, the mother's bearing and giving birth to a child foreshadows and constitutes her maternity and necessitates that the law protect that maternity (*Caban v. Mohammed*, 397). But just as technology, by making the identification of biological fathers possible, has threatened the traditional justification for the marital presumption and forced courts to justify that presumption on other grounds, so reproductive technology, by making identification of the biological mother uncertain and by reconstructing biological maternity into separate aspects, has undermined presumptions about what makes a mother a "mother."

That process is evident in the response of the law to "traditional," and to gestational, surrogacy. "Traditional" surrogacy usually involves a "surrogate" agreeing to be artificially inseminated with the sperm of the intending father, to gestate the resulting fetus, and at the birth of the baby to terminate her parental rights in favor of the intending parent or parents. Gestational surrogacy, involving more complicated reproductive technology, entails a separation of the genetic and gestational aspects of maternity. Typically, ova are removed from the intending mother, fertilized with sperm from the intending father, and implanted in the uterus (or fallopian tubes) of the surrogate, who gestates the fetus.[6]

Despite their similarities, "traditional" and gestational surrogacy present different dilemmas to courts. The primary conundrum identified by courts in the nongestational surrogacy cases revolves around the commodification of mothers and of the mother-child relationship; hardly a judge has issued an opinion in a surrogacy case without lamenting the risk of such commodification. In gestational surrogacy cases, the central concerns involve the potential disembodiment of motherhood and the collapse of the biological facts that previously guaranteed the identity of a child's mother.

In facing these issues, courts have used different approaches. But, as with the unwed-father cases, most judicial decisions about surrogacy or gestational surrogacy have aimed to safeguard the family either in general or in a particular case as an instance of the general form. On the whole, it has been harder to serve these ends in surrogate-mother cases than in unwed-father cases because understandings of the mother-child tie as an inexorable product of biological maternity have been deeply internalized in western societies at least since the Industrial Revolution.[7] As a consequence, the surrogacy and gestational surrogacy decisions have been more contorted than the decisions involving the rights of unwed fathers. In both surrogacy and gestational surrogacy cases, the courts, intending to preserve a traditional family or traditional families in general, have altered the terms of discourse so as to support changing definitions of "family."

These processes are evident in two recent surrogacy cases. The first, *In re Baby M*, decided in New Jersey, involved an agreement between Elizabeth and William Stern, the contracting parents, and Mary Beth Whitehead, the surrogate mother,[8] by which Whitehead agreed to be inseminated with William Stern's sperm, to carry and give birth to the resulting baby, and, at its birth, to terminate voluntarily her parental rights in favor of the Sterns. For this, Whitehead was to be paid $10,000. After the baby's birth in March 1986, Whitehead, unwilling to relinquish the baby, left for Florida with the child, her husband Richard Whitehead, and their two children. The Sterns commenced an action to have the baby returned to them.[9]

In the second case, *Johnson v. Calvert,* the California courts balanced the rights of a gestational mother against those of a genetic mother or, more accurately, against those of a genetic mother and father, together. In January 1990, Anna Johnson entered into a surrogacy agreement with Mark and Crispina Calvert providing that, for $10,000, Johnson would gestate a fetus produced from Mark's sperm and Crispina's ovum and would, at the child's birth, surrender it to the genetic parents. Crispina, whose uterus had been surgically removed, was unable to gestate a fetus, but, she did have healthy ovaries and produced eggs each month. Anna quickly became pregnant. During the pregnancy, relations between her and the Calverts deteriorated. Shortly before the baby's birth, Anna sued the Calverts, arguing fetal neglect[10] and seeking full parental rights. At the same time, the Calverts commenced an action to have the baby declared theirs. The child was born in September 1990, and in October the trial court declared the Calverts its legal parents.

In *Baby M* and *Johnson,* the courts granted custody, or full parental rights, to the parties most closely approximating traditional, two-parent, middle-class families. The New Jersey Supreme Court gave William Stern custody of Baby M and granted Whitehead limited visitation rights. Anna Johnson's maternal rights were flatly denied, and the child was given to the Calverts, its only parents under the law. In reaching these decisions, the courts either stretched the law or elaborated the biological facts. Each case, despite its explicit holding, questioned the sanctity of the traditions apparently being served.

While both New Jersey courts that issued decisions in *Baby M* gave custody to William Stern, the two courts' styles of discourse and modes of procedure could hardly have been more different. Yet each worked to preserve the family as a sacred form. The trial court, finding little statutory law to guide its decision,[11] examined the best interests of the child in detail and concluded that her "best interests" lay in the home of Elizabeth and William Stern. The state supreme court, in contrast, relied on and applied existing statutes promulgated to regulate the termination of parental rights and adoption in New Jersey. Both courts began with the assumption that Mary Beth Whitehead and William Stern were the baby's "natural" parents. The supreme court found this fact determinative, and restored Whitehead's maternal rights but left custody of the child with the Sterns. The trial court rewrote the biological script to eviscerate Whitehead's maternity.

At the start of its lengthy opinion, the trial court referred to Mary Beth Whitehead and William Stern as clearly, and equally, the child's parents. The court wrote: "Justice, our desired objective, to the child and the mother, to the child and the father, cannot be obtained for both parents" (*In re Baby M,* 525 A.2d 1132). The court defined its job as selecting between the two parents in the name of the child's best interests. Further along in the opinion, however, the court, describing Whitehead's decision to keep the baby, wrote: "Until then [the moment of the baby's birth], [Whitehead] understood what she promised to do, understood what she had to do, but when the time came to perform Mrs. Whitehead refused to perform her promise to give Mr. Stern his daughter" (*In re Baby M,* 1144). Even as he considered Whitehead's reaction at the baby's "moment of birth," Judge Sorkow began to obliterate her motherhood. Whitehead refused to give Stern "his daughter." And by the end of its opinion, the court completely displaced Whitehead's maternity. In the concluding pages of his opinion, Judge Sorkow referred to the child for the first time as Melissa, the name the Stern's had selected for her. Now the judge wrote:

> When Melissa was born on March 27, 1986, there were no, attendant to the circumstances of her birth, family gatherings, family celebrations or family worship services that usually accompany such a happy family event. . . . In reality, the fact of family was undefined if non-existent. The mother and father were known but they are not family. The interposition of their spouses will not serve to create family without further court intervention. (*In re Baby M,* 1172)

Thus, finally, Judge Sorkow himself created Melissa's family, a family that included her father, William Stern, and her mother, Elizabeth Stern.

Between the start of the opinion and its end, the court obliterated Whitehead's maternity where possible and rendered it moot where not. The court did this by relying, variously, on its own characterizations of Whitehead as mother and on the fact that Whitehead had entered the surrogacy contract. Under New Jersey state law, a legal parent cannot be deprived of parental rights absent a showing of unfitness, and clearly Whitehead neither abused nor neglected her children. Indeed, the court expressly found Whitehead to have been a fit parent to her two children with Richard Whitehead; for them, the court wrote, she was a "good mother." But, not so for Baby M (*In re Baby M,* 1170). Unable to terminate Whitehead's maternal rights under existing law, the court focused on the character of Whitehead as mother, in which the court found nature gone awry. As the court saw her, Whitehead, hysterical and selfish from the start, thwarted her own maternity by attempting to bargain it away. When, repenting, she tried to regain her place as mother, nature turned on her. She went too far.

What would have been normal maternal instincts were transformed and exaggerated, enveloping Whitehead and the child. Judge Sorkow explained:

> Mrs. Whitehead has been shown to impose herself on her children. Her emphasis on the infant may impair the parenting of the other two children for whom she has been, until now, a good mother. She exhibits an emotional over-investment. It was argued by defendant's counsel that Mrs. Whitehead loved her children too much. This is not necessarily a strength. Too much love can smother a child's independence. Even an infant needs her own space. (*In re Baby M,* 1168)

Whitehead, in short, made the fateful decision to ignore nature by selling her maternity. But when she regained her "natural" sense, sense had left her. In one of the many ironies of his opinion, Judge Sorkow explained this characterization of Whitehead by referring to her response to her contractual obligation: "This court is satisfied by clear and convincing proofs that Mrs. Whitehead is unreliable insofar as her promise is concerned. She breached her contract without regard to her legal obligation" (*In re Baby M,* 1169). Unreliable, and thus unable to function in the world of rational, autonomous individuals, Whitehead tried to reclaim her maternity. But her essential unreliability doomed even that effort. Thus, Whitehead is depicted as having failed the tests of nature *because* she failed the tests of culture.

A similar irony underlies the reasoning of the opinion on a grander scale. Clearly, under New Jersey law, a court could not terminate a fit parent's rights to his or her child. Neither could a court order an adoption without complying with the details of the adoption laws. Only by relying on the contract could Judge Sorkow bypass that law, and this he did. A significant section of his opinion discussed the surrogacy contract and its validity. Yet the court, basically traditional, favoring old-fashioned families and middle-class homes, dared not rest its decision directly on the contract. In the opening paragraph, the court wrote:

> The primary issue to be determined by this litigation is what are the best interests of a child until now called 'Baby M.' All other concerns raised by counsel constitute commentary.
> That commentary includes the need to determine if a unique arrangement between a man and woman, unmarried to each other, creates a contract. If so, is the contract enforceable; and if so, by what criteria, means and manner. (*In re Baby M,* 1132)

In this way, the court hedged its bets. By referring to the contract, the opinion gave legal justification to the termination of Whitehead's maternal rights and to its order effecting Elizabeth Stern's adoption of the baby.

But at the same time, it disclaimed any intent to approve or enforce the surrogacy agreement.

Logically, the response of the New Jersey Supreme Court to the lower court's reasoning was entirely correct. Either the contract was law or it was not. If not, state statutes precluded the termination of Whitehead's maternal rights and the order effecting Elizabeth Stern's adoption of the baby. The supreme court, which reviewed the reasoning of the lower court and not the behaviors and responses of the participants themselves, focused on the contractual issue and concluded that the surrogacy contract was "illegal, perhaps criminal, and potentially degrading to women" (537 A.2d at 1234). Looking at the issues in general more than at the parties to this specific case, the state's highest court chose to protect the family and the mother-child relationship, in particular, from the incursions of contract law. "There are," the court declared, "in a civilized society, some things that money cannot buy. . . . There are values that society deems more important than granting to wealth whatever it can buy, be it labor, love, or life" (537 A.2d at 1249).

Judge Wilentz, speaking for the New Jersey Supreme Court, thereby protected traditional families in general by refusing to permit the parent-child tie to originate contractually. But even in Baby M's particular case, the court preferred the family more closely approximating its image of a traditional family. Judge Wilentz, complimenting the trial court on its "comprehensive" and "perceptive" analysis of the child's best interests (537 A.2d at 1259), left the baby in William and Elizabeth Stern's custody,[12] and remanded the case for consideration of Whitehead's visitation rights. The court justified this conclusion by reference to the child's continuing residence with the Sterns for one-and-a-half years as well as to the character of the two households. While affirming the trial-court decision to grant Stern custody, the supreme court restored Whitehead's maternity, however flawed. The court did this not just literally in its decision to protect Whitehead's legal maternity but in its portrait of Whitehead's entering, and then backing away from, the surrogacy contract. Judge Wilentz wrote:

> [Whitehead] was guilty of a breach of contract, and indeed, she did break a very important promise, but we think it is expecting something well beyond normal human capabilities to suggest that this mother should have parted with her newly born infant without a struggle. Other than survival, what stronger force is there? We do not know of, and cannot conceive of, any other case where a perfectly fit mother was expected to surrender her newly born infant, perhaps forever, and was then told she was a bad mother because she did not. We know of no authority suggesting that the moral quality of her act in those circumstances should be judged by referring to a contract made before she became pregnant. (537 A.2d at 1259)

Whitehead's morality, and thus the story as a whole, were to be judged through the morals of motherhood, not those of contract. Her relation to the child, even if distorted by her presumption that that relation could be bargained away, was a maternal relation. Despite all, enough of Whitehead's maternity survived her own misguided acts to make her, indisputably, the baby's legal mother.

In the end, both opinions in *Baby M* were intended to preserve traditional families, the trial-court opinion by selecting the family that provided the clearer instance of a "good" family and the higher-court opinion by refusing to enforce the surrogacy contract altogether. Both courts, like the United States Supreme Court in the unwed-father cases, placed the child whose parentage was at stake with the family that provided a woman and a man living together as spouses or like spouses. The trial court's termination of Whitehead's maternal rights might have caused it to question the basic assumption of the unwed-father cases, that maternity is a consequence, and continuation, of gestation. But the court avoided that conclusion by obliterating Whitehead's maternity altogether. Judge Sorkow decided, and then declared, that Whitehead was not the mother, and thereby precluded the direct conclusion that her biological maternity counted for naught.

Finally, with gestational surrogacy, the question was asked openly. What exactly is the part biological maternity plays in making mothers "mothers?" Where one woman can claim gestational, but not genetic, maternity, and another can claim genetic, but not gestational, maternity, who is the mother? In *Johnson,* one mother opposed another mother—or, more accurately, another mother together with her husband. In this regard, the case differed from the unwed-father cases and from *Baby M* (cases in which fathers opposed mothers). Thus, *Johnson* provides a context in which to measure the generality of the assumption that the gestational role both produces and constitutes maternity.

Clearly, the unwed-father cases, by distinguishing biological maternity from biological paternity with reference to the deep significance of the parent-child bonds formed during gestation and birth, would seem to present a strong case for Anna Johnson. "The mother carries and bears the child," declared the United States Supreme Court in *Caban,* "and in this sense her parental relationship is clear." Certainly, Johnson had carried and given birth to the baby. Yet the state trial court, bestowing full parental rights on the Calverts, defined Johnson's role as incidental.

The opinion predicated parenthood—and thus the composition of family—exclusively on a genetic connection. "In this case," the opinion asserted, "we have a family unit, all genetically related. You have Mark Calvert, Crispina Calvert and their child they call Christopher; three people in a family unit." (*Johnson v. Calvert*, No. X 633190 at 10). In contrast, Johnson was described alternately as a business associate and a temporary caretaker.

The language of the court's finding was unequivocal. It declared "beyond a reasonable doubt that Crispina Calvert is the genetic, biological and natural mother . . . of the child, and that Mark Calvert is the genetic, biological and natural father of the child" (*Johnson v. Calvert*, No. X 633190 4–5). The court described Anna Johnson as a "gestational carrier," a "genetic hereditary stranger" to the child, who acted like a "foster parent providing care, protection and nurture during the period of time that the natural mother, Crispina Calvert, was unable to care for the child" (*Johnson v. Calvert*, No. X 633190 5). Like any foster mother, explained Judge Parslow for the trial court, Anna Johnson should have been aware during her pregnancy that "the day may come when the mother of the child will once again be able to take the child" and will "walk away with it" (*Johnson v. Calvert*, No. X 633190 6). Johnson's role as gestational "host," a matter of contractual choice and not family love, offered no evidence of maternity. She was paid for the "pain and suffering" that pregnancy brings, not for a child, not even for her willingness to disclaim all legal relationship with that child. It was not hers to disclaim. "She knew what her contribution would be." And she "knew that she had to give the child to the Calverts when it was born" (*Johnson v. Calvert*, No. X 633190 7). That knowledge, Judge Parslow explained, precluded gestational bonding between Johnson and the baby.

In a remarkable, though probably unintentional move, Judge Parslow differentiated the physical and psychological aspects of the gestational role of some mothers from the gestational role of other mothers. Those mothers most likely to bond with their babies *in utero*, most likely to benefit *as mothers* from the connection pregnancy affords, are mothers *in families*—most particularly married mothers with husbands, whose babies they carry.

So, Judge Parslow reserved the legitimating benefits of biological maternity for women like Crispina Calvert while denying them to women like Anna Johnson, women who represent, in his language, an "anti-child," "me first society" (*Johnson v. Calvert*, No. X 633190 14). He asserted that the biological "facts" had different implications and different consequences and were played out differently, depending on the parties with whom they were associated. Judge Parslow proclaimed:[13]

> People that are married and get pregnant and plan for a child, that contributes to the mother's feelings toward the child she's carrying. And in a situation . . . where the plan is from day one that the child is the genetic child of another couple but it's going to be given to that couple to raise exclusively when it's born means that there is less likelihood and *should be* less likelihood psychologically of a person carrying the child bonding with the child. (*Johnson v. Calvert*, No. X 633190 12) (emphasis added)

Biological facts, in Judge Parslow's view, respond to and reflect the situation and intentions of the woman who gestates a baby. In effect, the court described the occurrence of gestational bonding as a consequence of class and social context.

But what of Judge Parslow's central pronouncement—that the genetic, not the gestational, connection makes a mother a "mother?" Is that claim similarly conditioned by context and class? Certainly, in *Johnson*, the gestational mother, a black single parent and sometime welfare recipient, differed from the Calverts in class, race, and life-style.[14] The Calverts were not only middle-class professionals[15] but also, as a married couple, represented the family in its traditional form. *Johnson*, alone, does not allow conclusions about the comparative "value" that courts, and others, will attribute to the genetic donations of people from different classes, races, and social groups. However, when *Johnson* is read in concert with other cases, a pattern begins to emerge. As the *Johnson* decision was being issued, the media reported that six menopausal women had become pregnant through the implantation of donated ova, fertilized with the sperm of the pregnant women's husbands. No one suggested, noted Katha Pollitt in comparing gestational surrogacy with the case of the menopausal pregnant women, that the women who donated the ova be granted maternal rights (Pollitt 1990:826). In these cases, "the value women place on pregnancy and childbirth" made the babies the children of the gestational mothers (*id.*, 826).

The *Johnson* court did not need to decide whether the weight of a parent's genetic role is, like the weight of the gestational role, conditioned by social factors. Having defined Anna's gestational role as secondary and incidental, the trial court, like the courts in *Baby M, Michael H.*, and, more subtly, in the other unwed-father cases, represented the facts of parenthood so as to legitimate a decision that safeguarded tradition and the prerogatives of class. Faced with protecting a middle-class, old-fashioned family or reasserting accepted biological "truths," the judge aligned the biological facts to serve the social end. By defining gestational bonding as a matter of *choice*, Judge Parslow obliterated Johnson's maternity and declared Mark and Crispina Calvert the baby's "natural" and thus legal parents.

The California Court of Appeal concurred[16] and treated the case as if statutory law gave it no choice. In fact, however, the statutes in question, all written without a thought about providing for arrangements like those at issue in the case, could be read, as Judge Sills did, writing for the appellate court, either to support Judge Parslow's decision or to justify a declaration of Johnson's maternity. In a complicated journey through a series of California statutes, the court interpreted state law to demand a decision recognizing the maternity of the mother shown through blood tests to be the genetic mother.[17] But that conclusion was not inevitable. The law could be read as Judge Sills read it, but it could be read in other ways as well. For instance,

Judge Sills dismissed a provision of the state civil code that directed that "between a child and the natural mother [a parent-child relationship] may be established by proof of her having given birth to the child" (*Anna J. v. Mark C.*, 286 Cal. Rptr. 377). According to Judge Sills, the section in question was inapplicable because Johnson was *not* the baby's "natural" mother. Judge Sills's reading is plausible. So are others.

Assuming that a "natural" parent must be a genetic parent, the court easily dismissed Johnson's argument that the trial court's holding deprived her of a "liberty interest" in her child. Like the trial court, the appellate court reenforced the assumption that Anna was not the "natural" mother, and thus had no ground on which to rest her claimed maternity, by referring to Anna's *choice*. "Further," wrote Judge Sills, "we observe that Anna would not find herself in this position but for her own *choice*. She can hardly claim that state laws, which have the effect of confirming her own initial decision, arbitrarily infringe on her *liberty* without due process of law" (*Anna J. v. Mark C.*, 380).

Then, going one step beyond the trial court, the appellate court predicated the psychological bond between parents and children on genetic connections. The psychological bond between mother and child, described in *Caban* as flowing directly from a mother's gestational link with her child, was entirely displaced. Judge Sills declared:

> [G]enetics is a powerful factor in human relationships. The fact that another person is, literally, developed from a part of oneself can furnish the basis for a profound psychological bond. Heredity can provide a basis of connection between two individuals for the duration of their lives. As the trial judge in this case observed, 'we want to know who came before us and who's coming after.' (*Anna J. v. Mark C.*, 380–81)

Declarations about the roots of parental feeling thus came full circle. Recognized, but discounted in the unwed-father cases, resurrected but only in part in *Baby M*, the genetic tie between a parent and a child was described in *Johnson* as the heart and soul of family, in fact and in law.

Blood Is to Water[18] as Nature Is to Culture: or Is It the Other Way Around?

The judges in the unwed-father and surrogate-mother cases assumed[19] that family relationships and the "idea" of family are, and should be, different from and stronger than other kinds of relationships and ideas. Each of the unwed-father and surrogate-mother cases threatened or challenged traditional definitions of family, and in each case the court perceived a threat, not a challenge—a threat to the continued preservation of the parent-child relationship, and of the family more generally, as a *regulated* domain of love and loyalty, separate from the world of work and money.

The cases as a whole demonstrate the flexibility and multidimensionality of the symbols through which family relations are perceived and defined in American society, in general, and by the legal system, in particular. In each case, the court acknowledged biological "facts" but separated the legal definition of family relationships from those facts. Each court aimed to preserve a certain kind of family by protecting the rights of a certain kind of parent. In cases in which the biological "facts" failed to comport with that end, the facts were elaborated, displaced, or ignored.

The threat to family posed by the unwed-father cases was multidimensional. In those cases, the legal system was asked to approve a definition of paternity equating biological paternity with biological maternity. But that would have undermined the significance of paternal choice, which for centuries has been central to the definition of fathers as compared to mothers.

The unwed-father cases presented a curious twist on the assumption that blood is thicker than water. The biological fathers in these cases argued, in effect, that *their* ties to their biological children were more like blood than water, thereby contradicting the assumption that, for unwed fathers, biological paternity neither guarantees nor constitutes social fatherhood. In at least two of the cases, the Supreme Court was tempted to agree. But even in those cases, the Court continued to predicate paternity on a combination of biology *and* choice.

The first four unwed-father cases, read as a set, make sense only if interpreted to say that the strength and significance of a biological father's tie to his children depend on paternal choice—on the father's decision to establish a home with his biological children and their mother. The home need not be a "marital home," but it must at least approximate one before the law will declare a "natural" father to be the legal "father."

Michael H. made that reading explicit. The choice to become a social father, though fundamental to the very definition of paternity, is circumscribed. A biological father may choose fatherhood. Indeed, if he intends to be a legal father, he *must* so choose. But not any sort of choice will do. He must choose to relate to his child in the context of that child's mother—in the context of "family." Any other choice would undermine the distinctiveness of the kinship bond and would thereby menace the definition of family as a constellation of "compelling" relationships—of bonds "stronger than . . . other kinds of bonds." In *Michael H.*, for instance, the biological father's connection to his daughter was combined with a social commitment to the child. For the Court, that combination held no weight. Because the child's mother was married to another man, the biological father could not establish a "family" with the mother and therefore could not be a legal father in California. He could not, in short, expect the constitution to protect his paternity. Men get to choose how "thick" their blood will be, but the terms of the choice are set.

In the surrogate-mother cases, the threat to family was more obvious still. Commercial surrogacy suggests the commodification of babies and of the women who bear them, and for this reason, the practice has been widely condemned. However, in both *Baby M* and *Johnson,* the contracting parents' central hope was somehow to create a good old-fashioned, American family.[20] In both *Baby M* and *Johnson* the courts were convinced, and gave the contracting couple custody of, if not exclusive parental rights to, the child.

To achieve the desired result, the courts that heard *Baby M* and *Johnson* composed the biological facts so that the child was given to the parents with the more middle-class, traditional, home. In neither *Baby M* nor *Johnson* did biological "facts" render particular judicial decisions inevitable. In *Baby M,* the New Jersey trial court justified the decision to terminate Whitehead's maternal rights by distinguishing Whitehead's biological maternity from biological maternity in general. By arranging to sell her baby—or rather to sell her capacity to conceive and bear that baby—Whitehead forfeited the benefits biological maternity usually bestows. In *Johnson,* the decision to locate biological maternity in genetics was not only contingent but conflicted with the assumption found in the unwed-father cases that pregnancy and childbirth constitute the essence of maternity. Rather than deny that truth, the courts that heard *Johnson* displaced it. The prerogatives of pregnancy were reserved for proper women in proper homes. When asserted by a woman like Anna Johnson—poor, black, and single—the claim that pregnancy creates maternal bonds shows only bad faith. Judge Parslow wrote:

> There is substantial evidence in the record that Anna never bonded with this child until she filed her lawsuit, if then. And that at that point of course there may be questions about her bonding claim period. One of the problems with bonding is that it always involves credibility issues." (*Johnson v. Calvert,* No. X 633190 5–6)

Gestation carries one set of implications for the middle-class, married "mother"—and another set of implications, or perhaps no implications at all, for other "mothers."

Taken as a whole, the unwed-father and surrogate-mother cases confirm a legal understanding of family predicated on, but not inexorably connected to, "biological facts." Biological facts were called into judicial play only when they justified legitimizations of family desired on other grounds—when they justified the preservation of traditional families.

Thus, "biological facts" may provide a justification for, but not the substance of, parenthood, as in the unwed-father cases; they may be ignored, in effect denied, as in the trial-court opinion in *Baby M;* or, as *Johnson* suggests, they may be interpreted in light of the class or marital status of the "mothers" involved. In these cases, the courts invoked, elaborated, or denied "biological facts" so as to justify their holdings. And in each case, the court's holding sanctioned the creation, or the preservation, of traditional families, either in general or in the particular case. Uniformly, the courts in these cases rejected the suggestion that families be viewed as collections of autonomous individuals, joined by unfettered choice, and selected families that reflected traditional notions of spouses, together with their children.

Notes

I would like to thank Hofstra University for providing me with the research support that made preparation of this article possible. I have discussed the legal aspects of some of the issues considered in this paper in "Just a Gene: Judicial Assumptions About Parenthood," *UCLA Law Review* 40(3) (1993).

Parts of this article will be presented and elaborated in a book, tentatively entitled *Reproductive Technology and the Law,* to be published by New York University Press.

1. The New York statute upheld in *Lehr v. Robertson* gave some, but not all, biological fathers the right to notice of an adoption proceeding involving their children. Such fathers included, among others, those who were listed on the birth certificate, those who had signed a state "putative father registry," those who lived openly with the child and the child's mother at the time of the proceeding in question, and those who "held [themselves] out" as the fathers of their biological children.

2. Limited exceptions were available, but none that offered the biological father the chance to rebut the so-called "marital presumption."

3. Justice Scalia's opinion was not decisive since it was joined by only three other justices. However, Justice Stevens concurred in the opinion, thus rendering the holding law to the extent of Stevens's concurrence.

4. Justice Scalia's opinion referred at least six times to Michael as the "adulterous natural father."

5. The Court's decision did not *require* states to ignore the paternal claims of unwed, biological fathers. The decision only proclaimed that such schemes are not prohibited by any provision of the Constitution. In 1990, after the *Michael H.* decision, California, on its own, amended the statute at issue in *Michael H.* to allow men in Michael H.'s position to rebut the marital presumption if they seek to do so within two years of the child's birth (16 *Family Law Reporter* [BNA] 1520 [1990]). Such men were thereby given the same chance to rebut the marital presumption as the husband of the biological mother.

6. Alternatives exist. The ova may come from a third woman, either an anonymous donor or a relative or friend of the contracting parents or of the surrogate. In such a case, the genetic, gestational, and socializing aspects of motherhood would all be distinct. Three women could thus lodge cognizable claims to be the legal mother of one child. Similarly, the sperm may come from a third-party donor, thereby giving at least two men cognizable claims to paternity.
   The fee paid surrogates by intending parents in both "traditional" and gestational surrogacy cases has been about $10,000 (Andrews and Douglass 1991:672). In addition, if

such arrangements are set up by third-party brokers, the intending parents pay a fee, sometimes higher than that paid to the surrogate, to such mediators (*id.,* 672).

7. Before the last century and a half, understandings of paternity and maternity in the United States and Europe resembled more closely than they do now those delineated by Carol Delaney for Turkey (1991:30–42).

8. In fact, the contract involved in the case was signed by William Stern, Mary Beth Whitehead, and Whitehead's husband, Richard Whitehead. Elizabeth Stern did not enter the contract in order to avoid claims that the contract was for the sale of a baby. Richard Whitehead did enter the contract in order to deny paternity of the baby his wife would conceive and bear.

9. In fact, things were a bit more complicated than this. At the baby's birth, Whitehead relinquished it to the Sterns but the next day went to the Sterns' home, where she told the Sterns of her deep suffering at having lost the child. The Sterns agreed to let Whitehead take the baby home with her for a short time. When Whitehead refused to return the child to the Sterns, they went to court. An *ex parte* order demanding return of Baby M to the Sterns was issued, but when the process server went to Whitehead's home to execute the court's order, Whitehead handed Baby M out the window to her husband. Along with their two children and Baby M, the Whiteheads fled to Florida, where Mary Beth's parents lived. The Sterns commenced supplementary legal proceedings in Florida. On July 31, 1986, almost three months after the Whiteheads left New Jersey for Florida, local police enforced the Florida court's order that the baby be returned to the Sterns. The New Jersey trial court then reaffirmed its original order. At this time, Whitehead was given limited visitation rights.

10. Johnson's claim that the Calverts were guilty of fetal neglect was based on her assertion that they had put her under stress during her pregnancy and thereby risked the baby's health. (Healy 1991:96).

11. The trial court in *Baby M* ignored statutory law regulating adoptions and the termination of parental rights, presumably on the grounds that the legislature that promulgated those rules had no intention that the rules be applicable to surrogacy and that the contract's terms superseded statutes that might otherwise apply.

12. Custody was given to William Stern, alone, but it was the appeal of the stable two-parent Stern household, including both William and Elizabeth as parents, that convinced the court to grant custody to Stern.

13. Judge Parslow's opinion was rendered orally from the bench and transcribed by the court reporter. As a result, the language is not entirely grammatical or consistent.

14. In fact, Anna Johnson's heritage was black, Native American, and Irish. The media paid a great deal of attention to Anna's race, almost always identifying her as black. Mark Calvert was white and Crispina Calvert a Filipina. Katha Pollitt speculates that Crispina's marriage to a white man may have eroded the relevance of her own ancestry (Pollitt 1990:825). In addition, of course, in the American context, blacks are defined differently from other groups that are identified through heritage.

15. Crispina Calvert worked as a registered nurse. Mark was an insurance broker. Anna Johnson was a low-paid worker in the same hospital in which Crispina Calvert worked (Pollitt 1990:826).

16. When heard by the California Court of Appeal the case was called *Anna J. v. Mark C.* Since this paper was written, the decision of the California Court of Appeal was affirmed by the Supreme Court of California (1993).

17. Without reproducing the court's complicated journey through California law here, the uncertainty of the trip's conclusions can be suggested. The judge read state law correctly,

with regard to most cases, to allow demonstration of the mother-child relationship through application of provisions promulgated with reference to the father-child relationship (*Anna J. v. Mark C.,* 374). Thus, the court decided that the sort of blood testing used to indicate paternity could be used, identically, to indicate maternity. However, when the relevant sections of the California civil law were enacted, neither legislators nor anyone else were thinking about gestational surrogacy. That is suggested dramatically in the laboratory report indicating that Anna Johnson was not the child's genetic mother. The application of such testing to women was so novel that the laboratory results, reproduced in the opinion, *Anna J. v. Mark C.,* 373 n.12, actually described the test result as one of *nonpaternity.*

18. Explaining why kinship has been regarded in anthropological theory as a privileged system, David Schneider (1984: 165) wrote:

    I suggest that it has been so defined because there is an assumption that is more often than not implicit, sometimes assumed to be so self-evident as to need no comment, but an assumption that is, I believe, widely held and necessary to the study of kinship. It is the single most important assumption on which the premise of the privileged nature of kinship and the presumed Genealogical Unity of Mankind rests. It is the assumption that Blood is Thicker than Water.

19. In so assuming, these judges resembled the anthropologists whose work on kinship David Schneider analyzed in *A Critique of the Study of Kinship* (1984:97–177).

20. In a brief to the New Jersey Supreme Court, Elizabeth and William Stern's lawyers described the Stern family as follows:

    The Sterns live in Tenafly, New Jersey. The neighborhood consists mostly of younger families. There are many children living on the block. On either side of the Sterns' house there are families with children aged three to nine.

    The nearest commercial area is about a half a mile away from the Sterns' house. Bill Stern often takes Melissa in her stroller for a leisurely stroll around the small shops and area in general.

    One block from the Sterns' house is a park designed for little children. It contains swings, sliding boards and other recreation equipment for young children. Bill frequents this park with Melissa.
    The Sterns' home is on a tree-lined street. The rooms in the house are situated in such a way that the baby's crib may be seen from the Sterns' bed. A study in the Sterns' home has been turned into a playroom for Melissa.

    Bill and Betsy Stern enjoy a sociable and rewarding relationship with their neighbors. With their neighbors they engage in special family events, share advice on mothering and in other areas. The Sterns also get together with neighbors to play and to visit for dinner or for other social occasions. (*Brief on Behalf of Respondents William and Elizabeth Stern,* 33–44)

References

Books and Articles

Andrews, L., and L. Douglass. 1991. "Alternative Reproduction." *Southern California Law Review* 65:623.

Barnett, S., and M. Silverman. 1979. *Ideology and Everyday Life*. Ann Arbor: Univ. of Michigan Press.

Delaney, Carol. 1991. *The Seed and the Soil: Gender and Cosmology in Turkish Village Society*. Berkeley: Univ. of California Press.

Healy, Nichole 1991. "Beyond Surrogacy: Gestational Parenting Agreements Under California Law." *UCLA Women's Law Journal* 1:89.

Pollitt, K. 1990. "When is a Mother Not a Mother?" *The Nation* 215:825.

Schneider, D.M. 1968 (2d. ed. 1980). *American Kinship: A Cultural Account*. (2d ed.) Chicago: Univ. of Chicago Press.

————. 1984. *A Critique of the Study of Kinship*. Ann Arbor: Univ. of Michigan Press.

Strathern, M. 1988. "Enterprising Kinship: Consumer Choice and the New Reproductive Technologies." *Cambridge Anthropology* 14: 1–12.

————. 1992. "A Partitioned Process." In *Reproducing the Future: Anthropology, Kinship and the New Reproductive Technologies*. Manchester, UK: Manchester Univ. Press.

Cases and Briefs

In re Baby M, 525 A2d 1128, *aff'd in part and rev'd in part*, 537 A2d 1227 (1988).

Brief on Behalf of Respondents William and Elizabeth Stern, In re Baby M, 537 A2d 1227 (1988).

Caban v. Mohammed, 441 U.S. 380 (1979).

Hewitt v. Hewitt, 394 N E 2d 1204 (1979).

Johnson v. Calvert, 19 Cal. Rptr. 2d 494 (S.Ct. Cal. 1993), *aff'g sub nom. Anna J. v. Mark C.*, 286 Cal. Rptr. 369 (Cal. App. 4 Dist. 1991), *aff'g No. X 633190* (Cal. App. Dep't Super. Ct. Oct. 22, 1990).

Lehr v. Robertson, 463 U.S. 248 (1983).

Michael H. v. Gerald D., 491 U.S. 110 (1989).

Quilloin v. Walcott, 434 U.S. 246 (1978).

Stanley v. Illinois, 405 U.S. 645 (1972).

3

Heredity, or: Revising the Facts of Life

Rayna Rapp

Introduction

A word never has a single meaning except in one, limiting set of circumstances. When a word is being used within the very narrow confines of a rigidly controlled scientific utterance where the meaning is explicitly defined in unitary terms for that particular occasion or that particular usage, any other meanings that word might have are suppressed and the defined meaning is its only meaning. But since words are seldom used in this way, and rarely if ever in "natural" culture, this limitation can safely be ignored while the polysemic nature of words is kept firmly in mind. (David Schneider, *American Kinship: A Cultural Account*).

In studying the social impact and cultural meaning of amniocentesis for much of the last decade, I have been struck by the problems genetic counselors and geneticists have in constructing and imposing scientifically accurate descriptions of biogenetic inheritance. The science of genetics provides a well-developed lexicon for describing biological relationships forged through sexual reproduction. In the human species, reproduction entails the combination and recombination of chromosomes that carry the genes and that are contained in maternal and paternal gametes. During fertilization, each side ideally contributes an equal amount of genetic material in twenty-three pairs of chromosomes to the fertilized egg, which will in time develop from zygote to embryo to fetus and, finally, to neonate. This is the powerful universal description of human sexual reproduction which the conventional language of biomedicine in general, and genetics in particular, provides.

The amniotic fluid of a pregnant uterus contains cells that have been sloughed off by the growing fetus. By removing three tablespoons of that fluid by amniocentesis, fetal chromosomes can be cultured and analyzed in a cytogenetics laboratory. Standard genetic technologies probe for errors of cell division through which too much or too little hereditary material is passed on to every cell of the growing organism. The once-arcane discourse of genetics has taken on increased practical consequences for nonscientists as amniocentesis has become routinized. But pregnant women and their supporters often hold other ideas about parental contributions to pregnancies, about the causes of babies born with stigmatized disabilities, and about the means and meaning of a hereditary connection itself. The content of blood links, the existential status of Down's Syndrome children, the reasons for miscarriages and stillbirths—all are subjects ripe for social speculation as well as scientific explanation.

In this essay, I analyze differences between scientific and popular understandings of heredity, exploring variations in cultural constructs concerning the nature of relatedness. The essay does not evaluate the truth claims of biomedicine but rather contextualizes the sociocultural relations within which they are articulated and interpreted. I begin with an interpretation of the biomedical discourse and practical activities surrounding prenatal testing, attending to its powerful, universalizing claims on the definition of personhood and kin connection. I then suggest why translating genetics into "user-friendly" terms is an exercise that can never be completely accomplished, given the practical contests for meaning invoked by gendered and generational relations. The social relations within which the ties between sexual partners and parents and children are forged are far more complex and fluid than the processes of material exchange and transmission described within genetics. The discourse of genetics indexes topics—normative reproduction, disability, selective abortion—that are fraught with the range of values, emotions, and power arrangements through which family relations are lived out. But a scientific world view does not overtly reflect the complex social attachments invoked by pregnancy, abortion, and experiences with disability. The scientific meanings of heredity must therefore be continuously constructed, imposed, challenged, or resisted in light of these lived realities. In short, the dominion of science in social life is always the subject of a contest for meaning.

I have thus far been writing as if scientific and popular understandings were not only separate but also each internally unified. But of course, they are not. As a field-working anthropologist, it is important to assert the existence of variation among scientists (and biomedical service providers) concerning personal world views and styles of communication with patients. Nonetheless, training in biomedicine in general, and genetics in particular, provides a powerful vocabulary within which to construct a universalizing world view: an extra chromosome at the twenty-first locus (as geneticists pair them), for example, invariably causes Down's Syndrome wherever and whenever it is found. Scientific knowledge is powerful, and it easily tempts those who live under its penumbra to assume that its enunciation requires no further particularizing interpretation before the technologies with which it is associated can be beneficially applied.

But each pregnancy is embedded within concrete, historically shaped resources and aspirations that are far from uniform. And accommodation and resistance to scientific knowledge is always interpreted in social frameworks larger than the biomedical. In the face of the information on Down Syndrome, for example, one Evangelical Haitian husband I observed in genetic counseling firmly rejected prenatal testing for his wife, saying, "What is this retarded? They always say that Haitian children are retarded in the public schools. But when we put them in the Haitian Academy [a community-based private school], they do just fine. I do not know what this retarded is." In his experience, "chromosomes" seemed a weak and abstract explanation for the problems of prejudicial labeling a Haitian child may face. Moreover, in translating for counseling sessions, I discovered that there is no recognition of Down's Syndrome or mongolism among recent immigrants from the Haitian countryside: no word exists in Creole for the condition. In a country with the worst infant mortality statistics in the western hemisphere, babies may die from many causes, and this one may go unrecognized as a "syndrome." In this one small example, several contests for meaning are engaged. Most obviously, the power of science to define and intervene in what it defines as a biological problem here confronts uneven access to the benefits and burdens a scientific world view provides. Likewise, experiences of stigmatized and recent migration, Evangelical conversion, and the authority of husbands over wives are all in play. Multiple and intersecting power differences are thus engaged when prenatal testing is discussed. The working of those power differences inside ideas about heredity is the subject of this essay.

The Cytogenetics Laboratory is an Empire of Signs

The scientific field of genetics and popular American ideas about kinship appear to share a normative framework, for both agree that "one-half of the biogenetic substance of which the child is made is contributed by the genetrix, and one-half by the genitor. . . . 50% comes from his mother and 50% from his father at the time of his conception, and thereby is his 'by birth' " (Schneider 1980:23). Indeed, a standard session in genetic counseling centers on a discussion of eggs and sperm, haploid and diploid cells, meiosis and mitosis, and chromosome reduction division, all of which are narrated to suggest that the goal of reproduction is to get precisely 50 percent (and neither more nor less) of one's genetic inheritance from each parent if normalcy is to be produced. Thus, ideas about normative heredity seem to be shared by both specialists and laity, at the most basic level.

But enunciated scientific definitions and popular understandings also diverge. Most obviously, the substances in which these normative ideas are instantiated are not the same: the objects that geneticists investigate are chromosomes, while popular ideas about kinship center on blood. And it takes a lot of scientific work to transform the second into the first. While the realm of science-as-culture is properly beyond the scope of this essay, I should note the material resources and disciplines of a cytogenetics laboratory—the skilled combinations of eyes, hands, chemical reagents, cookers and coolers, centrifuges and pipettes, microscopes, and, increasingly, computers—that have allowed technicians, technologists, and geneticists to observe, characterize, and describe chromosomes in all their human variation. But analysis of "*Laboratory Life*" (Latour and Woolgar 1979) is another, if related, story. Here, I point to the discursive work that the construction of a scientific definition of heredity entails. Not only must popular meanings of hereditary transmission be suppressed in favor of scientific ones; scientific meanings must also be made sufficiently accessible so that patients (in this case, pregnant women and their supporters) can act upon them. This work is done through the practice of genetic counseling.

In the state of New York (and many other states), women recommended for prenatal testing must be offered genetic counseling before they can accept or refuse amniocentesis. This requirement functions through both professional code and regulatory law. The American College of Obstetricians and Gynecologists (ACOG) sets "prevailing standards of care," which in turn deeply influence the outcome of malpractice suits. It strongly recommends that its member-physicians inform pregnant women over thirty-five years of age of the existence of the test. In addition to age-related testing, a small number of women are also recommended for prenatal diagnosis because they and their partners are known carriers of specific conditions for which tests are available or because they have already given birth to an affected child. Regulatory statutes of both New York City and state health departments mandate that genetic testing be made available to those who are deemed appropriate candidates and who desire it, and funding must be made available for those unable to pay for it themselves. Pregnant women who fall within certain social groups—primarily, A.M.A. (advanced maternal age)—are thus virtually required to discuss scientific ideas about heredity and prenatal transmission of chromosomally based disabilities early in their pregnancy with a counselor. Relations between genetic counselors and pregnant patients are thus initiated by both profession and state.

Indeed, the development, diffusion, routinization, and resistance to prenatal diagnosis can only be understood once the nature of "relations of law" is fully explored, but this is a task that cannot be accomplished in a brief essay. Suffice it to say that the history of eugenics and its post–World War II transformation within and outside of the field of genetics—struggles over abortion legislation; statutory and regulatory public-health law at both municipal and, especially, state levels; our national and state-based policies concerning health insurance and hence access to testing—all these condition the medical contexts in which pregnant women and genetic counselors are encouraged to discuss "the facts of life." The legal and medical institutions within which prenatal diagnostic technologies are embedded profoundly shape their meaning and their acceptance. While a comparative and historical framework lies beyond the bounds of this essay, it is worth considering that in Scandinavian countries, for example, amniocentesis is universally available to all women deemed medically appropriate candidates for this test, and acceptance rates approach one hundred percent. In contrast, New York City probably offers and subsidizes amniocentesis for a higher percentage of medically appropriate candidates than does any other locality in the United States, but acceptance rates are highly variable, running as low as thirty percent in some city hospitals. The differential diffusion of prenatal testing in Scandinavia can be accounted for by a host of institutional factors, ranging from Scandinavia's relative homogeneity of educational and medical services available to all citizens; to its centralized, government-provided health care plans in which most people express satisfaction; and a concomitant absence of malpractice suits as a driving force in the routinization of services. Institutional history thus clearly frames the circumstances within which provision of the genetic counseling services (described below) occurs.

At an intake interview, the counselor explains the hereditary transmission of chromosomes, deciphers the risk of what is so antiseptically called "birth defects," describes the benefits and limitations of a sonogram-assisted amniocentesis, and tries to answer any questions a pregnant woman may have before she can make up her mind about using or refusing the test. The counselor also takes a personal and familial health history, focusing on reproductive and hereditary disabilities, in order to see whether pregnancy is at risk for conditions for which prenatal tests now exist.

The discourse of genetic counseling is resolutely medico-scientific, revealing and creating some meanings, masking or silencing others. Medical language commands great authority in the interview. While many counselors modulate their discussion of genetics according to their assessment of the individual client's scientific background, there is still a profound, potential gap built into much of their communication process. Genetic counselors are inherently bilingual, having been raised in one language community but having acquired science as a second (or subsequent) language. While this is undoubtedly true for many health-care providers, not all speak a dialect of science as resolutely specialized, statistical, and rapidly evolving as do members of the genetics community. Their professional discourse focuses, of course, on the human life-force itself. But they describe the biological basis of human life through erudite technologies. Genetic counselors learn to speak about risk figures and DNA probes with fluency, and their specialized vocabulary is ever expanding. As one workshop leader at a counseling conference held in Asilonar, California, in 1992 pointed out, "We all speak in anagrams. Can you remember when you learned to talk about—LMP, AMA, TOP, FISH, PCR, RFLPs? And when you learned to stop talking about RFLPs [because this tool for cutting into chromosomes and reproducing bits of them quickly became obsolete]?" Not only do counselors science-speak; they also lay claim to words that appear to have common-sense meanings, reassigning them specialized ones. Thus, a "positive family history," an "uneventful pregnancy," or "unremarkable family background"—even the concept of "reassurance" or the notion of "ethnic background"—hold specific meanings in counseling discourse. Often, these invert common-sense understandings: a "positive family history," for example, is anything but, as it refers to the presence of a serious, genetically transmissible condition. It is rare that a woman codes her own pregnancy as "uneventful," although this label marks the counselor's assessment that no further testing is indicated. "Ethnic background" for a genetic counselor has nothing to do with community traditions or tastes. Rather, it marks certain populations as "at elevated risk" for specific diseases. These inversions attempt the work of suppression to which Schneider's insight about scientific language referred.

But the work of suppression is more than lexical. The terminology of genetics comes attached to a scientific world view that suggests that adjusting the material world to human aspirations is a positive goal. This positive evaluation of intervention into the biological conditions of human life is shared by many, but certainly not all, pregnant women and their supporters sent for genetic counseling. Miscommunication as well as communication, silence as well as conversation, may thus characterize a genetic-counseling appointment, as patients and professionals negotiate both arcane idioms and core cultural issues.

These communicative scripts are played out in routine interactions. Every counselor develops an opening statement to pregnant patients with three goals in mind: to convey significant information about the risks of birth defects and the availability and nature of amniocentesis; to take a health and family history; and to communicate with the patient well enough so that her questions and concerns can be addressed. Most counselors adjust their standard speeches to the audiences they are accustomed to serving, as illustrated by these examples transcribed from my observations of counseling sessions to a group of working-class clinic patients, a counselor might say:

> Each time a woman gets pregnant, there is a two to three percent chance of a birth defect. Now, nobody likes to talk about birth defects, but we're

here today talking about them because there's something you can do to prevent some of them.

Have you heard of genes? Genes are the hereditary units. We all inherit many things from each of our parents: the way we look, the way we act, the way our bodies function.

But every woman has to make up her own mind if she wants to take this test. Today, we just talk, no needles. That's what counseling means.

Both the seriousness and reassuring nature of the test are also stressed when counselors speak to middle-class patients:

This procedure is designed to pick up birth defects. Mostly, we give out good news and reassurance, but occasionally we pick up something that will make you confront a very hard decision. . . . But remember, no matter what her age, a woman's chances are always in favor of producing a healthy baby.

The counselor is likely to present a middle-class group with richer technical descriptions and metaphorical elaborations:

Chromosomes are the basic units of heredity, carrying all the information on physical and mental makeup of their individuals. Genes are contained within chromosomes, and genes are made up of DNA. If your heredity is a library, then chromosomes are the volumes, and the pages and chapters are genes. There are forty-six volumes to the set.

This is a karyotype. It's a picture of chromosomes enlarged 8,000 times and put into order. To be normal, you need to have forty-six chromosomes in all the cells of your body. To an untrained eye, chromosomes look like sticks or caterpillars in the microscope.

Chromosomes are like a string of pearls. The genes are on that string. Our genes determine everything about us—our hair, our eyes, how tall we grow. They're even starting to say that our personality is genetic. So you can see how important chromosomes are. Look at the number on your chart, that number, forty-six, is very important. Any wrong number causes serious problems mentally, neurologically, physically, from having too much or too little genetic information.

If you were walking down the street and looking at a brick building, you'd be looking at a chromosome. Now, we know that the building is made up of individual bricks, just like genes. But what you see in the microscope are chromosomes, like whole houses.

Inside these descriptions, many kinds of work are being done. Metaphors are being used to move a potentially distant object closer, supplying known images to substitute for unknown (or incompletely known) objects of discussion: books, pearls, caterpillars, and brick buildings are easier to envision than the squiggly lines on the karyotype, which shows chromosomes paired and ordered. In such "user-friendly" descriptions, the authority of science is also being conveyed.

Making chromosomes "user friendly" entails more than just skilled translation services; it entails a practical problem that is also simultaneously a problem of emotion, knowledge, belief, and power. Chromosomes for prenatal diagnosis are located inside amniotic fluid, and amniotic fluid is, of course, located in the wombs of pregnant women. Getting chromosomes out entails getting not only needles but also ideas into a space that is highly charged: at once a sanctuary, a factory, and a site of struggle, women's wombs are attached to sentient persons, in all their various complexity, sometimes despite and ofttimes including the many constituencies such as neonatologists, right-to-life activists, and others (like husbands or mothers-in-law) who all claim interests in particular pregnancies.

One way to bypass the contradictory complexity of who controls the womb and its contents is for genetic counselors to assimilate amniotic fluid to blood. Blood is a deeply conventionalized fluid which belongs "to everybody," unlike the specifically female amniotic fluid about which much less is popularly known or imaged. Almost all counselors describe the process of having an amniocentesis as analogous to a blood test. Reassuringly routine, a blood test is understood by almost everybody to represent a virtually risk-free window into health and illness. Pregnant women give blood regularly, and most understand that a few tablespoons of this life-line substance can yield information on which important medical decisions will be made.

But pregnant women do not routinely give amniotic fluid, and women from many ethnic backgrounds fear the needle through which it is withdrawn. It is hard to get women to articulate the content of such fear: when observing, I often asked for an elaboration. Beyond the pain of being stuck, what did the needle connote? One Haitian patient refused the test, for example, saying, "It's not just the feeling, it's what's going in and coming out. I'm used to a blood test, I know what they're taking. But not this. They are taking something else." Her discomfort at the removal of amniotic fluid may condense many concerns, for example, fear of the new or uncertainty about the status of a liminal bodily fluid connecting herself to her fetus. This fluid has none of the obvious life-and-death valences associated with blood, but in contrasting amniotic fluid to blood, this woman invoked a substance that is simultaneously symbolic and material in its importance. As a conduit for both mortality and immortality, blood is obviously deeply embedded not only in the domain of medicine but in kinship and religion as well.

Amniotic fluid is harder to place: a salt-water medium that contains fetal urine and sloughed off skin cells that can be made to grow under laboratory conditions, it is the medium in which the growing fetus lives and excretes.

A medical text would speak of its electrolytic isomorphism with maternal blood, with which it shares most of its contents, excepting blood cells themselves. Pregnant women, however, often describe amniotic fluid in terms of the child, substantialized, acorn to oak, in the fluid itself:

> It will be OK. The fluid came out right, light. The doctor told me the fluid looked good, so I know the baby looks good. If the fluid comes dark, then you got problems, then they take action right away. (Luz Perez, 37, Puerto Rican home-care attendant)
> "Beautiful" the doctor said "beautiful," when he saw what was in the test tube. The baby will be beautiful. (Martha Freeman, 39, African-American school teacher)

Many women expressed astonishment, awe, or disbelief in the diagnostic powers of this substance:

> I never knew such a small amount of liquid could show so many important things. (JoAnna Lytel, White real-estate salesperson)
> I don't think I really believe in chromosomes, I mean, I could see the pictures, but I can't believe everything is in the chromosomes, and the chromosomes are really just floated in that stuff. Isn't it mainly baby's pee? (Aleta Mitchell, 36, White administrative secretary)

And they may feel quite proprietary:

> It's very surprising what they can find out from a little of my fluid. (Carol Jameson, 40, African-American bus driver)

For an anthropologist, ideas about amniotic fluid (and, of course, the chromosomes being cultured in it) are intriguing, for they raise the question of whether there might be new bases for symbolic and material representations of kinship, new canvases on which contributions of genitor and genitrix might be painted. By relocating the discourse of heredity onto chromosomes, themselves contained inside of amniotic fluid, might genetics be offering new bases for aligning scientific and popular understandings of kinship connections?

Gender and Substance Abuse

But before we wax eloquent over the miraculous representational powers of modern science, I think it is important to question the allegedly massive kinship transformations heralded in recent popular and scientific discussions of the new reproductive technologies. Scientific interventions into reproduction play themselves out on a much older engendered terrain. The insights of both feminism and fieldwork strongly suggest that

> when reproduction is viewed as a natural process, parental roles are also interpreted as primarily biological, an idea that obscures culturally authorized unequal distributions of power. (Collier and Delaney 1992:302) Definitions and practices of "reproduction" are always already constructed within fields of power. (Yanagisako and Collier 1987, cited by Collier and Delaney 1992:301)

Those fields of power are constantly and contradictorily constructed by different kinds of difference. Most obviously, gender differences construct the roles of parents unequally. No matter how many chromosomes a geneticist counts, nor how many relatives an anthropologist researches, men's contributions to baby–making across American cultures are considered creative, for they spark the fetus into existence. But the daily burden of producing a normatively acceptable fetus and child usually rests on the women. And women often blame themselves, or are blamed by family members, for the problems with which their children are born:

> I fell down during my pregnancy with her two times, and then this happened. (Dominican mother, 33, describing the birth of her daughter with cleft lip and palate)
> My mother-in-law says the cleft [in the first son] was caused by me using scissors during the pregnancy. This time, I've come for your counseling, but I won't use scissors during the pregnancy. (Chinese garment worker, 32)
> My mom don't want me near his retarded brother now, when I come up pregnant. She's worrying in case my baby catch it. (African-American student 17, sickle cell trait carrier)

Women and their supporters from many ethnic backgrounds believe that behavior they define as healthy or unhealthy is responsible for a pregnancy's outcome. This belief is undoubtedly helpful in linking smoking or alcohol consumption to low-birth weight or some congenital problems, for it suggests behavioral guides that many women can accommodate (although the punitive gaze focused upon pregnant women unto the point of criminalization of unhealthy behaviors is a highly contested domain, but that's another story). In any case, it doesn't aid in understanding chromosomes, whose patterns and pathologies are (theoretically) unaffected by maternal behavior.[1] Many Puerto Rican, Dominican, and Haitian women rejected prenatal testing, with a variant of "I don't smoke, I don't drink, I don't take drugs, I eat good food, I take good care of myself. What do I need this test for?" (Dominique Laurent, 39, Haitian garment worker).

Often, an assessment of age-related risks is personalized and folded into an interpretation of family history:

> My family's all healthy, they're all professionals, they're active, they take
> good care. Me, I cut out smoking, I've been off birth control pills for ages,
> and two of my cousins had babies when they were in their forties. I'm not
> at risk. (Angela Storrman, 41, African-American public school teacher)
> This only happens if you take drugs, that's when it happens. Nothing to
> do with me. (Maria Dominguez, 38, Dominican day-care worker)

Maternal health practices are frequently discussed in the language of epidemiology, substance abuse, and life-style choices, but they also engage a much older and enduring morality play. As feminist anthropologists have pointed out, women in many cultures, especially Euro-American cultures, are held, and hold themselves, responsible for nurturance. When something "goes wrong," that too is powerfully pictured as a failure of female responsibility. In our folk models of reproduction the "quality control" of children is construed as women's domain (Delaney 1986, 1991; Stolcke 1986).

Amniocentesis reveals this gender script at oblique angle, for it provides a forced-choice situation in which testing is either accepted or rejected. Women (and their supporters) must decide whether there are limits to maternal responsibility for disabling conditions. Among the most common reasons given for refusing the test was some variant of "My husband wouldn't let me." But what does this mean?

When women identified their husbands as the authority on whose behalf they were refusing the test, I often wondered whether I was witnessing male dominance or female invocation of a classic manly privilege in the service of their own polite resistance. Sometimes, I felt confident in making an interpretation. Hsia Chiu, for example, had only been in this country for three years when her husband decided she should have amniocentesis in her first pregnancy. While he was out of the consulting room, I asked what lay behind her silence at the counseling session and whether she wanted to have the test. She replied,

> My mother, my grandmother, they all had babies in China, and nobody
> did this. They wouldn't do it now, if they were here. Now is modern times,
> everyone wants to know everything, to know as soon as possible, in advance,
> about everything. What kind of information is this? I don't know, but I
> will soon have it, faster than I can understand it.

Ecuadorian-born Coralina Bollo felt pressured into having the test by her American-born husband. Flora Blanca had to keep her decision to have it secret from her disapproving *companero*. "He'll kill me for this, but I'm gonna do it," commented Puerto Rican–born Nilda Cintron. In such cases, I was persuaded that male dominance was driving a woman's "right to choose."

But gender scripts also revealed healthy doses of female manipulation: many women told me they brought their partners to see the sonogram to further their own ends. "Frank just isn't as committed to this pregnancy as he should be," commented white psychologist Marcia Lang, "but once he sees the baby moving, I know he'll get excited." Juana Martes, a Dominican home-care attendant, also thought men should see the sonogram that accompanies the test: "When the little creature moves, they begin to know what women feel, how they suffer for it to be born, and then they respect their wives."

Sometimes, conflicts between partners surfaced at the heart of counseling sessions, revealing the different interests women and men had constructed. One Colombian low-income couple I observed, for example, was being counseled because both were carriers of the sickle cell trait. The man appeared disinterested, staring into space as the amniocentesis was explained, but when the moment of decision making arrived, he sat up straight and firmly enunciated, "If it's normal, I want it, I want it for the rest of my life. From my position I say out, out if the baby is no good, if it comes out no normal."

The pregnant woman turned toward him and said quite firmly, "Who's carrying this baby?" The counselor tried to diffuse conflict, saying, "That's a decision you'll make together." The counselor was projecting the genetically equal contributions that science identifies onto the gendered stage. Not uncoincidentally, she was also promoting the middle-class norm of "companionate marriage" as a partnership of equals. The discourse of genetics thus advances scientific norms of egalitarian heredity that are highly consonant with other mainstream American values. But its practices focus on an object that cannot be harvested for scientific scrutiny without revealing deeply held gender tensions. The fact of decision making involved in amniocentesis reveals the existing gender negotiations within which any specific pregnancy is undertaken.

Disabling Kinship

Gender is not, however, the only marker of contested difference at work in the interpretation of hereditary relatedness and responsibility.[2] Prenatal testing is, above all, a practical activity, designed to diagnose fetuses with atypical chromosomes. Its purpose is to give women and their supporters the chance to decide to continue or end pregnancies in which a problem is revealed. Because termination of connection to the affected fetus is the silent interlocutor of prenatal testing, distance from abnormal chromosomes, as well as connection to normal ones, must be achieved. Difference as well as continuity, hierarchy as well as equality, can be embedded in biogenetic descriptions. If chromosomes can be discussed as objects of hereditary relatedness, genetic counselors can also describe them in terms that disconnect, as my field observations of counseling sessions indicate:

> We're only looking for fetuses whose inherited material won't give them a chance of a good life because they have too many chromosomes to be normal. The extra chromosomes cause severe handicaps, and life will become very hard for the whole family.
> Trisomy 21 was first described by Doctor Down, which is how it got its name. Regardless of who their parents are, these children look very much alike.

This idea that children with Down's Syndrome resemble one another more than they resemble their families of origin is enunciated not only by genetic counselors but also by pregnant women and by the parents of children with this condition. Indeed, the notion that people with Down's Syndrome could be removed from the kinship nexus that was theirs by birth and relocated inside their own separate tribe caused me to wonder if we might describe their symbolic predicament as a "kinship of affliction" (cf. Robert B. Edgerton, 1993) This is a problem to which I return below.

In speaking with women who have chosen abortion after receiving a prenatal diagnosis of Down's Syndrome, I was struck by the oft-repeated trope of alien kinship. One woman said,

> I had my abortion on June 30th and I was a mess. I was weeping all the time, I was inconsolable, and we went away for the 4th of July and I couldn't calm down at all. We were watching the parade on Main Street in Hamlet, at my in-law's cottage, and a family with a kid with Down's was standing in front of me. Right there at the parade, honest to God, like a sign direct to me. And the thing was, I really looked at the kid, how she dripped her ice cream all over, how she couldn't be made to do what the other kids wanted, I looked at her and thought, "She doesn't belong in that family." She didn't look like them, she looked like someone else. Like a lot of someone elses, not quite from the same race, if you know what I mean. And it made me feel, well, that I'd done the right thing, that the one I aborted wasn't quite from my family, either. (Emily Lockhardt, 37, White antiques restorer)

When mothers of children with Down's Syndrome tell the story of their pregnancies, births, and diagnoses, one common theme is the lack of familial resemblance:

So I had a home delivery and the midwife was very cool. Like she suspected something, but she didn't want to say anything, she just wanted me to enjoy the birth, to bond with Laney. But he was too sleepy, so she knew something was wrong, she called the doctor, and the pediatrician came and she said, "I hate to bring this up, I just have the vague suspicion he doesn't look like he's related to anyone in this family, I just don't think he resembles any of you." . . . At first, I just blocked what she was saying, and then I looked, and well, I had this uneasy feeling 'cause he didn't look like us. He looked like he belonged to some other family. (Judy Kaufman, 32, White nurse)

The first thing the doctor said was, he said, "If you had a lot of Irish moon faces in your family, I'd be happier about seeing this child. But she doesn't look like you, she doesn't look like she's from your gene pool at all." Then he explained why he thought it was Down's. (Laura Wishnick, 30, White lawyer)

The attribution of alien kinship does more than separate Down's Syndrome children from their genitors and genitrixes; it also provides an alternative kin group into which they can be placed.[3] As the sister of an adult with Down's said,

When she's at home, she loves her family, she really loves us. . . . But as soon as you bring her back to her workshop, or to her group house, she forgets you, she forgets you're there. She's with her people, her own people, you can't really talk to her about it, but you can see it. She's with her own people. (Carol Segal, 42, White college professor)

Alternative kinship may romanticize difference:

You know, you can think of Downs people as another beautiful race that the Lord created on this earth. (Bonnie d'Amato, 35, White social worker, mother of a six year old with Down's Syndrome)

I just thought about this negative stuff with the extra chromosome. Actually there's maybe something positive. Maybe its some genetic mutation that sets them all apart, that causes something positive, as well. I think that heart and that generosity and feeling one with the world, that's the positive side. They're different, they're oriented some different way. The extra chromosome doesn't just take something away, it gives something extra. It's like a special trait, they're all the same, and they're all different than us. (Judy Kaufman, 32, White nurse, mother of a five year old with Down's Syndrome)

Alternative kin connections can be used to build freshly imagined families:

There's a place in Pennsylvania where they adopt these kids with Down's. They've got twenty-four right now. (Q: you mean, like a school?) No, it's a family, it's a new family for people who fit there. (Irena Gotchalk, 40, white accountant, mother of a ten year old with Down's Syndrome)

Alternative kinship may also merge children with disabilities into kinship with other species:

Aleem was born with a lot of hair, I said, "Nurse, is this gonna fall off before I bring him home from the hospital?" Because I didn't want nobody to look at Aleem and think he was a little monkey, not a boy. (Johnella Cornell, 27, African-American hairdresser, mother of an infant with Down's Syndrome)
Having him in the house, it's like having a gorilla. (Cynthia Foreman, 38, White law professor, mother of a four year old with a chromosome anomaly)

Relatives and potential relatives of chromosomally disabled children construct a genealogy of affliction that works to both exclude and include, placing marked members outside their families of birth and inside imagined communities of difference.

These imagined communities take on much broader significance when evoked by parent-activists in the service of disability rights. Relatedness and connection is rhetorically restored by the kinship discourse of activists. During my two years of participation in a support group for parents whose children had Down's syndrome, I was struck by how frequently members articulated an inclusive, collective sense of parental responsibility:

You also feel a sense of parenthood for everyone's child, there's a sense they're all my children, you know. Which I don't think you feel with your normal children. (Bonnie d'Amato, 35, White social worker, mother of a six year old with Down's Syndrome)
Our kids need special classrooms in caring schools. Our kids need speech therapists and physical therapists who know their special needs. But most of all, our kids need respect. As a mother, it's my job to get those things for our kids. (Linda Degracia, 34, White secretary, mother of a five year old with Down's Syndrome)

The restitution of kinship here serves to enlarge the human family, claiming a natural base for a social challenge against discrimination.

Conclusion

Normative descriptions of heredity that are developed inside of science can never be completely aligned with popular understandings of relatedness.

Scientific descriptions naturalize a terrain on which power is continuously negotiated in social life beyond the consulting room. Scientific discourse about biogenetic links provides powerful resources that appear neutral. Yet this discourse is available to be invoked and challenged in the daily experiences of living with both difference and inequality. In this essay, I have tried to illustrate how unitary scientific norms are continuously constructed, imposed, challenged, and sometimes resisted in popular understandings of both prenatal diagnosis and disability.

A cultural analysis of genetic discourse opens up another window on the foundational assumptions of the natural basis of Euro-American kinship. When experts instruct lay patients about "the facts of life" involved in prenatal testing, the equality of genitor and genetrix are overtly described, while gender differences are simultaneously denied and reproduced (cf. Strathern 1992, 1993; Edwards 1993). Likewise, the stigma attached to chromosomally disabled fetuses and people can be both constructed and contested using scientific and genealogical resources.

Describing genealogy as a fact of nature is widespread throughout American culture. But it is the naturalization not only of genealogy into biology but also of the power differences attached to biological descriptions that is contested by new social movements like feminism and disability rights. Feminists and disability-rights activists both struggle against notions of difference that are naturalized, embodied, centered in kinship, and hierarchically organized. Such naturalizations are deeply entrenched in Euro-American culture and are not easily overcome. But in examining them again and again and again, unto the very level of the genome itself, we may someday recognize the highly political nature of our cultural obsessions. Then we may better appreciate how constituencies marked by a stigmatized difference may invoke it to claim the necessity of transformation.

Notes

Funding for this study was provided by the National Endowment for the Humanities, the National Science Foundation, the Rockefeller Foundation's "Changing Gender Roles Program," the Institute for Advanced Studies, the Spencer Foundation, and a semester's sabbatical from the Graduate Faculty, New School for Social Research. I am deeply grateful for their support and absolve them from any responsibility for the uses to which I have put it. I especially thank the scores of pregnant women, health care providers, and family members who took the time and energy to engage in my research questions. Faye Ginsburg applied her usual and quite extraordinary humor and editorial insight to a nascent draft of this essay, and Dorothy Nelkin, Terry Turner, and the editors of this volume also provided extremely useful comments at round two. I am grateful for their encouragement and help.

1. Of course, guidelines on smoking and alcohol consumption during pregnancy also add surveillance as well as reassurance, and are potentially woman blaming, as recent debates on public warnings to pregnant women indicate. And there may well be contributions to chromosome damage that can be socially influenced, but of which we are currently unaware.

Factors such as radiation exposure and diet have been suggested as responsible for reports of "outbreaks" of Down's Syndrome, but have never been confirmed using epidemiological research methods. While there are no obvious, known environmental causes of this (or any other) chromosome problem, we cannot rule out such a possibility. The search for environmental influences of neural tube defects, for example, also used reported "outbreaks." It took several decades of research to eventually link vitamin B/folic acid deficiencies as a contributing cause. Unlike Down's Syndrome, however, neural tube defects tend to cluster ethnogeographically, suggesting the possibility of a dietary link.

2. Indeed, much of my research focuses on ethnocultural, class, and religious diversity in women's responses to the offer of prenatal testing, e.g. Rapp (1993a, 1993b); 1994.

3. I should point out that I have never heard this discourse of displacement/relocation of Down's Syndrome children in African-American or Hispanic families, only in White ones.

References

Collier, Jane F., and Carol Delaney. 1992. "Reply to Cris Shore, Virgin Births and Sterile Debates." *Current Anthropology* 33 (3) (June): 302–303.

Delaney, Carol. 1986. "The Meaning of Paternity and the Virgin Birth Debate." *Man* 21(3): 494–513.

———. 1991. *The Seed and the Soil: Gender and Cosmology in Turkish Village Society.* Berkeley: Univ. of California Press.

Edgerton, Robert B. 1993. *The Cloak of Competence.* Revised and updated. Berkeley and Los Angeles: Univ. of California Press.

———. 197?. "Anthropology and Mental Retardation." In *Cultural Illness and Health,* 11–22. Washington, DC: American Anthropological Association.

Edwards, Jeanette. Sarah Franklin, Eric Hirsch, Frances Price, and Marilyn Strathern. 1993. *Procreation: Kinship in the Context of the New Reproductive Technologies.* Manchester: Manchester Univ. Press.

Latour, Bruno, and Steve Woolgor. 1979. *Laboratory Life.* Beverly Hills, CA: Sage.

Rapp, Rayna. 1993a. "Accounting for Amniocentesis." In *Knowledge, Power and Practice: The Anthropology of Medicine in Everyday Life,* edited by Shirley Lindenbaum and Margaret Lock. Berkeley: Univ. of California Press.

———. 1993b. "Amniocentesis in Sociocultural Perspective." *Journal of Genetic Counseling.* 2 (3): 183–96.

———. 1994. "Risky Business: Genetic Counseling in a Shifting World." *Articulating Hidden Histories: Anthropology, History, and the Influence of Eric R. Wolf,* edited by Jane Schneider and Rayna Rapp. Berkeley: Univ. of California Press.

Schneider, David M. 1980. *American Kinship, a Cultural Account.* Rev. ed. Chicago: Univ. of Chicago Press. Original published by Univ. of Chicago Press, 1968.

Stolcke, Verena. 1986. "New Reproductive Technologies: Same Old Fatherhood." *Critique of Anthropology* 6(3) (Winter): 5–31.

Strathern, Marilyn. 1992. *Reproducing the Future: Anthropology, Kinship, and the New Reproductive Technologies.* Manchester: Manchester Univ. Press.

————. 1993. "Displacing Knowledge: The Consequences of Technology for Kinship." In *Conceiving the New World Order: Anthropology and the Politics of Reproduction*, edited by Faye D. Ginsburg and Rayna Rapp. Berkeley: Univ. of California Press.

Yanagisako, Sylvia, and Jane Collier. 1987. "Toward a Unified Analysis of Gender and Kinship." In *Gender and Kinship: Essays Toward a Unified Analysis*, edited by Jane Fishburne Collier and Sylvia Junko Yanagisako. 14–50. Stanford, CA: Stanford Univ. Press.

4

Forever Is a Long Time: Romancing the Real in Gay Kinship Ideologies

Kath Weston

"If it's real, it's got to last!" The place was a small cafe in San Francisco's Mission District; the topic, kinship. Tony Paige was attempting to explain his reluctance to recognize lesbian and gay families as a legitimate form of relatedness.[1] In the beleaguered tones occasionally adopted by heterosexual residents of this "gay city," Tony protested, "When 'the gays' talk about their 'chosen families,' they're telling me that anybody can be a relative. How will we know who's family and who's not? Where will it all end, I ask you? Besides, gay relationships are notorious for their instability. If people come and go, how can you call them kin?" In response, I noted that the jury was still out on the question of the relative length of gay versus heterosexual relationships.[2] In the eyes of many gay men and lesbians, I continued, "biological" relationships were no less subject to termination than relationships with the friends, lovers, and children that gay people incorporate into their chosen families. As Tony listened to me recount portions of coming-out narratives in which "biological" kin severed family ties after learning that relatives were gay, his look changed to one of perplexity and concern. "I just can't understand that," he responded. "Parents are parents and blood is blood. What kind of person could cut off a child that way?"

For years, anthropologists constructed genealogies and generated accounts of kinship that incorporated a set of cultural presuppositions remarkably congruent with the ones that framed Tony's views on gay families. Kinship ties were, by definition, ties that endured. Unalterable biogenetic connections accounted for the permanence of this very special sort of social relation. In the United States, cultural expectations associated with bonds of kinship incorporated a belief in what David Schneider (1968) called "diffuse, enduring solidarity." Diffuse, because relatives were presumed to interact in a variety of circumstances for a multitude of purposes. A cousin could show up to fix the family car but, unlike a professional auto mechanic hired specifically for the task, the cousin might well stay for dinner and return the following week to celebrate someone's birthday. Enduring, because bonds of kinship should not be broken or substantively transformed in response to life's vicissitudes. Relatives were not supposed to keep a strict accounting of services rendered or make loyalties contingent upon a person's conduct. At the time of my fieldwork in the Bay Area during the mid-1980s, a broad spectrum of people continued to describe relatives as "the ones who are always there for you," a select group upon whom an individual could rely, regardless of context or crisis.

Those who accepted this analysis of a kinship constituted through biological connection and "code for conduct" acknowledged that nonfamilial ties might also be marked by the sort of diffuse, enduring solidarity called "love." Friends, coworkers, old army buddies could be—indeed, were often expected to be—"there" for a person. What social scientists believed distinguished these "other" sorts of relations from kinship ties was their voluntary, and therefore "fragile," character (Allan 1989; Norman 1989).[3] "You can pick your friends, but not your relatives" went an old saying that made its way into monographs on kinship during the 1950s and 1960s. Friends might be loved "just like" family, but they remained "fictive," "pseudo," or "artificial" kin. Whereas friendships and other "nonfamilial" relationships marked by enduring solidarity could be terminated at will, a person was saddled with relatives for life, whether she despised them or eagerly anticipated the next family gathering.[4] Implicit in the distinction between friendship and family—like the distinction between "fictive" and "real" kinship—was a contrast between ties supposed to be freely chosen and ties understood to be given, usually at birth. Procreation determined "true" kinship, and what was "genuine" was not subject to change.

When Schneider (1968, 1984) developed a critique of the reduction of kinship to genealogy, that critique focused less on the permanence attributed to kinship ties than on the notion of the biological infrastructure alleged to support the cultural edifice of an array of kinship terms and practices that varied widely from one society to another.[5] To Schneider and his colleagues, biogenetic connection appeared as nothing more (and nothing less) than a peculiarly Western mode of demarcating a certain set of social ties, a culturally specific way to signify belonging. In the long shadow cast by the critique of kinship, *all* kinship ties (indeed, all social ties) could be characterized as fictive. No justification remained for privileging biogenetic connection as a presocial "fact of life" that ordained certain relationships to be of central importance to social organization. As is the case whenever an insurgent critique casts doubt upon a field's most cherished paradigms, not everyone accepted this novel view of kinship. Scholars on either side of the constructionist debate fortified their positions by drawing upon already well-entrenched relativist versus universalist lines of argument. While some ethnographers resolved to define family as "the natives" defined family and refused to assume that all societies "had" kinship, others continued to perceive a (usually nuclear) family in any assemblage of genitor, genetrix, and progeny.

In the course of deconstructing genealogy, the critique of kinship simultaneously deconstructed kinship as a domain. Without a biological referent, kinship studies seemed in danger of losing its object (Schneider 1984; Yanagisako and Collier 1987). As proponents laid siege to the genealogical nexus that defined the discipline, participants on both sides of the constructionist debate began to echo Tony Paige's lament: "Where will it all end?" Having dismantled the subfield's procreative underpinnings, what more was there for kinship specialists to do but document how kinship was meaningfully constituted for those who employed the concept? After years of being treated as an ethnographic staple, kinship virtually disappeared as a category in advertisements for teaching positions in anthropology.

Ironically—but perhaps not coincidentally—this stagnation in the field of kinship studies occurred at the very historical moment when controversies over so-called "new family forms" were heating up in the United States. By the late 1980s and early 1990s, even the *New York Times* had begun to run stories about gay relationships under headlines such as "How to Define a Family" and "What Makes a Family?" (Gutis 1989; T. Lewin 1990). The disputes chronicled in such media coverage announced the coming of age of kinship ideologies, which contested the narrow interpretations of "the family" that had previously dominated public discourse. Cases were not limited to gay people seeking recognition for their partnerships. In one instance, a woman fought to overturn prison policies so that she could see the child she had raised to adulthood but never formally adopted; in another, a surrogate mother asked for custody of the child she had borne but contracted away. Unmarried heterosexual couples sued to get the family discount rate at the local health club, while friends who considered themselves "part of the family" demanded hospital visitation rights.

Illuminating as the critique of kinship has been in exposing the ethnocentrism built into kinship studies, thus far it has contributed little to an understanding of the conflicting interpretations of kinship that gained currency in the United States by the late twentieth century. As a critical and textual endeavor, it has not developed ways to account for the appearance of kinship ideologies that challenge received wisdom about what constitutes a family. Without detailed reference to historical and material context, kinship studies cannot assess what has made procreative ideologies of kinship seemingly resilient in the face of such challenges. Neither can it evaluate the relative efficacy of the various strategies employed to gain recognition for chosen families and other reconfigurations of kinship ties.

This is not the place to explore in depth the limitations of what might now be considered a deconstructivist project. Suffice it to say that in targeting "biology" and the procreative nexus for deconstruction, anthropologists who subscribed to the critique of kinship approach allowed other key constituents of kinship ideologies in Western societies to maintain their taken-for-granted status.[6] Left largely untheorized are questions about how kinship ideologies arise, how people bring them into play in everyday arenas of dispute, the effect of specific lines of argumentation on power relations between dominant and subordinate groups, what possibilities emergent ideologies open or foreclose, how contests of meaning are themselves socially structured, and how social struggles to legitimate particular forms of kinship end up reshaping the very ideologies they deploy. Addressing these questions requires something more than a straightforward investigation of what different people mean when they invoke categories such as "blood," "love," "choice," or "forever."

To move beyond oversimplified arguments that "alternative" families either totally mirror or completely counter "hegemonic" forms of kinship requires a less dichotomized understanding of the dynamics of ideological change. To move toward an approach that encompasses the interplay of history, meaning, and practice involves reconstructing as well as deconstructing kinship. Rather than marginalizing the study of kinship after exposing the latter as "a special custom distinctive of European culture" (Schneider 1984:201), this focus on contests of meaning reframes the study of families in Western societies in ways that break through the narrow conceptualization of kinship studies as a discrete domain of inquiry.

Competing interpretations of "the family" in Western societies draw upon broader themes of voluntarism, permanence, genuineness, and imitation that historically have mediated the conception of kinship as genealogy. It is no accident that the same country that successfully marketed a soda pop as "the real thing" has conducted a national debate on what makes a family in terms that require participants to come up with arguments as to why their preferred forms of family should be considered "the genuine article." The notion of kinship as a biogenetic connection that brings with it diffuse enduring solidarity represents only one among a number of what Arjun Appadurai (1988) has called "ideologies of authenticity." In the United States, a cultural preoccupation with authenticity is evident across domains that range from "the family" to gender, ethnicity, and cultural politics. Chromosome tests to determine the "true" sex of athletes, advertisements that tout the "authentic" cuisine of ethnic restaurants, museums that scrutinize their collections for forgeries, global tours that pull in customers with promises of a look at "how the natives really live," all speak of a society that continuously reinvents and romanticizes "the real."[7]

Within Tony Paige's objection to the concept of chosen families—"How will we know who's family and who's not?"—dwells a desire to seek and to separate the genuine from the imitative by linking authenticity not only to biology but also to duration. Why should scholars and "subjects" alike be so preoccupied with the adjudication (or dissolution) of authenticity? Why the temptation to elide history through the deep-seated conviction that what is "real" cannot, should not, be subject to change? What, in terms of power, is at stake? It is, after all, rather peculiar (at least to the ethnographic eye) that permanence—mediated by particular conceptions of time and biology—should be integral to both scholarly and popular discussions of kinship. To pose and then investigate such questions offers an opportunity to reinvigorate kinship studies by linking the subfield to important and theoretically vibrant research on history, time, class relations, colonialism, gender studies, and the construction of "the Other."

The concept of gay families is the product of a population whose lesbian, gay, bisexual, and queer subjectivities have been shaped, in part, by the fear of having kinship ties sundered in response to disclosure of a stigmatized sexual identity. Like the anthropological critique of kinship, the gay kinship ideologies that emerged in the United States during the 1980s refused to naturalize familial ties by equating biogenetic connection with kinship per se. At the same time, these ideologies problematized the attribution of permanence to "blood" ties and impermanence to "nonbiological" relationships such as friendship. The same gay kinship ideologies that warn of the fragility of "blood" ties celebrate friendship as an enduring bond that can assume the status of kinship. Within discourse on gay families, friendship turns on its head the cultural association of biogenetic connection with permanence by presenting friendship as the *most* reliable and enduring of kinship relations.

For Once and For Always: Gay Kinship Ideologies of the 1980s–1990s

Light from the restaurant spilled over into the bus stop on the corner. Inside diners were too preoccupied with their mussels marinière to notice the small reunion. Since Debra Lee and Gloria Salcido last met, the better part of a summer had passed. Now they gazed at one another fondly, anxiously, across a suddenly endless expanse of table. Over the years, first as friends, then as partners, and now as "ex-lovers," they had shared the goal of making their connection last. Although each had had time since the breakup to adjust to the changes in their relationship, neither was eager to put feelings about those changes into words. Only after the waitress ended her shift, leaving behind two cups of coffee and the check, did the conversation turn to the matter both knew had brought them here. "You'll always be family to me," Debra said with conviction. Gloria reached out for Debra's arm, then seemed to think better of it. With an ear to the ground and an eye to the future, they began to speak in low tones about the prospects for "working" on their friendship.

The concept of gay or chosen families first began to achieve wide circulation among lesbians and gay men on the West Coast while I was conducting fieldwork in the San Francisco Bay Area during the mid-1980s. At that time, few went so far as to disallow a rather vaguely defined category called "blood" or "biology" as the basis for some type of family tie.[8] Instead they began to speak of "blood" ties as socially negotiated rather than biologically mandated, one among many possible forms of familial relationship.

Before exploring the linkage between friendship and enduring solidarity in gay kinship ideologies, I want to stress that not everyone self-identified as lesbian or gay subscribed to these ideologies or articulated them in the same fashion. A small number believed that "blood" relations could never be terminated or resisted the notion that friends could count as family. When I speak of "gay kinship ideologies," then, I do so with some sense of irony, since this rhetorical tactic resurrects an ethnographic vision of timelessly enduring, discretely bounded cultures (see Thomas 1991:309). Gay "communities" are hardly homogeneous, and they have no neatly demarcated borders. Yet the rhetorical tactic of writing about "gay kinship ideologies" is useful to the extent that it allows me to focus on recurrent *formal* features, such as references to relationships that last, which tended to cross lines of gender, class, race, and ethnicity in discussions of kinship.

In *Families We Choose* (Weston 1991) I explored some of the ways in which differences of identity and interpretation have inflected kinship among lesbians and gay men in the United States.[9] This essay develops a line of inquiry opened in the concluding chapter of that volume: How useful are the terms "same" and "different" for describing the complexities of social change? Can similarities encode difference, and differences similarities? What does it mean that people of different colors, classes, and sexualities consistently alluded to the length of friendships and partnerships in discussions of kinship? Does it make a difference that lesbians and gay men often voiced these remarks in the context of seeking legitimation for their closest relationships? An anniversary celebration for a gay male couple may appear related to a party that commemorates twenty years of heterosexual marriage, but what about the mention of a "longtime friend" in the death notice of a middle-aged lesbian?

For my present and limited purpose, I have posited a (far from) unified gay population as the source of "gay kinship ideologies" in order to throw everyday notions of the permanence that is supposed to be embedded within kinship into strange and startling relief. That move enables me to consider how ostensibly similar formal features of kinship can carry conflicting meanings and embed subtle ideological shifts, allowing "new" family forms to be read simultaneously as radically innovative and thoroughly assimilationist. In the end, they are intrinsically neither.[10]

As constituted during the late 1980s and early 1990s, gay families could encompass gay and heterosexual friends as well as lovers, ex-lovers, and children who might or might not be biogenetically connected to the gay person doing the parenting. Although Gloria Salcido's and Debra Lee's relationship had shifted from one of friends to lovers and then ex-lovers, the two women considered one another "family" throughout the difficult months of their separation and breakup. The size and composition of gay families varied tremendously. Because chosen families generally took the form of a network of kin radiating out from the particular lesbian or gay man who had done the choosing, members frequently spanned several households. Like many others who spoke of having lesbian or gay families, Gloria and Debra described a limited number of friends they considered kin.

Among gay men and lesbians in the Bay Area, a utopian outlook tended to shape discussions of "alternative" family forms. "[Building gay families] is very complicated, I think," explained Paulette Ducharme, "because there's not necessarily a model. So people try a lot of different things. What[ever] works." In practice, however, this sense of creating kinship in the absence of precedent gave way to social arrangements that were meaningfully structured and choices that were inevitably constrained. The *formal* criteria used to differentiate chosen kin from nonkin incorporated signs of diffuse, enduring solidarity that did not differ substantially from those featured in dominant discourse on kinship. Ideally, gay families incorporated relationships forged and tempered over the course of years. Chosen kin were expected to "be there" for one another through ongoing, reciprocal exchanges of material and emotional support.

Sometimes gay families formed in the context of a life crisis, such as a chronic illness that required exceptional levels of social support (see Dorrell 1991; Hays, Chauncey, and Tobey 1990).[11] During the 1980s AIDS provided one "catalyst" for the movement to incorporate chosen kin into prevailing definitions of family (Levine 1990:39). For gay men, a diagnosis of HIV+ often forced the issue of coming out to heterosexual relatives, which generally brought changes to "blood" relationships that could take the form of outright abandonment or unexpected levels of support. Members of a person's gay and straight families might find themselves interacting—in cooperation or in conflict—for the first time. In many cases friends and other peers became the primary caregivers, although in high-incidence areas a person's friendship network might prove too decimated by illness to offer effective support (Lovejoy 1990). Incredible efforts of formal and informal organization yielded the essentials of daily life: housecleaning and shopping services, transportation to medical appointments, pet care, cooking rotations, conversation. Families of friends, backed up by a range of new community-based organizations, occupied a central position in these activities.

Long before gay kinship ideologies referred to friends as family, anthropologists and sociologists had approached friendship as one of kinship's liminal categories. Along with institutions such as *compadrazgo* in Latin America and "going for sisters" in urban Black communities of the United States, friendship became a focus of research on what social scientists once called fictive kinship.[12] In North America, researchers documented numerous instances of people who claimed that they considered certain friends to be family or "like family." Unlike bonds of marriage or descent, however, these friendship ties were not systematically organized through a sexual relationship or a procreative nexus. Also unlike bonds of marriage or descent, friendships remained systematically peripheralized in studies of belonging (Jerome 1984; Paine 1969). Even today, many researchers continue to relegate friendships to the status of "fictive kinship" when they do not minimize the importance of these ties or ignore them altogether.

In scholarly treatments of friendship, it is not at all unusual to find analysts placing a lighter value on friendships than those relationships carry for the people subjected to scholarly scrutiny. An early study of relationships between gay men and heterosexual women, for instance, referred to friendships that "achieve high levels of understanding that enable [their participants] to relate in imaginative, creative ways" (Nahas and Turley 1979:121). Having characterized these ties in glowing terms, the authors hastened in the next sentence to christen these bonds "marginal relationships." Friendship generally fares no better in popular treatments. As gay kinship has become a topic of controversy and debate in society at large, the friends incorporated into chosen families have received little attention, despite the respect historically accorded to friendship by many lesbians and gay men.[13] For every newspaper article devoted to lesbian mothers or an attempt by a gay couple to acquire a marriage license, another that could have covered a family of friends remains unwritten.

The scholarly literature portrays friendship as the most unpredictable of social ties precisely *because* most people in the United States construct friendship as a chosen, or voluntary, relationship (Allan 1989; Gouldner and Strong 1987; Rubin 1985; Wiseman 1986). What can be freely entered should be just as readily subject to termination, or so the cultural reasoning goes.[14] Through an implicit contrast with biogenetic connections, which are taken to be irrevocable, friendship becomes assimilated to a contractual model of relationships. Even accounts that treat friendship as a form of "fictive kinship" cast friendship as a less reliable and less enduring tie than relationships calculated through "biological" connections. In *All Our Kin*, for example, Carol Stack recognizes the significance of the participation of friends in the "personal kindreds" of poor African-Americans in urban communities, yet then describes friends as people who "drop in and out of one another's [kinship] networks" (1974:54). Similarly, Christopher

Ellison's (1990) tendency to view friendships in African-American communities through the lens of voluntarism and fragility leads him to characterize friendships as likely to be "less supportive and reliable" than "family ties" (299–300) despite his claim that "blacks are more likely to receive support from friends than from family members" (306).

Given this combination of a cultural legacy that subordinates friendship to kinship and a scholarly legacy that tends to depict such "fictive kin" as fair-weather friends, why should friendship appear as a signifier of stability in gay kinship ideologies? An African-American from The Flats (the neighborhood where Stack [1974] recorded beliefs regarding the relative unreliability of friends as kin) would likely have encountered conflicting attitudes toward the stability of friendship relations if s/he later came out as as a lesbian, moved to the Bay Area, and became active in "the gay community." The same gay kinship ideologies that highlight friendship as an important, even distinctive, aspect of social relations among lesbians and gay men have also portrayed friendship as a bond more likely to endure than ties of "biology," marriage, or partnership. As one man put it, "Your straight family may reject you because you're gay. Your lovers may or may not stick around. But good, solid friendships can last you a lifetime." In most cases people elaborated this emphasis on the reliability of friendship through comparisons that drew attention to the uncertainties attendant upon relationships with lovers and "blood" or adoptive kin.[15]

When gay kinship ideologies depict friendship as an enduring relationship, more is involved than a logical inversion of the cultural categories of belonging linked to permanence (fragile friendships and enduring biogenetic ties in the dominant ideology, lasting friendships and terminable biogenetic ties in discourse on gay families). Understanding why gay kinship ideologies associate friendship with permanence and other forms of belonging with impermanence requires an understanding of the specific historical circumstances in which these ideologies have emerged. This inversion of the dominant ideology has been structured through the lived experiences of individuals who make their relationships not as they please but rather within the context of a society where heterosexuality remains normative.

Like the fragility often attributed to friendship, the permanence customarily attributed to "blood" ties (and sometimes marriage) became problematized for people who claimed a lesbian or gay identity in the wake of the gay movement. Elsewhere I have argued that the gay movement of the 1970s contributed to the emergence of a discourse on lesbian/gay families in the 1980s by encouraging people to "come out" to "biological" and adoptive kin (Weston 1991).[16] In previous decades, individuals sometimes disclosed their homosexuality to relatives, but not in any systematic fashion. By the 1980s coming out had become a possibility to be contemplated, if not always a plan of action to be implemented. At the time of my fieldwork, I did not meet a single lesbian-, bisexual-, or gay-identified person who claimed never to have considered coming out to parents and other "close" relatives.

The prospect of being disowned by "blood" or adoptive relatives was the greatest threat recognized by people preparing to disclose their lesbian or gay identity to "straight family." Coming-out stories consistently focused on the prospect of "losing" kin and highlighted the devastating emotional impact when rejection ensued. Although outright rejection may not have occurred with great frequency, neither was it uncommon. Perhaps more important than the incidence of rejection was the generalized *fear* of being "cut off" that pervaded these narratives. A lesbian need not actually come out in order to realize that heterosexual relatives might not "be there" for her, precisely because she is gay.

Many anthropologists have argued that "biological" connection must incorporate social connection to make kinship. Whether biological, adoptive, or chosen, all kinship ties are optative, in a sense. Even for those who restrict themselves to a biogenetic paradigm for calculating kinship, selectivity is built into the classification of certain relatives as "closer" than others and the editing of "family trees" (Schneider 1968). For gay people contemplating disclosure to "blood" relatives, the contradiction between prescriptions for enduring solidarity and the selectivity built into this ostensibly most durable of ties often became evident. At issue was not so much the outcome of disclosure—"rejection" or "acceptance"—but rather a growing recognition of the potential for the termination of ostensibly indissoluble ties.

Even coming-out stories that featured a happy ending tended to reaffirm, rather than assume, kinship. In many cases, the narrator resolved the suspense leading up to disclosure through a phrase that evoked the specter of the terminability of kinship ties in the very act of affirming a solidarity that endures: "You're still my son! You're still my daughter! I still love you!" Family trees dropped branches or sprouted new foliage as relatives embarked upon the complex process of coming to terms with a stigmatized sexuality. Coming out set in motion a personal politics that reconfigured, when it did not sever, now apparently mutable "blood" ties.

If "biological" and adoptive ties no longer seemed fixed, people coming out into gay "communities" during the late twentieth century also encountered conflicting views on the stability of relationships between lovers. Most were already well acquainted with stereotypes of gay relationships that circulated in the larger society. Among lesbians and gay men in the Bay Area, opinions differed as to whether (or to what extent) gay relationships could be considered more transient than heterosexual relationships. Those who questioned the longevity of gay relationships tended to attribute the instability they perceived to a lack of social legitimation and institutional support. "It's funny," said Frank Maldonado. "With my straight, married friends, there's that awareness: 'Well, they're gonna be around a long time.'

Whereas sometimes, with some of my [gay male] friends, they might have a boyfriend for a couple of months or a year or whatever. There isn't that stability." Lourdes Alcantara complained about gay friends who thought that she and her lover of five years were eventually going to break up. "People don't trust gay relationships. They think it's just for a while, that we are too *inconstantes*, that we're going to find somebody else. . . . [Yet] I'm monogamous, we are monogamous, and I believe in forever." Diane Kunin was careful to qualify her remarks on the challenges facing lesbian couples with a reference to the historical rise in heterosexual divorce rates: "[It's] not that marriages really last, straight marriages. Not that the divorce rate isn't astronomical, but I've watched some of my friends who are lesbian mothers deal with lovers moving in and out of their lives, and it's a hard thing."

In contrast, Roberta Osabe saw lesbian relationships as more stable than heterosexual *or* gay male relationships: "I always saw a lesbian relationship as being pretty constant. . . . My experience has been that women tend to stay together pretty much longer than men do. Straight relationships—the kind of people I see or friends that I have who are together—a lot of them don't stay together for that long, just because things are so different [between women and men]." And cynicism about what had happened to his friends' relationships did not prevent Frank Maldonado from planning to remain with his partner "forever":

> If you're going to make a commitment, you have to make a commitment and stand behind it. So when Bobby and I got together . . . we told each other that, hey, we're going to look at this as a lifelong endeavor until death do us part, better or worse, sickness or in health. It's not like a dance partner—if you step on my foot, I'm getting another partner. It's the real world and we're going to go all the way with it.

There were those who expected a relationship with a lover to last "only as long as it's good," and those who wanted their partnerships to endure "for always." Like Frank Maldonado, many mentioned the ideological stability accorded heterosexual marriage, despite ample evidence in an era of no-fault divorce that a large number of marriages do not begin to approach "forever."

Significantly, categories of transience and permanence organized the entire discussion of gay relationships. "I'm not saying this instability, or whatever, is a bad thing," insisted Paulette Ducharme. "I'm not putting any judgment on that." Using years spent together as an index of commitment had little to do with whether a particular person wanted a life partner or valued long-term relationships in the abstract. A "strong" relationship meant, among other things, a relationship that had endured the test of time.

Whether or not people expressed interest in building a lasting relationship with a lover, almost all sought commitment from the friends they considered family. Some of the same people who wanted their partnerships to endure also cited a variation of the old gay adage: "Lovers may be passing through, but friends stay." Knowledge of the importance placed on friendship within gay "communities" often came in the form of advice given by an older lesbian or gay man who had "been around," someone who had seen people disowned by "blood" relatives, someone who remembered all too well the pain that people go through when relationships end that once aspired to "forever." Drawing upon over sixty years of experience, Harold Sanders was but one of many who had concluded: "That's the way one builds a good life: a set of friends."

If friendships are the relationships believed most likely to endure, one way to create long-lasting kinship ties is to transform ex-lovers into friends who are also kin. In theory, if not always in practice, former lovers could be recuperated as friends (Barrett 1989; Becker 1988). According to Diane Kunin, "After you break up, a lot of people become as if they were parents and sisters, and relate to your new lover as if [the new lover] were the in-law." While lesbians seemed more likely than gay men to attempt to transform ex-lovers into friends, this distinction was by no means absolute.[17] One man, for example, met another man in the military who introduced him to "the beauties of sex and how it could make you feel. It was a wonderful thing. Then, shortly after Roger and I met, we both received orders for overseas. I went to Guam, and he went to Germany (laughs). So we were separated, but we always remained friends." It was as friends, not simply ex-lovers, that former sexual partners became reincorporated into gay families.

When the Time Comes: "Fictive Kin," Reconsidered

After considerable thought and several sessions with a calculator, Bruce Edelman decided to install new wall-to-wall carpeting in his modest Sunset home. With the money from his second job, he figured he could just afford to rip out the coffee-stained shag rug that had come with the house and send it the way of other relics of decades gone by. Because he could not miss any days from work, Bruce estimated that it would take him two months to finish the task alone. Depressed by that thought, he placed a ten-minute phone call which initiated a chain of communications that crisscrossed the city. The following weekend, seven of his closest relatives converged on his home with hammers in hand. Bruce contributed pizza, beer, soft drinks, and all the necessary materials. To the accompaniment of music from the boom box that followed Bruce wherever he went, this improvised work crew installed the entire carpet in a day.

Although Bruce Edelman made it quite clear to me that he included in his chosen family each of the people who helped him lay the carpet, none were related to him by "blood" or marriage. In earlier decades, an ethnographer might well have described the relatives in Bruce's narrative as "pseudo-kin." At a minimum, the ethnographer would have placed quotation marks around the term "relatives" to mark it off from "real" kinship ties, still the point of implicit (if not explicit) contrast where friendships are concerned.[18]

This dichotomy between real and imitative, authentic and inauthentic, continues to inform much of the research conducted under the rubric of kinship studies. To categorize some forms of friendship as fictive kinship—or even "alternative" families—is to presume that "blood" relations, organized through procreative heterosexuality, not only constitute "true" kinship but also provide a model for all possible derivative forms of family. When viewed through the lens of an ideology that refuses to recognize biology and marriage as the foundation for all conceivable types of kinship, however, gay families no longer appear as "alternative," "fictive," or "substitute" formations.[19] Once "the" (nuclear) family, organized through heterosexual procreation, is dislodged from its position of preeminence, to what would gay families (or single-parent families or postmodern families) pose an alternative?

Rather than rejecting the quest for authenticity, gay kinship ideologies have tended to portray gay families as "just as real" as other forms of kinship. Attempts to authenticate gay families have occurred not in an ideological vacuum but in a context of social struggle. As gay people have confronted dominant constructions of kinship that deny chosen families legal or social recognition, they have framed litigation and legislative strategies over issues that range from hospital visitation privileges to joint adoption and property rights. The consequence of the success or failure of such bids for legitimacy can be very concrete: it can mean the difference between being able to take time off for a partner's funeral or holding back unexplained tears for weeks at work.

To comprehend the relation between ideological transformations and social change in contemporary debates over what makes a family requires an understanding of not only the claims advanced but also the *manner* in which advocates of chosen families have made their case. Having rejected the equation of biological connection with the sort of "genuine" kinship supposed to lead to enduring solidarity, many gay men and lesbians looked to enduring solidarity as sufficient basis for laying claim to familial status for their relationships. By stressing the lasting character of certain "nonbiological" ties, they cast as kin friendships and partnerships that were not organized through a procreative nexus.

Intentionally or unintentionally, advocates began to highlight the length of time two people had remained "in a relationship" in cases that argued for gay people's rights to bereavement, rent-controlled apartments, child custody, and benefits packages offered by employers. Lesbian/gay organizations helped frame domestic-partnership legislation that stipulated coresidence for a specified waiting period (anywhere from three months to a year) before an unmarried couple could register to attain the legal standing that entitled them to benefits available to married couples.[20]

With very few exceptions, media coverage of court cases relating to gay families also emphasized markers of enduring solidarity.[21] A *New York Times* article on Sandra Rovira, who sued AT&T for death benefits, portrayed Rovira as having "formalized" her relationship to her deceased partner "in a 1977 ceremony for relatives and friends" (T. Lewin 1990). *Gay Community News* characterized Rovira as the partner in "a 12-year committed relationship with Marjorie Forlini, who for 10 years had also served as co-parent to Rovira's two children from [a] previous marriage" (Graham 1990). In a report on *Alison D. v. Virginia M.*, a suit before the New York Court of Appeals that sought visitation rights for a "nonbiological" lesbian parent, a couple was described as having separated "after a seven-year relationship" (Nealon 1990). Similarly, the lead sentence of a *New York Times* story on custody battles between lesbian coparents described Michele G. and Nancy S. as having "lived together for 11 years" before their decision to raise children (Margolick 1990).

Because friendship has minimal legal standing in the United States, families made up of friends have not become a focus of court cases and the accompanying media coverage. Yet, it is not at all uncommon in nonlegal arenas for gay men and lesbians to emphasize the length of time a friendship has endured as a way to establish its importance and kinship character. "The closest people in my life are not my blood family," Frank Maldonado explained. "The people I surround myself with now are mostly gay. And lesbian. I have a number of straight friends that I see day to day, or week to week, whatever. And they're my family. They take care of me, I take care of them. . . . Some of my friends I've known for fifteen years. You get attached." Others, like Bruce Edelman, distinguished people who were "just friends" from friends who were also family by referring to events that he and other members of his chosen family had experienced together. A few spoke of encouragement—even pressure—from gay peers to remain in "close" friendships and partnerships once those relationships had passed a high-water mark of five or ten years. In such cases, longevity could offer reason to "work" to extend those relationships and justification for naming them kin.

As authenticating narratives—narratives that say "these are real families"—gay kinship ideologies invert the assertion that "what's real is not subject to change" in order to argue that "whatever endures is real." This transformation of Tony Paige's deep-seated conviction—"If it's real, it's got to last!"—sets aside syllogistic reasoning in favor of a cultural logic that plays upon the widespread interpretation of kinship ties as ties that bind.

Like their heterosexual counterparts, most lesbians and gay men in the United States during the 1980s and 1990s were looking to the future when they constructed kinship ties and argued for their authenticity. They spoke of their gay families as a source of "security," expecting chosen kin to "be there" for them at some unspecified time of need in days to come. Unlike most of their heterosexual peers, however, they were also looking to the past when they contended that gay families were every bit as legitimate as other forms of kinship *because* those relationships had lasted. In this discourse, "stability," "strength," and "commitment" were measured by the months and years that a person had remained in an erotic or nonerotic relationship.

Forever can, indeed, be a long time. At certain points in arguments for the legitimation of gay families—especially (but not exclusively) families made up of friends— enduring solidarity recasts itself as a temporal rather than a timeless concept. It matters little whether the time span cited is five or fifteen or fifty years, whether the figure given reflects the finality of death or the unexpected dissolution of a friendship. The result is a different kind of "forever" than the one envisioned by those lesbian, gay, bisexual, and heterosexual couples, who, like Frank Maldonado, took as their own the marriage vow "till death do us part." "Forever," in this alternate reading, represents neither a will to eternity nor an immutable biogenetic connection, but rather the outcome of the day-to-day interactions that organize a relationship. Only in retrospect can a set number of years be attached to a relationship in order to assert its legitimacy as a form of kinship. Only with hindsight and the passage of time can such a bond be termed "lasting." In this transformation of the biogenetic paradigm for kinship, permanence in a relationship is no longer ascribed ("blood is blood"), but produced.

When all is said and done, are these "new family forms" simply old-fashioned institutions in queer clothing? To the extent that questions of transience and permanence organize discussions about chosen families, gay kinship ideologies do appear to stake their claims on the terrain of a dominant discourse on kinship. After all, one can imagine other possible constructions: an open-minded curiosity regarding what will come to pass rather than a value placed on accumulating years, or discussions of relationships in which a time orientation hardly figures. Gay kinship ideologies recreate an authenticating vision of social ties each time they bring forward evidence to demonstrate enduring solidarity or argue that what perseveres is "real" (if not everlasting) kinship.

Yet gay kinship ideologies represent neither a simple case of assimilation into the dominant discourse nor an "alternative" ideology that breaks completely with the terms of a biogenetic paradigm for kinship. Shifts in the *concept* of time embedded in gay kinship ideologies emerged from developments in *historical* time that associated sexual identity with a particular mode of organizing a family and labeled the latter "gay."[22] The very process of contending for the legitimacy of chosen kin tended to introduce subtle changes into the notion of enduring solidarity. Even as gay kinship ideologies built upon prevailing beliefs about what makes a family, they transformed those beliefs by putting duration into forever and persistence into permanence.

Authority, Authenticity, and the Reconstruction of Kinship

A woman lies dying. In a small apartment on 18th Street, the friends Helen Reynolds names family gather around the handmade quilt that covers Helen in her hospital bed. Over the last six months, these have been the ones who carried Helen to the doctors and carried daily sustenance back to Helen. Now, amidst the tubes and medicine jars they hover, speaking softly or not at all, reaching out to grasp Helen's hand or sparing her the effort. Someone risks a joke. Everyone laughs; no one feels like laughing. Sometimes her chosen kin look over at Helen, watching her grow ever smaller in the bed, but increasingly they exchange glances with one another. In and out of the tiny rooms they wander, staring at the walls or the floors, serenading Helen with a haphazard choreography of movement and sound. There is nothing left to do but wander, and hover, and wait.

For all its apparent material substantiality, "biology" has operated within procreative kinship ideologies as a floating signifier of both permanence and authenticity. As Johannes Fabian astutely notes:

Kinship, on the surface one of the most innocent descriptive terms one could imagine, is fraught with temporal connotations. From the early debates on "classificatory" kinship systems to current studies of its *continued* importance in Western society, *kinship* connoted "primordial" ties and origins, hence the special strength, persistence, and meaning attributed to this type of social relation. (1983:75)

Through the biogenetic paradigm that has constituted kinship and dominated kinship studies, the social relations known as "family ties" have been turned into the "stuff of nature and primitivized" as a procreative, rather than political, arrangement (Levy 1989, 1991).[23] Like gender and sexuality, nationality and ethnicity have also been constructed through ideologies of authenticity, first naturalized in the course of attribution by birth, then immobilized to the extent that biological ties continue to be conceived as immutable.

If anthropology has credited "other" societies with timeless traditions, it has simultaneously ascribed to Western societies a category of belonging called kinship that places social ties outside time's reach. Yet it is not enough to expose "biological" connection as a culturally contingent mode of reckoning relationships. In Pierre Bourdieu's terms, "Genealogies kill the properly strategic dimension of practices which is related to the existence, at every moment, of uncertainties, indeterminations, if only subjective ones" (1990:385). After a lifetime of independence, Helen Reynolds initially resisted the efforts of her gay family of friends to supply her with food, medicine, and daily companionship. Bruce Edelman could not have known for certain whether his chosen kin would respond to his call for assistance. Gloria Salcido and Debra Lee saw one another four times before each felt confident that they would find a way to preserve their friendship. Examination of the link between timelessness and authenticity offers one way to place such strategic moves by individual actors in the larger context of the historical and material conditions in which kinship ideologies emerge, challenge the status quo, and change.

In and of itself, nothing about "biological" connection implies permanence, much less ongoing relationship or enduring solidarity. When people in the United States speak of "blood" ties, they do not have in mind the ever-shifting biology of Darwinian evolution or a neurology that has documented the degeneration of nerve cells in the absence of use or a body in which cells are continuously sloughed off and replaced. More commonly, they picture biology as an unchanging "natural" bedrock believed to support superstructures of "culture" and "society." This particular reading of "blood ties" transforms two of life's most evanescent events—death and birth—into foundational episodes that establish kinship. Genealogies forge links between people at the point of procreation, making birth the focal point of alliance and "blood." Only a biological process (death), as opposed to a social process (rejection, neglect), is supposed to be capable of sundering "blood" ties. In this reading, death becomes the terminus that marks attainment of "forever" in a relationship. From mortality and procreation to the perpetual renewal of tissue at the cellular level, biological processes might just as easily constitute a signifier of change and flux rather than continuity and control. Instead, Anglo-European societies historically have pressed birth and death into the service of a permanence supposed to establish authenticity in social relations.

When people enumerate the years a relationship has lasted in order to support a custody claim or explain the classification of friends as kin, they appear to assimilate terms such as "enduring solidarity" directly into their arguments. In this sense the gay kinship ideologies that have emerged during the late twentieth century seem to stake their claims to legitimacy on the same ground of authenticity occupied by the biogenetic paradigm they seek to displace. But by inverting the cultural logic that links genuineness to endurance (moving from "what's real must last" to "what lasts is real"), these emergent ideologies have produced some unforeseen effects.

Ideologies of authenticity are "about" much more than belonging. In context, authenticity can establish authority to speak, to order, to act, to control. Attributions of permanence obscure power relations by locating relationships outside of time and therefore beyond social intervention. What exists in perpetuity, like what occurs "in nature," appears impossible to contest. Arguing for the enduring character of a relationship can then become a way to assert authority, making kinship a political project in both its scholarly and strategic guises. In contrast, narratives of authenticity that cite persistent (but not timeless) solidarity in relationships reconfigure authority "not as border-patrolling, boundary-engendering, but as meaning-giving" (K. Jones 1991:123).[24] Rather than attempting to fix the meaning of kinship from the perspective of a lesbian or gay identity, the claim that chosen families are "real" families effectively highlights the indeterminate and ultimately contextually defined meaning of "family" as a category.

Gay kinship ideologies undermine the authority ceded to authenticity even as they utilize its terms precisely *because* they build duration into "forever." Pictured as a steady state, "forever" veils the manufacture of stability in both "biological" and "nonbiological" relationships. In contrast, when "forever" surfaces in discussions of chosen families, it tends to represent not so much irrevocability as an *intention* to forever that shapes practice and perception. Diane Kunin described herself as gradually "realizing . . . how hard it is to find people that you're really willing to make that kind of commitment to, and who are willing to make it back. And then how hard it is to set it up." Attempting to build a lasting friendship or emphasizing the years that a sexual relationship has endured become part of a process of creating kinship.

Recasting "forever" as a temporal concept is but one possible outcome of claiming a lesbian or gay identity under historically specific conditions. In a situation in which partnerships may appear unstable and "blood" ties can be sundered in response to disclosure of a gay identity, no relationship—not even friendship—is taken for granted. Yet in the absence of any axiomatic association of a particular type of social tie with permanence, anyone can "work" to turn a relationship into kinship. Paradoxically, at the very moment gay kinship ideologies conceal the historical context of their own emergence by speaking in timeless fashion of the authenticity of gay families, they democratize the prospects for laying claim to kinship ties.

At stake in the arenas where gay people seek legitimacy for chosen families is something more than conflicting values or beliefs or definitions of family. Determinations of who shall count as kin have material as well as social and ideological consequences. When those who contest the authenticity of chosen families ask in fear or exasperation, "Where will it all end?" theirs is not the scholar's concern with the fuzzy boundaries that demarcate social categories but more often an implicit acknowledgement of a cultural link between authenticity and control over valued resources. For the person seeking access to a partner's health-insurance plan or input into the treatment of a friend who lies in a coma, how family ties will be determined and what specific reconstructions of kinship will gain legitimacy remain compelling questions. With issues such as these hanging in the balance, it would certainly be premature to raze the forest of kinship studies or condemn ethnographers to wander about identifying the "family trees" that constitute culturally specific constructions of relatedness.

Although I have focused here on contests of meaning, my intent is not to move "American kinship" from the study of symbols in the clouds to the study of symbols in the storm. When Tony Paige and I discussed the legitimacy of gay families in a Mission Street cafe, we unwittingly linked bodies and biology to permanence and authenticity in a way that opened up new possibilities for reconstructing kinship studies as an undertaking that is not only symbolically but also politically, economically, and historically engaged. Ideological conflicts are nothing without the historical and material conditions that give them life. Only after the gay movement encouraged people to risk rejection by coming out to relatives did gay families emerge as a cultural category that highlighted choice and recast "close" friendships as kinship. As the concept of chosen kin undercut the reification of time in procreative constructions of kinship, arguments for the legitimation of gay families drew attention to the everyday activities involved in producing and maintaining relationships. Nowhere was the politics of the definition of kinship more apparent than in the United States of the 1980s, where drastic cuts in government funding of social services resulted in the increasing mediation of subsistence and assistance through categories of "blood" or "marriage."

If contemporary controversies about what makes a family are evaluated within the minoritizing framework of a civil-rights model, attempts to authenticate gay families may appear as a bid for inclusion by "a people" historically denied the most basic claims to kinship. Particularly for those who have something to lose if power relations are renegotiated to give lesbians and gay men access to entitlements allocated through families, it is tempting to take refuge in an overly neat and ultimately much too reassuring dichotomy between hegemonic ideologies belonging to "us" under attack by counterhegemonic ideologies assigned to "them." But it is misleading to speak of "gay kinship"—or, for that matter, "biogenetic kinship"—as a freestanding paradigm. This sort of polarization into dominant and subordinate, straight and gay, seriously underestimates the potential of contests of meaning to span sexual identities and other cultural domains. And in doing so, it misses all the complexity of social struggle.

Lesbian and gay families cannot be dismissed as a fiction predicated upon a heterosexual model for constituting kinship. Yet, they have incorporated prevalent symbols and appeals to authenticity in ways that make it difficult to separate dominant from "alternative" constructions of family. Through paradox and inversion—blood relations are chosen, ties that last create real families—gay kinship ideologies have used common categories to generate uncommon meanings. Sometimes, with ideologies as with relationships that endure, *plus c'est la même chose, plus ça change*. The more things stay the same, the more things change.

Notes

My thanks to David Halperin, Marilyn Ivy, Ellen Lewin, Radhika Mohanram, Geeta Patel, David Schneider, and Sylvia Yanagisako for their thought-provoking comments on this essay. Linda Watts and Alison Stratton provided invaluable assistance in locating research materials. Grants from the American Association of University Women and the National Science Foundation funded field research for the study. An earlier version of the essay was presented at the 1992 Matrilineality and Patrilineality in Comparative and Historical Perspective conference, University of Minnesota.

1. Here and throughout, I have changed names and (in the vignettes) developed composite portraits to preserve the anonymity of individuals I worked with while in the field. In addition to participant observation in the San Francisco Bay Area from 1985–87 (with a follow-up visit in 1990), this study draws upon a set of eighty interviews with self-identified lesbians and gay men. People of color made up approximately one-third of the interview sample. About half of the interviewees could be described as coming from a working-class background, with a similar percentage of the whole employed in working-class occupations at the time of the study. For further details on the composition of the interview sample, see Weston (1991:215–21).

2. When I employ the term "gay" without qualification, I intend the category to embrace self-identified gay men and lesbians. At various points in the essay, I substitute the phrase "lesbians and gay men" to remind readers that gendered differences (as well as differences of age, class, language, nationality, racial identification, and so on) crosscut this population.

3. For a feminist critique of the liberal individualism that frames discussions of friendship as a voluntary relation, see Friedman (1989).

4. For classic elaborations of the contrast between "real" and "fictive" kin, see Eisenstadt (1956) and Pitt-Rivers (1968).

5. See also Rapp (1987) and Yanagisako and Collier (1987).

6. What I call "the critique of kinship approach" refers to a theoretical tendency within kinship studies rather than a single school of thought or mode of analysis. Considerable variation exists in the research agendas of anthropologists who have built upon Schneider's work. Yanagisako and Collier (1987), for example, have argued that gender constructs permeate the symbolism of bodies, biology, and procreation in U.S. understandings of kinship. Elsewhere, Yanagisako (1985) has explored how the historical construction of

ethnicities inflects the meanings carried by core symbols such as "love" that are ostensibly held in common by participants in "American culture."

7. See Handler (1988), M. Jones (1990), Orvell (1989), and Sedgwick (1990).

8. On the ways "biology" figures in discourse on lesbian and gay families, see E. Lewin (1993) and Weston (1991).

9. E.g., African-American, Puerto Rican, and American Indian gay men and lesbians raised the topic of genocide in discussions of parenthood more often than Whites, whose racial identification inserted them into the history of race relations in a different way.

10. In the United States, features of kinship that scholars sometimes treat as paradigmatic also tend to be already (if not always) raced and classed. But that is the subject of another essay. For an investigation of differences in the meanings carried by terms such as "love," especially in association with cultural constructions of ethnicity, see Yanagisako (1985).

11. Cf. Nardi (1992a:118), who contends that illness in general, and AIDS in particular, heightens the importance of friendship in the lives of lesbians and gay men.

12. *Compadrazgo* institutionalizes the relationship between a child's godparents and parents. When people "go for sisters (brothers, etc.)," they formalize their relationship by applying kinship terminology to a "nonbiological" tie.

13. Urban gay male and lesbian populations in the United States have long celebrated the "strength" and centrality of friendship (Nardi 1994). On the historical developments associated with the successive institutionalization of nonerotic friendships among homosexuals, followed by the concept of "gay community" and finally "gay families," see D'Emilio (1983), Nardi (1992a), and Weston (1991).

14. Friendship has not always been construed as a temporally contingent relationship in Anglo-European societies (cf. Cicero 1898; O'Hara 1991). For a speculative treatment that links the construction of homosexuality as an identity to the devaluation of friendship, see Foucault's comments in Gallagher and Wilson (1987).

15. In one study, gay people were the only respondents likely to turn to friends before "blood" or adoptive relatives when seeking emotional support (cited in Nardi 1992a:110).

16. Lesbians and gay men applied kinship terms to one another well before the 1980s, but these older usages were not organized by the cultural category of "choice" (see Weston 1991:127, 135–136). Contemporary discussions of gay families are marked by a relative absence of kinship terminology, with at least two important exceptions: (1) terms of address used by children for adults (Mama, Tío, Aunt, etc.), and (2) the house system that organizes the African-American drag balls documented in Goldsby (1989) and the documentary "Paris Is Burning." For more on lesbian/gay community formation in the years leading up to the 1980s, see D'Emilio (1983, 1989), Herdt (1991), Kennedy and Davis (1993), and Newton (1993).

17. Also at issue is who counts as an ex-lover. See Nardi (1992a, 1992b), who found sex and sexual attraction to be common elements in "best friend" relationships among White, middle-class gay men. When friendships persisted, sexual involvement tended to diminish over time.

18. Though this practice was more common in the past, it has not disappeared from anthropological accounts of friendship and other "nonbiological" kinship relations. See, for example, Uhl, who distinguishes the female friendships she studied in Andalusia from "special friendships instituted through . . . fictive kinship" (1991:90).

19. See Gilmore (1975), who argues in a very different context against the tendency to view friendship as a substitute for kinship or as a residual category used to describe meaningful ties in the absence of kinship organized through a procreative nexus.

20. "Common-law marriage," which grants legal status to heterosexual couples who have not formally registered their union with the state, relies upon a similar criterion of coresidence over a specified period of time. Despite this apparent continuity with domestic partnership, common-law marriage today takes effect by default, incorporating heterosexual couples into the institution of marriage with little effort on their part. In contrast, domestic-partnership policies have been hard won through political battles that have brought into play strategic depictions of long-term lesbian and gay relationships.

21. Significantly, this pattern seems to hold for coverage in both the gay and nongay press.

22. On the distinction between metaphorical and historical time, as well as the importance of analyzing the historical processes associated with the transformation of cultural constructs, see Thomas (1989).

23. Levy discusses anthropology's part in creating a model of kinship grounded in a biologized concept of sexuality and gender difference. This new formulation was "a class- and culture-specific model to be sure, but one that appeared universal and natural. . . . The formation of this new family model out of older historical materials lent the emergent middle classes an appearance of legitimacy and permanency it [sic] would not otherwise enjoy" (1991:59). On the dehistoricizing impact of ideologies that naturalize social relations, see also Eagleton (1991:59).

24. Jones's concept of authority is more useful for understanding the claims for entitlement and open-ended definitions of family advanced by gay kinship ideologies than the more customary equation of authority with determinate meanings and social control. I am grateful to Ellen Lewin for drawing my attention to this source.

References

Allan, Graham. 1989. *Friendship: Developing a Sociological Perspective.* New York: Harvester Wheatsheaf.

Appadurai, Arjun. 1988. "Putting Hierarchy in Its Place." *Cultural Anthropology* 3(1): 36–49.

Barrett, Martha Barron. 1989. *Invisible Lives.* New York: William Morrow.

Becker, Carol S. 1988. *Unbroken Ties: Lesbian Ex-Lovers.* Boston: Alyson.

Bourdieu, Pierre. 1990. "The Scholastic Point of View." *Cultural Anthropology* 5(4): 380–391.

Cicero, Marcus Tullius. 1898. *De Amicitia.* New York: Century.

D'Emilio, John. 1983. *Sexual Politics, Sexual Communities: The Making of a Homosexual Minority in the United States, 1940–1970.* Chicago: Univ. of Chicago Press.

———. 1989. "Gay Politics and Community in San Francisco Since World War II." In *Hidden From History: Reclaiming the Gay and Lesbian Past,* edited by M. Duberman, M. Vicinus, and G. Chauncey, Jr., 456–73. New York: Meridian.

Dorrell, Beth. 1991. "Being There: A Support Network of Lesbian Women." *Journal of Homosexuality* 20(3–4): 89–98.

Eagleton, Terry. 1991. *Ideology: An Introduction.* New York: Verso.

Eisenstadt, S. N. 1956. "Ritualized Personal Relations." *Man* 96:90–95.

Ellison, Christopher G. 1990. "Family Ties, Friendships, and Subjective Well-being among Black Americans." *Journal of Marriage and the Family* 52:298–310.

Fabian, Johannes. 1983. *Time and the Other: How Anthropology Makes Its Object*. New York: Columbia Univ. Press.

Friedman, Marilyn. 1989. "Feminism and Modern Friendship: Dislocating the Community." *Ethics* 99:275–90.

Gallagher, Bob, and Alexander Wilson. 1987. "Sex and the Politics of Identity: An Interview with Michel Foucault." In *Gay Spirit: Myth and Meaning*, edited by M. Thompson, 25–35. New York: St. Martin's.

Gilmore, David. 1975. "Friendship in Fuenmayor: Patterns of Integration in an Atomistic Society." *Ethnology* 14:311–24.

Goldsby, Jackie. 1989. "All About Yves." *Out/Look* 2(1): 34–35.

Gouldner, Helen, and Mary Symons Strong. 1987. *Speaking of Friendship: Middle-Class Women and Their Friends*. New York: Greenwood.

Graham, Julie. 1990. "Lesbian Sues AT&T." *Gay Community News* (Nov. 3–9).

Gutis, Philip S. 1989. "How to Define a Family: Gay Tenant Fights Eviction." *New York Times* (April 27).

Handler, Richard. 1988. *Nationalism and the Politics of Culture in Quebec*. Madison: Univ. of Wisconsin Press.

Hays, Robert B., Sarah Chauncey, and Linda A. Tobey. 1990. "The Social Support Networks of Gay Men with AIDS." *Journal of Community Psychology* 18:374–85.

Herdt, Gilbert, ed. 1991. *Gay Culture in America*. Boston: Beacon.

Jerome, Dorothy. 1984. "Good Company: The Sociological Implications of Friendship." *Sociological Review* 32:696–718.

Jones, Kathleen B. 1991. "Trouble with Authority." *differences* 3(1): 104–127.

Jones, Mark, ed. 1990. *Fake? The Art of Deception*. Berkeley: Univ. of California Press.

Kennedy, Elizabeth Lapovsky, and Madeline D. Davis. 1993. *Boots of Leather, Slippers of Gold: The History of a Lesbian Community*. New York: Routledge.

Levine, Carol. 1990. "AIDS and Changing Concepts of Family." *Milbank Quarterly* 68(Suppl. 1): 33–58.

Levy, Anita. 1989. "Blood, Kinship, and Gender." *Genders* 5:70–85.

———. 1991. *Other Women: The Writing of Class, Race, and Gender, 1832–1898*. Princeton: Princeton Univ. Press.

Lewin, Ellen. 1993. *Lesbian Mothers: Accounts of Gender in American Culture*. Ithaca, NY: Cornell Univ. Press.

Lewin, Tamar. 1990. "Suit Over Death Benefits Asks, What Is a Family?" *New York Times* (September 21).

Lovejoy, Nancy C. 1990. "AIDS: Impact on the Gay Man's Homosexual and Heterosexual Families." *Marriage and Family Review* 14(3/4): 285–316.

Margolick, David. 1990. "Lesbians' Custody Fights Test Family Law Frontier." *New York Times* (July 4).

Nahas, Rebecca and Myra Turley. 1979. *The New Couple: Women and Gay Men*. New York: Seaview.

Nardi, Peter M. 1994. "Friendship in the Lives of Gay Men and Lesbians." *Journal of Social and Personal Relationships* 2:11.

————. 1992a. "That's What Friends Are For: Friends as Family in the Gay and Lesbian Community." In *Modern Homosexualities: Fragments of Lesbian and Gay Experience,* edited by Ken Plummer, New York: Routledge.

————. 1992b. "Sex, Friendship, and Gender Roles Among Gay Men." In *Men's Friendships,* edited by Peter M. Nardi, Newbury Park: Sage.

Nealon, Chris. 1990. "Lesbian Seeks Visitation Rights in Custody Battle." *Gay Community News* (Nov. 25–Dec. 8).

Newton, Esther. 1993. *Cherry Grove, Fire Island: Sixty Years in America's First Gay and Lesbian Town.* Boston: Beacon.

Norman, Michael. 1989. *These Good Men: Friendships Forged from War.* New York: Crown.

O'Hara, Daniel T. 1991. "Michel Foucault and the Fate of Friendship." *boundary 2* 18(1): 83–103.

Orvell, Miles. 1989. *The Real Thing: Imitation and Authenticity in American Culture, 1880–1940.* Chapel Hill: Univ. of North Carolina Press.

Paine, Robert. 1969. "In Search of Friendship: An Exploratory Analysis in Middle-Class Culture." *Man* 4: 505–524.

Pitt-Rivers, Julian. 1968. "Pseudo-Kinship." In *International Encyclopedia of the Social Sciences,* 408–413. New York: Macmillan/Free Press.

Rapp, Rayna. 1987. "Toward a Nuclear Freeze? The Gender Politics of Euro-American Kinship Analysis." In *Gender and Kinship: Essays Toward a Unified Analysis,* edited by J.F. Collier and S.J. Yanagisako, 119–31. Stanford: Stanford Univ. Press.

Rubin, Lillian B. 1985. *Just Friends: The Role of Friendship in Our Lives.* New York: Harper & Row.

Schneider, David M. 1968. *American Kinship: A Cultural Account.* Englewood Cliffs, NJ: Prentice-Hall.

————. 1984. *A Critique of the Study of Kinship.* Ann Arbor: Univ. of Michigan Press.

Sedgwick, Eve. 1990. *Epistemology of the Closet.* Berkeley: Univ. of California Press.

Stack, Carol B. 1974. *All Our Kin: Strategies for Survival in a Black Community.* New York: Harper & Row.

Thomas, Nicholas. 1989. *Out of Time: History and Evolution in Anthropological Discourse.* Cambridge, UK: Cambridge Univ. Press.

————. 1991. "Against Ethnography." *Cultural Anthropology* 6(3): 306–322.

Uhl, Sarah. 1991. "Forbidden Friends: Cultural Veils of Female Friendship in Andalusia." *American Ethnologist* 18(1): 90–105.

Weston, Kath. 1991. *Families We Choose: Lesbians, Gays, Kinship.* New York: Columbia Univ. Press.

Wiseman, Jacqueline P. 1986. "Friendship: Bonds and Binds in a Voluntary Relationship." *Journal of Social and Personal Relationships* 3:191–211.

Yanagisako, Sylvia Junko. 1985. *Transforming the Past: Tradition and Kinship among Japanese Americans.* Stanford: Stanford Univ. Press.

Yanagisako, Sylvia Junko, and Jane Fishburne Collier. 1987. "Toward a Unified Analysis of Gender and Kinship." In *Gender and Kinship: Essays Toward a Unified Analysis,* edited by J.F. Collier and S.J. Yanagisako, 14–50. Stanford, Stanford Univ. Press.

Yukins, Elizabeth. 1991. "Lesbian/Gay Parents Dealt Legal Setback." *Gay Community News* (May 12–28).

The Birds and the Bees:
An Uncontrolled Comparison

5

Empowering Nature, or: Some Gleanings in Bee Culture

Anna Lowenhaupt Tsing

The chiefest cause, to read good bookes,
That moves each studious minde
Is hope, some pleasure sweet therein,
Or profit good to finde.
Now what delight can greater be
Than secrets for to knowe,
Of Sacred Bees, the Muses Birds,
All which this booke doth show.
—A. Crosley, "To the Reader"[1]

Sometime in 1984, a swarm of "African" bees—also known as killer bees—hitched a ride from somewhere in Latin America to Lost Hills, California. In June 1985, a machine operator working in a Lost Hills oil field saw bees kill a rabbit and reported it to the authorities. In an extensive official campaign over the next few months, twelve colonies containing African bees were found in the area—most discretely tucked away in abandoned drain pipes or college campus trees, but some in the managed apiaries properly reserved for "European" bees. The newspapers went wild. "Aggressive Bees Rout Entomologist." "U.S. Enters Bee Fight With Own Quarantine." "Invader Bees Reproducing." "Bee Battalions Mopping Up Killer Bee Invasion." This time, briefly, the mulattos would be removed and destroyed for a Europeans-only California. "Africanized Bees Won't Take Over Country Just Yet" (Whynott 1991: 152–55).

Hitchhiking, border-crossing aliens who hide out in abandoned places and run from the restless gaze of the immigration authorities, who are capable of savage and unpredictable acts, and who reproduce much too quickly on U.S. soil: These are familiar U.S. stories of the non-European human outsider. How did they come to infect and infuse stories about bees? The workings of nature, including the lives of bees, are not so mysterious that we cannot talk about them; and we must talk about them in human, cultural ways. But are natural facts merely transmutations from human lifeways? The bee scientist protests that it is the popular press that creates popular stereotypes; scientists learn from the bees themselves. The cultural analyst returns to cite assumptions that cross technical-popular lines—those that create norms of bee labor and reproduction, those that categorize "Africans" as outsiders. The dialogue breaks off; but "nature" is confirmed. "Nature," like the bee, is both a tireless laborer and a provoker of great crises. She confirms our prejudices but then escapes from our best-laid schemes of domestication. She provokes us to both recycle and reform conventional knowledge. And in the bee she has found a worthy representative.

Nature

Naturalizing power requires empowering nature. Empowering nature means attributing to nature forms of agency we can understand. Yet "nature" is also, by definition, that which escapes human attributions. This essay argues that the work of nature in U.S. American culture is to create the space for a tension between those forms of agency we best know and those we imagine to be outside our ken.

This is a tension that cultural analysts rarely recognize. We tend to write of "naturalizing" social relations as a synonym for "justifying" them, thus ignoring the cultural specificity of the justification through reference to nature. When we do acknowledge "nature," we tend to highlight the ways nature can be whatever we want it to be. Fashion sets the agenda for understanding nature; political virtues congeal into scientific laws. Nature is molded and melded into a reflection of human cultural concerns. The historically shifting imagined differentiations of gender and race are the (still so intransigent to be infuriating) best example: Cultural agendas create the frameworks and technologies in which observers find natural difference where they need to see it.

These insights are certainly truthful ones; yet, it is also worthwhile to pay some attention to the specificity of "nature." Inequalities can also be legitimated through reference to religion, civilization, progress, and other things. Naturalizing has its own peculiarities—including, for example, its development in dialogue with Christian notions of the deity. Nature, like God, is both lawful and mysterious; it requires human efforts to know it, yet always slips away from full knowledge. Thus, although cultural analysts over and over demonstrate the cultural shaping of so-called natural attributes, we can never thus unseat "nature": It is an aspect of nature to be partially and ultimately wrongly labeled by human cultural efforts; this is what gives nature its majesty.

Unfortunately, we can get little insight about the cultural specificity of nature as an object of knowledge from most of those who write about nature.[2] Nature writers, like cultural analysts, take the domain for granted, although they tend to emphasize the other side of the tension. Nature writers, environmentalists, and scientists tend to be fascinated by the Otherness of nature—its wildness, its mystery, and thus its capacity to provoke cultural renewal. The human experience in nature about which they write is an experience of awe because of nature's basic unknowability. Sometimes even in the deepest forest, a wild animal acts like it knows you, they write, but it is the undependability and transience of this moment that makes it so poignant. All we can depend upon is difference: Natural history catalogues this difference; natural science analyzes its dynamics.

Both cultural analysis and nature writing depend on their mutual tension in understanding nature even as they reject the other as insignificant, unfortunate, and downright wrong. Even radical difference is codified in culturally familiar exoticizations (as anthropologists have learned in painful self-recognition). And the idiom of the cultural "making" of nature separates the plastic medium (with its own possible refusals and unpredictabilities) from the cultural template. If it is the unmentionable possibility of knowing unknowable nature that is intriguing to the nature writer, it is the unmentionable possibility of politically docile nature getting away that is intriguing to the cultural analyst. But thus neither approach tends to discuss the constitution of the domain of "nature" on which its analysis depends. My argument here is not that we should "mix" culture and biology or humanistic and scientific approaches; it is about the cultural shape of "nature" that makes these kinds of statements sound so appealing, so natural.

Let me turn from these abstract and high-minded concerns to the domain that interests me here: domestic animals. Domestic animals are those nonhuman animals we most expect to act like people—or, at least, act in culturally familiar ways. We expect them to act like humans, but they are not humans. It seems to me that domestic animals exemplify the tension I have set forth here; almost by definition, domestic animals are shaped by yet escape the cultural models of agency we thrust upon them. I leave it to my readers to worry about what they think about their pets. Here my subject is honeybees—that is, the culture of bee nature and the "nature" in bee culture.

To "domesticate" an animal is to bring it into the orbit of the human family. In the history of most domestic animals—here I confine myself to European and European-diaspora traditions—this has meant not only a relation to the human-species family but also to specific human-kinship—defined families who rear and train animals. Domestic animals are supposed to behave as family members and work within the family unit. Like other family members, they receive care and subsistence for their devotion to the family. Most domestic animals are supposed to have families of their own under the wing of the human family. Middle- and upper-class urban pets in the United States are a "hyperdomesticated" exception; they are expected to join a particular human family directly and often are required to remain celibate and/or childless as family dependents. Most other domestic animals in the United States, including farm animals and rural pets, are encouraged or required to form supervised families that work under human headship. Even in industrialized stock raising, domestic assumptions still chart the course for human notions of stock genealogy, socialization, the division of labor, and patterns of productivity; animals as workers are often organized in family-like firms. Thus the social lives of domestic animals tend to be shaped by two kinds of human kinship attributions: First, they should have appropriate kinship relations with humans, to work with and under them; second, they should have appropriate kinship relations with each other, to make them both productive and proper human companions. In these ways, the agency of domestic animals is understood in relation to (human, culturally specific models of) kinship.

There are a large number of human-animal relationships that challenge and confuse the lines between "domestic" and "wild," and it is commonly recognized that human kinship attributions may be only awkwardly appropriate in these cases.[3] Honeybees are not like this. North American beekeeping derives from a long European tradition in which bees have been, if anything, emblematic of domesticity. Honeybees are devoted to their home in a hive; busy, they work hard; helpful, they cooperate within a natural division of labor; loyal, they protect their home altruistically; parental, they provision their brood; frugal, they save up a full larder. All of these characteristics of bees, and many more, have been taken as indications of the affiliation between honeybees and human families.

Yet even this emblematic species will not fully cooperate; after all, bees are not people. Bees are problematic for, as well as emblematic of, domestic ideals. That's why, more than people, honeybees are "just part of nature."

Origins

This essay enters a conversation begun with a story David Schneider tells about his research on Yap, published as a letter to the editor of *Man* (Schneider 1968). Schneider was investigating Yapese beliefs about human procreation; people had insisted over and over that sexual intercourse was not necessary for conception. "Conception was the reward arranged by happy ancestral ghosts, who intervened with a particular spirit to bestow pregnancy on a deserving woman" (126). In support of their beliefs, they offered him examples of sexually active women who had never had children as well as sexually undesirable women who had. But Schneider, weighed down by his "own version of the forms of western European thought" (127), was puzzled by this belief until the following incident. The story is lively enough to quote at some length:

> One fine day, walking along a path I did not often take, I came upon four large men removing the testicles of a small pig. Always the anthropologist, I did not assume that I knew why; I asked. Makes the pig grow much bigger, they said. But, said I slyly, could a sow ever get pregnant from such a boar? Not from that one! they affirmed. It needed a boar whose testicles had not been removed.
>
> I was unnerved, I admit. So I went back over the whole matter slowly and carefully. Castrate the pig and he grows larger than if he is not castrated. Right! But a castrated pig cannot get a sow pregnant. Right! And then they added once again, if you want a sow pregnant you must get a boar which has not been castrated. They copulate, the sow gets pregnant, the pigs are born.
>
> But, I protested, everyone has been telling me that coitus does not make women pregnant. That is correct, they said. But they were puzzled, and so was I. We did not understand one another. I had presented them, I felt, with logically inconsistent statements that fairly cried out for some explanation. They could not see what my problem was since they had provided me with the full array of necessary, correct facts and to them there was no problem.
>
> So we kept at it until I again put the contradiction to them; if you castrate a pig he cannot get a sow pregnant. Surely that proved that copulation causes pregnancy! But suddenly one man saw what my problem was, for he put it plainly and emphatically: "But people are not pigs!" Once that point was made, the rest followed in happy, logical order. I had obviously assumed that biological processes operate for all animals and had included man [sic] among them. But they had assumed that no one but a fool would equate people and pigs. (127–28)

Why couldn't Schneider tell the difference between people and pigs? One could argue that Schneider's work after he returned to the U.S. from Yap was devoted to just this question. He touches upon his answer in referring to "biological processes" in the quote above: U.S. Americans, like himself, can't tell the difference between people and pigs—especially when it comes to issues of sexuality and reproduction—because U.S. Americans assume that pigs and people are similarly creatures of nature. An extensive research project developed this insight. In *American Kinship* (1980), Schneider describes understandings about kinship that create a realm of natural social association for U.S. Americans. Turning structural-functionalism on its head, he argues that kinship solidarity, rather than being a requirement of social structure and function, is a symbolic commitment, a cultural assumption shaping the realm of social associations imagined as natural. At the center of this kinship solidarity, he finds sexual intercourse, which creates both the love and the continuity of the "diffuse, enduring solidarity" of kinship.

Yet in order to further explore the realm of nature, I would argue, we must return to the pigs as well as the people. What makes human nature "natural" is the fact that people and pigs—and other animals—share in it. Schneider's insights about people take us in the right direction: For U.S. Americans, sexual intercourse creates cohesion and reproduction not just for humans but for all species. Sexual intercourse is discussed by both animal lovers and animal scientists as the central dynamic of species and kin-line reproduction; species and kin-line reproduction, in turn, are seen as forging the pattern of animal social relations. When animal biologists explore "reproduction" they focus almost entirely on the organization of sexual intercourse, to the neglect of feeding, maturation, and much more.[4] One could argue that U.S. American "nature" is that cross-species realm created by the species-specific kinship solidarities formed through sexual intercourse. (And, thus, gender and race—so central to U.S. American notions about the possibilities of sexuality—are always already key to constituting "nature.") As with human kinship, functionalist assumptions about the evolutionary importance of sexuality-based kinship solidarities can be turned on their head to reveal cultural assumptions. In this sense, sociobiology has only formalized a common popular assumption: Sexually created kinship is the diffuse, enduring solidarity that makes for both family and species cohesion and continuity. It is thus no surprise that a U.S. American can't tell the difference between the sex life of a person and a pig.

Schneider's story also alerted me to an entirely different aspect of cultural analysis: its rhetorical effectiveness. The story is purposely sly: an understated, dry humor makes fun of the anthropologist as it forces the reader to think critically about his or her own assumptions. The story made me think about the rhetorical strategies of Schneiderian cultural analysis more generally: Even when the text is deadly serious in tone, it tends to depend for its effectiveness on an ear-tweaking irreverence. It confuses the common-sense and the unheard of, the respectable and the risqué. To be done well, it must pull the rug from under the reader, but entirely quietly and calmly.

By the time I was receiving my graduate training, Schneiderian cultural analysis was being taught as a partial analysis—the symbolic part of a more ambitious agenda that should include history, social practice, and structures of inequality. This is a useful project that continues to excite me. However, now that anthropologists have begun to pay more attention to the ways writing and style shape varied forms of analysis, it may be a good time to restore Schneiderian cultural analysis to a status of completeness. Thus, a rug-pulling, ear-tweaking style of cultural analysis works rather differently from the more conscientious puzzle solving of structural-Marxist–type analyses that begin with inequality. It is unfulfilling to puzzle solve with just symbols and meanings; but it is also difficult to ear tweak with social relations of inequality.

It is in this spirit that I can continue to a companion story that also serves as a stimulus point for this essay. When I was doing fieldwork in the Meratus Mountains of South Kalimantan, Indonesia, I became fascinated with Meratus Dayak honey-hunting practices and their related bee lore. The prime honey producer in the Meratus Mountains is the bee called, in Latin, *Apis dorsata* or, in English, the "giant honeybee." In the Meratus Mountains, *Apis dorsata* colonies build single large combs hanging from the high branches of specially prepared forest trees; Meratus Dayaks scale those trees in the dark of moonless nights to take down the honey.[5] One evening I was talking with some Meratus friends about bees; I explained that I had learned that a colony of bees had a queen—I used the word *raja*, "ruler"—surrounded by many workers. Raja locally refers to the head of government and the spirit of authority; it looms over more politically precise postcolonial terms such as *presiden* and *gubernur*. One of my friends laughed at me and suggested that my view of bees was derived from political propaganda spread by my government to make its subjects think that even animals accepted hierarchy with obedience. I had to stop and think: As a cultural analyst, he had pulled the rug from under me. In imagining government, could I really tell the difference between bees and people? There was "nature" again, staring me in the face.[6]

I went back to the United States and tried to learn a lot more about honeybees. But what has kept startling me—with the help of my Meratus ethnographer—has been the inability of the sources I have tapped to disengage bee agency and human agency, even for those that take their "natural" difference for granted. Because it never occurred to Meratus to treat honeybees as "domestic" home-and-family mates, I became particularly fascinated by how stuck Europeans and U.S. Americans have been in the domestic model. The tensions of working with bees through this model have informed the challenges of beekeeping and bee knowledge. And because I had started out with Southeast Asian bees, I couldn't avoid the discussions of (bee) race and nationality that pervade U.S. storytelling about the "domestic." Stubborn assumptions about the necessities of bee-and-human kinship and nationality inform both scientific and popular bee lore. New apicultural challenges recycle old cultural assumptions even as current versions prove useless. Yet even the familiar returns with the force of the uncanny.

Bee science is distinctive in its popular-technical hybridity. Much bee research is still done by individual curious beekeepers and small apicultural research stations without expensive equipment. Bee journals for the "serious hobbyist" as well as the commercial apiculturalist abound; at the same time, bee research is visible in high-profile journals such as *Science* and *Nature*. Here is a realm then, where natural kinship is created for a distinct but diverse cross section of U.S. Americans.

Honeyed Households

"Honeybee" can refer to all the species of the genus *Apis,* but in the United States the term most commonly refers to the European "races" of the species *Apis mellifera.* No species of *Apis* are indigenous to the New World; the familiar pollinator and honey producer *Apis mellifera* (which in this section I'll call honeybees or bees) was brought over by European colonists as part of the ecological package in which they conquered and transformed the New World with Old World flora and fauna. Once having settled down on American soil, of course, the conquerers forgot not just their own foreignness but also that of the flora and fauna they brought with them; they made themselves at home and began to worry about properly socializing somewhat later-arriving aliens—or else keeping them out. But that is a story I will tell later.

Technical books on honeybees often remind their readers that the bees are not fully and properly "domestic" animals, since they do not rely on humans for their care, subsistence, or reproduction.[7] Yet in European and European-diaspora traditions, bees are always treated as domestic, first, because this is the dominant model of husbandry, and, second, because bees have so many home-endearing qualities, as I mentioned above. It is this tension between their domestic embodiments and refusals that makes honey-bees interesting as creatures of nature; they defy human control even as they exemplify domesticity. Their home life proves that "home" is natural law; yet they refuse to stay home as they should.

The biggest problem with bees, as far as domestication-minded people are concerned, is their independence. Honeybees gather nectar and make honey for themselves and their brood. Queens mate with multiple drones in nuptial flights high above the ground in a difficult arena for humans to intervene. And while bees may consent to live in human-constructed hives, making them stay in a particular hive is another matter. European *Apis mellifera* build their nests in enclosed spaces, where they have protection from cold and predators; besides hives, they live in holes in trees, spaces between walls, and other convenient nooks. Bees in a hive may "abscond," that is, take off as a whole colony with the queen to build a nest elsewhere. They may also "swarm," that is, take off with a queen and part of the colony, leaving the rest of the colony with another queen to continue working in the original nest.

The assumptions and practices of U.S. beekeeping and bee lore derive originally from European peasant traditions in which the tentativeness and tensions of bees' domestic positioning was a major feature of bee culture (that is, human cultivation of bees). In these traditions, people aimed to consolidate the domestic status of bees but expected that they would never be fully successful. Thus, European beekeepers worked hard on symbolic-practical fronts to keep bees from absconding from the hives in which they produced honey within and for the human household. One might consider the European custom of "tanging," in which beekeeping families clanged kitchen implements—pans, kettles, spoons, hearth irons—to keep the bees from absconding. The loud sounds produced may have helped keep the bees from flying off, at least temporarily: Certain kinds of sounds, transmitted through the substrate of the comb to the bees' legs, cause bees to freeze (v. Frisch 1967:286).[8] Yet the symbolism of tanging, as the sounding of the tools of the home, is even more apparent. Bees continually had to be reminded of their domestic loyalties. In this same vein, European beekeepers used charms to calm the bees and keep them home. Here is an Anglo-Saxon charm, addressed to potentially absconding or swarming bees, which makes its "domestic" reminders quite clear:

> Sit ye, my ladies, sink
> Sink ye to earth down;
> Never be so wild
> As to the wood to fly.
> Be ye as mindful of my good
> As every man is of meat and estate. (Fife 1939:336)

Another example of efforts to keep the bees in the family is the English custom of "telling the bees," practiced in rural areas through the early twentieth century: When a death occurred in the human family, the bees were to be told about it. Bees needed extra respect as household members because they could always leave; no one bothered to tell the cow.[9]

Given domestic models for understanding quandaries about bees, it is not altogether surprising that discussions of gender involving bees come back to family and household—and the debates and insecurities they gather in combining the laws and mysteries of nature. European bee scientists and beekeepers have been in agreement about the gender classification system for bees since the seventeenth century: The queen lays the colony's eggs; the workers are nonsexual females; the drones are nonproductive (for subsistence) male sexual agents. However, the question of how to interpret these gender classifications is, of course, never closed. An amusing interchange between U.S. bee commentators at the end of the nineteenth century lit upon the ambiguous gender status of the sexually and reproductively inactive worker bee. If sexual intercourse and the reproductive families it makes orders nature, is the worker bee a real woman?

> What are the absolute facts of the case? The worker (barring a few exceptions) is *anatomically* a female but *functionally* a neuter.

Thus argued a Mr. E. E. Hasty, writing in the correspondence pages of *Gleanings in Bee Culture* (1899b:81), a journal for bee enthusiasts and beekeepers. He claimed that it was more appropriate to write of a bee as "he," because a worker bee is not only an insect but also not a particularly female one.

> Our little squad of bee-writers . . . want an insect which isn't a female, after all, called "she." This alleged reform, if it could be successfully inflicted on the language, would at once create an urgent need for some other pronoun than "she" to express the *real* feminity of the queen. (81)

But the defense from a Dr. Miller was gallant and passionate.

> Did you ever see such audacity as that displayed by that man E.E. Hasty? I called his attention to the fact that he owed Mrs. Bee an apology for calling her "Mr." Bee, and, instead of promptly apologizing to her, as any gentleman ought, he just gets stubborn, and insists he is going to keep right on being impolite, and will call her "Mr." whenever he likes. (80)

Dr. Miller does not consider a bee either an "it" or a "he"; after all, even if she is not the mother of the family, she is truly the angel of the house. Thus his reply to Hasty's charge of gender ambiguity reclaims the feminine domestic of the household, not the reproductive pair:

> But *is* the worker functionally a neuter? Her function is to keep house, nurse the babies, and hustle around to get something to put on the table. If those are neuter functions, then all of our household goddesses should be addressed as *it*. (80)

Miller then accuses Hasty of being inadequately domestic himself; he has been "living so long on one meal a day" that he must have become dyspeptic and "soured on the female persuasion" (80). How could he recognize the domestic, and thus feminine goodness of the bees?[10]

The editor sides with Hasty but is willing to "compromise" with Miller by changing his use of "he" for worker bees to "it." It is with some hesitation, for he thinks: "But somehow it took the 'life' out of much that is said" (82). He continues, "Like Hasty I associate with 'he' smartness and wickedness; and with 'she' softness and goodness" (82). But readers get involved, mainly in defense of women's domestic roles. One reader argues that it is (properly domesticated) women—including worker bees—that nurture and save the race.

> The queen . . . can do nothing to keep her race from becoming extinct; the worker must come to the rescue; the worker performs the other half of the work of the true female. . . . When the time comes that the relative missions of queen and worker are not only fully understood, but to each the credit given that to each belongs, then . . . each will be addressed as it properly should—Mrs. Queen and Mrs. Worker. (Greiner 1899:213)

Even the queen is demoted to a wifely service status within the natural household: Mrs. Queen. But a second reader warns the editor of domestic revolutions:

> Man smarter than a woman? Not much! We have seen women who could peel the bark off a hickory sapling, the equal of any male gender. Better to continue to say *she*, young man, when you think of the worker-bee; this is the age of "woman's rights," and you may wish you had if you do not. *She* is not so "soft and good" as she might be when you get her aroused. (Abbott 1899:213–14)

From Family Beekeeping to Industrial Apiculture

U.S. beekeepers and bee scientists inherited a European domestic model for thinking about bees; their changing practices, questions, and debates have continued to be informed by issues of domesticity. However, bee knowledge and beekeeping practices in the United States have moved through a national trajectory understood as entrepreneurial and progressive. In this trajectory, bees have seemed to grow closer and closer to becoming the model "modern" industrial workers: Already exemplars of routine, industriousness, and orderliness, new bee-handling technologies have made them interchangeable and movable units of labor power. Bees have become part of a nature that could be technologically grasped and controlled—but only by recognizing nature's inherent resistance to full capture. Indeed, the struggle between natural resistance and human modeling creates technical progress. As one bee manual put it,

> There is continual confrontation between bees and man. Man seeks to find the most efficient equipment for the bees' use according to his own ability to handle it. The bees, however, only accept and use man-made equipment if it suits their own needs. It can be very frustrating, but this learning

... is what makes beekeeping one of the most fascinating nature studies. (Stephen 1975:331)

Books on bees in the United States almost always begin their story with a nineteenth-century *national* event, the invention of the movable-frame hive by a U.S. citizen, Reverend Lorenzo L. Langstroth. Before the Langstroth hive, one gathers, there was timeless tradition in all its sticky variety. After Langstroth, there was clean, progressive, modern bee culture. The following presentation is representative:

> Before Langstroth, and the Langstroth hive, there were log hives, gum hives, box hives, skep hives, and many others. . . . What Langstroth saw, that day in 1851, was that he could suspend wooden frames in the hive, three-eighths of an inch from the walls, and the bees would leave the spaces between the frame and the hive wall free of wax. . . . The Langstroth movable-frame hive brought on an era of commercial beekeeping. (Why-nott 1991:18)

The Langstroth hive allowed U.S. beekeepers to remove honeycomb without destroying the hive, thus allowing them to work with more hives more easily.[11] Other late nineteenth-century inventions, such as bee-dispersing smokers and centrifugal honey extractors, were equally important to the new bee culture. The queen excluder, a screen large enough for worker bees to pass through but too small for the queen, let beekeepers separate the brood comb, where the queen laid eggs, and the harvestable honeycomb. Supers, boxes of empty comb layered above the hive, induced continuous honey production beyond bee needs.[12] Indeed, the new manipulable hive, with its coerced segregation of the queen in her nursery and its rising tiers of insatiable supers, became an industrial production module in which bee labor is valued as much for its regular efficiency as for its products.

In the late nineteenth century, U.S. popular science, invention, and publicly proclaimed family values were closely intertwined. Science outlined the necessities of hygiene and efficiency, including family and industrial hygiene and efficiency, which kept organisms in line with new technologies. In dominant understandings, the organization of families and industries were not at odds with each other; family order was the basis of industrial order. U.S. Americans were learning about and shaping a kind of nature that blossomed in the hands of entrepreneurs; this was a nature that kept up with the times, even as it held on to its true value. Those who worked with bees were part of this. Even smallholder beekeepers were embued with an entrepreneurial spirit in which they hoped to turn morality and knowledge to the expansion of production. Bee journals combined science, commercial schemes, practical wisdom, and family morality. (*Gleanings in Bee Culture* ran a column on "Our Homes" that referred specifically to human family relationships.) The importance of the scientific and moral code of hygiene was highlighted in campaigns against American foulbrood, a bee disease spread by "contaminated" food. Inventions such as the queen excluder and the movable-frame hive worked with ideals and dilemmas of "domestic" production, intensified their possibilities, and extended them into the basis for a commercial and industrial apiculture.

Immobile queens and efficiently designed hive-homes were only the beginning of this process of "domestic" rationalization in which—as for the more well-known schemes of factory Fordism—kinship models and industrial efficiency became difficult to extricate from each other. A series of inventions and new beekeeping practices made bees increasingly easy to replace, transport, and sell in large quantities. Bees became easily interchangeable labor units. The rearing of queen bees became a commercial proposition as bee men learned to isolate and organize provisions for queen cells; mated queens sent in small boxes could spawn industries of worker families across the continent. By the turn of the century, it also became profitable to send out larger packages of workers, sold by the pound; beekeepers could let their colonies die back in the winter but supply the family firm with new "packaged bees" in the spring. Or one could buy two pounds of bees and a caged queen for an instant family in a hive (Whynott 1991:45–51). Finally, in the 1940s, bee scientists perfected artificial insemination techniques that allowed them some control over bee reproductive lines. Only then could they attempt to breed for specific characteristics: bees resistant to American foulbrood, or bees with a preference for alfalfa. Still, "man is just beginning to modify honeybees through artificial selection" (Seeley 1985:16).

By the middle of the twentieth century, bee science was flourishing. The excitement lay not in the study of bees as individual organisms but rather in the systems of cooperation and communication developed by the bee colony as a social unit. The study of forager bee "dancing" as a communicative vehicle, initiated by German bee scholar Karl von Frisch, aroused enormous interest among both scientists and the educated public in the United States (v. Frisch 1967). Von Frisch is quoted as saying, "The bee's life is like a magic well: the more you draw from it, the more it fills with water" (Ioyrish 1974:187). And indeed, this well of knowledge about institutionalized coordination and communication has continued to yield (see, for example, Michener 1974; Moritz and Southwick 1992). That the water from this well tastes a little like time-and-motion and organizational studies of industrial labor should not be too surprising. And, of course, the influence is not just one-way: Insect studies—as in the sociobiology of E.O. Wilson (1971)—can also boomerang to inform ideas about human interactions. Indeed, the latest craze in bee studies brings together kinship moralities and the ideally efficient division of labor through investigations of the genetic "kinship" basis of both the social coherence and the internal divisions of bee society (see, for example, Robinson and Page 1988; Page, Robinson, and Fondrk 1989). Tellingly, even scientific critics argue that the glowing results are an artifact of the method (Carlin and Frumhoff 1990; Oldroyd, Rinderer, and Buco 1990).

Meanwhile, a new form of beekeeping practice has further intensified the commodification and transferability of bee labor: migratory beekeeping. Migratory beekeepers haul truckloads of hives back and forth across the United States each year, following the agricultural blooming seasons (Whynott 1991).[13] This practice owes its profitability to the massive use of pesticides in U.S. agriculture, which wipe out local insect pollinators; bees must be trucked in to pollinate the crops. (The invention of forklifts and the vast sums spent on U.S. highways also deserve credit.)

Surprisingly, most of the peddlers of migratory bee labor are families. "The other day," said one major beekeeper to a journalist, "I'm riding down 1–95, heading to Miami with five loads of bees, with my three daughters and two sons-in-law, and I looked out there and saw my grandson and my daughters, and they're all in the bee business, they grew up in it, and that's gonna be their life too" (White 1991:43–44). Many such families move with the hives ("We're in it to make a living and have a good family life," said one beekeeper [Mairson 1993:91]); some use their family to promote their business (" 'When Jim goes by himself [to find farms on which to set his hives], he gets no locations,' she says. 'When he takes me and the kids, he never gets any refusals. The landowner can't refuse; he sees you have a family to support' " [Mairson 1993:86]). But unlike earlier generations of beekeepers, these families do not attempt to stretch to include the bees. The humans are the labor recruiters; the bees are the labor. What kinship they have with the bees is managerial. Like other migrant workers, the bees are replaceable. And they love to labor.

But like the natural hive home, the naturally fully mobile factory doesn't always work, and migratory beekeepers must build contingencies into their plans. The trip from one region to another—collapsed into timeless irrelevance in bee-labor management plans—in fact takes its tolls, and migratory beekeepers' stories are full of the never-fully-planned-for hazards of travel.

A migratory beekeeper from Florida once paid a beekeeper in North Dakota $10,000 to shake bees into several hundred hives. The bees were shook and the hives were loaded on a truck and the driver left for Florida. But along the way, because of the heat, the bees left the hives and pressed against the nets, which puffed out from the truck. In the beekeeper's yard in Florida, when the nets were pulled off the truck, most of the bees absconded. As the beekeeper put it, "Ten thousand dollars flew into the trees." (Whynott 1991:48)

Furthermore, the bees encounter localizing hazards—situations that mark them as noninterchangeable. One crisis was the honeybee tracheal mite, which appeared first in Texas and then in Florida in the mid 1980s (Whynott 1991:21–22).[14] States began to ban the transport of bees across state lines. Florida was placed under federal quarantine; no bees could leave the state. Bee-labor power was no longer so easily manipulable. But from the perspective of the 1990s, this episode seems a minor mobility setback in comparison to the entry of "African" bees into the United States. By the early 1990s, California had already weathered one major quarantine-and-exterminate incident (described in the introduction); Texas was gearing up for its own more extended quarantine program (Winston 1992:136); the first U.S. death attributed to "killer bees" had occurred in Texas (*New York Times* 1993). Bee migrant labor was suddenly a charged issue, and the industry might never be the same. In order to make sense of this new alien hazard, however, it seems important to think about the long-term significance of race and nation in U.S. bee culture.

Before leaving industrial models, it may be useful to consider that the model worker in the U.S. American imagination has always been a white worker and a national representative. Indeed, the forms of labor discipline, hygiene, morality, and orderliness that constitute the model U.S. American working family could be said to be founded on a "natural" contradiction: On the one hand, they depend on the energy of immigrant assimilation; on the other hand, they depend on the social purity of strong racial and national borders. So too with bees. I have so far presented European-origin bees as if they homogeneously and alone occupied the conceptual space of bee-nature; yet, in fact, their traits have come to be understood in relation to a much more multicultural bee space.

Eyeing the Other

In the United States, kinship, as well as nationalism, relies on two contrasting and contradictory understandings of Otherness, which one might call romance and reproduction. The romance of the stranger brings into kinship the seductive draw of the unfamiliar. Family making requires it in the form of marriage to an/other (another gender, another family); the romance of the stranger is the converse of the incest taboo. In the national arena, the romance of the stranger takes a variety of forms: imperial expansion; immigrant assimilation. For animals, including bees, hopes for the "hybrid vigour" created by cross-breeding bring strangers into the family. In contrast to this model, reproduction wants the continuity of the same, "a chip off the old block." Otherness is a terrifying threat to the possibilities of reproducing the same. The children must be protected from it. The nation must be protected from it. Labor productivity—including that of bees—must be protected from it. These two versions of the Other exist in uneasy tension, together threatening the stability of family and national morality. If romantic strangers are incorporated, can dangerous strangers be rebuffed? Not really. The stability of the family, industry, and the nation stand in "natural" vulnerability from this dilemma. The stability of bee kinship and labor arrangements are also vulnerable.

How are differences among bees understood? Otherness among animals is generally talked about in terms of the categories of *race* and *species*. In theory, animals of different races can mate and produce fertile hybrid offspring, while animals of different species can not. Yet, applied to actual animals, the contrasts between these kinds of group differentiations are not always very clear—and certainly not for honeybees.[15] Groups of honeybees achieve labels as distinctive because of geographical isolation, and the question of whether they would mate with individuals of other groups is often unknown.[16] Conflict still rages among honeybee scientists about which groups constitute a distinctive species and which a race. Contemporary experts calculate the number of known *Apis* ("honeybee") species as low as four and as high as twenty-eight (see, for example, Ruttner 1988:3; Otis 1991). Furthermore, groups now firmly seen as species were once thought to be races, and vice versa. In this context, in which experts continually make "practical"—i.e., culturally sensible, useful—decisions about classification, it may be important to note the cultural assumptions behind these terms: *Species* difference points, by definition, to difficulties of coexistence. Since mating is understood to make kinship and solidarity possible, and animals of different species supposedly won't mate, they eye each other across an unbridgeable abyss; even if they were similar, they would not know how to communicate or cooperate. A different species is inscrutable. In contrast, *race* difference always points to the problem of miscegenation. The sense of similarity is plenty strong; the difficulty is enforcing segregation.

Perhaps we can view it as an historical accident that the difference between European and Asian honeybees is currently seen as an inscrutable species difference, while the difference between European and African honeybees is seen as a segregation-inciting racial difference. (If it is not an accident, then it draws on intertwined histories of animal and human travel, science, and politics that are much too large for consideration in this paper.) From the perspective of those whose knowledge begins with the unmarked European-origin honeybee, Asian bees are difficult to understand and African bees are potential rapists.[17] As a result, contrasting dilemmas arise as U.S. beekeepers are forced into contact with Asian and African bees. The rest of this section offers one crazy yet serious example of each: the attempt to capture and domesticate the "big bees of the Philippines," and the attempt to fight off the "invasion of the African bees." Each attempt has been unsuccessful, reminding those who care about bees that bee nature is there for a moment and then off and gone. Each episode plays the tension between romance and reproduction rather differently; but both show the strains.

In the late nineteenth and early twentieth centuries, U.S. interest in honey-bee races—as well as human races—was focused on the differences among *European* races. There were German bees, Italian bees, Caucasian bees (from the Russian Caucasus), Cariolan bees (from Austria and the Balkans), as well as a variety of less-discussed Middle Eastern, or "Oriental" bees—Syrian, Macedonian, and more. Although judged in many ways like human races, they had their colors backwards: the northern races were dark and the southern ones blond. During this entrepreneurial period, most U.S. beekeepers advocated appropriate hybridization among these races, with a strong preference for the light-colored Italians. (Despite the disapproval of experts, who promoted hybridization, U.S. beekeepers selected even among Italians for the most light-colored bees.) Work on hybridizing bees, as well as other plants and animals, was tied to U.S. eugenic theories in which for people, too, the nation was built up by combining the best of the European races.

This was a period of U.S. expansion as well as European immigrant assimilation. One expansion particularly tested and modified U.S. ideas about cultural borders: the turn-of-the-century U.S. acquisition of Cuba and the Philippine Islands after the Spanish-American war. Certainly, U.S. responses to this new status as colonial ruler were varied. U.S. beekeepers' reactions showed both excitement and wariness; yet the romance of imperial incorporations was particularly visible. Two kinds of imperial romance were in particular evidence: First, beekeepers were excited to colonize Cuba with their already familiar bees and beekeeping techniques; they spoke glowingly of the possibilities of expanding into this new and favorable space. Second, rumors of a big, long-tongued honeybee in the Philippines excited many beekeepers who thought U.S. colonization gave them the rights to all Philippine labor. Here, I focus only on the latter and tell the story through excerpts from the 1899 *Gleanings in Bee Culture*.

Going the rounds of the daily papers is a statement, more or less modified, that in taking control of the Philippine Islands our government has obtained full possession of the giant bee, *Apis dorsata*, which bee is to be immediately brought by the government to this side of the world. . . . Those who are favorably inclined to the new bees, and desirous to obtain them, may feel assured that they will receive information promptly through GLEANINGS whenever anything authoritative is to be said; and those who oppose their introduction may possess their souls in patience; for, if we are to believe those who say *Apis dorsata* would be no acquisition, we may also believe them when they say that it could not live in our climate. (1899a: 57–58)

Gleanings was cautious, but interested. And their interest grew after receiving a letter from a U.S. soldier stationed in the Philippines, who offered to get the bees. The letter shows the intimate intertwining of the animal and human colonization:

> Dear Sir:—After reading the above address perhaps you are wondering who it is that is sending you a letter accross 11,000 miles of ocean and land. Well, to explain who I am, and the object of this letter, I will say that my residence is in Dallas, Polk Co., Oregon, and at the breaking-out of the Spanish-American war I was a law student in the office of Daly and Hayter. . . . When the war against Spain was declared I enlisted with the 2d Reg. Oregon Vol. Infantry, and we came with the first expedition to the Philippines. Our regiment was the first to land on Philippine soil. . . . Now, what I want to do is to get some of these bees [*Apis dorsata*] to the United States. . . . Will you kindly help me out by sending advice, cages, and instructions for using? (Uglow 1899: 228)

Gleanings replied enthusiastically, but noted the danger in the project because the Philippines was not yet fully conquered. (Filipinos had declared themselves an independent republic before the arrival of the United States; the U.S. army fought for several bloody years before convincing Filipinos of their revived colonial status.) *Gleanings* offered a reward ($25.00 for one queen alive) and begin to gloat:

> If this young soldier friend has not been shot down in the late battles we may expect shipments of *Apis dorsata* in the near future. . . . It will be a joke if GLEANINGS gets ahead of the government in securing the big bees. . . . The daily press has given us enough free daily advertising of these big bees to create a large demand for them already. We are already getting calls. (1899c 228–29)

Yet evidence of a struggle around the question of bringing the aliens to the United States was also clear in the pages of the journal.

> When left to herself, Nature takes good care of her own. Out of her infinite resources she gives each form of animal and vegetable life its appropriate place and rank. The importation of foreign species is contrary to Nature's intention, and often results disastrously. (Cutts 1899)

> Dr. Doolittle reproves Dr. Miller very gently for not wanting *Apis dorsata* to be fooling around in the neighborhood of the doctor's home. He asks: "How came you, doctor, to have any territory exclusively for your own use in this world? Did God give you a right to turn the rays of sunshine on the flowers around Marengo, that they might bloom for your Italian bees and not for *Apis dorsata?*" The same question might have been asked

about the introduction of common rabbits into Australia in 1864. . . . The government spent millions of dollars in killing them, but to no purpose. Locusts were a blessing in comparison. Dr. Miller has a right to feel some degree of fear in view of such facts. (Stenog 1899)

Both sides of the controversy tended to conclude that aliens would not do well in the United States. As Stenog, the author quoted above, put it, "*Apis dorsata* will, in all probability, flourish about as well in Marengo, Ill. as lemon-trees would there outdoors" (1899:387). Yet readers responded to the competition to get the bees and offered information about sightings of *Apis dorsata* in various places in South and Southeast Asia. In each case, the problems of human colonization loomed as large as those of bee colonization; the bee-seekers could not get natives to help them, and they asked no questions about native bee-handling practices. Thus they approached each bee encounter with the hope that the bees would act like their model Europeans. Finally, the headline called out "Apis Dorsata Caught at Last" (Rambo 1899a: 424). A missionary named, of all things, Rambo had found them in India and captured half a swarm with great difficulty. His romantic enthusiasm was enormous: "If the bee friends could but see these beautiful bees as I saw them through field-glasses they would want to have them, if only for their beauty. . . . They looked so innocent as to make me itch to catch them in my hands" (Rambo 1899a:425).

The assumption of innocence so great to make one "itch to catch them" describes U.S. attitudes toward Filipinos as well as toward Philippine bees. In each case, the innocents were to be caught and colonized for their own good. Despite worries about the incompatibilities between U.S. Americans and Filipino humans and bees, the dominant sense was that they could and should be brought into the safety and productiveness of the U.S. cultural and political economy. Like wild children, they could be socialized in their new family setting. Schools were brought to the Philippines. U.S. democracy became the authoritarian standard. But the bees, among others, were recalcitrant. Even when caught, no one could make them stay put. The honeybee swarms absconded and returned to the forest branches on which they made their combs. As one *Gleanings* headline put it, "Caught and Gone Again; the Giant Bees not Willing to be Confined to Hives" (Rambo 1899b:466). By the 1920 edition of *The ABC and the XYZ of Bee Culture*, the authors were able to say of efforts to domesticate *Apis dorsata*, "For the last 20 years there has been very little said about them" (Root and Root 1920:643).[18]

By the middle of the twentieth century, for both people and bees, a sense of unmarked "Americanness" had emerged. No contenders to European-origin bee hegemony in the New World had appeared for some time, and, just as for humans, there was less talk of racial differences among Europeans. But race emerged at the forefront of bee talk again when the issue became the newly arriving "Africans."[19] Bee scientists speak of numerous races of bees in Africa, but in the U.S. discourse on beekeeping, these have been entirely collapsed into a globally frightening Africanness. Such continental homogenizations are also at work in the discourse on people.

The story of African bees in the New World is astounding. It began in Brazil, where a geneticist named Warwick Kerr imported queens from South and East Africa to cross-breed with the European-origin honeybees in Brazil. Kerr had heard about the large honey harvests in southern Africa, and wanted to bring some of that productivity to Brazil. In 1957, Kerr took those bees that survived the journey and had been selected for further testing to a eucalyptus forest in Sao Paulo. They were set up in hives, and the queens were kept from escaping by screens. But someone "apparently" removed the screens, and twenty-six swarms escaped, including one East African queen and twenty-five queens from the Transvaal. These twenty-six swarms reproduced and formed a feral population in the area.[20] This population continued to reproduce, and it spread out to surrounding territory at the amazingly rapid rate of 300–500 kilometers each year (Winston 1992:11). They soon moved beyond the borders of Brazil into neighboring nations.

Moving southward into Argentina, the African-derived population was blocked by cold weather. A 1991 report showed only northern Argentina as "saturated" by African bees; the middle latitudes had become a zone of intermediate European-African hybrids, while the southern area was free of an Africanized bee population (Sheppard, et al. 1991). Moving northward, however, there was no such obstacle. In 1976, the "African" bees reached Venezuela. In 1980, they arrived in Columbia. In 1982, they were in Panama. In 1986, they had found their way to southern Mexico (Winston 1992:12). By this time, agricultural bureaucrats, beekeepers, and politicians in the United States were crazed with anxiety.

Back in 1965, *Time* coined the term "killer bees" to name this population for its propensity to sting those who disturbed the nest. The sting from an African-derived bee is no more serious than the sting from a European-derived one but the former come out faster and in much larger numbers (Collins, et al. 1982). Killer-bee lore continued to grow. In 1974, the *New York Times* compared "the northward swarm of vicious African honeybees" to "the monster creations of science fiction" (Winston 1992:5). In 1977, a movie called *The Swarm* depicted African bees invading Texas: They overturned trains, attacked children, killed thirty-seven thousand people, and destroyed a nuclear missile site before the Army Corps of Engineers could bomb the national menace out of existence (White 1991:38; Winston 1992:5). Bee scientists and beekeepers spoke out against tabloid journalism (e.g., Winston 1992:1–7). But their "objective" rhetoric, while less hysterical, was also, of necessity, charged with culturally specific concerns about race, nationality, and kinship. The two fears that have dominated U.S. research agendas—fears about the domestic stability and the agressiveness of African-derived bees—have spawned bee programs that further reify racial distinctions for the cause of segregation. And just as in *The Swarm,* agricultural bureaucrats have turned the protection of racial purity into a national security mandate.

The bees that have been spreading through South America have tropical habits in many ways comparable to those of the Southeast Asian bees that interested U.S. beekeepers at the turn of the century. Writers for whom European standards are culturally normative always describe tropical bees as strange. (For example, one serious journalist calls the African bee "hyper-sensitive, hyperactive, and hyperprocreative" [White 1991:37].) Yet it seems more useful to see the European-derived bee as the odd creature. European honeybees have specialized their colony-building practices to cope with cold winters. They pick protected cavities, such as hives, to build their nests, and once they find a good cavity, they are likely to stay there for some time. They build up big colonies in which the warmth of numbers can keep up winter temperatures. In contrast, tropical honeybees, including the African-derived Brazilian population, are not winter specialized. The African-derived bees of South America sometimes build their combs in the open, even seeming to taunt European-oriented beekeepers by building beneath—instead of inside of—human-constructed hives (Winston 1992:31). Furthermore, they have no need for huge colonies, preferring to form new swarms that can take advantage of scattered nectar-producing areas. The whole colony absconds easily, following the nectar. These are practices that scare domestication-minded beekeepers. And, although a reasonably large literature is available on indigenous African methods of honey production (see, for example, Irvine 1957; Isack and Reyer 1989), it seems never to have occurred to anyone in the Americas to learn from African bee culture.[21]

The other problem with African-derived bees is their aggressive response to disturbance. Sometimes these bees come out to protect the colony when a person or animal merely approaches the nest. A person who is not allergic to bee stings can take several hundred stings without major ill effects. However, those who for some reason do not run away from defensive African-derived bees may be stung several *thousand* times. Penned or tied-up livestock are especially vulnerable. (The joke is told in Mexico that the latest get-rich-quick scheme is to tie your sick old horse next to your neighbor's beehive; when the horse is stung to death, you sue the neighbor [White 1991:45].) Three hundred fifty people may have been killed by excessive stinging in Venezuela between 1975 and 1988, or about 2.1 deaths per year per million people (Winston 1992:52). Opinions differ about whether this is an unacceptable death rate, considering that quite a few people—although not quite as many—die from stings by European-derived bees. But many North Americans have been frightened.

U.S. fears are put in perspective by their contrast with the Brazilian response. Brazilian beekeepers *like* the new bees; when the government passed out European queens to bring back European strains, beekeepers killed them (White 1991:56). Brazilian beekeepers claim that the African-derived bees are better honey producers than the German bees they once managed. After an initial fall in honey production, with fears about the introduction of the new bees, Brazilian honey production has risen dramatically. Brazilian bee scientists are also among the most vocal advocates of the view that these bees are all-American hybrids: They are not "African" nor "European"; they mix the best of each for an American setting. The scientist who originally introduced them has continued to sponsor efforts to create the best hybrid qualities; by 1960, he has argued, all "pure-African" bees had been eliminated. "A new generation of beekeepers began to take over in Brazil," he recalls, "and, with techniques that we had helped develop, they began to thrive, and the bees' less desireable qualities began to be bred out. Today, our beekeepers overwhelmingly prefer Africanized bees. . . . And do you know how hard these bees work?" (White 1991:59)[22]

In contrast to this enthusiasm for hybridization, U.S. bee research has been aimed at separating out the traits of each bee race to make them properly distinguishable. The dominant U.S. view is that the African-derived bees are really, essentially "African"; their mitochondrial DNA is similar to bees in Africa (Fletcher 1991; Hall 1991). (Mitochondrial DNA studies are also a key technology in contemporary U.S. scientific efforts to produce "race" among humans.) The contrast between Brazilian and U.S. views is striking. It is hard not to think about Brazilian national ideology, in which it is the melding of African, European, and indigenous American (human) races that has produced the energy and passion of Brazil. The bees, too, have found their "American" potency in racial blending. In contrast, U.S. American beekeepers and officials campaign for European racial purity as the guarantor of the nation.

The most dramatic U.S. effort to enforce bee segregation occurred in the mid-1980s, when the U.S. Department of Agriculture decided to create a barrier across Mexico to stop the African bees from coming north. Like the missile-stopping barrier called Star Wars, to which the idea seems closely related, the Bee Regulated Zone was supposed to create a safety net around the United States to block out alien invaders. "The zone was to be 225 kilometers long and 170 kilometers wide, encompassing the narrowest part of Mexico. . . . The plan itself, couched in semi-military terms, gave the impression that we were going to war against the Africanized bee, using sophisticated technology at the cutting edge of scientific progress" (Winston 1992:127).[23] As with Star Wars, many scientists objected that the scheme was impossible. By the time any money was approved and resources ready, in 1987, African bees had already moved north of the zone. The two small "Operational Units" that were implemented anyway did nothing to stop the bees' northward spread. And thus, on October 15, 1990, African bees were found in Hidalgo, Texas. In July 1993, newspapers reported the first "killer-bee"–related U.S. death (*New York Times* 1993). As one bee writer put it, the United States had begun "the transition to a post-Africanized America" (Winston 1992:133).

The Department of Agriculture's reaction to the African bees combines fears of Mexican immigrants creeping over inadequately patrolled borders and fears of Black-White racial miscegenation. Agricultural bureaucrats are afraid of the out-of-control reproduction of African bees, of the heady sexuality of the males (African bees produce more drones than Europeans), and of their unwillingness to settle down in domestic stability to work at human honey production. A serious journalist worried: "Africanized bees are skilled robbers. . . . and—in a rather macabre practice—they have been known to invade a European colony, kill the queen, install their own queen, and enslave the resident population" (White 1991:38). In other contexts, bee writers have spoken of the "incorporation" or "assimilation" of bees from another colony; why is it "enslavement" here? Is the author, perhaps, invoking "reverse discrimination"? Do we hear a tie between "African" racial terror and threats to national sovereignity?

Then too, there are the threats to the family. The mobility and aggressiveness of the African bee family, its unwillingness to settle into working-class stability, are often cited as threats to the order and efficiency of production. The national economy will suffer. There are also dangers for the human family.

> "The thing that bothers me the most," [the USDA inspector said], "has to do with the quality of life. If you can't open your doors and let your children play in the yard because there are bees nearby . . . what about them? Or if there is a grandmother or grandfather out in a chair, what about them?" (Whynott 1991:168)

Yet perhaps the most telling piece of all is the admission one hears that segregation has not worked and will never work despite the intense desire— for the nation, for the economy, and for the family—to make it work. Segregation, on which so much depends, is an aspect of nature that is naturally undependable. And if the model working family, in its segregated "modern" world, is still the law of nature, it is not one that can stand against its own natural disasters.

> The Texas Action Plan, to be administered by the Texas Department of Agriculture, will impose quarantines within a 150-mile radius of any find

of Africanized bees. Every hive inside the circle will be sampled. Initially, there will be depopulations, but once the Africanized bee is firmly established [and despite every precaution, it will come], depopulations will cease and a Management Plan will take effect. . . . No unmarked queens will be permitted. Beekeepers will have to maintain 10 percent of their stock for drone production, so as to saturate the area with European stock. All wild colonies will be destroyed. (Whynott 1991:168)

Envoi

In a time of massive transnational migrations and flexible industrial readjustments, the U.S. discourse on kinship and the family has taken on rapidly multiplying challenges to articulate the dilemmas of race, class, nationality, and gender. Through competing frameworks of "romance" and "reproduction," family models have entered into social agendas for national expansion and ethnic assimilation as well as national and racial protection. These are gendered agendas. Taming the "big bees of the Philippines"—and the human men and women—was a feminizing strategy in which domestication was the goal. (Although Philippine bees are no longer a political issue, Filipino people still struggle to understand and move beyond this colonial legacy.)[24] Programs to fight off the "invasion of the African bees" invoke a different gender agenda: the protection of gentle European females (that is, bees) against the uncontrolled sexuality of the savage Other.

The most visible feminist discussion of gender in "nature" argues that women and nature are similarly treated as objects rather than subjects of knowledge. The split that divides male knowers and objectified women, animals, and other others in European–derived thought helps explain the predominance of white male scientists as well as the omissions and false stereotypes of masculinist theories that give no agency to women and nature. However, this approach does not help explain the gendered quality of those forms of agency that *are* attributed to nature. By beginning with the centrality of sexuality and kinship solidarity to the constitution of animal and human "nature," as I have here in following a Schneiderian lead, it becomes possible to examine the importance of gender and race in constituting what is imagined as "natural" behavior. This is, of course, precisely where feminist sociobiologists begin when they argue that the centrality of sexuality to evolution creates assertively feminine forms of agency appropriate to female roles in sex and reproduction (e.g., Hrdy 1981). But instead of accepting and building from these natural facts, I have tried to make sense of their cultural construction.

Making "nature" a realm of legitimacy for human social relations requires extensions from humans to nonhuman creatures. We know what is natural by comparing ourselves to animals. Where the feminist critics of science mentioned above tend to argue that scientists do not think of nature in subjective-enough terms—instead viewing nature without human passion—I find that nature is always, as a realm of cultural legitimacy and truth, infused with human lifeways. The "objectivity" of science is always culturally and politically charged because scientists, like other people, cannot think and talk without culture and politics. Yet our views of nature are not a simple reflection of our valued standards and ideals: our observations of non-humans present continual challenges to our cultural agendas that require new inflections and transpositions of our cultural "sense." It is in recognition of such challenges that bee scientists argue that they work to understand bees on bees' own terms. Of course, such scientific appreciation of bees' terms reflects scientists' ideas about the possibilities of agency, which are always culturally defined. Yet, still, attention to bee life ways can raise new, unexpected issues, as the bees refuse cultural expectations and social programs. It is the tension between these two facets of our knowledge that allows "nature" to both tell us the law and open the doors of mystery.

Notes

Gleanings in Bee Culture is the name of a U.S. journal of beekeeping, bee science, and bee commentary. I borrow the name in admiration of the breadth of possibility it opens. Harriet Whitehead and I first discussed this paper as part of an intertwined project on "the birds and the bees." Donna Haraway kindly read and commented on a draft. I am also grateful to Jane Atkinson, Paulla Ebron, Roberta Nieslanik, Troels Petersen, and Patty Zischka for letting me talk to them, at odd moments, about bees.

1. This is the opening to Charles Butler's classic text, *The Feminine Monarchy, Or, A Treatise Concerning Bees, and the Due Ordering of Them*, 1609.

2. In making a general point of this sort, one necessarily forgets many fine exceptions, including the work of all those that made it easier for the generalization to be argued. I might begin by acknowledging Donna Haraway's *Primate Visions* (1989) as a key study of the constitution of nature and one that makes others, like this one, possible.

3. A domestic animal, like a domestic human family, should be settled and home centered; animals whose rearing involves lots of movement disturb ideals of domesticity. This disturbing state can rub off on their caretakers, who, even as humans, are flung with their animals from the settled domestic to the edge of the wild: The cowboys who once drove cattle across the U.S. West are one obvious example. In another direction of confusion, as the wild has increasingly needed to be reinstated as protected terrain, human-reared animals must be turned wild. Game animals—trout, pheasants—are raised and let loose; emblems of diversity—endangered raptors, orangutans—are replaced in their "wild" niches. But these animals must be denied domestic status; for the fisherman or the tourist to remember that the stream is stocked or the birds are fed would ruin the effect.

4. There are important exceptions to this generalization. For example, the pioneering work of Adrienne Zihlman on chimpanzee life histories has challenged the equation of sexual intercourse and reproduction to show a much longer series of "reproductive" events.

5. Tsing (n.d.) describes Meratus honey hunting and the Meratus ecological models that connect people, bees, and honey trees in the Meratus Mountains.

6. Contemporary U.S. understandings of "nature" do not privilege political order in the same way as they privilege sexuality. Yet in earlier European traditions, the political hierarchy of nature was important. According to Ioyrish (1974:190), "Napoleon Bonaparte (1769–1821) saw elements of the state in the bee colony. In drawing up the Code Napoleon, he made use of the ideal order, collectivism, and total commitment to the queen of the bee 'empire.' He adopted the bee as his emblem, and during his reign the curtain of the Grand Opera was decorated with a bee pattern." And, according to Shakespeare (*King Henry V*, quoted in Free 1982:37):

> . . . for so work the honey-bees,
> Creatures that by a rule in nature, teach
> The art of order to a peopled kingdom.
> They have a king, and officers of sorts:
> Where some, like magistrates, correct at home;
> Others, like merchants, venture trade abroad;
> Others, like soldiers, armed in their stings,
> Make boot upon the summer's velvet buds;
> Which pillage they with merry march bring home
> To the tent-royal of their emperor:
> Who, busied in his majesty, surveys
> The singing masons building roofs of gold;
> The civil citizens kneading-up the honey;
> The poor mechanic porters crowding in
> Their heavy burdens at the narrow gate;
> The sad-eyed justice, with his surly hum,
> Delivering o'er to executors pale
> The lazy yawning drone.

7. The only insect bred to rely on human care is the silkworm (Bailey and Ball 1991).

8. Until recently, bee scientists thought that bees were incapable of sensing sounds transmitted through the air. Recent research, however, has suggested that bees are sensitive to the air-particle movements of airborne sound rather than the pressure oscillations that most vertebrates detect. Thus, for example, worker bees take clues in finding nectar sources from the air-particle movements emitted by sound-emitting dancing bees (Towne and Kirchner 1989).

9. Free (1982:105) reports that bees were informed of marriages as well. He quotes Rudyard Kipling:

> A maiden in her glory,
> Upon her wedding-day,
> Must tell her Bees the story,
> Or else they'll fly away.

Free (1982:117) also reports the custom of "telling the bees" practiced in the nineteenth-century United States.

10. The cultural specificity of Miller's argument is perhaps easier to see by holding it up in contrast to an argument about the gender of bees that derives from a non-European

tradition. Bodenheimer (1951) reports the following conversation between a Middle Eastern beekeeper named Ahmed from the Wadi Do'an of Hadramaut and an Englishman named Ingrams:

"The bees have a father," said Ahmed. . . . On Ingrams' reply that the father is a queen, Ahmed answered: "But it is the leader, and who ever heard of a woman leading an army like that?" Referring to the males, he answered: "But they are soldiers, they have the swords to sting with. The bee women (i.e., the drones) are bigger and don't sting." (226–27)

The passage is of interest here not only for Ahmed's argument that bees are male but also because he uses imagery that is foreign to European smallholder beekeeping. The model of an army of bees sets up rather different dilemmas for human-bee relationships than the model of the household of bees.

11. The portrayal of Langstroth as the father of "modern" bee culture disguises the national aspirations of this narrative—a story of growing U.S. preeminence in defining global "modernity." It is easier to see the nationalism of the story in comparing U.S. accounts with those produced in other places. Thus, for example, a book on bees written in the former Soviet Union (Ioyrish 1974) introduces the rationalization of beekeeping with a different figure: Peter Prokopovich. The storyline is similar to the Langstroth tale in its portrayal of the line between traditional and modern, but it is set thirty-seven years earlier:

In 1800, at the age of 24, Prokopovich took up beekeeping. For fourteen years he bred bees in the traditional non-collapsible log-hives of the Ukraine, Russia, and neighbouring countries. But his ingenious mind was not satisfied with the primitive techniques used then in beekeeping. In 1814 he invented the collapsible hive, an invention that was of great importance as it served to rationalize beekeeping and promoted increased productivity and profitability . . . (Ioyrish 1974:193)

Later, indeed, Langstroth comes up without much fanfare:

The Rev. L.L. Langstroth (1810–1895) invented and developed a frame hive widely used in America. (Ioyrish 1974:195)

12. Various ways of manipulating the brood and honeycomb, made possible by movable frame hives, reduce the problems of swarming and absconding. But only to a certain extent, as one contemporary beekeeper testifies, even as she advocates these manipulations: "[Providing available brood comb and foundation for new honeycomb] is not a guaranteed method of keeping bees from swarming—there are no guarantees of anything, with bees" (Hubbell 1988:80). Indeed, the increase in scale these new technologies allow themselves reduce their effectiveness as tools of domestic stability. The beekeeper above goes on to say that she worked hard at the manipulations necessary to keep her hives from swarming when she had less than a hundred hives. "But with three hundred, it became impossible. I now accept the fact that a certain number of my hives will swarm" (Hubbell 1988:80). After all, bees are still predictable yet unpredictable creatures of nature.

13. One journalist reports the following figures: 300,000 hives a year moved between California and the Dakotas; 300,000 hives a year between Texas and the Dakotas/Minnesota; 180,000 hives a year between California and the Northwest; 70,000 hives between Florida and the upper Midwest; 60,000 hives between Florida and the Northeast (Mairson 1993:77).

14. The question of why this mite provoked a major crisis is itself culturally rich—and worth further investigation. A British source (Bailey and Ball 1991:78–88) describes *Acarpis woodi* mite infection as a much exaggerated problem; infected bees die only slightly sooner than uninfected ones and appear normal until they die. U.S. American beekeepers were probably particularly upset because infection rates before 1985 were very low, allowing fantasies of purity, when suddenly these rates shot up. The origin of infection was assumed to be Mexico; economic practices that moved bees across the country—that is, the sale of bees as well as migratory beekeeping—were blamed.

15. The term "race" is used for many other domestic animals to refer to the distinctive products of long histories of human breeding; this offers a different set of conceptual problems. Because human breeding plans have not been significant in producing honeybee "races," these races are more relevantly tied to uses of the term for humans.

16. The best contemporary studies tend to use the time of day during which drones fly out to mate with queens as a measure of reproductive distinctiveness. But even this method cannot produce definitive predictions of mating possibilities because it ignores localized environmental factors affecting drone flying times.

17. Asian *Apis* include "giant" and "dwarf" honeybees (*A. dorsata, A. florea,* and possible others) as well as cavity-dwelling bees (*A. cerana*) similar to European honeybees. African honeybees are all considered races of *Apis mellifera* and include more than ten scientifically named groupings.

18. Efforts to domesticate Asian bees on European models have not, however, stopped. Thus, for example, in the 1980s bee ecologist Robert Whitcombe tried to domesticate the "little bee" *Apis florea* in Langstroth hives (Whitcombe 1984). His efforts, he admits, were "inconclusive." Surprisingly, he learned a good deal about local beekeeping techniques in Oman, where he conducted his research, before embarking on his own beekeeping efforts. Yet, because he considered Omani knowledge and practices to be archaic folk survivals in a properly modern world, he was unwilling or unable to apply local knowledge in his experiments.

19. Debate rages about what to call these bees: Some call them "Africanized," some "African." (Spivak, Fletcher, and Breed 1991:5; Winston 1992:69). The debate reflects differences of opinion about just how hybridized these bees are from the East African "race" called *Apis mellifera scutellata.* I don't like the term "Africanized" because it actively unmarks European-origin bees (the ones being "Africanized"). I use "African" or "African-derived."

20. Kerr later admitted that he had handed out some other African queens to local beekeepers, and their progeny may have added to the group; but it was still quite a small genetic nucleus (Spivak, Fletcher, and Breed 1991:3; White 1991:56).

21. Contemporary U.S. scientists learn from a long colonial tradition in which "nature" in the Third World can be approached in oblivious disdain of the mediation of local human knowledge and practice (Pratt 1992). As one bee scientist put it when describing new advances in thinking about African-derived bee populations, "The best teachers are the bees themselves" (White 1991:39). To learn about African bees, no one, of course, consults Africans.

22. Compared to European-derived bees, African-derived bees mature slightly more quickly, forage slightly more actively, and die slightly sooner (Winston 1991). Kerr also claims that African-derived bees forage on moonlit nights (White 1991:59); certainly, other tropical *Apis* do (Roubik 1989:137). Goncalves, Stort, and De Jong (1991) discuss the history of Brazilian beekeeping, the beekeepers' preference for African bees, and the rising production statistics for Brazilian honey.

23. Winston (1992:127–129) lists the following components of the plan: (1) quarantines on moving bees out of the zone; (2) destruction of African swarms and colonies; (3) maintenance of European colonies; (4) European drone flooding; (5) drone traps to kill African drones; and (6) education to discourage intentional introduction of African bees. There is nothing particular high technology about these measures except, perhaps, the imagined scale at which they were to be employed.

24. My understanding of "colonial domesticity" in the Philippines is indebted to Vicente Raphael's insightful paper on this topic (Raphael 1993).

References

Abbott, E. T. 1899. "He, She, or It. A Little Advice to the Editor." *Gleanings in Bee Culture* 27(March 15): 213–14.

Bailey, L., and B. V. Ball. 1991. *Honey Bee Pathology*. 2d ed. London: Academic.

Bodenheimer, F. S. 1951. *Insects as Human Food*. The Hague: W. Junk.

Carlin, Norman, and Peter Frumhoff. 1990. "Nepotism in the Honey Bee." *Nature* 346(August 23): 706–707.

Collins, Anita, Thomas Rinderer, John Harbo, and Alan Bolten. 1982. "Colony Defense by Africanized and European Honey Bees." *Science* 218(October 1): 72–74.

Crosley, A. 1609. "To the Reader." In *The Feminine Monarchy, Or, A Treatise Concerning Bees, and the Due Ordering of Them*, by Charles Butler. Reprint, New York: Da Capo Press, 1969.

Cutts, J. M. 1899. "Apis Dorsata. A Note of Warning." *Gleanings in Bee Culture* 27:499.

Fife, Austin. 1939. *The Concept of the Sacredness of Bees, Honey, and Wax in Christian Popular Tradition*. Ph.D. dissertation, Stanford University.

Fletcher, David. 1991. "Interdependence of Genetics and Ecology in a Solution to the African Bee Problem." In *The "African" Honey Bee.*, edited by M. Spivak, D. Fletcher, and M. Breed, 77–94. Boulder, CO: Westview.

Free, John B. 1982. *Bees and Mankind*. London: Allen and Unwin.

Frisch, Karl von. 1967. *The Dance Language and Orientation of Bees*. Translated by Leigh Chadwick. Cambridge, MA: Harvard Univ. Press.

Gleanings in Bee Culture. 1899a. "Apis Dorsata from the Philippines; Some Big Stories." 27 (Jan 15):57–58.

———. 1899b. "He or She. Confab between Dr. Miller and E. E. Hasty." 27 (Feb 1): 80–82.

———. 1899c. "Apis Dorsata in the Philippines; A Chance to Get Them to the United States." 27 (March 15): 228–29.

Goncalves, Lionel, Antonio Stort, and David De Jong. 1991. "Beekeeping in Brazil." In *The "African" Honey Bee*, edited by M. Spivak, D. Fletcher, and M. Breed, 359–72. Boulder, CO: Westview.

Greiner, F. 1899. "He or She: Its Use in Different Languages." *Gleanings in Bee Culture,* 27 (March 15): 213.

Hall, H. Glenn. 1991. "Genetic Characterization of Honey Bees Through DNA Analysis." In *The "African" Honey Bee,* edited by M. Spivak, D. Fletcher, and M. Breed, 45–73. Boulder, CO: Westview.

Haraway, Donna. 1989. *Primate Visions: Gender, Race, and Nature in the World of Modern Science.* New York: Routledge.

Hrdy, Sarah. 1981. *The Woman That Never Evolved.* Cambridge, MA: Harvard Univ. Press.

Hubbell, Sue. 1988. *A Book of Bees.* New York: Random House.

Ioyrish, Naum. 1974. *Bees and People.* Translated by Glynis Kozlova. Moscow: MIR.

Irvine, F. R. 1957. "Indigenous African Methods of Beekeeping." *Bee World* 38(5): 113–28.

Isack, H. A., and H. U. Reyer. 1989. "Honeyguides and Honey Gatherers: Interspecific Communication in a Symbiotic Relationship." *Science* 243(10 March): 1343–46.

Mairson, Alan. 1993. "America's Beekeepers: Hives for Hire." *National Geographic* 183(5): 72–93.

Michener, Charles. 1974. *The Social Behavior of the Bees: A Comparative Study.* Cambridge, MA: Harvard Univ. Press.

Moritz, Robin, and Edward Southwick. 1992. *Bees as Superorganisms: An Evolutionary Reality.* Berlin: Springer-Verlag.

New York Times. 1993. "Death of a Rancher in Texas is Attributed to Killer Bees." 142(July 20): A8.

Oldroyd, Benjamin, Thomas Rinderer, and Steven Buco. 1990. "Nepotism in the Honey Bee." *Nature* 346(23 August): 707–708.

Otis, Gard W. 1991. "A Review of the Diversity of Species Within *Apis.*" In *Diversity in the Genus Apis,* edited by Deborah Smith, 29–49. Boulder, CO: Westview.

Page, Robert E., Gene E. Robinson, and M. Kim Fondrk. 1989. "Genetic Specialists, Kin Recognition, and Nepotism in Honey-Bee Colonies." *Nature* 338(13 April): 576–79.

Pratt, Mary Louise. 1992. *Imperial Eyes.* New York: Routledge.

Rambo, W. E. 1899a. "Apis Dorsata Caught at Last." *Gleanings in Bee Culture* 27 (June 1): 424–27.

———. 1899b. "Apis Dorsata: Caught and Gone Again; the Giant Bees Unwilling to be Confined to Hives; Their General Appearance Much Like Italians, only Larger." *Gleanings in Bee Culture* 27 (June 15): 466–67.

Raphael, Vicente. 1993. "Colonial Domesticity: White Women and United States Rule in the Philippines." Paper presented at the University of California, Santa Cruz.

Robinson, Gene E., and Robert E. Page. 1988. "Genetic Determination of Guarding and Undertaking in Honey-Bee Colonies." *Nature* 336(26 May): 356–61.

Root, A. I. and E. R. Root. 1920. *The ABC and the XYZ of Bee Culture.* Medina, OH: A. I. Root.

Roubik, David. 1989. *Ecology and Natural History of Tropical Bees.* Cambridge, UK: Cambridge Univ. Press.

Ruttner, Friedrich. 1988. *Biogeography and Taxonomy of Honeybees.* Berlin: Springer-Verlag.

Schneider, David. 1968. "Virgin Birth." *Man* N.S. 3(1): 126–29.

———. 1980. *American Kinship: A Cultural Account.* 2d ed. Chicago: Univ. of Chicago Press.

Seeley, Thomas. 1985. *Honeybee Ecology: A Study of Adaptation in Social Life.* Princeton, NJ: Princeton Univ. Press.

Shepard, Walter, Thomas Rinderer, Julio Mazzoli, J. Anthony Stelzer, and Hachiro Shimanuki. 1991. "Gene Flow Between African- and European-derived Honey Bee Populations in Argentina." *Nature* 349(February 28): 782–84.

Spivak, Marla, David Fletcher, and Michael Breed. 1991. "Introduction." In *The "African" Honey Bee*. edited by M. Spivak, D. Fletcher, and M. Breed, 1–9. Boulder, CO: Westview.

Stenog. 1899. "Some Pickings From Our Neighbors Fields." *Gleanings in Bee Culture* 27(May 15): 387.

Stephen, W. A. 1975. "For the Beginner." In *The Hive and the Honey Bee,* edited by Dadant and Sons. Rev. ed. Hamilton, IL: Dadant and Sons.

Towne, William F., and Wolfgang H. Kirchner. 1989. "Hearing in Honey Bees: Detection of Air-Particle Oscillations." *Science* 244(12 May): 686–88.

Tsing, Anna. N.d. "Cultivating the Wild: Honey Hunting and Forest Management in Southeast Kalimantan." In *Culture and the Question of Rights in Southeast Asian Environments,* edited by Charles Zerner. In preparation.

Uglow, John. 1899. "Apis Dorsata in the Philippines; A Chance to Get Them to the United States." *Gleanings in Bee Culture.* 27 (March 15): 228.

Whitcombe, Robert. 1984. "The Bedouin Bee." *Aramco World Magazine* 35(2): 34–40.

White, Wallace. 1991. "A Reporter at Large: The Bees From Rio Claro." *The New Yorker* (September 16): 36–60.

Whynott, Douglas. 1991. *Following the Bloom: Across America with the Migratory Beekeepers.* Boston: Beacon.

Wilson, E. O. 1971. *The Insect Societies.* Cambridge, MA: Harvard Univ. Press

Winston, Mark L. 1991. "The Inside Story: Internal Colony Dynamics of Africanized Bees." In *The "African" Honey Bee,* edited by M. Spivak, D. Fletcher, and M. Breed, 201–212. Boulder, CO: Westview.

———. 1992. *Killer Bees: The Africanized Honey Bee in the Americas.* Cambridge, MA: Harvard Univ. Press.

6

The Gender of Birds in a Mountain Ok Culture
Harriet Whitehead

Introduction

The problem is more one of stopping, or conventionalizing the flow of analogies—the "pull" from one analogy to all others—than of finding analogies.
—Roy Wagner, *Symbols That Stand for Themselves*

Sometimes a good cigar is just a good cigar.
—Attributed to Freud

Among the Mountain-Ok–speaking Seltaman people of western Papua New Guinea, the highly plumaged bird of several sexually dimorphic bird-of-paradise species is spoken of as the "big sister," while the drably plumaged bird is spoken of as the "little brother." Seltaman observe with some amusement that the "little brother" will one day grow up and "take the place" of his big sister. The Seltaman genderization of these species is the reverse of what ornithologists tell us. In "ornithological reality," the highly plumaged birds of the species in question are always adult males and the drably "plumaged birds are the females and the juvenile males;" a transitional plumage is apparent in males that are reaching full sexual maturity. As we shall see, however, most Seltaman really "mean" this genderization: "big sister" and "little brother" are not just a manner of speaking. The type bird of the sexually dimorphic birds treated in this fashion is the locally common Raggiana bird of paradise (*Paradisaea raggiana*), called *karom* in Seltaman speech.

Seltaman constitute one territorial group among approximately sixteen culturally distinct populations of a larger regional culture that has come to be called Mountain Ok, after the name of the language family to which most of the regional dialects belong. Inhabiting the rainy Central Ranges of the island of New Guinea, Mountain Ok speakers are primarily low-intensity, root-crop horticulturalists and suidologists with a strong hunting and foraging component in their economy. The social orders of the smaller groups are not highly differentiated. Much of community life is ordered through the multilayered male cult initiation system. Out of this cult system has poured a voluminous body of puzzlingly connected myths, ritual themes, and lore concerning ancestral events and natural species. Each Mountain Ok subgroup has its own distinct blend of sacred knowledge (see Barth 1987), much of it entrusted to the memories of a few ritually senior men. Among Seltaman, the knowledgeable elders in question do not exchange mythic material among themselves and many are negligent of their obligation to pass it on to sons. Thus Seltaman sacred knowledge tends to cling to existence in isolated tidal pools, each seemingly cut off from the others and from the main sea of Seltaman secular culture. Yet at the same time, these fragments and the secular whole *seem* tantalizingly related. The question being raised here is: Are they? If so, in what way?

The gender and kin relationship of birds of paradise furnishes a good case for investigation. Faced with bird lore that is, to borrow a phrase, "so patently farfetched that the motivation for it must be elsewhere" (Riffaterre 1987:382), one turns a natural suspicion in the direction of the "power discourse" of the area, the sacred corpus of myths and lore. And on first take, one is not disappointed. Among the sacred secrets of the Seltaman there are several versions of a myth in which the regional culture heroine, *Afek* ["the ancestress"] is displaced in ritual authority by her little brother. Inasmuch as the bird lore and the secret ancestral lore are connected by the intriguing intertext, "the little brother takes the place of his big sister," the question is raised whether the two contexts in which this phrase appear are "interpretants" of each other: the birds of the sacred saga, or the sacred saga of the birds.

Though frustrated in my attempts to uncover an explicit relationship of this sort while I was in the field, I nevertheless posed the problem to a group of (western) bird watchers who were, under the guidance of a prominent ornithologist, visiting Tabubil, the regional mining town, where I happened to be camped one week. The ornithologist rather contemptuously dismissed the issue. "Of course there's a connection," he snapped, proceeding to change the subject. His subtext was "*You* have simply failed to uncover it." The essay that follows is addressed to this unnamed ornithologist. He is, of course, a stand-in for all of us who, whether inspired, as I suspect he was, by a vision of tribal sacredness as some sort of higher nature wisdom, or simply exercising our unrestricted license to interpret, glibly assume connections wherever we espy the connectable.

I would like to argue here that the peculiar Seltaman treatment of their birds of paradise must be assessed in terms of three relatively distinct domains of Seltaman culture and meaning production. First and most obviously, there is the sacred corpus, which contains the Afek saga and other myths and myth fragments as well as sacred songs and the compendium of ritual scripts and types of ritual paraphernalia. There is, almost as obviously, a corpus of secular stories and songs used by Seltaman to entertain each other. Finally there is an area that I will call, for lack of a better term, "nature lore" in which one finds both secular explanations ("lore") and secular stories about wild creatures, both ostensibly addressed to the forms, habits, and ecological relations of natural types.

The real questions raised by the big sisters and little brothers of bird and myths are questions concerning what we might variously call "meaning environments" or "discursive fields" or "semiotic spaces"—those areas within any culture that manifest a genre-like boundedness. The peculiarity of bird-of-paradise gender and kinship plainly has a position in the discursive field of secular nature lore, but it appears to be intertextual with the sacred corpus. While traditional anthropological analysis has always licensed ignoring and thus reading "across" meaning environments of this sort, and would thus immediately encourage us to see in bird lore a stamp of the sacred, recent intellectual trends, in particular those in which the concept of the intertext is featured, have called such practices into question. Readings must now be informed by an understanding of the "reading rules" of the particular culture. Daniel Boyarin has framed the issue elegantly in his *Intertextuality and the Reading of Midrash*. In defining the nature of the midrash, the rabbinical elaborations on biblical scripture, he writes:

> The way that midrash works is by introducing into the fissures in the [biblical] text new narrative material, largely created out of other biblical texts. This practice is founded again on the insight that the Bible is a single semiotic system, a self-glossing text. However, this work is not . . . a free, individual response to the text, but one which is constrained by a very specific ideology. Only certain plots and certain associations of text to text are allowed. I would suggest that this is true of any reading in any culture, but it is usually unconscious. (Boyarin 1990:92)

What I want to suggest is that Seltaman "readings"—and I will be dealing, for the most part, with the "readings" of initiated Seltaman men—implicitly constitute certain relations and not others as "gaps" to be filled, implicitly demarcate certain discursive boundaries within which to confine new meanings, and implicitly respect certain rules of glossing that are distinctive to each genre-like field. In places, the Seltaman "reading" project overlaps with readings anthropologists have traditionally wanted to pursue, in other places it does not.

Obviously this divergence of reading projects does not mean that we, as interpreters, have no license to "read across" boundaries in a way that Seltaman would not. Social science, as an interpretive science, has always produced and will continue to produce theoretical mandates for doing exactly this. The danger is one of hasty leaps. The forces and motivations that social-science reading projects are aimed at uncovering cannot plausibly be disconnected from a people's self-understanding, and this self-understanding is what is revealed in their own reading rules. Once it becomes clear to us how people, or a people, are going about self-interpretation, our theorized forces and motivations may cease to appear relevant, or they may still appear relevant but differently distributed in their relevance. When we launch our own analysis prematurely, we are in danger of misapplying our analytic tools.

It would be all too easy for such misapplications to occur when we turn the concept of "naturalizing power" upon the Seltaman materials. It is true that, in the perspective of initiated Seltaman men, some wild species are indeed encompassed by the "power discourse" of the culture, the initiated men's sacred knowledge. But as I hope to show, there are other less power-laden semiotic fields encompassing wild species as well, and it behooves us to grasp the processes of meaning production in these other fields too lest we, in our interpretive prematurity, "deform" this area of Seltaman self-understanding. I also hope to indicate, though I cannot fully develop the point, that the very basis for distinguishing the power-laden, sacred encompassments from the less-charged variety of cultural glossing inheres in the implicit "reading rules" of the power discourse itself and tells us something of its social nature.

I can do no more than sketch the argument here, throwing in suggestive ethnographic tidbits and familiarizing readers with the requisite background to the puzzle. In respect to the birds-of-paradise problem, the "reading rule" situation is edged with a certain ambiguity and thus the question of whether there is the sort of "connection" that the ornithologist and I disagreed over cannot be absolutely settled here. But my point here is to reframe this sort of question, not particularly to answer the exemplary one.

Nature Lore as a Semiotic System

The meaning environment upon which I will concentrate in this exposition, because it involves a great number of matters unfamiliar to most readers, is the area of what I have called "nature lore." The idea that speculations and explanations about natural species might constitute a distinct arena of meaning production, separable in some important respects from the rest of the culture, was originally broached by Peter Dwyer in his rather neglected essay, "Animal Metaphors: An Evolutionary Model"

(Dwyer 1979). Here, he suggests three areas of "ideological interest" in natural creatures that will bear upon the natural taxonomies; these are the economic, the ritualistic, and the "objective." Dwyer's "objective" area, which he explains as "that set of complementary metasignifiers dealing in similarities and contiguities in animal morphology, behavior and ecology," (Dwyer 1979:15) strongly foreshadows the "nature lore" domain that I have arrived at here by taking a different path through Dwyer's and others' works. His "objective" area is also embedded in a rather different argument from mine, but one to which I will turn once the appropriate illustrations have been assembled.

Dwyer's sense of the distinctiveness of this dimension of "interest" resonates with the findings of other naturalists, ecological anthropologists, and folk taxonomists such as Jared Diamond and Ralph Bulmer and his collaborators.[1] In the course of correlating their in-field zoological, ornithological, and ecological findings with the naming systems and local knowledge of the New Guinea peoples whose environment was under investigation, all of these scholars have at times had to wrestle with the issue of reputed creatural habits or relationships that are, in biological terms, unreal. As it turns out, gender-reversed birds of paradise, as examples of the "unreal," have plenty of company. Butterflies that transmogrify into bats, rodents that turn into marsupials, monotremes ("echidnas") that hatch from the eggs of a species of bird, species of bird that are nonreproductive themselves and whose numbers must be replenished with the assistance of different bird species, worms that become snakes that become eels—all have cropped up in the researches of these nature-attentive scholars (Diamond 1966; Bulmer and Menzies 1972–73; Dwyer 1976b, 1980; Flannery 1990:42–43). Cultural anthropologists have under-reported such phenomena, but here and there a note is found. Stephen Feld, whose cultural and musicological studies among the Kaluli of the Mt. Bosavi area carried him onto the topic of birds, reports a gender-reversed situation for local paradises and certain other birds (Feld 1982:53ff, 243; 1991:209). So too do Gilbert Lewis, for the Gnau of the East Sepik Province (Lewis 1980:162–63), and Philip Guddemi, who recently worked among the Sawiano of the same province. Guddemi's case, though it differs from the Seltaman one, helps to focus the issue. He reports,

> The drab bird of paradise, a young male in their view, is the egg-layer of the two sexes. ("Yes, males can lay eggs too!") But as he matures, he will turn into a female, the highly decorated bird. This now female bird, once plumaged, ceases to lay eggs. "Why should she [lay eggs]?" Sawiano ask. "She's now decorated." I was so boggled by this I was unable to frame the question, What then does female mean? (Guddemi, personal)

In peculiar beliefs such as this, the particular concepts of gender, mating, gestation, birthing (or egg laying), age development, and age-stage metamorphosis become disembedded from their naturalistic contexts and reapplied, apparently earnestly rather than metaphorically, where they do not biologically belong. The question before us is whether the semiotic space in which such nonnaturalistic and nonmetaphorical reapplications occur is largely under the sway of a particular kind of motivation that thus bounds it and sets implicit rules, in other words whether it is a distinct semiotic space, or whether such peculiarities represent the invasions into "normal commonsense classification" of any one of a variety of cultural agendas yet to be specified (such as the ideological need to shore up gender inequality). If the first, then there is hope that some general set of principles can be worked out that helps resolve all of these peculiar cases. These general principles would then simultaneously obviate the resort to the sorts of hidden mythic-connection hypotheses that the ornithologist proposes.

Our confidence in the particular bird-myth connection with which we started the essay is already weakened by the foregoing survey, which reveals both the commonness and the diversity of regional origin of these peculiar loric twists and, especially, the greater regional spread of bird-gender "falsehoods," which obviously are not confined to areas with the Afek tradition. Subtracting from our confidence as well is the typically off-hand manner in which such bits of knowledge are embraced, both among Seltaman and apparently among these other cited peoples as well. It is my guess that naturalists and taxonomists report these matters in New Guinea far more often than do cultural anthropologists studying "the belief systems" not just because their certainty in biological truth makes them rise to the dare but also because their work leads them into these topics, whereas work on rituals, myths, and cosmological beliefs often does not. (Guddemi, who was devoting full research time to the study of Sawiano ritual and religious cosmology, stumbled upon their bird-gender lore inadvertently when one day he whimsically compared decorated Sawiano male dancers to birds of paradise. The Sawiano men corrected him.) When the cultural anthropologist does encounter such lore, he or she often files it in the miscellany pile, for in most cases it simply does not carry the smell of the sacred.

What on earth is it about then? The question tends to lead us straight to *The Savage Mind* and to the problems inherent in Levi-Strauss's framework, chief of which is that no influences on "biological belief" are excluded. While Levi-Strauss may have correctly hit the "tone" of this sort of material—it is speculative, sometimes playful, shrug-of-the-shoulders stuff—the effect of his work is to extend this tone to everything that is connectable to living species or construable as a form of intellectual play with species, which means in many societies virtually everything.

While in the end it may be necessary to declare the realm of nature lore in New Guinea a permeable one and thus capable of being invaded by other cultural projects, I think it worthwhile to give some thought to the post–Levi-Straussian attempts that have been made to relimit it. The anything-goes assumption about folk classification, an assumption frequently reaffirmed in the writings of various authors by reciting Foucault's favorite John Louis Borges extract from "a certain Chinese encyclopaedia" (where animals are divided into "(a) belonging to the Emperor, (b) embalmed, (c) tame, (d) sucking pigs . . . etc." [Foucault 1970:xv; Ellen 1979:6]) has not held up well among those working directly with folk taxonomies. Bulmer and his collaborators, as well as Dwyer and Diamond, attempt to read their data on peculiar lore in light of certain now rather widely accepted tenets that they themselves have helped to established. One of these is that peoples in vital interaction with a wild natural environment, whether as foragers or shifting horticulturalists or some combination thereof, are keen natural observers who produce "folk biologies" that are remarkably concordant with the classifications that visiting naturalists eventually produce (Bulmer 1970, 1973, 1979; Atran 1990; Berlin 1991). The second tenet, in many ways a corollary of the first, is that some form of the notion of species is practically universal and is the foundation of folk as well as scientific biotaxonomies. Whatever disagreement over finer distinctions may arise between the folk classifier and the scientist in a given natural environment, and whatever nomenclatural practices either uses, both will arrive at a remarkably similar set of irreducible groupings based on "multiple distinctions of appearance, habitat, and behaviour" (Bulmer and Tyler 1968:335). Bulmer has dubbed the folk-recognized natural unit the "specieme." In most cases where scientists recognize a "species," the local folk will have designated a "specieme" (335). Bulmer is careful to hedge his definition of the specieme, however, so that it rests upon most, but not necessarily all, of the criteria encoded in the concept of biological "species":

> The "natural kinds" that Karam are distinguishing are "natural" in the logical sense, that is, based on possession of many attributes, both morphological and biological, in common. To the extent that Karam recognize that creatures reproduce after their kind, we might say that these kinds are "natural" in the biological as well as the logical sense. However, there are a handful of cases . . . which suggests that they do not see separate ancestry and reproductive isolation as necessary features of the units they distinguish. (335)

This maddening situation, where New Guinea peoples see certain biological criteria as *frequent but not invariable* attributes of the morpho-ecological types that they recognize—their "speciemes"—can be spelled out better if we encompass the findings of Diamond and Dwyer, who are in general agreement with Bulmer and his collaborators. Specifically, naturalist-anthropologists have found that while most of the "speciemes" that New Guinea peoples recognize are seen as autonomously reproducing and breeding true to kind in the manner of (scientific) biological species, in any given area a few are not so viewed. Those few are typically viewed as the outcomes of metamorphosis of certain changeable members of a different specieme (Diamond 1966; Lewis 1980:162–163; Dwyer 1976a, 1976b; Dwyer 1980; Bulmer and Menzies 1972–73:101–104). Correlatively, while most of the creatures in any given area that are thought to reproduce autonomously and breed true to kind are indeed true biological species, a few are not. Those few are most often age or stage subtypes within a true biological species (Dwyer 1976a). Correlatively once again, the notion of metamorphosis is very frequently *accurately* invoked to cover biologically true age and stage transformations, such as the growth from smaller to larger, and the metamorphosis from tadpole to frog, pupa to butterfly, and immaturely plumaged bird to maturely plumaged bird. But in a few cases, in any given area, it is also *inaccurately* invoked to link biologically unrelated speciemes. Extrapolating from Dwyer's illuminating work on the Rofaifo Siane, in those few inaccurate instances, the two linked creatures typically share some striking morphological or behavioral similarity or some intimate ecological relationship (Dwyer 1976b). An ecological relationship example would be two speciemes that share two ecozones, but one predominates in one zone while the other is scare therein and the other predominates in the other zone while the first is scarce therein. Each creature appears as a furtive relict presence in the other's domain. A shared morphological/behavioral trait example would be the correspondence between the fluttering wings of the butterfly and those of the small bat, which make the two difficult to distinguish in twilight (Dwyer 1976b).

In working with examples like this, Dwyer has hit upon two very important contextualizing perspectives on these beliefs. First is their system embeddedness. That is, the beliefs tend to make sense within the ecology of the people involved—its particular repertory and configuration of creatures and habitats—and within the corresponding system of morpho-ecological and behavioral distinctions that the people inhabiting this environment operate. Second, many of these beliefs seem to betray the typical wishes of hunter/foragers as they go about their work within this same environment. Though he does not interpret the Rofaifo case in these terms, Dwyer points out that their "false" species transformations almost always lead from plentiful but small or otherwise uninteresting creatures to scarcer but large or otherwise interesting ones (e.g., those valued for meatiness, plumage) (Dwyer 1976b). The Seltaman themselves provide us with a good illustration of this: The Rainbow Bee-eater (*Merops ornatus*), a small bird that is a seasonal visitor to the Seltaman hunting range, is thought to transform (upon the hunter's instructions!) into a specieme of succulent bandicoot (*Microperory-ctes longicauda*). Both bird and bandicoot are characterized by a similar striking eye-stripe and "long nose." In this case it is especially clear that the believed-in transformation is the offspring of the hunter's wish; yet at the same time, it is clear that this wish is disciplined by adherence to the details of objective correspondence between the two creatures.

Even when the wishful component is not evident, the hunter/forager's perspective often shines through. Some animal tales seem to say no more than that two creatures, though similar in some ways, are nevertheless quite distinct from the hunting perspective, and here's why. My field notes recorded this, from the Seltaman and their neighbors, the Angkayak:

> One day, Yakhail (Long-beaked Echidna) and Dubol (Doria's Tree Kanga-roo) had climbed a tree and were up there talking. Dubol spoke first: "I've got a tail like a fence-rail, and I've broken it off and am eating it." He made a chewing noise as he said that, meanwhile sitting on his long tail. Yakhail responded, "I've broken off my tail and am eating it [too]." Dubol jumped to another tree, climbed higher [letting his undamaged tail hang down], then looked down at Yakhail triumphantly and said, "Look, my tail is still long, see!" Then Yakhail said, "You have a long tail so dog and man will always kill and eat you, while I [now] have a short tail. I'll stay inside the ground and only occasionally will they kill and eat me." (field-notes)

In a short paper on "bird stories" that partially anticipates the points I am trying to make here, Stephen Feld writes of the day a particularly astute Kaluli bird expert made him aware of the way in which Kaluli creature stories are working out, often in exquisite detail, the natural-history peculiarities of local species. He reflects that his own "bias toward symbolic (and presumably 'deeper') readings" of these nature stories forces into the background this Kaluli interest in the "discontinuities in nature" (Feld 1991:211).

If we follow Dwyer's suggestions about the local systemic embeddedness of peculiar beliefs, adhering as well to his and others' findings concerning the perspicacity of local observations, we transform Levi-Strauss's *pensée sauvage* playing field (as regards New Guinea nature lore) into one on which primarily one meaning game, rather than many, is being played. In other words, New Guinea nature lore shapes up as a distinctive semiotic field.

The meaning game in question is the game of conceptually organizing a task-oriented, and usually quest-oriented, experience of wildlife within the local hunting, foraging, and gardening range. Elements of Levi-Strauss's pronouncements still ring true here and we will turn to one of these below, but I would call into question his implicit notion that any old cultural project—divination, cosmology spinning, etc.—may express its meanings through the type differentiation (what one might call the "speciation") of the local natural environment. The viewpoint taken here is that the local "speciation" of a natural environment and the penumbra of "nature lore" associated with it tends to express, on one level, certain cognitive universals in the perception and differentiation of living kinds—which is the reason for the extensive overlap between local folk and scientific classifications in any area (cf. Atran 1990, 1994; Berlin 1991)[2]—and, at a second level, the effects on perception and interest wrought by the purposes that typically bring people into contact with wild natural kinds. To evoke, without rehashing, the perennial debate in ethnobiology between "intellectualist" and "utilitarian" approaches (cf. Berlin 1991; Hays 1991), I am attempting, from within a primarily intellectualist framework, to add two faintly utilitarian qualifications. One is that peoples in interaction with a natural environment can only classify out and intellectualize about those creatures that are reasonably accessible to their observation, and their observational practices are heavily governed by the nature of their interaction. If we make "practices" (in this case observational practices) rather than "practicality" the keyword in the discussion, we avoid many of the difficulties of the utilitarian position. My second qualification addresses that element of wishfulness in nature-lore speculation that Dwyer unearthed; this, along with the observational practices, will have some grounding in the purposes that are bringing any given people into sustained interaction with natural species.

Regarding purposes in the present case: In the New Guinea mountains, the gardening cycle involves some invasion of primary and advanced secondary forest and thus undoubtedly has bearing upon encounters with wild species, but hunting and foraging are the primary purposes that carry people out into the bush. Even in the Highlands where utilization of wild foods has been drastically diminished and where, in the past, a state of war often impeded trips to the forest, a lively foraging experience was still possible—as the self-account of a Melpa big-man, Ongka, makes apparent (Strathern and Ongka 1979). I thus feel it sufficient for now to characterize the typical New Guinean's "vital interaction" with the environment as hunting, foraging, or simply "quest" oriented. In these terms, I think it necessary to suggest that the intellectual leeway that many New Guinea peoples find for some of these peculiar elements of nature lore is set in place by incomplete knowledge of the creature. If hunting and foraging is associated with a certain sort of wishfulness—that the tiny might turn into the big, for instance—and if this wishfulness leaves its imprint on the cultural formulation of nature, surely hunting and foraging also constitute a set of practices, and these practices do not encourage equally all forms of nature study.

The sorts of biological facts that New Guinea peoples "get wrong" are, more often than not, ones that are hard to get right unless one invests a good deal of time in observational activities that, being unproductive, are unlikely to be undertaken for foraging purposes (or usually any other local purposes). Consider how one might discover that the Long-beaked Echidna (*Zaglossus bruijni*), which is only sparsely present throughout New Guinea and which spends much of its life hidden underground, is an egg layer that nurses its young! The Seltaman, who happened to capture an echidna while I was in residence, had no idea about the egg laying; I give them credit for having the nursing at least partially figured out. Even more credit goes to the Hatam people of the Arfak Mountains, who claim that the echidna hatches from the egg of the Buff-tailed Sicklebill (Ian Craven, cited by Flannery 1990:42–43; see also Dwyer 1980).

Sometimes the requisite observation for a particular process is all but impossible. Seltaman, for instance, could easily describe the undeveloped "fetal" condition of newborn marsupials, for they had removed such creatures from the pouches of slain females. But as to how this creature enters the pouch in the first place, they could only surmise that it must be born directly into the pouch, rather than having to migrate to it from the vagina. This surmise in turn led them to the next: that in mating, marsupial males must ejaculate directly into the female's pouch. I feel quite confident that the western zoologist who first established the "truth" about marsupial neonatal migration did not do so under Seltaman observational conditions.

Qualifications are in order. I encountered, as did Dwyer, Bulmer, and Menzies, individual variations in the acceptance of these peculiar items of lore. These included not just cultural skeptics of one sort or another but also individuals who have a more biologically accurate take on the matter in question, a fact that suggests variable observational experience.[3] And certainly if one does a survey of New Guinea cultures in a similar ecological region, one will find that the same "mistakes" are not made by all of them. But this does not circumvent the fact that the areas in which "mistakes" tend to be most made are those areas that one might call "observationally underdetermined." As I will argue in a moment, bird-of-paradise gender is just such an area.

When we turn to the folk differentiation of local nature, we see that what is most baffling about it in relation to the scientific "speciation" of that same local nature is not that the folk make use of different morpho-ecological and behavioral distinctions in cutting up their creatures into types, for here, in fact, they are strikingly concordant with the invading scientists. It is that they are willing to *inconsistently* apply the principles of reproductivity, gender, development, and metamorphosis when no firm counterevidence regularly gets in their way. Some speciemes are autonomously reproductive, but a few aren't. Some follow a progression from smaller to larger as they age, but some don't. Indeed, the "differentness" in other folks' notions of gender, age, etc., that emerges from this is really a difference in the consistency of application of notions that are otherwise remarkably similar to those of the West.[4] Without speculating as to the source of the kernels of similarity between our and others' notions of gender, mating, age-stage, and so on, I will confine myself to agreeing with Bulmer that these notions cannot be treated as the bedrock part of the folk differentiation—"speciemization"?—of the natural landscape, however intimately they "hover around" this differentiation. The bedrock components are the reasonably observationally accessible "multiple distinctions of appearance, habitat, and behaviour" (Bulmer & Tyler 1968:335).[5]

We are brought back here to Levi-Strauss's argument that

> there are two distinct modes of scientific thought. These are certainly not a function of different stages of development of the human mind but rather of two strategic levels at which nature is accessible to scientific enquiry: one roughly adapted to that of perception and the imagination: the other at a remove from it. (Levi-Strauss 1966:15–16)

His restriction of modes and levels to two can be debated, but the general point is well taken. In our urge to make nonliterate peoples "scientific" in their own way, we still persist in asking that they engage in the sorts of unusual and technologically assisted modes of observation that only people who are scientific in our way typically practice.

Birds of Paradise in the Nature-Lore Semiotic

Let us now examine how, within the semiotic field of Seltaman understanding of their natural landscape, they might, *with no assistance from the sacred corpus,* wind up with the genders of a particular taxon reversed.

It is important to note first of all that Seltaman do not reverse the gender of all birds. Most familiar bird species are gendered "accurately": that is, the egg layer and the one that is mounted in intercourse is designated as the *yangus,* a term that refers to the female of an animal species; and the other, the one that mounts her in intercourse, as the *kimok,* a term that means both (human) husband and the male of an animal species, roughly "stud." This "correct" mode of designation holds even when there is some sexual dimorphism apparent, as with certain fruit doves, the domestic chicken, and the brush turkeys.

The "big sister" (*yen*) and "little brother" (*ning*) mode of classification puts in its appearance only when one subtype of a bird taxon is notably decorative while the other is drab. Behind this usage lies the presumption that the decorative feathering emerges from the drab, in other words, that "brothers" turn into "sisters" later in the course of development, well after initial fledging. The late emergence of decorative plumage from drab is indeed a feature of all the local paradise types, *karom*—the Raggiana (*Paradisaea raggiana*), *firak*—the Magnificent (*Cicinnurus magnificus*), *kirang*—the Superb (*Lophorina superba*), and *kasiim*—Carola's Parotia (*Parotia carolae*). For these species, juvenile males look like females until they begin to attain full maturity. Transitional plumage specimens can be seen or collected in the course of hunting, and Seltaman will say of these specimens, "Look, he's starting to become a sister."[6,7]

The main counterevidence for the Seltaman theory would be egg bearing, egg laying, and copulation. Nest sitting, though it is in fact female exclusive for most of the transforming paradise types, is seen by Seltaman as a function either bird gender can perform (and indeed many species are joint sitters); thus it cannot figure into confirmation or disconfirmation of their genderization of the paradises.

The more significant counterevidence of egg bearing becomes an issue when eggs are discovered in the cloaca of slain "little brothers." Though no Seltaman drew my attention to it, I suspect this discovery is made not infrequently, and I suspect too that it plays a role in a "revisionist" version of bird-of-paradise lore that one Seltaman produced for me. One day, when I carefully pressed two Seltaman hunters—Lucas and Edmund—on the question of Raggiana gender, Edmund stuck to the idea that the "big sister" is the egg layer, but Lucas suddenly informed us both that there are in fact some *female* "little brothers." As he was my most knowledgeable source on birds, I take Lucas's answer as probably reflective of better observational experience.

Lucas's revisionist belief is instructive in other respects. One notes that it is half-way to a perception that the "sister" and "brother" classification was, after all, a manner of speaking; but in its half-way state, it succeeds in protecting the idea that the decorated bird is female against one of the common-sensical problems with the unmodified formula, namely the idea that the drab bird must change sex to become decorated. For Lucas the matter was quite simple: only the female "little brother" can turn into a "big sister." The male "little brothers" simply "stay nothing" all their lives.

Now this is not the formulation one wants to hear if one is arguing that the local avifauna are the locus for a representation of the Afek saga. Let us return for a moment to our original problem, the relationship of bird and myth, and elaborate on the mythic analogue. Afek is the ancestress who endowed Seltaman and related Mountain Ok cultures of the region with their ritual system. In the mythic past, she came into Central Ranges accompanied by her little brother. Setting up habitation, she built and dwelt in the culthouse among the sacred ritual paraphernalia and was the important member of the pair. Her little brother dwelt in a simple "woman's house" and was "a little nothing person." Various typical mythic things happen to this mythic couple—the brother spies on the sister, the brother tricks the sister, the sister just finds herself unhappy with the arrangement, whatever (there are different versions)—but the denouement of it all is that Afek's little brother is depicted as eventually "taking the place of" his big sister. He moves to the culthouse and takes over the ritual paraphernalia, while she moves to the woman house. Thus it is that in the present men, not women, are the custodians of the ritual system and the ritual paraphernalia; moreover, senior men—identified with Afek in specific ritual practices— initiate boys so that these boys will grow up to take their, the initiators', places. Thus it is that women now remain just "nothing people."

Without a blink, Lucas ruined this dimension of the correspondence. Females are the ones who grow up to be sisters, while it is the males who "stay nothing" all their lives. Lucas is of course only one source. Nonetheless, minimally his reformulation indicates that nature lore, when pushed, has directions of its own in which to move, ones at variance with the supposed sacred analogue.

Let us continue with the issue of disconfirmatory bird evidence. Nesting activity has been neutralized, and witnessing egg laying on the part of the drab birds, even finding eggs in their cloacae—providing one accepts egg laying as a female exclusive activity, and Seltaman apparently do—only serve to introduce females into the population of "little brothers," not to rule them out in the population of "big sisters." This leaves copulation as the main form of potential counterevidence. At first it seems astonishing that the bird types whose mating activity is the most clamorous, public, and visually stunning of any in the world are the very ones whose genders the Seltaman are "getting wrong." Questioned closely, Seltaman turn out to be familiar with bird copulation in their domestic chickens, in brush turkeys, and in pigeons and fruit-doves, which can be watched from bird blinds in fruiting trees. But if asked whether they had witnessed the same activity in any of the transforming paradise species, all of my informants demurred. When asked more specifically whether the display behavior had anything to do with copulation, they again demurred. Most likened the paradise display to a "sing-sing"—human dancing and celebration. One or two men were even startled to hear me suggest a sexual component. "*Karom* (Raggiana) must copulate," one man opined, "but I think they hide to do it." Many Seltaman men and women too had witnessed, at least fleetingly, Raggiana display, since there were known "leks" (display trees) within walking distance of the two villages. Many Seltaman male hunters had also witnessed display behavior in the Carola's Parotia as well.[8] How is it then that all who were asked denied ever seeing bird-of-paradise copulation?

In a culture where one has learned to regard the decorative plumage type as the female while at the same time to regard bird mating as consisting of a male-on-top position, it is a distinct possibility that persons witnessing bird-of-paradise mating would fail to recognize it as such. But before we make this speculation, it is worth asking whether the mating rituals of birds of paradise renders, even in western eyes, an unambiguous answer to the question of which plumage type is which gender. I have not found adequate material on the other species in question, but for the Raggiana this is far from being the case. Naturalists' painstakingly accumulated record of Raggiana display patterns reveals several potentially "misleading" features. Beehler (1988) found that, first, drably plumaged birds can be seen displaying to each other (in one observed case two captive females, just off their nests, displayed to each other; often, however, the displayers are immature males); that highly plumaged birds can be found executing displays in pairs or groups even in the absence of drably plumaged admirers; and that birds of either plumage not infrequently do solo displays that may include the final or "copulatory sequence." The display itself, in other words, is not securely linked to one plumage type or to a pairing of opposite plumage types. Second, there is a point in the male Raggiana's display at which he inverts himself on the perch, presenting a rear view to the attending female, and awaits her inspection; at this point it is not unusual for the interested female to mount him, briefly. Last, when copulation occurs, it is preceded by a sequence in which the male appears to pummel the female with his outstretched wing; this pummeling lasts about four times as long as the actual copulation (twenty to thirty-five seconds versus five to eight seconds). In effect, Raggiana male-on-female mounting, which climaxes the display patterns only 11 percent of the time in any case, is a brief detail in a variable and heterogeneous sequence of behaviors that may include female-on-male mounting, excited interactions between same-plumaged birds, and bouts of what appear to be a sort of ritualized pummeling. We might add here as well that a Seltaman observer, most usually a hunter, is very likely to cut short any ongoing display with an attempted shot before the display reaches its climax. In any event, it is easy to see that the probable range of Seltaman observations of Raggiana courtship—and, I am speculating, the courtship of the other local displayers—could provide material for a number of ornithologically inaccurate takes concerning the gender-age characteristics and interactional patterns of the two markedly different plumage types that congregate for it.

In short, the highly plumaged class of bird of the transforming paradise types could easily be construed as composed of either gender alone or as having both male and female members. The Gnau of the East Sepik Province treat their local one (apparently the Lesser, *Paradisaea minor*) as a female-only taxon into which certain members of a "consort" male-only taxon (the drab birds) transform (Lewis 1980). The Kaluli treat their various brightly plumaged birds as the females of their taxon, while the drabs are the males and immature females (a construction parallel to Lucas's revision above) (Feld 1982:53–54). The Rofaifo treat their local King of Saxony bird of paradise (*Pteridophora alberti*) and Stephanie's Astrapia (*Astrapia stephanniae*) highly plumaged types as nonreproductive taxa into which certain other taxa (corresponding to the drabs of each species and which are viewed as fully autonomously reproductive) selectively transform (Dwyer 1976b). An Oksapmin informant explained to me that the Oksapmin (who traditionally shared the Afek saga with their Mountain Ok speaking neighbors) view the highly plumaged Raggiana as a nonreproductive "advanced age" stage of a single taxon that includes the younger drab birds who are the ones who do the reproducing. Both age-stage classes encompass both genders. The Sawiano case was detailed earlier in this chapter, and the Seltaman are, of course, as I have just described them. With one exception to be noted momentarily, those cultures in which the highly plumaged bird is considered male only are usually not singled out for comment in the ethnographic literature because their choice is the "unmarked" one, from the western perspective.

If the bird can go either way, why so often female? I cannot answer for every case but two very revealing answers emerge from the Seltaman, the Kaluli, and the Kalam materials. The Seltaman answer, from my field note, is:

> Edmund explained that if you examine transitional *karom ning* (Raggiana) "brothers" that are in the process of changing into "sisters," you'll see that their long plumage begins at the breast. On either side of the bird's chest, these plumes erupt and grow longer and longer, paralleling and partly underlying the wings, until eventually they are long enough to join in the back and make a tail plume. "You think these are their tail feathers? No, they're not. They're breasts."

Edmund's description and western ornithology are in agreement. The developed plumage of the *Paradisaea* birds of paradise, which include the Raggiana, starts its development from the breast or "armpit" area. The other local paradise species of the Seltaman area develop breast shields, or—as in the case of Carola's Parotia—both breast shields and a pectoral plume. For Seltaman, the development of breasts is a more salient signal of a girl's sexual maturation than is menarche. Accordingly, the development of breast-like plumage is easily seen as the maturation of a female bird.

The Kaluli and the Kalam, however, suggest a rather different line of explanation that could well bear indirectly upon Seltaman. The Kaluli, who gender reverse virtually all dance-plumage–yielding bird species, simply consider *attractiveness* (Feld's term) to be a female trait (Feld 1982:66ff). The Kalam, by comparison, do not gender reverse their plumage-yielding birds of paradise—here is one ethnographically accessible group that gets bird-of-paradise biology "right"—but they metaphorically feminize the plumage itself, likening the decorative plumes to women's skirts or the beauty of these plumes to the beauty of young women (Majnep and Bulmer 1977:57, 70, 135). As it happens, there are distinct echoes of this "attractiveness is female" thinking in the dance usage of Seltaman as well, in that the love-charms that men use to make themselves desirable in the dance are typically composed of female-referring elements. In effect, we seem to be looking at a "genealogical" relationship between three versions of male bird-of-paradise "feminization." The Kalam are biologically "correct" in their construal of bird gender, but entertain a metaphoric association between beautiful plumes and beautiful women. The Kaluli appear to have "literalized" this metaphor by attributing female gender to the beautiful plumage bearers and, accordingly, positioning the mates of these females among the drably plumaged members of the taxon. Going a step further, the Seltaman have carried literalization to the point of treating the "beautiful" attribute, the plumes, as the breasts of a female and confining the gender-reversal theory to those species, the transforming birds of paradise, in which the breast argument makes the most sense. Were we to imagine that all these groups started, historically, with a similar metaphor—"beautiful plumes are like women/women's attributes"—we would see in this spectrum of Kalam to Kaluli to Seltaman the progressive pull of a metaphoric image into the force field of the "nature-lore semiotic," a movement that involves the conversion of a metaphor into a concreteness and the "rearrangement" of those other creatures (the drab mates, the other nontransforming but decorative birds, etc.) that are in the "semiotic vicinity" of this concreteness in such a way as to accommodate it.

With this speculative illustration, my argument converges with Peter Dwyer's larger argument, alluded to earlier. In "Animal Metaphors," Dwyer (1979) envisions a semiotic process in which the decay of metaphor in one "ideological area" (related to taxonomy) may provide the materials for the rise of new meaning arrangements in another such area.

"Dead-metaphor" arguments of this sort are slippery, however, and form a locus of theoretical contention in cultural anthropology, being for some theorists simply ruled out (see for example Lakoff and Johnson 1980). Whatever its state of apparent decrepitude, a "decaying" signifier may, with the appearance of new contexts, reintrude some aspect of its old meaning, giving rise to new inadvertencies in social discourse. This fact of history fuels the refusal by some interpretivists to ever quite let a good trope die, and this refusal in turn supports the very sorts of interpretations—seeing "intertextuality" in every overlap—that I am here arguing against. Were I to admit into Seltaman bird-gender meaning, a prior historical meaning in which the plumaged bird's female gender was a metaphor regarding the femaleness of beauty, I would have opened a door through which "big sister" Afek could easily walk as well. But to exclude a possible prior historical meaning from a contemporary semiotic field is not the same thing as to exclude that prior history itself. Certainly for Seltaman it is possible that a more metaphoric feminization of beautifully plumaged birds once reigned; it is possible as well that at one time an Afek allusion stood behind "sister and brother" birds. Indeed, it is the choice of kinship relation between the reversed male and female birds—elder sister and younger brother—that most strongly hints that here, if nowhere else, the sacred corpus may have extended a tentacle of meaning. But traces of a prior usage do not establish the presence of a contemporary meaning. As the remainder of this essay is devoted to showing, there are other strong reasons for concluding that contemporary Seltaman simply lack any sacred dimension to their birds of paradise.

To round off our discussion of the "nature-lore semiotic," contemporary Seltaman treatment of bird gender has all the appearance of the sorts of interpretative moves that are characteristic of the semiotic space in which the natural landscape is intellectually differentiated and grasped from the experiential perspective of the hunter/forager. The "gaps" that appear in this "natural" text would be, in this view, the puzzling associations of seemingly distinct types: the two types that "visit" each other's territory, the two that seem always to perch in the same tree, the one that is sometimes found in the process of turning into the other, or the one that reinscribes on its own body some distinctive feature of the other. The material that is used to fill these "gaps" is typically of a very limited sort and usually encompasses the concepts of gender (one type is the male, the other the female), of mating (and they are "married" to each other), of birth or egg laying (the one occasionally lays an egg for the other), of kinship relation (the two are uncle and nephew), of maturation and aging (one is the older, the other the younger), and of stage metamorphosis (some of the one type turn into the other). This view is heavily anthropomorphic: a kinship relation may be secondary, like uncle-nephew; mating may be "marrying"; becoming like an X may be "taking the place of X"; and so on. Yet while not applied with a view toward consistency—"Yes, males can (sometimes) lay eggs too!"—the connective conceptual material is intriguingly congruent with nature's own repertory of associational devices. And with this material, nature is culturally "landscaped out" in a way that is intriguingly congruent with the foragers' hopeful or disappointed gaze. The negligible creature is, on the one hand, a sign that its transform, a desirable creature, is somewhere about; and, on the other hand, the thing one stalks or strikes down pointlessly when expecting the other—the butterfly instead of the bat.

All of the little nature puzzles itemized here resonate with David Schneider's "People aren't pigs" story cited in the present volume by Sylvia Yanagisako and Carol Delaney and by Anna Tsing and with the other stories he resorted to in order to convey that in one way or another our Western notions of biology and reproduction set us up for some rude surprises when we visit other cultures. What the "pigs and people" example illustrates is precisely an "inconsistent" application of a "folk-biological" notion, and Schneider would be the first to point out that when inconsistencies of this sort are present, the notions in question are something other than a direct apprehension of biology. I quite agree. For lack of space to enter into any protracted discussion of what these notions should be called, I will persist with the familiar term "folk biology" and simply point out that our own Western "folk biology" too will offer some rude surprises to the scientific visitor. How many New York City apartment dwellers, for instance, speak of the smaller of their two species of cockroach as "the baby cockroaches"?[9] We certainly cannot excuse New York apartment dwellers for this blunder on the grounds that they are not in vital interaction with a wild environment, for in this case they are: their apartments. And how many freshwater-bass fishermen call the huge specimens, which are always female (and heaviest when gravid), "Grandaddy bass" or "Mr. Lunker," reflecting the perspective of the sportsman (not the forager) who prefers to see his quarry as a worthy male opponent instead of a pregnant mother? In a word, the principles under discussion here are not confined to any one culture, though any particular instantiation of them is entirely relative to the culture or cultural position of the formulator.

Natural Types in the Sacred Semiotic

The foregoing elaboration of nature lore as a semiotic space with its own associated mode of meaning production, and the positioning of Seltaman bird-of-paradise lore within this space, should, I feel, reduce the initially puzzling elements of this bird lore to the point that we refrain from rushing so readily to the sacred corpus as the ultimate decoder of every puzzling natural feature. The gender reversal of these birds no longer seems particularly far-fetched, and their age differentiation (older sibling, younger sibling) fits the nature-lore semiotic both in (accurately) addressing the age-stage difference between the two and in making the scarcer and more valued bird the transformative outcome of the more plentiful bird. But as noted above, the reduction is not without remainder. One still has to ask: Why sister and brother? Other kinship relations are available in which to cast an older female and a younger male, or an older female and youngsters of both sexes. Mother-child is especially appropriate for the latter if we put aside any incest queasiness as the Seltaman themselves seem to do in considering sister and brother birds.

It is tempting to argue that within this more restricted area of choice, the birds' kinship relation, a sacred motivation could easily intrude. The possibility of a meaning intrusion from the sacred corpus which is, after all, the "master semiotic" of Seltaman culture is made all the more enticing by the fact that the sacred corpus does indeed operate its own set of glosses on natural species. Not every natural species hides a sacred "story," to be sure, but some do. For instance, the (nonlocal) Lowland cassowary is traditionally considered the embodiment of Afek, and there are stories that encompass her change into this creature. Her brother, in one myth fragment, is portrayed as becoming the Great cuckoo dove. Certain local marsupial species are held to be ancestors, while others are considered appropriate ritual sacrifices because of some quality that associates them with abundant taro. Red-streaked tangket, the species planted around settlements and gardens, is an offspring of Afek in some myths or stained by her menstrual blood in others. Most intrusively, ordinary pythons tend to have mythical properties attributed to them that are expressly the properties of truly mythic giant serpents (*anangamtemkaak*), whose stories are part of the sacred corpus. And so on.

In a word, the natural environment is very clearly "landscaped out" by both a sacred semiosis and the secular one that I have just portrayed. It is a daunting task to untangle the two if they are, as I am arguing, tangled by our theoretical misunderstandings instead of seamlessly fused by Seltaman culture. I hasten to admit that, in an earlier draft of this paper that far exceeded the size limitations, I was able to find numerous points of teasing and rather indirect contact between the sacred corpus and the Raggiana bird of paradise, but they were all, in some sense, "near misses." None either led to or constituted a secret element in which Afek or her brother appear as, change into, give their names to, or share their attributes with, any of the paradise species glossed as "sister" and "brother," including the Raggiana. Indeed, as one can see from the sacred designations of species just listed, Afek and the other mythical characters of the sacred corpus are dotted around the natural landscape in a different set of creatures from those that I have been discussing.

Reading Rules of the Sacred Semiotic

The final argument against glibly fusing the two dimensions of Seltaman nature discourse, however, rests on a different basis from the cataloguing of near misses and the suspicious interrogation of analogues. It rests upon the implicit rules of reading of the sacred corpus itself. The generic ("genre-like") distinctiveness of the Seltaman sacred corpus (*weng abem*) can be approached by briefly comparing it to the corpus of Seltaman secular stories (*sung*—"stories," or *fasela sung*—"old folks' stories"). To initiate a secular story, a Seltaman typically starts off with a sort of "once upon a time" expression and ends with a "that's all there is" expression. In between, not only are mood and audience response thrown into a particular modality but also the elements that unfold exemplify a mix of favorite and familiar subjects (the food quest), characters in relationships (family members), plot motifs (supernatural encounters), and entertainment devices (the insertion of songs) that conform to certain unspoken limits of novelty. A feature of secular stories as a genre is that the characters of *fasela sung* are unnamed; they are designated by relationships: a man and his family, two sisters-in-law, a pair of cross-cousins, etc. The appearance of a person's name in a story usually betokens a lapse out of the *fasela sung* genre and into an account of something that "really" took place—a recent event, news from another community, an historical event involving people who, though now deceased, were known to some of the audience.

Sacred stories are never introduced or concluded with the "once upon a time" and "that's all there is" formula, and they always contain some named characters. The implication in both cases is that sacred stories are making a "reality" claim. The names used in sacred stories are typically their most fundamental secret element. To change a sacred story into a secular one it is sufficient—from what I can gather—to remove the names and alter part of the plot, usually the ending, then bracket the story in the formulaic introduction and conclusion. That is all. In the corpus of over one hundred *fasela sung* that I collected from the Seltaman and their immediate neighbors, the Angkayak, I was able to detect a handful that are close transformations of sacred stories.

What this means is that there will be virtually the same story appearing in two different genres or meaning environments. It can easily be the case, then, that part of the audience for the secular version will experience an evocation of the sacred version. And any new audience for the sacred version will have the surprise of discovering an old friend dressed up in new clothing. An appreciably similar situation obtains in regard to natural speciemes that have sacred glosses. Some of the participants in a discussion of a local specieme will know that it leads to a sacred story or appears in a key ritual sequence. And, comparably, those admitted to new levels of the secrecy system will find parts of the ordinary natural environment becoming, in Dan Jorgensen's apt phrase, "defamiliarized" by a new meaning load (Jorgensen 1987:5). These meaning carryovers from semiotic field to semiotic field are frequently singled out for theoretical focus in interpretive anthropology, with the general idea being that these linkages are psychologically central to the cultural enterprise under discussion.

While insightful, this point should be contextualized within a larger vision. This is that the new initiate, in discovering these old familiar secular items dressed up in new sacred clothing, is getting his first glimpse of an alternate discursive game. He is very apt at first, as anthropologists are, to confuse the game with the elements upon which it is played. But the elements within the game are one dimension; the rules of concatenating them, of producing meaning from them, are another. Here it becomes useful to distinguish the sacred corpus from its reading and glossing rules—its "genre" characteristics—just as one distinguishes "jazzed-up" tunes from the principles of "jazz." Though in the case of the Mountain Ok sacred, elements and rules are probably more mutually implicated than are tunes and jazz rules, nonetheless the Mountain Ok sacred is arguably a *way of thinking* and not just a body of thought objects. In theory, any item could be drawn into this game. In practice, only someone who understands the game and is recognized as understanding it, only someone who is a master of the discourse, can perform this drawing in—or, alternately, perform an exclusion. In effect, it is up to recognized masters whether a good cigar is just a good cigar or whether it is something else. The efforts of the less adept will be treated with suspicion, pegged as uninformed, or, if the listener is also a sympathetic instructor, corrected. Since it is only through exposure to a range of examples that a person comes to assimilate the rules of the sacred corpus (they are not abstracted and taught separately from the content upon which they operate), it would follow that "masters" are also men with large element repertories and a history of social connectedness to earlier masters. In the end then, the semiotic space of the sacred maps onto a particular set of social relationships and a characteristic mode of sociality. One could even go so far as to speculate that once a man is a thorough insider to these relationships and this sociality, he could turn anything that came to hand into sacred knowledge and find believers who would listen to him.

Before touching further on the sociology of sacred discourse, let us return for a moment to the issue of the initiate's subjectivity, which arguments such as Jorgensen's address, and add to this (admittedly speculative) psychology another (admittedly speculative) chapter. It seems likely to me that the meaning carry-overs from secular to sacred that initiation stirs up, which are undoubtedly quite stunning to new initiates, give way over time and with the increasing acquisition of sacred genre rules to an equally definite meaning severance or, perhaps better, meaning compartmentalization. When raw and fresh, the sacred secrets spill over into the initiates' daily lives, intruding on their minds during commonplace activities and making them conscious of their new differentness. A particular marsupial is captured by some hunter and, hearing the news, a new initiate likely thinks, "The ancestor!" But with greater sophistication comes a greater sense of when an element is "in play," as it were, and eventually few thoughts will be provoked by the occurrence in a secular context of some element found also in the sacred corpus. Subjective experiments in fusing together meanings from two generic areas would, I am suggesting, become of less interest once it sinks in that the methods of meaning production in the two areas are simply different. This "sinking-in" process need not be a conscious one nor the result of express training; more likely it is part and parcel of the doxic practices of initiated-male sociality.

Thus an element, whether it be a local specieme or a narrative fragment, that is found simultaneously in the sacred corpus and a secular semiotic space (such as *fasela sung* or the space of "nature lore") is participating, I would argue, in two different meaning environments, two different historical trajectories, two different forms of life. Especially since the secular corpus is productively manipulated by people unacquainted with the sacred corpus (such as women), secularized elements easily become launched on paths of meaning entirely unrelated to their meanings in the sacred context. Conversely, those elements taken up into the sacred genre begin to participate in configurations of meaning that leave behind their meanings in secular life.

The contrast between the destinies of sacred and secular elements is best illustrated, again, with stories. It is brought out most critically when we turn to the issue of how Seltaman respond to evocations in the two different contexts of secular storytelling and sacred storytelling. Within either corpus, stories and their elements manifest numerous points of contact, and one story may evoke another through shared character relationships, narrative elements, creatures, or items. Overlapping features or analogous structures may even cause one story to map onto another in memory; I noted a number of apparent memory conflations of this sort. (The more stories a person knows, the richer his or her associational network and conflationary potential.) But for Seltaman, the overt and principled response to these associations—or "elicitations," in Roy Wagner's useful formulation (1986 a:xiv–xv)—in the two genres is markedly different. In the secular genre, they serve only to keep the storytelling session alive by stimulating the recollection of further stories. This is by no means an insignificant function, and it has the distinct social consequence of drawing more storytellers into a storytelling session and of spreading both social attention and entertainment responsibility more widely around the circle.

In the sacred genre, elicitations provide the stimulus for a quite different game. The participants in an exchange of sacred information are most often two people who have forged or are forging bonds of a master-disciple sort.[10] Elicitations that appear in this setting and that are noticed by the disciple are often treated coyly by the master. Their appearance forms the occasion for his implying that there are further hidden connections, connections leading to less widely shared and thus more magically potent sacred elements. Here the idea of hidden glosses, of elements behind elements, is not simply an idea that the anthropologist holds. It is held by the Seltaman as well; indeed, it is one of the "generic" principles of the sacred corpus.

This principal is one I became unconsciously aware of (if I may phrase it that way) when working with Walter [not his name], an elderly ritual expert who had consented to "sell" me his repertory of sacred stories and ritual practices. Trying not to load questions, I nevertheless would try in a gingerly way to query the associational linkages that appeared in the material we were discussing: pointing out shared names or plot elements in stories, asking if there was a story behind a ritual object or a creature used in sacrifice, and so on. I grew accustomed to Walter's knowing chuckle. It was proffered to tantalize me with the prospect of further hidden material that he would get around to telling me in his own good time, even though in many cases he never did. It was simultaneously a compliment for my perceptiveness and a prelude to his asking me for the secret knowledge that he was sure *I* was withholding from *him*. We were involved in a complex dance, but the main rule was clear: points of contact between sacred elements led somewhere. There were occasions upon which, pressed harder on a matter, Walter would make (or fake) the admission that he personally didn't know quite where a point of contact led, only that it led somewhere and there were those with greater savvy who could tell me—experts in Telefomin, for instance, or Oksapmin. Another elderly ritual expert who refused to communicate any secrets to me nonetheless also, on occasion, employed the knowing chuckle (wicked giggle might be a better characterization) as a taunt.

By contrast, when my interpreter, who always worked with Walter and me on the sacred material and who understood the protocol of that situation, chose to regale me with *secular* stories from his own extensive repertory, his response to my occasional probings for a hidden meaning was always, "Yes, but this is just a story!" This response occurred even when we two were alone and at liberty to indulge in sacred talk. This response occurred even in two cases when the eliciting element in question was something almost never mentioned except in restricted conversations. In effect, seemingly blatant elicitations of the sacred, because they occurred in a secular story, categorically led nowhere. To inquire about them was not offensive; it simply missed the point.

Let me suggest accordingly, that the local transforming paradise species are, despite their sister- and brotherhood, in Seltaman eyes, "Just birds!" The argument is reinforced by the fact that I learned most of the sacred glosses on natural species from Seltaman without deliberate probing. It was sufficient that the creatures be under discussion for some men to begin to offer friendly hints ("There's a story to this one") and others whispered promises ("When the other people leave, I'll explain this one"). Sometimes men would know there was a sacred story even though no one could be found who actually knew the *sacred story*. The point remained: when a taxon had a position within the sacred corpus, Seltaman men generally would, in one way or another, indicate this. They would, in effect, put the taxon "in play."

It is significant, then, that despite my numerous discussions of "sister" and "brother" birds with Seltaman, no story or explanation of this type ever emerged for these birds. No one ever put them in play. Most strikingly, when Seltaman (including Walter) whispered to me the matches they perceived between the images on the Papua New Guinea currency and their sacred taxa (the cassowary on one coin was Afek, the marsupial on another was "the ancestor," etc.) the image of the Raggiana bird of paradise in full courtship display, which appears on two of the coins and on the Papua Niugini flag as well, provoked from them the following formula: "The women will tell you this bird is *karom keit* ("decorated Raggiana") or *karom yen* (Raggiana "sister"), but it's not. It's really ———." At this point, they would produce the secret name of a myth-entailed nonlocal species of bird.[11] In effect, given maximum opportunity to locate the Raggiana within the sacred semiotic, Seltaman instead found a way to get it out of their path. No hints, no promises, no knowing chuckles.

Nature, Power, and Discourse

Readers will be forgiven for wondering, at this point, whether this essay is in any way about "naturalizing power." My positing of the "nature-lore" semiotic, while certainly relevant to David Schneider's perspicuous problematizing of biology, which in turn is ancestral to the central concept of this volume, itself seems at odd angles to this concept. Indeed, it has been one of the goals of this essay to attempt to show that the funny things we do with nature (we Americans, we Seltaman, we whomever) are not always necessarily power implicated.

But the roots of social power are multiple, and if Nature has been, in this limited example, set to one side, a different root, the mastery and guardianship of a discourse, has come more clearly into view. Even though it cannot be spelled out in any detail here, it is clear that the implicit reading and glossing rules of the Seltaman sacred corpus are constitutive of and constituted by a form of hierarchical sociality. For men who enter into this form, the gradual mastery of the sacred genre traces a trajectory of social empowerment that in each generation places at the apex of the initiatory system—a system that indirectly governs communal life—certain initiated men who, in addition to other qualifications, have learned well the right points at which to chuckle knowingly. Even as the rules and corpus of sacred material can be perceived as "dialogically emergent" from a characteristic sociality (cf. Mannheim and Tedlock 1991; Mannheim n.d.), the power associated with that sociality is, in part at least, (and leaving aside grosser contingencies), emergent from the ability of those in the know to manipulate these rules and command this corpus. Comparably, there is a dialogic emergence of the secular story genre from that matrix of day-to-day relaxed communal sociality in which power distinctions are of less interest. As Seltaman put it (and as I found to be true), "All Seltaman can tell you stories. Men, women, and children."

Nature lore remains something of a cipher in this regard. Of what sociality is it constitutive? Out of what sociality is it constituted? Nature lore fits into multiple strands of conversational coactivity that tend most often to occur out in the bush: some male only (but assorted ages), some female only (but assorted ages), some of mixed sex and age. While nature lore is anthropomorphosing and thus inevitably somewhat "reflective" of what Seltaman think people do, it lacks social didacticism and is marked, rather, by a playful but astute sizing up of the nonhuman, creatural "other" that this lore takes as its object. Perhaps here we are in an area of sociality, the human-creatural, as yet little theorized by social science.

Summary

In overview, I have argued that discursive fields or sites of meaning production (such as the three Seltaman semiotics just discussed) tend to have canonical and rule-dependent boundaries that, under normal (unmarked) circumstances and social conditions, limit the intertextuals that anybody takes seriously. Just as we (educated Westerners) do not take seriously the sexual slang intertext when we speak of "The Big Bang Theory" of the universe (even when, as so often happens with sexual intertexts, a nonserious interlocutor brings them to our attention), or the Biblical intertext when we call a kind of seed "Job's tears," or the Sesame Street intertext when we describe an eagle as a big bird, so comparably Seltaman do not take seriously the sacred big sister and little brother intertext that occurs within the social-cum-"generic" contexts of a secular discursive field.

Notes

I am indebted to Susan Gelman and Bruce Mannheim both for general discussion and for extensive help with the literature and theory of folk classifications; and I am indebted to Susan Harding for steering me toward the concept of reading rules. Extensive discussion with Eytan Bercovitch on the Mountain Ok materials, and Peter Dwyer's laser-like reading of an earlier draft, have also been crucial to my final formulations. Others whose discussions of earlier drafts have benefited the current one are Fredrik Barth, Philip Guddemi, Sherry Ortner, Anna Tsing, and Sylvia Yanagisako. Research among the Seltaman was funded by grants from the National Science Foundation and the National Geographic.

1. Bulmer's main collaborators are the zoologists James Menzies and Michael J. Tyler, and Ian Saem Majnep, a Kalam expert on the Kalam natural world.

2. Building on many of the arguments cited here, as well as extensive additional research, is Scott Atran's articulation of a cognitive foundation for the apprehension of living kinds. Atran assembles an impressive brief to the effect that, whatever secondary projects may be mounted on their initial orderings, the core taxonomizing principles of living kinds are the same in every culture and relate humans to the natural world in a stubbornly common-sensical way (Atran 1990, 1994; see also Sperber 1994). The present argument is less ambitious than this, though it converges on a similar point.

3. There is a corollary of this, which is that the local differentiation of the environment may embed accurate bits of wisdom that many individuals have never arrived at from observation and indeed do not know. For instance, the Seltaman call some beetles "caterpillar's mother." When asked directly, "Does this mean that when a beetle 'puts children' these will be caterpillars?" or further, "Will this caterpillar grow up to become a beetle?" some Seltaman would stammer out, "I don't know! Maybe!"

4. Atran entertains a functionalist explanation of these inconsistencies, pointing out that the mentality that is able to mistakenly allow that, for instance, a beetle may become a frog, will be able to assent to the idea that a tadpole may become a frog. This point presumes there is a mental structuring of the living world by innate intuitions (Atran 1994:334).

5. Because in nature speciation occurs on a gradient, and thus the reproductive isolation of types is so often partial, Western biological classification itself grades into "typological" rather than "genetic" uses of the term "species." This is evident in any field guide to regional fauna. Michael J. Tyler remarks that with the current genetic notion of species, "We are trying to squeeze a dynamic 20th century concept into a static 18th century mould" (Tyler 1991:167).

6. When Seltaman were sorting through bird illustrations and encountering examples of unfamiliar or less familiar species for whom fledging characteristics were unknown, they would tend to loosely apply the "sister-brother" classification to those instances in which one member of a pair is decorative and the other drab.

7. There are two local parrot species, the Papuan King Parrot and the Eclectus Parrot, that are notably sexually dimorphic, with each gender being equally decorative. The sexes of the two species fledge differently from the nestling or pinfeather stage. Neither of these are spoken of as "sister" and "brother." Seltaman see the male and female Papuan King Parrot as "correctly" male and female. They see the male and female Eclectus Parrots as two different taxa related in a mother's brother- sister's child relationship.

8. Both species are common in the vicinity of the village, indeed the Raggiana is among the four most common birds in the area. Both may be hunted for meat, though the Raggiana is a successful eluder for the most part. Seltaman do not currently hunt any of their local birds of paradise for plumes, although there is evidence that they did so episodically in the past and a newly burgeoning market for plumes in Tabubil may induce them to do so again.

9. I am indebted to Susan Gelman for this example.

10. Should there be a larger congregation present, as in a limited number of ritual contexts, a consensus forms over who will be the designated authority for the session, and this decision again frames a master-disciple relationship, but with a temporary plurality of disciples.

11. Though knowledge of this bird and the sacred tradition associated with it seems to be historically recent for the Seltaman, contingent on their wider regional contacts following the opening of the Ok Tedi mine, the tradition comes to them from other distant Mountain Ok groups who share the Afek tradition. In some of these groups, the tradition surrounding

this bird is conflated with the Afek tradition. I hope to devote a later publication to this issue.

References

Atran, Scott. 1990. *The Cognitive Foundations of Natural History,* New York: Cambridge Univ. Press

———. 1994. "Core Domains versus Scientific Theories: Evidence from Systematics and Itza-Maya Folkbiology." In *Mapping the Mind,* edited by L. A. Hirschfeld and S. Gelman. New York: Cambridge Univ. Press.

Barth, Fredrik. 1987. *Cosmologies in the Making.* New York: Cambridge Univ. Press.

Beehler, Bruce. 1988. "Lek Behavior of the Raggiana Bird of Paradise." *National Geographic Research* 4(3): 343–58.

Beehler, Bruce, Pratt, T. K., and Zimmerman, D. 1986. *Birds of New Guinea.* Princeton, NJ: Princeton Univ. Press.

Berlin, Brent. 1991. "The Chicken and the Egg-head Revisited: Further Evidence for the Intellectualist Bases for Ethnobiological Classification." In *Man and a Half: Essays in Pacific Anthropology and Ethnobiology in Honour of Ralph Bulmer,* edited by A. Pawley, 57–66. Auckland, NZ: The Polynesian Society.

Boyarin, Daniel. 1990. *Intertextuality and the Reading of Midrash.* Bloomington, IN: Indiana Univ. Press.

Bulmer, R. 1970. "Which Came First, the Chicken or the Egghead?" In *Echanges et Communications,* edited by J. Pouillon and P. Maranda, 1069–91. Paris: Mouton.

———.1973. "Why is the Cassowary Not a Bird?" In *Rules and Meanings,* edited by Mary Douglas, 167–94. New York: Penguin.

———.1979. "Mystical and Mundane in Kalam Classification of Birds." In *Classifications in Their Social Context,* edited by Roy F. Ellen and D. Reason, 57–80. New York: Academic.

Bulmer, R., and Menzies, J. 1972–73. "Karam Classification of Marsupials and Rodents." Parts 1 and 2. *Journal of the Polynesian Society* 81:472–99; 82:86–107

Bulmer, R., and Tyler, M. J. 1968. "Karam Classification of Frogs." *Journal of the Polynesian Society* 77:333–85.

Diamond, J. 1966. "Zoological Classification of a Primitive People." *Science* 15:1102–1104.

Dwyer, Peter. 1976a. "An Analysis of Rofaifo Mammal Taxonomy." *American Ethnologist* 3:424–45.

———.1976b. "Beetles, Butterflies and Bats: Species Transformation in a New Guinea Folk Classification." *Oceania* 14:188–205.

———.1979. "Animal Metaphors: An Evolutionary Model." *Mankind* 12:13–27.

———.1980. "Habomi ae Etolo: A Footnote to Monotreme Taxonomy." *Mankind* 12(4): 348–50.

Ellen, Roy F. 1979. "Introductory Essay." In *Classifications in Their Social Context,* edited by R. F. Ellen and D. Reason, 1–29. New York: Academic.

———1991. "Grass, Grerb, or Weed? A Bulmerian Meditation on the Category *Monote* in Nuaulu Plant Classification." In *Man and a Half,* edited by A. Pawley, 95–101. Auckland, NZ: The Polynesian Society.

Feld, Stephen. 1982. *Sound and Sentiment*. Philadelphia: Univ. of Pennsylvania Press.

————.1991. "Cockatoo, Hornbill, Kingfisher. In *Man and a Half*, edited by A. Pawley, 207–213. Auckland, NZ: The Polynesian Society.

Foucault, Michel. 1970. *The Order of Things*. NY: Vintage.

Flannery, Timothy. 1990. *Mammals of New Guinea*. Qld, Australia: Australian Museum, Robert Brown & Associates.

Hays, Terence. 1991. "Interest, Use, and Interest in Uses in Folk Biology." In *Man and a Half*, edited by A. Pawley, 109–114. Auckland, NZ: The Polynesian Society.

Jorgensen, Dan. 1980. "Secrecy's 'Turns': Revelation in Telefol Religion." Paper delivered at the meetings of the American Anthropological Association, Chicago, Illinois.

Lakoff, George, and Johnson, Mark. 1980. *Metaphors We Live By*. Chicago: Univ. of Chicago Press.

Lewis, Gilbert. 1980. *Day of Shining Red*. New York: Cambridge Univ. Press.

Levi-Strauss, Claude. 1966. *The Savage Mind*. Chicago: Univ. of Chicago Press.

Majnep, Ian Saem, and Bulmer, R. 1977. *Mnon Yad Kalam Yakt: Birds of My Kalam Country*. Auckland, NZ: Auckland Univ. Press.

Mannheim, Bruce. n.d. A program for Andean mythography

Mannheim, Bruce, and Tedlock, Dennis. 1991. Introduction to *The Dialogic Emergence of Culture*. Chicago: Univ. of Illinois Press.

Riffaterre, Michael. 1987. "The Intertextual Unconscious." *Critical Inquiry* 13:371–85.

Sperber, Dan. 1994. "The Modularity of Thought and the Epidemiology of Representations." In *Mapping the Mind*, edited by L. A. Hirschfeld and S. Gelman. New York: Cambridge Univ. Press.

Strathern, A., and Ongka. 1979. *Ongka: A Self-Account of a New Guinea Big-man*. New York: St. Martin's.

Tyler, Michael J. 1991. "Biological Nomenclature, Classification and the Ethnozoological Specieme." In *Man and a Half*, edited by A. Pawley, 164–67. Auckland: The Polynesian Society.

Wagner, Roy. 1986a. *Asiwinarong: Ethos, Image and Social Power among the Usen Barok of New Ireland*. Princeton, NJ: Princeton Univ. Press.

————.1986b. *Symbols That Stand for Themselves*. Chicago: Univ. of Chicago Press.

The Origin of Nations

7

Father State, Motherland, and the Birth of Modern Turkey

Carol Delaney

Introduction

This paper will analyze the familiar and familial images of Father State (*Devlet Baba*) and Motherland (*Anavatan*) through which Turkish national identity is conveyed. The language of kinship is so commonplace that most people hardly ever pay any serious attention to it. And anthropologists, for whom kinship has been a major focus of study, often dismiss as merely metaphor its use outside the context of kinship. However, it could also be argued that, because family and kinship relationships are felt to be natural, the imagery of the family used in other contexts helps to naturalize them as well. Anderson seems to have been thinking of something like that when he suggested that nationalism might be more productively treated "as if it belonged with 'kinship' and 'religion' rather than with 'liberalism' or 'fascism' " (1983:15). That is, nationalism should be understood not in terms of explicit political ideologies, as is conventional, but in terms of larger cultural systems (kinship and religion) from which Anderson thought it derived (ibid.: 19). Anderson's intuition had already been preceded by David Schneider (1969), whose article noted the *conceptual* similarity between the categories of kinship, nationality, and religion.

One becomes a member of a family (or kinship unit), a nation, and a religion in remarkably similar ways: either by being born into it or in some cases by being naturalized. Schneider suggested that perhaps the boundaries between nationality, religion, and kinship were not so well marked, at least in cultures influenced by Judaism and Christianity, and, I would add, Islam—in other words, the Abrahamic religions. All three terms—family, nation, and religion—are usually felt to demarcate separate domains or areas of human experience but, at the same time, "they all seem to say one thing. They are all concerned with unity of some kind," which Schneider defined as "diffuse and enduring solidarity" (1977:67). Although Schneider did not use the word, he appeared to be talking about identity and the *similar* ways in which *different* sorts of identity are constructed. Alternatively, one might say that the same rhetoric is used in different contexts, contexts that tend to become concretized as distinct, and even natural, domains. Yet, while Schneider raised the question of the blurred boundaries between the seemingly distinct social domains of family, nation, and religious community, he did not ask: Why is the head of the family, the nation, and the church symbolically, as well as normatively, male? In other words, he did not ask who is on top!

The fact that the family, nation, and church are each spoken of, and imagined as a unit obscures both the internal stratifications and the gendered hierarchies in these institutions. For example, the conceptualization of the family as a "natural" unit has been a staple not just of kinship theory but also of political theory going back at least as far as Aristotle.[1] The notion of family as a natural unit not only naturalizes (and thus universalizes) western notions of kinship as derived from (i.e., constituted by) blood relations resulting from sexual intercourse, but it also naturalizes power as it submerges asymmetries of age and gender as well as differing interests.[2] In Turkish, the word commonly translated as "family" is *aile*, but this has different meaning for women and men. *Aile* refers to wife and children; thus only men really *have* families; women are part of one.[3]

The fusion of gender, sexuality, and kinship and the "forgetting" of the different structural places each person occupies within the image of the unified family is comparable on the personal level to that required of different groups by the inclusive rhetoric of nationalism. "Forgetting," said Renan more than a century ago, "is a crucial factor in the creation of a nation" (1990:11).

My goal in this paper is not just to highlight the differential placement of men and women in and to the nation—an issue that has been addressed by some feminist scholars,[4] but notably not by Anderson, Gellner, or Hobsbawn—but more importantly to show the role that the symbolism of mother and father play in the conception of the nation. By attending to these procreative images and meanings of gender, I hope to extend the theoretical import of Schneider's argument as I contextualize it with material from Turkey. The implications of the material suggest that the concept of the nation-state is itself gendered and therefore that gender inequality vis-a-vis the nation is not an accidental feature but is inherent in the notion of the nation as it has been historically conceived in the West. The geographical and temporal origin does not, of course, preclude its being exported to and adopted by peoples elsewhere.

Conceiving the Nation

Father State (*Devlet Baba*) and Motherland (*Anavatan*) are concepts familiar to all Turks and were well known to peoples living under Ottoman rule. Thus, although they were not newly invented with the Republic of Turkey in 1923, they were used in a new way. In shaping the nationalism that would help to create the new nation, Mustafa Kemal, later known as Atatürk, drew upon these familiar concepts but changed the referents.

Father State epitomized Ottoman rule. The state was both patriarchal and paternalistic, and the people, organized into *millet* ("nations"), were dependent on its benevolence and its protection. Confessional groups, whether Muslim, Jewish, or one of various forms of Christianity such as Greek Orthodox, Armenian, or Syrian, were the basis of the *millet* system. Religious identity most often coincided with ethnic and linguistic identities and membership was a matter of birth. Within the Ottoman Empire were many nations.

The land was owned by the state and imagined both as the vast amorphous expanse of state patrimony and as the small area of the earth one was reared on. But in either case, *Arravatan* ("Motherland") was a generalized medium of nurture, under the control of the state but without specific boundaries or identity.

People were familiar with the concepts of nation and state, but these did not go together naturally; indeed, in certain circumstances they could be seen as opposed. The notion of a circumscribed body of land isomorphic with the body politic was absent. In order to bring the nation-state into being, the conceptual ground first had to be laid. The power and success of the nationalist movement was due, I believe, not only to Mustafa Kemal's military strategy but also to his rhetorical strategy. He *refigured the imaginative terrain as he sought to redefine the physical.*

The transformation from the sprawling Ottoman Empire to a European-type, territorially based nation-state of Turkey did not occur in a vacuum, nor was it inevitable. Even before the collapse of the Ottoman Empire at the end of World War I, two other powerful ideologies for fostering solidarity were competing for peoples' allegiance: pan-Islam and pan-Turkism. The same two options have once again come to the forefront of political consciousness: on the one hand, the rise and spread of militant Islam calls for an extended Muslim brotherhood; and on the other, the end of the Cold War has made porous the boundaries separating Turkey from other Turkic-speaking groups in the former Soviet Union.[6] As people's allegiances are pulled in different directions, Turkey is being divided and, in the process, its future is being charted.

Pan-Islam, as its name implies, is based on the unity or brotherhood provided by Islam. This was the most accessible ideology, since Islam was the source of identity and the primary cultural context in which the majority of people lived their lives. A great many Turks still continue to identify primarily as Muslims and as people from a particular area in Turkey— Konyalı (of Konya), Ankarkalı (of Ankara), etc.—rather than primarily as Turks. Pan-Islamic identity would include most of the various Arab peoples in the empire but would exclude the Christians and Jews living in their midst.

Pan-Turkism, in contrast, was a nationalist theory based on linguistic affinities with other Turkic-speaking peoples in Central Asia, Russia, and even as far as China, some of whom were at least nominally Muslim, while others practiced local varieties of shamanism. Since many of these peoples were not at that time within the empire, this theory had quite definite expansionist aspects. Drawing on notions of a glorious pre-Islamic past, pan-Turkism could easily be seen to be in conflict with Islam. For this reason, it would hardly appeal to the Ottomans of the ruling class or to the majority of the people who were villagers. It did, however, captivate the imaginations of a number of the urban intelligentsia.

Pan-Turkism was a romantic and mystical ideology that drew a compelling portrait of an "imagined community" (Anderson 1983) called "Turan." The notion of Turan had become widely known through a famous poem by Huseyinzade Ali in the late nineteenth century—a poem that, according to Ziya Gökalp, "heralded the beginning of a new revolution in Turkish life" (Gökalp 1968:6). It supposedly provided the inspiration of the Young Turk movement of 1908–1909 to unite all Turkic-speaking peoples. The notion of Turan was further immortalized in another poem, this time by Gökalp himself (1876–1924), who is often credited with laying the foundations of Turkish nationalism; he promulgated his ideas in short essays and poetry that were printed in journals, newspapers, and pamphlets and widely disseminated. In a 1911 poem, he wrote: "The fatherland of the Turks is neither Turkey nor Turkestan; their fatherland is the vast and eternal Turan" (Landau 1984). It is more than a curious footnote to mention that a number of U.S. & European historians and political scientists have exposed their biases by translating *vatan* and even *anavatan* as "fatherland" rather than "motherland," which is how Turks understand the words.[7] Such an oversight on the part of the analysts reveals that they have not fully comprehended the gendered significance of the terms and the sentiments they can arouse.

Nationalist ideas on the European model had also been discussed in Turkey since the late nineteenth century among the intellectual elites, some of whom had even been educated in Europe, but such ideas had not captured the popular imagination. Mustafa Kemal was well aware that in order to capture the imagination as well as the allegiance of the majority of the people, he would have to communicate his ideas and plans for the country in a language and genre with which they were familiar. The language of the people was not the language of the Ottoman court, and the language of the Ottoman court was hardly Turkish. According to Gökalp,

> there were two languages side by side in Turkey. The first, known as Ottoman, was recognized officially and had a virtual monopoly on writing. The second, which was limited almost entirely to speech among the people, was referred to contemptuously as Turkish and was considered as the argot of the common people. Nevertheless, it was our real and natural language, whereas Ottoman was an artificial amalgam created out of the grammar, syntax, and vocabulary of three languages: Turkish, Arabic, and Persian. (1968:24)

He goes on to say how there were two prosodic systems and two musical forms, and that a similar dichotomy existed in literature, comprising myths, tales, proverbs, ballads, legends, epics, anecdotes, and folk plays (ibid.:24). Another intellectual at the turn of the century ruefully reflected that Ottoman "was not the language of one nation. It is not Persian, Arabic or Turkish. The masterpieces of our literature cannot be understood by an Arab or a Persian . . . [and] we do not understand it either. Are we getting to be a nation without a language?" (Ahmet Midhat Efendi, 1884–1913, quoted in Başgöz 1978:124).

Both men encouraged the modernizing, nationalistically inclined intellectuals to turn to the "common people" and to folklore for inspiration. It was in folklore—tales, proverbs, and especially folk poetry, often communicated by traveling minstrels—that the sentiments and values of the *Turkish* people could be found. This was the language and the genres that the people understood, enjoyed, and preserved. "The language of this poetry had served as a viable means of communication for centuries among uneducated peasants, a means which the new intellectuals had been searching for to bridge the gap between the rulers and ruled" (Başgöz 1978:128). While much of the folk poetry and song contained religious ideas, these were, nevertheless, often cast in terms of secular images and themes, especially of nature and romantic love.

A large part of the appeal of Mustafa Kemal was his ability to utilize this vast store of familiar folklore and poetry as a catalyst for change. Social scientists, especially in the United States, have failed to understand or take account of the political role of poetry in other cultures because it is so devalued in their own.[8] The focus on folk traditions helped to enhance the self-perception of Turks, to bring out the uniqueness of their language and customs, their culture. It was also meant to help fashion a notion of the integrity of their culture and institutions, to foster a notion of the nation-state as one integrated entity unlike the Ottoman regime in which state and nation were split. Here Mustafa Kemal drew upon not just familiar imagery but also imagery of the family. In order to understand the power of that imagery and how it figured in the conception and creation of the Republic of Turkey, it is important to explore in more detail the meanings of the gendered images of *baba* ("father") and *ana* ("mother").

The creation of a modern, secular, western-type of nation-state was the goal of Mustafa Kemal; ironically, as will become clear shortly, something of the power of religion gets built into the structure by means of those very things felt to be most natural, namely reproduction and gender. Images configure the imagination; not only is gender utilized in the conceptualization of the nation, but that conception has the potential to affect the way people think about men and women (cf. Helmreich, 1992). What is emphasized, however, is not just gender, but gender in the context of reproduction.

It is easy, even natural, to discuss the creation and existence of a nation in terms of procreation and birth: "a nation in travail," "the birth of a nation," a "nation reborn." Each concept has been used in the title of a book about the emergence of modern Turkey, but they all could apply to any number of other nations.[9]

Notions of Conception

If it is easy to use the language of procreation and birth to discuss the nation, it is even easier to assume that procreation and birth are *natural* givens in human existence. While not denying that certain physiological processes do occur, most of us do not entertain the theoretical possibility that the processes of coming into being are constructed and interpreted within specific cultural frameworks of meaning and value in which the very meaning of "nature" derives from its place in a specific cosmological/ religious system. While it is common in the West to figure nature as symbolically female,[10] there is nothing natural about that designation; instead, "nature" and "the natural" come imbued with gender associations that are embedded in a particular religious or cosmological system.

The system that has been dominant in the West for millenia construes nature as created by God, who is figured symbolically as masculine; nature, that which is created by God, is both inferior to and dependent upon God and is symbolically construed as female. The laws that govern nature were implanted by God, and early modern scientists thought they were exploring these God-given laws and regularities. "Nature," therefore, could not possibly have the same meanings and associations in different cosmological systems, in different views of how things came to be. Something is lost when God drops out of the picture, as has happened in modern science, and it is not just God. What has also been lost is the awareness that our notion of "nature" has been constructed within a culturally specific cosmology, and therefore our understanding of "nature" is neither natural nor universal. Even when women are associated with the "natural world" elsewhere, one must consider the cosmological context in which that world has a place and the meanings of gender in that context. Today, most of us think of procreation as a natural phenomenon; yet in other contexts, as will become clear shortly, only one aspect of it, namely the woman's role or contribution, is considered natural, the other is associated with the divine.

Much of what I say will be familiar because the symbols and theory are not confined to Turkey. These were the terms in which I first learned about procreation; they are widely known, and still taught to children in much of the United States and Europe as well as Turkey. Despite scientific theory, these images still continue to operate in less explicit contexts such as poetry and song as well as nationalist discourse, and thus assumptions about gender are seamlessly incorporated and reinforced in the construction of the nation.

Baba and *ana* are defined by their culturally perceived roles in procreation. These words, I argue, are not merely labels attached to male and female parents but are also meaningful terms that are differentially coded and hierarchically ordered as is clear when used in the phrases "to father" vs. "to mother." Thus, understanding their meaning and role may help to understand their significance when they are deployed as *Devlet Baba* and *Anavatan*.

In the theory of procreation I have been investigating,[11] men are believed to be the generative agents; they provide the "seed." Women, in contrast, are imagined as "soil," which can be either barren or fertile. They receive the seed-child and, if fertile, provide the generalized medium of nurture of that helps to make it grow. Villagers used to cite the *Qur'an* in order to legitimate their view. In Sura 2:223 it is stated, ["Women are given to you as fields; Go therein and sow (your seed) as you wish."] Note also in this passage how God speaks *to* men *about* women; God and men are in an I-Thou communicating relationship, women are objectified. This is hardly a unique example in the *Qur'an*; it is also a common form in the Bible.

Through "seed," men provide the spiritual identity that distinguishes one person from all others. In a non-Turkish religious context, this rhetoric and imagery was made explicit by Elijah Muhammed in relation to the creation of the nation of Islam, and more recently by David Koresh, the Waco cult leader who saw his mission as increasing the "seed" of the House of David.[12] And in a nationalist context, I can recall reading that Herder, the German theorist of cultural nationalism, said something to the effect that neither the land nor the climate is the source of the national spirit, which comes from the seeds of the fathers.

Women are symbolically associated with the earth—what was created by God. And women come to be defined by their physical and nurturing, rather than generative, qualities, which come to define their social role. The differences between men and women are seen as both natural and in the order of things. These ideas are embraced by many Turkish-Muslim women. According to Nükhet Sirman (1989:24), such women applaud the challenge that feminists have made against the objectification and commoditization of the female body and sexuality, but they conclude that the solution is for women to embrace their true nature as wives but more especially as mothers. In order to do that women must work for the "restoration of the original Islamic community . . . which requires a total submission to their nature as the only possible form of true existence. Motherhood constitutes a crucial element of this essential nature" (Sirman 1989:25). What they do not realize is that the "essential nature" they esteem has itself been constructed within a specific theory of procreation.

This *theory* of procreation, hardly the "facts" open to observation, is what I have called a "monogenetic" theory of procreation, for there is only one principle of creation. Although women are necessary for procreation and are valued for their contribution to the process, men, in their pro*creative* function, are associated with divine creativity and partake of its power and authority. There could have been a variety of conceptual possibilities for the male role: that (1) in sexual intercourse he merely opened the way for the fetus, (2) he merely was feeding it, (3) that he contributed something to its substance. But none of these are equivalent to what has been meant by paternity. The paternal role has been conceptualized as the generative, creative role; the father is the one who bestows life as well as essential identity via the soul; thus he is the means for the divine entering into human society. This ability is what has allied him, symbolically at least, with God.[13] Procreation, then, has hardly been viewed as merely a natural process; instead it has been a highly charged arena for naturalizing divine power.

This is captured succinctly, but perhaps unwittingly, by Seyyed Hossein Nasr, a well-known Muslim scholar: "The Muslim family is the miniature of the whole Muslim society. . . . The father and his authority symbolizes that of God in world" (Nasr 1985:110). God, the Head of State, and the father form a devolving but unilineal structure of authority. During the Ottoman period, the Sultan or Padishah was not only the Head of State, he was also "the direct representative or shadow of God in the world" (Berkes, cited in Tachau 1984:59). The only legitimate order was that decreed by God. Binnaz Toprak, a Turkish political scientist, notes that for Muslims, "political *legitimacy* is primarily a theocratic question rather than a political one" (Toprak 1981:25). Theoretically, at least, "there is one God in heaven, who gave one law to mankind and established one ruler to maintain and enforce that law in his one community" (B. Lewis 1988:46).

The reality, of course, is not and was not so simple. There was an Ottoman Empire and an Ottoman state but no Ottoman nation; Ottomans were part of the Muslim nation. More importantly, perhaps, there was no Turkish nation; Europeans may have referred to the Ottomans as Turks, but that was not a term of self-reference. Indeed, not all Ottomans were Turkish.[14] In fact, it has been said that the greatest sufferers of Ottomanism were the Turks!

"Turk" was a derogatory term that referred to the Anatolian peasants. It was a great achievement of Mustafa Kemal to turn that derogatory term into *the* defining term of national identity. Not until the birth of the republic was announced did Mustafa Kemal make the claim "How happy is the person who can say 'I am a Turk'." But how did he do that, and what or who *is* a Turk? This is an important question, but the answer is not so simple. The people who today call themselves "Turks" have "Turkic, Kurdish, Albanian, Bosnian, Armenian, Bulgarian, Greek, Circassian, Georgian, Laz, Abkhazian, Arab, and Iranian origins" (Meeker 1992:413); they can hardly be seen to be the direct descendants of the ancient Turkic tribes from central Asia. Therefore, any answer to the question "Who is a Turk?" involves a specific narrative of origin.[15] Despite Mustafa Kemal's belief that national identity was primarily a matter of language and culture, there was always slippage into an ethnically based notion of Turkishness. Some have suggested that the Republic of Turkey ought to have been named Anatolia or the Ottoman Republic in order to avoid the conflation of language with ethnicity. Indeed, these did become conflated by Atatürk's researches into history and language whereby he promulgated the theory that Turkish was the Ur Language and Turks the original people (see G. Lewis 1984). His theory was given institutional legitimacy by the establishment in 1932 of the Türk Tarıhı Kurumu (Turkish History Association) and, in the same year, the Türk Dil Kurumu (Turkish Language Association).

The Birth of Turkey

The task of Mustafa Kemal was to create a national consciousness and to instill sentiments of "diffuse, enduring solidarity." But the inclusive rhetoric of nationalist beliefs and strategies was diametrically opposed to the policy of the Ottoman Empire. That policy was to preserve the distinctiveness of the various nations rather than to assimilate them—a policy that in a benign mode could be seen as the essence of multiculturalism, but given a more sinister cast could be seen as an expression of a kind of "divide-and-conquer" strategy. At the conclusion of World War I, the latter strategy prevailed when the Allied powers agreed to divide and distribute the territory among the British, French, Italians, and Greeks. The breakup of the Empire may have stirred the hopes of other groups to take advantage of the situation to stake claims for autonomy, but at the time, it seems, their best hopes were with the nationalists, who sought liberation from the Allied powers.

Mustafa Kemal wanted not to conquer but to regain possession of the land about to be dismembered. At the capitulation of the Ottomans to the Allied powers, Kemal, distinguished in the Battle of Gallipoli, was ordered to relinguish his commission and demobilize his troops. He refused, and for his disobedience was condemned to death by a military court.

Eluding the military police, he made a whirlwind tour of the country and rallied the people to resist the partition and claim the country as their own. The appeal was made to their sense of honor; they must come to the defense of the *Motherland* that, he claimed, had been prostituted under the capitulations and was about to be mutilated by the partition.

The power of his plea was immediate. According to two of his biographers, the emotional appeal may have been the result of the fact that he identified his own mother with the motherland and felt injuries to the latter as if they were to the former (cf. Volkan and Itzkowitz 1984).[16] He used a popular poem by Namik Kemal (no relation) that very clearly drew an analogy between land and mother. Mustafa Kemal changed the last sentence and thus also drew attention to his vision of his own role. The last two lines of Namik Kemal's poem read: the foe thrusts his knife into the heart of the land/there was none to save our ill-fated mother. Mustafa Kemal who imagined himself as the land's savior changed the last line to read "but yes, one is found to save our ill-fated mother." Peasants did not have to understand the idea of a nation-state to be motivated to protect their own threatened soil if it was understood as their mother who was being raped and sold into captivity. Once their sense of honor was called upon, they rose up against the intruders and ejected them from their soil.[17]

Fixing the boundaries was equivalent, I suggest, to restoring the integrity or virtue of the motherland:[18] this land would henceforth be the *physical basis* for the nation. All those born upon and nurtured by her soil were henceforth to be related like siblings. *Vatandaş*, the word coined to mean "citizen," is literally "fellow of the motherland"; it is like the word *kardeş*, which means both brother and sibling, literally "fellow of the womb." The physical substance (consubtantiality) of siblings is from the mother, but their essential, eternal identity comes from the father. Although both men and women can be citizens, it remains the male's perogative to transmit it.

Political Procreation

The transformation of political structures was paralleled by a transformation in the structure of personal life. The change from the Empire with its many nations, like the Sultan and his harem, to a modern nation-state was accompanied by a transformation in marriage laws—from the polygamy permitted in Islam to monogamy as practiced in the western nation-states. This was not to suggest that monogamy was the ideal and/or that women were not also oppressed in monogamy but that the relationship was changed. In Turkey, divorce could no longer be unilaterally declared by the man.

The nation-state was imagined as an inviolable union—a wedding—that presupposed a notion of differentially sexed, valued, and situated people; but in this case, the union was of Father State and Motherland—now the vast Anatolian heartland. In Turkish this is called *Anadolu,* which in folk etymology means "mother filled" or "filled with mothers." These mothers, identified with the rich, fertile soil of Anatolia, are nevertheless represented by the state, which is symbolically masculine. In her fine analysis of Güntekin's famous *Çalıkuşu* (the first "nationalist" novel set in Anatolia), Sibel Erol (1991), argues that the family was the central image through which national identity was communicated. At the same time, she did not fully examine the gendered and heterosexual implications.

Mustafa Kemal, the founder of the Republic, was renamed Atatürk—Father Turk or Father of the Turks. If the land of Anatolia was symbolically the Mother, Mustafa Kemal surely was the Father, not so much Father State but Father of it. And while he would have rejected the dependency encouraged by the image of Father State as the primary benefactor, it could also be argued that his personal style in relation to the people was paternal, if not patronizing. A law passed in 1934 "forbade the use of Atatürk by anyone else. Thus, he became the *one and only* Father Turk" (Volkan and Itzkowitz 1984:302) (emphasis added), though most people referred to him simply as "Ata," which is another word for father or ancestor. He became the symbolic progenitor of the people as well as Father of the State that he ruled with one party.

Scholars both inside and outside Turkey (e.g., F. Ahmad 1977; Yerasimos 1987) have called this a "monoparty" rather than a single party rule. By this they mean to show that there was a conflation of party and state during the early years of the Republic. The difficulties encountered with the shift to multiparty politics have been discussed in terms of legitimacy, specifically about the problem of "dual legitimacy" (Hotham 1972:63).[19] Although the discussion is about *political* legitimacy, the language and theory of procreation in which there can be only one principle of legitimacy, that which comes from the father, are helpful in grasping the nature of some of the problems.

The rhetoric of kinship and descent that provides for a person's identity and legitimacy was deployed to give national identity and legitimacy to the new citizens. They could claim legitimacy from the *ata* ("ancestor-father") Atatürk who bestowed it, and recognize their common substance by being born and nurtured from the same soil, *Anavatan.* Building upon familar concepts and meanings, Atatürk used them symbolically to bind a people to a land and to provide a more general and more inclusive identity.

Notions about procreation seem to be implicitly behind considerations about who is a citizen. The new Turkish constitution of 1982, drafted over several years following the military coup of 1980, makes it clear that the child of a Turkish father or a Turkish mother is a Turk (Dodd 1990:172). But only a child with a Turkish father is a citizen; thus, nationality and citizenship do not necessarily coincide.[20] Children with foreign fathers but Turkish mothers are not automatically citizens, nor can a Turkish woman married to a foreign man acquire property in Turkey. Clearly, citizenship is not gender neutral.[21]

Lessons in Nationalism

As soon as the boundaries of the new nation were drawn, the major problem confronting the victors of the war of independence was that of forming a national consciousness and sentiments of solidarity. While nationalism had been discussed among the intelligentsia, it needed to be taught to the majority of the people whose notion of nation was *millet*, i.e., a concept of nation that meant group of people, not territory. Ziya Gökalp, whose ideas greatly influenced Atatürk, rejected all definitions of the nation based on ethnic or racial identities and stressed instead common culture. His inclusion of religion in common culture made Atatürk nervous, even though Gökalp's ideas about religion, influenced by Durkheim, were hardly traditional. Atatürk felt that Islam would compete with the new nation for people's loyalty, for he knew that "the primary loyalty of individuals is to the *umma* rather than to the state" (Toprak 1981:25). In order to create a modern, secular, westernized nation-state in a Muslim context, religion had not to be so much separated from the state as subsumed by the state. Atatürk, like Gökalp, stressed the moral superiority of ancient Turkish culture, a move that Meeker (n.d.) suggests was "a prescription for loosening the ties of the people of Asia Minor with their Ottoman and Islamic past and thereby easing the way for a program of secularizing and Westernizing reforms."[22]

Atatürk's idea of nation, incorporated into his party's program, "is a political and social body composed of citizens who are bound together by language, culture, and ideals (Heyd 1950:63). In order to bring a western-type nation-state into being, a national identity had to be created. Since culture is not a natural but an acquired characteristic, it can be learned, and education was to play a key role in creating a national consciousness. Not surprisingly, Atatürk often presented himself as the quintessential teacher with blackboard and chalk as he went around the country giving lessons in nationalism. Two subjects were especially important—the position of women, and language.

The Position of Women

The position of women in society, for both Gökalp and Atatürk, was an issue of major importance. Both argued that among the ancient Turks women were much more highly regarded than in Islam, and both believed that a modern nation could not come about without the elevation of women.

"Is it possible," asked Atatürk, "that one-half of the nation can be developed and the other half neglected? Is it possible that one-half of the nation can be uplifted while the other half remains rooted to the ground?" (Taşkiran 1976:62). Although he believed that women should be emancipated, educated, and uncovered, he also said "[T]hey must be virtuous, dignified, and capable of gaining respect" (ibid.: 63). His explicit discourse on the liberation of women was, however, undermined by his view that "the highest duty of women is motherhood" (ibid.: 56). "Their duty is to bring up and educate a strong new generation of people who will defend the country with determination and courage and pass on the spirit of our nation to future generations" (ibid.:62–63). In this way, Atatürk reinscribed Muslim notions of womanhood in the modern state. Kandiyoti goes further and suggests that despite the fact that "the woman question became a privileged site for debates concerning questions of modernization vs. cultural conservatism" (1989:127), women were actually pawns in the process.[23]

Regardless, Atatürk initiated revolutionary reforms affecting personal status, usually the last bastion of religious conservatism. In place of the *Sharia* (Islamic law), Atatürk substituted the Swiss Civil Code and thereby instituted changes in laws dealing with marriage, divorce, property, education, and enfranchisment. Ironically, Turkish women were given the vote years *before* their Swiss sisters! Although women can vote and stand for office, there has been a steady decline in the number and the enthusiam since the beginning of the Republic, which suggests, to me, that something else continues to interfere with these efforts. Clearly, one part of the problem has to do with the lack of theorization and implementation of what is necessary to make women's full participation possible, for example, education and day care. But another part of the problem is related to the way the imagery and symbolic associations of the nation and citizenship continue to undermine the democratic intentions. As Nükhet Sirman noted: "Representation thus becomes primarily a gender specific relationship: it is men, and not just any men but household heads, who by virtue of their position become representatives and women, [who become] the represented, *par excellence*" (1990:45).

Women do not represent, they are what is represented. Perhaps this was behind the statement I heard Kenan Evren make on television a few months after the 1980 coup: "Turkey is a nation of men, not women." He meant to express the feeling that the virility of the nation had been restored (why virility?); but he also implied that men defend as well as represent the Motherland. His choice of words perpetuates the indigenous symbolism, as it also reinforces traditional meanings of gender. This observation opens theoretical space to think about the differences between symbolization and representation, often held to be the same. In many countries, not just Turkey, *women may symbolize the nation, but men represent it.*

Women's symbolic function operates in a number of ways. In common speech, the nation is often referred to as "she." She is also often fashioned into a generalized statue to embody and display the special virtues and honor of a particular nation, for example, France, America, or Germany (cf. Mosse 1985).[24]

Language Reform

Another important reform had to do with language. The language of the Ottoman court was Osmanlıcı. It was written in Arabic script and many of the words and expressions, as well as some of the flowery sentence structures, were considered foreign. Atatürk wanted to purge the language, as he had the land, of foreign influences that he felt were defiling and polluting the *anadil,* the mother tongue. While the *anadil* was the generalized medium of expression, it was the sayings of the fathers, *atasöz,* that gave shape and distinctiveness to it.

In his desire to foster literacy among the people, Atatürk ordered that Turkish be written in Latin letters, which were able to represent the vowel harmony of Turkish far better than Arabic. At the same time, however, Turkish was no longer written in God's script but in that of the infidels. This shift was felt by some religious people as a terrible affront, and even today it continues to irritate some of them.

The changes have been enormous; indeed, Osmanlıcı is about as different from modern Turkish as Chaucerian English is from contemporary English (Henze 1982:108). But the change has occurred within sixty years and is an ongoing process. Every year, the Turkish Language Association creates new words from Turkish roots and publishes them; these new words are referred to as Öztürkçe (real, true Turkish). Turkish national identity, therefore, can hardly be seen as based on linguistic or scriptual *continuity,* as Anderson supposes. Instead, the people were given a new identity and a new language with which to express it, but they were also cut off from their past. While nationalism may have been fostered in the late nineteenth century by the emergence of several Turkish (as opposed to Ottoman) language newspapers, the language was still written in Arabic script and was, of course, incomprehensible to all but the educated elite. Anderson bemoans the fate of the various Turkic-speaking peoples of Turkey, Iran, Iraq, and the USSR. He assumes that this "family of spoken languages [was] once everywhere assemblable, thus *comprehensible,* within an Arabic orthography" (1983:48) (emphasis added) and thus that Atatürk destroyed their unity when he imposed compulsory romanization. What Anderson fails to note is that these languages were incomprehensible to the majority of the people and that Atatürk's language reform made literacy attainable for them. Furthermore, the vernacular Turkish that Atatürk wished to emphasize was far more comprehensible to the far-flung Turkic speaking peoples than was the artificial creation, Osmanlıcı.

Additionally, Anderson never addresses, nor considers, the gendered components of language—that the transnational use of Arabic orthography, like Latin of an earlier time, was accessible only to educated men (Ong 1982). Nor does he consider the fact that even when the vernacular became the standard written language, women were not automatically educated to read, and that gender disparity in literacy continues today.

Atatürk's belief that national identity was a matter of language and culture also, of course, posed problems for groups who persisted in their own ethnic and/or religious definition of nationality. The familial rhetoric undergirding the construction of Turkish nationalism and the nation-state is pervasive and tends to undermine the democratic intentions. It is easier to see how it obscures the interests of the various ethnic groups who did not accept Atatürk's inclusive notion of nationality and descent and persisted in their own ethnic and/or religious definition of nationality. It is usually much more difficult to see that *the differential implications for men and women are not natural.*

Gendered Nation

Although the imagery I have been discussing is specific to Turkey, much of it has a familiar ring. It suggests, I believe, that the very conception of the nation and the discourse of nationalism is itself an inherently gendered discourse. Because of their symbolic association with land, women are, in a sense, the ground over which national identity is played out. This becomes quite clear in war and was commented upon during the recent Gulf War, where all sides used the language of penetration, attack, "scoring," and conquest that clearly drew upon notions not so much of heterosexual intercourse but more significantly of rape.[25] In a less explicit way, national identity is also played out in the civilian context of national sport (cf. Appadurai 1990; Archeti 1991; Maurer 1992), the national "ground" in this case having shrunk to the size of the playing field. Yet the scholars who have begun to explore this phenomenon have rarely attended to the gender implications, namely that is is still men who represent the nation on this field and "fight" for its honor.

The discourse of nationalism is not only a gendered discourse, it has been historically, at least, also a western discourse. "The roots of nationalism spring from the same soil as Western civilization" says Hans Kohn (1960:41). While the nation-state is a modern political formation associated with events of the American and French Revolutions, its conception goes back to ancient Greek and especially Hebrew culture: "Three essential traits of modern nationalism originated with the Hebrews: the idea of the chosen people, the emphasis on a common stock of memory of the past and of hopes for the future, and finally national messianism" (ibid:41.)[26] He is hardly the first or the only person to have called attention to this. In a series of lectures given at Harvard in 1987 and published in *God Land: Reflections on Religion and Nationalism,* Conor Cruise O'Brien noted:

> Nationalism, as a collective emotional force in our culture, makes its first appearance, with explosive impact, in the Hebrew Bible. And nationalism, at this stage, is altogether indistinguishable from religion; the two are one and the same thing. God chose a particular people and promised them a particular land. (1988:2)

When nationalism and religion coalesce, there is always a danger of deifying the nation, making it almost a sacred entity. Although Atatürk wished to subsume Islam under the state, the nation-state did take on some of the aura of the sacred. In addition to being called Ata, he was also called the "Gazi," a word that usually referred to a "defender of the faith"; clearly in this context the meanings were transferred to the "sacred" nation. The first sentence of the new constitution justifies the military intervention of 1980 because of the threat to "the integrity of the eternal Turkish nation and motherland and the existence of the *sacred* Turkish state" (Dodd 1990:154) (emphasis added).

O'Brien's focus was religion and nationality; yet implicit in the idea of "one people" is the element that is the focus of David Schneider's paper, namely kinship. Schneider notes that "in the tradition of Judaism nation, state, and kinship group are one" (1977:69). At the same time, neither Schneider, Kohn, nor O'Brien consider the way the age-old but pervasive imagery of procreation and gender is incorporated into the discourse of nationalism and is thus intimately involved with the very conception of the nation.

The words nation, native, natal, and nature are all derived from the Latin roots for birth or being born, as Vico, an Italian philosopher, pointed out long ago. He talked about the way a "nation is etymologically a birth or a being born and hence a race, a kin or kind having a common origin or more loosely a common language and other institutions" (1986:xx). But he was even more specific: nations developed out of Chaos which he "defined as the confusion of human *seeds* in the state of the infamous promiscuity of women" (Vico 1986:260) (emphasis added). Certainty of offspring was thought to bring Order out of Chaos and civil society out of barbarism. Like Aristotle before him and Engels after him, Vico saw the beginnings of civil society as coincident with the so-called discovery of paternity, which "just naturally" demanded the control of women and the institution of heterosexual and monogamous (for the woman) marriage so that the paternity and legitimacy of children could be established.

Paternity was taken as a natural fact rather than as a cultural construction within a particular theory of procreation. It is not, of course, the same theory we hold today, in which, at the very least, "seed" would have to be imagined as the *combined* entity created from the contribution of both male and female. But in the earlier idea, the father as contributor of "seed" was imagined as the "author" of the children; because of that authority, he became the ruler in the family; and this, according to Vico, was felt to be not just a reflection of nature but also a reflection of the Divine order (Vico 1986:420) as it is inscribed in the Bible. In other words, the "natural" and the "divine" converged in this most important example of naturalizing power.

The interrelation between kinship, nationality, and religion has been integral since the beginning when God promised Abraham: "I will make of thee a great nation and give to you and your seed all the land of your wandering"[27]—the land flowing with milk and honey; images often used to symbolize woman in western European and other nations influenced by Judaism, Christianity, and Islam. Kinship, nationality, and religion are interrelated, but the means of their integration is a specific theory of procreation in which specific definitions of gender are absolutely central.

Notes

This paper has been through several versions. An abbreviated version was first presented in March 1991 at the meetings of the American Ethnological Society in Charleston, NC, on an invited panel on "Nationalism and Gender." It was later presented at a workshop on "Gender, Islam and Democratization" at UCLA in January 1992, and in February 1992 to a faculty seminar on "The State and the Construction of Citizenship" at the University of California, San Diego. Most recently, a version was presented at the AAA, November 1992 in an Invited Session in honor of David Schneider. Over time, a number of people have offered helpful comments, some of which I hope have found their way into this version.

1. See especially *Politics*. However, the theoretical basis for his ideas about the "natural" gender roles can be found in *Generation of Animals*. See also Locke's *Two Treatises on*

Government, Filmer's *Patriarcha*, and Pateman's *The Sexual Contract* for an excellent discussion of the gender assumptions in political theory about the family.

2. David Schneider (1965, 1968, 1972, 1984) has been in the vanguard of showing how anthropological concepts and theory about kinship have derived from and reinforce western notions of kinship. Picking up from there, Sylvia Yanagisako and Jane Collier (1987) have shown how kinship theory incorporates notions of gender and that they are both part of the same system. My own work (Delaney 1986, 1991) shows how our notions of kinship and gender are not just about biology but incorporate cosmological or religious ideas as well.

3. This notion is not unique to Turkey. Engels reminds us that the very word family derives from the Latin *famulus*, which "means a household slave and *familia* signifies the totality of slaves belonging to one individual." It came to "describe a new social organism; the head of which had under him wife and children and a number of slaves, under Roman paternal power, with power of life and death over them all" (Engels 1972: 68).

4. See especially Pateman (1988), Stolcke (n.d.), and Yuval-Davis (1987). The male scholars of nationalism seem to assume a generic individual without recognition that the generic image is male.

5. From my own observations and those of other scholars of Turkey (cf. Jenny White 1994; Nükhet Sirman 1990), this attitude of dependence is still very much a part of Turkish culture. For example, in the village she studied, Sirman notes: "the dominant image of the state is that of a paternalistic provider" (24) and "The state, *devlet*, is in the same structural position to the villagers as a father is to his sons" (44).

6. In the summer of 1992, I revisited the village I had lived and worked in from 1980 to 1982 and found to my surprise that the daily television news included a map and weather reports from towns such as Alma Ata and Tashkent—places the villagers had previously little knowledge of or interest in. Bringing them into the homes by way of television seemed to be a way of bringing them closer, into the extended Turkish family.

7. Despite the fact that *vatan* is the Turkish form of *watan* (an Arabic word), which I have been told does mean "fatherland," it does not necessarily follow that it will have that meaning in Turkish. Similarly, the fact that some peoples do use "fatherland" or *patrie* rather than "motherland" does not mean that the labels are interchangeable; they convey different images and emphasize different qualities. And even in those countries which use "fatherland," I believe that the land as a physical entity is still imagined symbolically as female. "Fatherland" may have more to do with spiritual identity than with material substance.

8. Redressing this bias, several recent anthropological works have drawn attention to the political importance of poetry, especially in a Middle Eastern context. See Abu-Lughod (1986), Caton (1990).

9. *Turkey in Travail: The Birth of a New Nation* (Armstrong 1925); *Turkey Reborn* (Bigelow 1941). *The Rebirth of a Nation* (Kinross 1964); *Turkey: Rebirth of a Nation* (Ahmed 1961); *Turkey—Decadence and Rebirth* (Paneth 1943); *The Rebirth of Turkey* (Price 1923). No doubt there are others.

10. See Bacon (1964), MacCormack and Strathern (1980) and Easlea (1983); and from a different culture an alternative view, Strathern's "No Nature, No Culture" (1980).

11. It was the subject of my anthropological research in Turkey from 9/79–7/82, twenty months of which were spent in an Anatolian village. The results of that work have been published in a number of articles and in *The Seed and the Soil: Gender and Cosmology in Turkish Village Society* (1991).

12. Elijah Muhammed is quoted in the recent film, *Malcolm X*, and David Koresh's statements were cited in numerous newspapers, news magazines, and on television. Both men used this rhetoric as the rationale for legitimizing their taking of many girls and women as "wives." The notion that the identity of a child is given by the man also became clear in the rape of Bosnian Muslim women, who said they did not want to have a "Serbian" baby. The rape might have been reason enough not to want the child; their statement, however, reinforces the logic that men give identity.

13. These ideas have been presented in greater detail in Delaney (1986, 1991).

14. Wives and concubines of the Sultan (and other elite Ottomans) often came from different racial and ethnic groups and different areas of the world, and Sultans too were ethnically mixed. In addition, the elite Janissary Guard was composed of men taken as boys from Christian families and adopted by the court. They were provided with the best food and clothes and brought up and educated along with the Sultan's sons.

15. Levent Soysal (n.d.) in "The Origins of the Ottoman Empire: Narratives of (Dis)Continuity" argues that modern histories are constructed around a number of different and even mutually exclusive origin stories. In stressing the Ottomans and Islam, one must naturally suppress Turks and pre-Islamic origins; yet in another scenario, the reemergence of the Turks is equated with the authenticity of pre-Islamic practices.

16. The associations are well known among Turkish men, since all are familiar with "duelling rhymes"—taunts in which one man can humiliate another by sexual slurs against his mother (Dundes, Leach, and Özkök 1972). Clearly, the use of such imagery on a grand scale touched a sensitive nerve.

17. In one of the most mismatched battles in the history of war, the tattered "nationalist" army defeated the Allied powers. An especially interesting article is that by Gawrych (1988). But see also Kinross (1965); B. Lewis (1968); and Volkan and Itzkowitz (1984).

18. It is not surprising that during the turbulent decade of the 1970s, when the country was again seen as divided against itself and in danger of splitting apart, these familial images were again evoked. After the period of military rule, it was a political coup on the part of Türgüt Ozal and his supporters to use the comforting image of *Anavatan* as the name of the party. Despite predictions to the contrary, it won by an overwhelming majority.

19. What they refer to by this term is the conflict about the basis of the nation, especially secularism and democracy, both principles advocated by Atatürk. But what happens, they ask, when the will of the people (the democratic principle) acts against the principle of secularism in an effort to reestablish Islam?

20. Despite universalistic claims of citizenship, I would agree with Pateman (1988) and Stolcke (n.d.) that women in a number of European nations do not really have a nationality of their own; it comes from descent and marriage, that is, a woman's nationality follows that of her father or her husband. Nor can she pass her own nationality down to her children except in the case of illegitimacy. While nationality laws are concerned with the control of reproduction, that is, who shall reproduce the nation, they also incorporate and restate much older conceptions of gender.

21. Nira Yuval-Davis (1987) discusses the Jewish notion that it is the mother who bestows nationality—that is, only the child of a Jewish mother is a Jew. She states that this practice came about among a persecuted minority population that was often subject to pogroms and rape. She goes on to say that it does not in any way diminish the importance of paternity. The child takes the name of the father, and all laws pertaining to family matters of marriage, divorce, child support, legitimacy are in the hands of Orthodox religious leaders, all male. She also discusses the way nationalist policies to "increase" the nation often conscript women into reproductive labor.

22. At the same time, Meeker draws attention to the fact that such a move eclipsed notions of descent and cultural heritage of other groups in the Empire.

23. Today, when there is resistance against the West, it is women who are called upon to display loyalty to Turkey and to Islam—by becoming covered. Again, I would say they are pawns (see Olson 1985; Mandel 1989; Delaney 1994).

24. At the same time, real women in Turkey must also often display national symbols on or with their bodies, for example by female circumcision or by the less violent form of female enclosure, namely veiling.

25. G. Lakoff (1990–91) gave a talk about the metaphors of war at Stanford during the Gulf War; he had also circulated a paper on that topic over the computer networks. I, too, spoke about the sexual metaphors of war during the crisis.

26. Conor Cruise O'Brien (1988), also notes the way in which these elements figured in conceptions of the nation among Americans, French, and Germans, and I would add, Zionists. The image of "the promised land" and the notion of "manifest destiny" of the Americans draw heavily upon biblical stories.

27. This is a paraphrase of Gen. 17:2–8, but similar notions occur in numerous passages in Genesis (12:2–3; 14:14–16; 15:5, 18; 18:18; 22:17–18).

References

Abu-Lughod, L. 1986. *Veiled Sentiments*. Berkeley: Univ. of California Press.

Ahmad, F. 1977. *The Turkish Experiment in Democracy, 1950–1975*. Boulder, CO: Westview.

Ahmed, G. 1961. *Turkey: Rebirth of a Nation*. Karachi, Pakistan: Ma Aref.

Anderson, B. 1983. *Imagined Communities: Reflections on the Origin and Spread of Nationalism*. London: Verso.

Appadurai, A. 1990. "Nations and Passions." Talk given in October to Dept. of Anthropology at Stanford University, Stanford, California.

Archeti, E. 1991. "Masculinity and Soccer: The Formation of National Identity in Argentia," paper presented at the AES meetings.

Aristotle. 1932. *Politics*. Loeb Classics. Cambridge, MA: Harvard Univ. Press.

Aristotle. 1942. *Generation of Animals*. Loeb Classics Cambridge, MA: Harvard Univ. Press.

Armstrong, H. 1925. *Turkey in Travail: The Birth of a New Nation*. London: John Lane.

Bacon, F. 1964. "The Masculine Birth of Time or the Great Instauration of the Dominion of Man Over the Universe." In *The Philosophy of Francis Bacon,* edited by Benjamin Farrington, 61–72. Chicago: Univ. of Chicago Press.

Basgöz, I. 1978. "Folklore Studies and Nationalism in Turkey." In *Folklore, Nationalism and Politics*, edited by Felix J. Oinas, 123–37. Columbia, OH: Slavica.

Bhabha, H., ed. 1990. *Nation and Narration*. New York: Routledge.

Bigelow, R., ed. 1941. *Turkey Reborn*. Scotch Plains, NJ: Flanders Hall.

Caton, S. 1990. *Peaks of Yemen I Summon: Poetry as Cultural Practice in a North Yemeni Tribe*. Berkeley: Univ. of California Press.

Delaney, C. 1986. "The Meaning of Paternity and the Virgin Birth Debate." *Man* 21(3): 494–513.

———. 1991. *The Seed and the Soil: Gender and Cosmology in Turkish Village Society.* Berkeley: Univ. of California Press.

———. 1994. "Untangling the Meaning of Hair in Turkish Society." *Anthropological Quarterly* 67(4).

Dodd, C. H. 1990. *The Crisis of Turkish Democracy.* 2d ed. Cambridge, UK: Eothen.

Dumont, Paul. 1984. "The Origins of Kemalist Ideology." In *Atatürk and the Modernization of Turkey,* edited by Jacob M. Landau. Boulder, CO: Westview.

Dundes, A., Leach, J., and B. Özkök. 1972. "The Strategy of Turkish Duelling Rhymes." In *Directions in Sociolinguistics,* edited by J. Gumperz and Dell Hymes, 130–60. New York: Holt, Rinehart and Winston.

Easlea, B. 1983. *Fathering the Unthinkable: Masculinity, Scientists and the Nuclear Arms Race.* London: Pluto.

Eickelman, D. 1978. "The Art of Memory: Islamic Education and Its Social Reproduction." *Comparative Studies in Society and History* 20(4): 485–516.

Engels, F. Zurich: 1884. 1972. *The Origin of the Family, Private Property and the State.* Reprint, New York: Pathfinder.

Erol, S. 1991. "Güntekin's *Çalıkuşu:* A Search for Personal and National Identity." *The Turkish Studies Association Bulletin* 15(1): 65–82.

Filmer, Sir R. 1887. *Patriarcha; or, the Natural Power of Kings.* Included with J. Locke's *Two Treatises on Civil Government.* London: George Routledge.

Gawrych, G. 1988. "Kemal Atatürk's Politico-Military Strategy in the Turkish War of Independence, 1919–22." *Journal of Strategic Studies* 11(3): 318–41.

Gellner, E. 1983. *Nations and Nationalism.* Ithaca, NY: Cornell Univ. Press.

Gökalp, Z. 1968 *The Principles of Turkish.* Translated from the Turkish by R. Devereux. Leiden: E. J. Brill.

Güntekin, R. N. 1949. *The Autobiography of a Turkish Girl.* Translated from the Turkish by Wyndham Deeds. London: Allen and Unwin.

Helmreich, S. 1992. "Kinship, Nation, and Paul Gilroy's Concept of Diaspora." *Diaspora* 2(2): 243–249.

Henze, P. 1982. "Turkey: On the Rebound." *The Wilson Quarterly* 6(5): 108–35.

Heyd, Uriel. (1950) *Foundations of Turkish Nationalism.* London: Luzac.

Hobsbawn, E. J. 1990. *Nations and Nationalism Since 1780.* Cambridge, UK: Cambridge Univ. Press.

Hotham, D. 1972. *The Turks.* London: John Murray.

Kandiyoti, D. 1989. "Women and the Turkish State: Political Actors or Symbolic Pawns." In *Woman-Nation-State,* edited by Yuval-Davis and F. Anthias, 126–149. London: Macmillan.

Kinross, L. 1965. *Atatürk: The Rebirth of a Nation.* London: Weidenfeld and Nicolson.

Kohn, H. 1960. "Hebrew and Greek Roots of Modern Nationalism." In *Conflict and Cooperation Among Nations,* edited by Ivo Duchacek, 39–41. New York: Holt, Rinehart and Winston.

Lakoff, G. 1990–91. "Metaphor and War." Paper circulated on computer networks, December 1990, and presented at Stanford University, January 1991, during the Gulf War.

Landau, Jacob M., ed. 1984. *Atatürk and the Modernization of Turkey.* Boulder, CO: Westview.

Lewis, B. 1968. *The Emergence of Modern Turkey.* Oxford: Oxford Univ. Press.

————. 1988. *The Political Language of Islam*. Chicago: Univ. of Chicago Press.

Lewis, G. L. 1984. "Atatürk's Language Reform as an Aspect of Modernization in the Republic of Turkey." In *Atatürk and the Modernization of Turkey*, edited by Jacob Landau, 295–320. Boulder, CO: Westview.

Locke, J. 1887. *Two Treatises on Civil Government*. London: George Routledge.

MacCormack, C., and M. Strathern, eds. 1980. *Nature, Culture and Gender*. Cambridge, UK: Cambridge Univ. Press.

Mandel, R. 1989. "Turkish Headscarves and the Foreigner Problem." *The New German Critique* 46:27–46.

Maurer, B. 1992. "Striking Out Gender: Getting to First Base with Bill Brown." *Public Culture* 4(2): 24.

Meeker, M. n.d. "Turkish National Identity and the Ancient Oghuz: How Basat Killed Tepegoz." (Personal copy on file with author.)

————. 1992. "The Dede Korkut Ethic." *International Journal of Middle East Studies* 24(3): 395–417.

Mosse, G. 1985. *Nationalism and Sexuality*. New York: Howard Fertig.

Nasr, S. H. 1985. [1966] *Ideals and Realities of Islam*. London: Allen and Unwin.

O'Brien, Conor C. 1988. *God Land: Reflections on Religion and Nationalism*. Cambridge, MA: Harvard Univ. Press.

Olson, Emelie 1985. "Muslim Identity and Secularism in Contemporary Turkey: The Headscarf Dispute." *Anthropo logical Quarterly* 58(4): 161–171.

Ong, W. 1982. *Orality and Literacy: The Technologizing of the Word*. London: Methuen.

Pateman, C. 1988. *The Sexual Contract*. Stanford, CA: Stanford Univ. Press.

Paneth, P. 1943. *Turkey—Decadence and Rebirth*. London: Alliance.

Price, C. 1923. *The Rebirth of Turkey*. New York: Seltzer.

Renan, E. 1990. "What Is a Nation?" In *Nation and Narration*, translated and edited by H. Bhabha, New York: Routledge. Given originally as a lecture, 1882.

Schick, I., and E. A. Tonak, eds. 1987. *Turkey in Transition*. Oxford: Oxford Univ. Press.

Schneider, D. 1965. "kinship and biology." in *Aspects of the Analysis of Family Structure*, edited by A. Coale, et al., 83–101. Princeton: Princeton Univ. Press.

————. 1968. *American Kinship: A Cultural Account*. Englewood Cliffs, NJ: Prentice-Hall.

————. 1977. "Kinship, Nationality and Religion: Toward a Definition of Kinship." In *Symbolic Anthropology*, edited by J. Dolgin, D. Kemnitzer, and D. Schneider, 63–71. New York: Columbia Univ. Press. Originally published in *Forms of Symbolic Action*, edited by Victor Turner (1969).

————. 1972. "What Is Kinship All About?" In *Kinship Studies in the Morgan Centennial Year*, editing by P. Reining, 32–63. Washington, DC: Anthropological Society of Washington.

————. 1984. *A Critique of the Study of Kinship*. Ann Arbor: Univ. of Michigan Press.

Şeni, Nora. 1984. "Ville Ottoman et Representation du corps Feminin." *Les Temps Modernes* 456–457 (July–August): 65–95.

Sirman, N. 1989. "Feminism in Turkey: A Short History." *New Perspectives in Turkey* 3(1): 1–34.

————. 1990. "State, Village and Gender in Western Turkey." In *Turkish State, Turkish Society*, edited by Andrew Finkel and Nu--aukhet Sirman, 21–51. London: Routledge.

Soysal, L. n.d. "Origins of the Ottoman Empire: Narratives of (Dis) Continuity." (Unpublished paper on file with author.)

Stolcke, V. n.d. "The Individual between Culture and Nature: The Nature of Nationality." (Personal copy on file with author.)

Strathern, M. 1980. "No Nature, No Culture." In *Nature, Culture and Gender,* edited by C. MacCormack and M. Strathern, 174–222. Cambridge, UK: Cambridge Univ. Press.

Tachau, F. 1984. "The Political Culture of Kemalist Turkey." In *Atatürk and the Modernization of Turkey,* edited by J. Landau, 57–76. Boulder, CO: Westview.

Taşkiran, T. 1976. *Women in Turkey.* Istanbul: Redhouse.

Toprak, B. 1981. *Islam and Political Development: Turkey.* Leiden: E. J. Brill.

Vico, G. 1986. *The New Science of Giambattista Vico.* Translated from the Italian by Bergin and M. Fisch. Naples: 1744. Ithaca, NY: Cornell Univ. Press.

Volkan, V. D., and N. Itzkowitz. 1984. *The Immortal Atatürk: A Psychobiography.* Chicago: Univ. of Chicago Press.

White, J. 1994. *Money Makes Us Relatives: Women's Labor in Urban Turkey.* Austin, TX: Univ. of Texas Press.

Yanagisako, S., and J. Collier, eds. 1987. *Gender and Kinship: Essays toward a Unified Analysis.* Stanford, CA: Stanford Univ. Press.

Yerasimos, S. 1987. "The Monoparty Period." In *Turkey in Transition,* edited by I. Schick and A. Tonak, 66–100. Oxford: Oxford Univ. Press.

Yuval-Davis, N. 1987. "The Jewish Collectivity and National Reproduction in Israel." In *Women in the Middle East,* 60–98. London: Zed Books.

8

Classification Systems Revisited: Kinship, Caste, Race, and Nationality as the Flow of Blood and the Spread of Rights

Brackette F. Williams

With the demise of "kinship" as an autonomous analytic unit, despite interests in ethnobotany and other such taxonomies, analyses of classificatory systems were also largely relegated to the backwaters of the disciplines. Few discussions of the now central concern with ethnic boundary constructions, "ethnogenesis," and other category qua group-generating processes in contemporary nation-building proceed without comment on what Charles Keyes (1981) has called the "aura of descent" that surrounds lay and professional conceptions of ethnic identity and its links to culture and territory. Nonetheless, too few conscientious efforts are made to examine the continuities between cultural constructions of kinship and those of other categorical distinctions such as race, nation, and caste.

Yet when social classification meets hierarchy, their union is made possible by myths that fold social space back on itself to naturalize power differences that are legitimated in particular representations of the historicity of kin substance. The apex of the classification system does not simply sit atop the social order. Classification of social types are situated in an ideology of power and reproductive distribution which must be all-inclusive. The apex as source, and persons it categorizes, must be the product of cultural reckonings according to which all substance—pure and impure, high and low—originate. It is of this process for the production and recognition of a unitary substance that myths of category, group, and family origins seek to remind us when they proclaim that the lowly of a social order are products of those of the highest category of that order.

Smith (1988) building on the work of Alexander (1977), who identifies myths of interracial origins to be charters for the middle class in Jamaica, notes that, in defining the apex of family genealogies, these myths set the terms for the interpenetration of race, class, and the status of kin substance in Jamaica.

It is interesting that the origin myth . . . does not say that the child takes the slave status of the mother, though historically that was the legal position. It discusses status in two separate ways related to two separate cultural domains. The father decides, according to the myth, to educate his children and arrange for their manumission, and he does this out of a sentiment and affection. They become the Free People of Colour. In the kinship domain the diffuse, enduring solidarity appropriate to those sharing a common blood impels the father to act in this way. However, class separates the father from his mistress and her children, decrees that the union is non-legal, and the children illegitimate. Racially, the children are in the middle in terms of *both substance and status*. . . . Ideologically, the existence of the middle class depends on these unions. (Smith 1988:90) (emphasis added)

Huggins invokes this same process to comment on the relation between "truth" and "myth" in the story of when Sally Hemings met Thomas Jefferson:

The desire to merge national and racial identity into a single myth explains the compelling persistence of the story of Sally Hemings—the slave and servant of Thomas Jefferson who, the story goes, bore his children. . . .

Why the fuss? Sally Hemings was certainly not the first or the only black woman to have been so used by a master. It is Thomas Jefferson who makes this story.

Jefferson was a "founding father" of the nation, and it is rumored that he sired children by an African-American woman, his slave. It does not matter whether the story is *actually* true. It is *symbolically* true and will, as a result, never be fully discredited for those of either side. Like other legitimizing myths the Sally Hemings story ties a people to the founding of the nation, reinforcing birth-right claims. (1990:xlvii)

Likewise, as Tambiah has noted for the union of high and low varna, "there is a method to the madness" (1975:208) that afflicts those who would proclaim themselves the categoric, group, or individual outcome of a structural illegitimacy.

The consequence of this mythical derivation of castes propounded by Brahmans is that a number of castes, many of them indeed beyond the pale, can and do relate their mythical origins to a Brahmanical ancestor male or female who was degraded. . . . This mythical charter which the impure use to bolster their claims also implicitly and tacitly reinforces the fact that the Brahmans are—because they are the point of reference—the fountainhead of purity and the apex of the pyramid (Tambiah 1975:208).

In the general production of a social order, this melding of high and low substances, when mediated through kinship, simultaneously locates and legitimates a source—an apex—of a system of classification for a social order to which all can lay claim. To understand how this is possible requires that we return to kinship studies and the issue of how peoples produce the nature out of which they, as individuals, families, and categoric groupings, are reproduced.

This essay returns to Marshall (1977) and Wagner (1977) and their efforts to develop an approach to kinship that challenges the boundary between nature and nurture. The aim is to utilize their conclusions as a context for examining Schneider's (1977) discussion of kinship and nationality in U.S. culture, in contrast to Cox's (1948) critique of the caste school of race relations, and in relation to particular aspects of Dumont's (1970) and Tambiah's (1975) work on issues of categoric boundaries, pollution, and the production of caste in India. Tambiah, I will argue, provides analytic procedures that suggest the utility of considering the common ideological precepts that permit the production and ranking of persons of mixed descent in caste-stratified and racially divided societies. The concern is to situate these arguments in relation to contemporary efforts to understand the symbolism of mixed "substance" in the production of "peoples," "races," and "nations" as suggested by scholarship on intermarriage and identity formation among persons produced of mixed unions in the United States. The overall objectives are to contribute to an analysis of how systems of classification might be understood in relation to "socially recognized" race as an aspect of the production of "nations" and national cultures. Special attention will be given to how these concepts and processes move people to resources and resources to people as the means by which power differentials are naturalized and legitimated.

Following a summary of Cox's cautionary critique of the limits of race and caste analogies,[1] we will turn, first, to some aspects of Dumont's discussion of caste, the hierarchicalized civility embodied in caste types, and the problem of moral degeneracy ideologically presumed to flow from improper mixing of category types. We will then be positioned to benefit from Tambiah's insights on the interpenetration of *hierarchy* and *key* as alternative modes of classification, which makes possible the recognition and ordering of categories produced through mixed unions. Our final concern is to return to U.S. society, focusing on Schneider's analysis of kinship and nationality, to suggest how a synthesis of these approaches to kinship and caste can inform an analysis of the interpenetration of U.S. kinship and nationalist ideologies in the socialization of nature and the naturalization of power. In the end, the essay suggests that it is the interpenetration of social ideologies of power and classification that allows us to make cultural sense of myths of origins and shared substance. Attention to interpenetration of ideologies allows us to examine how the naturalization of power differentials operates in the production of kinship, ethnicity, and class-stratified races and castes in contemporary nation-building.

Nurturing a Socialized Nature: A Trukese Love Story

In "The Nature of Nurture," Marshall directs our attention to the dialectical construction of nature by nurture. Based on his work among the Trukese of Micronesia, he advocates a reexamination of western-derived assumptions that presume kinship and friendship to be "necessarily separate, mutually exclusive domains" (Marshall 1977:623), as in you can pick your friends but you cannot pick your kin. Marshall and other scholars recognized that, to the extent that the creation of kinship out of biological and legal "facts" was recognized to be a culturally constructed act, it was also understood that it was not limited to the consanguineal and affinal features of such constructions. The question was what else should be included in a definition of kinship. How could anthropologists determine analytically what kinship was "about"? How could the particulars of the cultural construction of relations between "biology" and "law" within a society be approached in such a manner that cross-cultural comparison, at the heart of the anthropological enterprise, would remain possible?

Marshall argues for an analytic approach to interpersonal relationships that would allow anthropologists to view *all* connections among persons within a single framework and, thus, to learn what unifies or differentiates the various types of connections. To make such an approach possible, he suggests, requires a formulation of synthetic connections among several strands of anthropological inquiry: analyses of fictive and ritual kinships, treatments of the systems of symbols that represent the meaning of kinship among different people, and analyses of the meaning and uses of friendship in social processes of adaptation within or between groups.

Marshall opts for the expression "created kinship" to describe important types of social relationships in Greater Trukese Society (GTS), while avoiding the a priori assumptions that those not based solely on consanguinity and affinity are "fictive" or "ritual," rather than "real," kinship. He uses created kinship to cover three types of relationships—clientship, *määräär* ties, and adoptions—that differentially employ the "facts" of consanguinity and affinity in relation to other criteria of bonding and commitment. In GTS, he notes, clientship allows a lineage to count among its members persons who are neither born to the lineage members nor adopted by them as children. The creation of clients, motivated by political and economic expedience, allows GTS lineages to recruit new members and to "incorporate outsiders into a community on a permanent basis" when such is useful "to form or strengthen intercommunity and interisland alliances" (Marshall 1977:645).

Unlike the client ties, the *määräär* relationship is presumed to be based on a link of either consanguinity or affinity as evidenced by a shared clan name, although the actual link to a common ancestry is no longer traceable. Hence, the presumption of ancestral linkage is a necessary but not sufficient criterion for any particular *määräär* tie. The ties are actually established on the basis of mutual interests and consent by the lineage members who desire the relationship. In adoptions, consanguineal ties are a sufficient but not necessary criterion of choice and motivation in that, statistically, adoptive parents are most frequently consanguineally related to the children they adopt, even though children known to be unrelated by this criterion also may be adopted.

Overall, the process of kin creation in GTS belies the possibility of a clear-cut distinction between ties of consanguinity and affinity—shared genealogy—and those based on other criteria of relatedness. First,

> once established for one or two generations, clientship usually alters clan membership, the application of incest and exogamy rules . . . , and matters of inheritance. Clientship provides a major vehicle for moving people to resources and resources to people in GTS. (Marshall 1977:644).

Second, both *määräär* ties and adoption serve as mechanisms to convert distant kin into close kin, but do so differently; adoption, like clientship, can also convert nonkin into kin (645). Therefore, third, "presuming such methods for creating kin to have existed for many generations, we see that over time a great many 'fictions' have become 'facts' " (646). And, finally, interest in the identification of persons as kin is directly related to interest in creating mechanisms to socialize nature for the purpose of producing the synchronic and diachronic diffuse, enduring patterns of solidarity that are necessary or useful in social action. The motivation to create kin directs the selection of criteria above and beyond shared physical substance as well as what meaning-in-action[2] is given to "facts" of shared physical substance.

On these issues, Marshall concludes that Trukese do not simply overlook or lack knowledge of the unsocialized facts of nature, but rather shape and transform these in conjunction with particular and general motivations for social action: to move people to resources and resources to people. Consequently, for the Trukese, kin are defined in relation to the sharing of land, food, labor, residence, and support. Shared genetic substance is important but does not necessarily determine "who chooses to acknowledge each other as kin" (Marshall 1977:651). Instead in the "Trukese view, those who nurture one another through acts of sharing *validate* their natural [potential] kinship or become created kinsmen as a consequence of these nurturant acts" (651). It follows that those who do not maintain the proper pattern of sharing "*may* cease to recognize each other as kin" (651). The genetics of kin affiliation is socialized by the recognition and the motivation to recognize affiliation.

The motivation to move people or resources precedes the motivation to define kin, to move distant kin closer, and to move nonkin into close or distant-kin categories. Hence, people are prior to the consequences these moves have for the overall system of social relationships. What kinship is about is people trying to figure out how to create, and what to make of, shared substance as one criterion among criteria on the basis of which they can move goods, services, and obligations across the social order in a manner that is consistent with their individual or group goals and motivations within that order. Ideologically and in practice, the consequence is a Trukese kinship system constituted of shared biogenetic substance mediated by "shared biography and shared understandings about mutually created bonds" (Marshall 1977:656). The term *ttong* glosses this interpenetration of biology and biography and indicates the code for conduct—the pattern of care and nurturance—available to those who would "prove their kinship" (657).

The process of creating kin cannot then be seen as influencing the kin networks only of those persons actively engaged in such creations at a particular moment in time. Because these actions are embedded in the historicity of the system, "the nature of nurture determines the quality of interpersonal relationships and the span and effectiveness of everyone's kinship universe" (Marshall 1977:652). Hence, while we might be surprised to find a human group that makes no use of the criteria they can generate out of a theory of procreation, we ought not to be surprised that these criteria are likely to be insufficient for the production of complex and overlapping forms of sociality necessary to the distribution of goods, services, and obligations. Nonetheless, whatever the theory of procreation by which physical substance is made and exchanged, once it is available for socialization, physical substance can be made either a necessary or a sufficient criterion with which to *begin* the process of creating the requisite range and types of intensive social relationships.

Under these conditions, to say that the meanings and implications of the "facts" of consanguinity are culturally constructed, rather than biologically given in a western-derived sense, is also to say that they are historically constituted. Any kinship system displaying these characteristics provides a social representation of the historicity of relationship formation and transformation. Kinship is about the "facts" of consanguinity and affinity, but these "facts" are not solely about the formation of a kinship system. They are representations of the effective aspects of the historical processes by which sociality (individual and group) has been naturalized in conjunction with how "natural" connections of substance (i.e., blood/shared biogenetic substance) have been socialized. In GTS no law, customary or formal, declares that blood, as a shared biogenetic substance, is made solely by sexual intercourse. Consequently, we need not be surprised that same-sex as well as cross-sex partners can make and distribute, within the system of intensive social relationships, the proper substance of kinship: socialized nature and naturalized culture as a code for conduct built around the criteria for recognizing this socialized nature.

Marshall demonstrates this dialectic of mutual construction in his analysis of friendship relations among the Trukese. Beginning with the fact that, within GTS views of shared substance, the same-sex sibling bond is considered to be the closest and strongest tie in the social order of relationships, he notes that "Trukese can create siblings in a manner *analogous* to the other categories of created kin" (Marshall 1977:646) (emphasis added). Distinguishing created siblings from adopted siblings (reserving the latter term for siblingships created when persons who are already parents adopt additional children), he argues that the character of the relationship between created siblings satisfies most of the criteria anthropologists use to define friendship. That is to say, a created siblingship is an intimate, voluntary, dyadic tie that, based on mutual consent, is mutable and may be of brief duration, though it may also last a lifetime.

Challenging the tendency in anthropology to treat kinship and friendship as separate, mutually exclusive domains, Marshall notes that "Trukese use a single generic term to talk about [friendship created on the idiom of siblingship]: *pwiipwi*, a reduplicated form of the root *pwii-*, which means 'same-sex sibling' when coupled with suffixed possessive pronouns" (1977:647). Trukese distribute these types of relationships across four categories: (1) *pwiipwi chëk* (for those in one's own descent line or lineage), (2) *pwiipwi winisam* (for codescendants of men of a lineage), (3) *pwiipwi winipünü* (for "siblings by a spouse," persons who are married to *pwiipwi chëk*) and (4) *pwiipwin äsineey* (for "siblings by recognition") (647). With respect to this classification, Marshall offers the following qualifications:

> *Pwiipwi chëk* is regularly applied to one's siblings in the same subclan (*fütük*), that is, its use is not necessarily restricted to siblings in the same lineage or descent line. In addition, this term is occasionally used in reference to individuals of the same clan either on one's own island or from other island communities in GTS. Similarly, the term *pwiipwi winisam* is applied to all co-descendants of the men of a subclan, and occasionally this term may be extended to co-descendants of the men of a single clan when it becomes useful to do so. (647)

Moreover, the link between the process of creating close and distant kin and that of making friends is further strengthened by his discussion of *pwiipwin le sopwöne wa* ("siblings by recognition created of sharing an adverse situation or extreme hardship"), a term used on Namoluk as a synonym for *pwiipwin äsineey*. What these various types of siblings by recognition have in common is that they make the *character*, but not the (biogenetic) substance, of kinship the source of necessary criteria for the designation and maintenance of the social relationship. Marshall's analysis of *pwiipwi* relationships, combined with his treatment of clientship, *määräär* ties, and adoption, quite rightly leads him to conclude that what is at issue in the social process of relationship formation is how individuals, whatever their connections of biogenetic substance and links through law, move one another in and out of a category of "intensive interpersonal relationships" (Marshall 1977:654). Noting that, in general, social systems tend to contain "a limited set of relationships to which individuals feel a very strong commitment" (654), Marshall argues that in GTS these relationships are characterized by "intense commitment, complete trust, diffuse reciprocal obligations coupled with explicit rights and duties, intimacy, confidentiality, privateness, and regular, unquestioning mutual aid, support, and cooperation" (654–55). These features all reduce to the common denominator of "one central idea: *sharing*" (655).

From this standpoint, Marshall argues that for Trukese, "created sibling relationships are not only as good as natural ones, they are potentially better. . . . [A]n *improvement* on nature in the sense that they allow for the purest expression of 'brotherly love' in Trukese culture" (Marshall 1977:649). For this reason, although sharing and the criteria that define appropriate patterns of conduct so identified are at the center of processes for the production, transformation, and maintenance of such intensive interpersonal relationships, Marshall cautions us that the emphasis on sharing should not lead us back to an overemphasis on shared biogenetic substance. Instead,

> recognition of this [code for sharing and its symbols] directs our attention away from the traditional view where only one symbol of sharing—*shared genealogy*—has been taken as viable for a cross-cultural definition of kinship and turns our sights . . . toward sharing relationships as these are expressed *through a variety of culturally specific symbolic and interactive media* . . . [such that] what is common to kinship, then, is not shared physical substance alone, but the concept of sharing, itself. (655)

Thus, he argues further that as we examine these media of sharing we must aim to "distill . . . certain recurring themes (for example, blood, land) that combine in various ways to give us the complex skein we call kinship and friendship in human societies" (655).

Marshall's analysis allows us to understand that whereas "blood is thicker than water," some blood is thicker than other blood for having shared water and that still other blood can be culturally, rather than biologically, *made* and thickened by shared adversity. It also allows us to understand better that if by "you cannot pick your kin . . ." we mean that no individual has the unilateral ability to alter any given theory of procreation and its constitution of shared substance, then the statement is quite "factual." However, if by that statement we imply that the processes by which we socialize nature have no impact on the content of nature, then we commit a "fiction"; an understandable one, but a fiction nonetheless. If by such propositions we must distinguish these categories of natural (as opposed to created) kin in relating them back to one another, it would seem more accurate to say we can pick our friends precisely because we know how to create our kin. Selective interpretations of the interactional meanings (the meaning-in-action) of biological facts (i.e., prescribed amity or experienced enmity) allows us to recognize the necessary and sufficient criteria of both kinship and friendship, because both social ties are, as Marshall's analysis demonstrates, potential members of a broader category: "intensive social relationships."

For all its considerable accomplishments, Marshall's argument leaves us dangling on a critical point. Throughout his discussion, we are aware that, whatever comforts and joys may be individually acquired in the amassing and exchanging of "brotherly love," when viewed from a group perspective the motivation to share is intricately linked with processes of boundary formation within and across groups sharing a territory or adjacent territories—forging intercommunity and interisland alliances, and moving people to resources and resources to people in such territories. In this Trukese love story, there are no visible Romeos and Juliets, no Montagues and Capulets. Hence, the question must be asked as to how the opposite of sharing—*interdicts* on the flow of forms of substance, and on the sharing of people and resources—are implicated, diachronically and synchronically, in conceptions of who, in terms of sociopolitical conditions, has the right to share what, with whom, and when.

Analogs and the Dammed Flow of Relatedness

Wagner's (1977) discussion of kinship as an analogic process for the creation of morally appropriate forms of differentiation—interdicts on the flow of relatedness—in essence takes up where Marshall's demonstration concludes. Wagner begins with the proposition that "all human relationships are analogous to one another" (623). Rather than assume the naturalness of notions about the significance of shared genealogy, with its emphasis on a search for integrative principles for the formation of kinship systems as a separate (or separable) domain, Wagner proposes that anthropologists "consider . . . a situation in which all kin relations and all kinds of relatives are basically alike, and it is a human responsibility to differentiate them"

(623). Consistent with Marshall's conclusions concerning the centrality of sharing as a cultural code for conduct linking various ways of *making* types of intensive social relationships, Wagner argues that all kin relations are defined by "a certain solicitude (perhaps epitomized by Schneider's 'enduring, diffuse solidarity') [which] is quintessential to all ideal kin relationships regardless of how they may be defined or in what form this solicitude is expressed" (623). Recognizing the multivocality of symbols, he suggests that, to the extent that one symbol can represent the basic analogy of relatedness, solicitude represents "all kin relationships to one another" and speaks of "one essential kin relationship, which is encompassed and varied in all the particular kinds of relationships that human beings discern and differentiate" (623).

From this perspective, for example, Wagner contends that this flow among relationship types is why we sometimes see a mother as another kind of father and why we may deem a sister a better sister for the fact that she is a "little mother," etc. Moreover, he adds, "in spite of every effort one may make to differentiate them, "this essential similarity *flows* between and among" (Wagner 1977:623) types of relatives (and, as we have seen in Marshall's case, more generally among types of intensive social relationships). Thus Wagner proposes that

> for precisely this reason . . ., man's obligation and moral duty is to differentiate, and to differentiate properly. For if the appropriate distinctions are drawn, and the proper modes of avoidance, respect, deference, and even burlesque are observed, then the resulting "flow" of similarity will be realized, perceived as an expression of inner morality. But if these distinctions are not drawn, or drawn improperly, or if the wrong or inappropriate ones are made, then the flow of similarity will appear as a kind of contagion, a moral degeneracy spreading from one kinsman to another. This is what the celebrated "incest taboo," which has been identified by so many anxious classifiers in so many diverse societies, seems to be all about. For incest—treating a mother or sister as a wife or lover or treating a son or brother as a lover or husband—is a morally undesirable flow of similarity. (623–24)

Wagner's key point is that the act of "being related"—moved into the proper position for particular kinds of solicitude—is a consequence of an act of differentiation rather than simply an act of recognizing a given "nature" of shared and exchanged substance. This differentiation is made possible, in his view, through a directing of the flow of similarity contained in analogic representations. Without such analogic direction, otherwise similar beings could not be distinguished from one another for purposes of morally appropriate social actions. And it is morally appropriate social action rather than the mere recruiting of individuals to a group that is at issue. Following Wagner's logic, whether for lineal or collateral definitions of type, the conceptual process by which similarity and difference are recognized, distinguished, or otherwise placed in ordered relation is never merely focused on "group recruitment" but rather always includes an act of differentiation whereby the group to be recruited and that from which recruits can be taken are mutually created.

For Wagner, understanding the process by which realizations of controlled flow are made possible requires that we note carefully the manner in which analogies of flow are culturally created—the organization of symbols and their meanings—making possible the drawing of distinctions within a whole. This possibility directs attention to the interlocking uses of metonymn and metaphor in the production of analogues out of homologues.

> Every particular "kind" of relationship exemplifies this essence in some particular way, and comprises a ("metonymic") *part* of a potential *whole,* a totality of which the aggregate of all kinds of relationships represents a homologue. Each particular kind of relationship, since it incorporates the underlying context of relational solicitude, can be seen as an ("metaphorical") analogue of each other kind of relationship. (Wagner 1977:624)

Wagner contrasts the methodological consequences of beginning with similarity and the problem of analogic differentiation with those of earlier approaches, which are differentially based on assumptions about the importance of consanguinity and affinity in the form and function of kinship systems. He argues, first, that functionalist, structuralist, and cognitive kinship studies remain within a "homological frame of reference" wherein "kin differentiation (the genealogical 'grid') becomes an invariant control against which the sociological alignments and stresses of various tribal peoples are contrasted" (Wagner 1977:625). Second, his argument continues, approaches such as that of ethnosemantics substitutes "culture-specific kin classification for 'mode of relationship' or 'kin attitudes,' " (625). Although Wagner concedes that the latter approach is valuable in that it allows for a "close specification of particular homological transformations," he charges that its usefulness, like that of other "homological schemes," is "ultimately contingent upon the validity of the idea of natural kin differentiation" (626).

In addition to this dependency on the primacy of natural kin, he rightly notes that the utility of such approaches is further limited because they are essentially synchronic insofar as, relying on the genealogical method and kin diagrams, they emphasize the systematic deployment of relational correspondence across an invariant grid. The history of particular connections between an ego and a kin universe, therefore, can be drawn only by ignoring the historicity of the system's production and transformation—reducing the matter within and across generations to "real," "fictive," or "in-law." That is say, each such study begins as if it enters the social process at its beginning, to taking as real those who, at that point, have traceable links to ego either through "blood," legal, or "fictive" connections. That fictions have become facts is not the problem. The problem is that the anthropological methods merely graph the outcome rather than analyze how and why intensive social relationships are made and transformed through the definition and regulation of relatedness. Those methods also neglect to analyze linkages between relatedness and the varieties of social actions which give intensive social relationships their meaning-in-action.

In an effort to transcend the privileging of "natural" kin differentiation and to accomplish an analysis of the alterations that occur as a result of analogic processes (or, in the terms employed here: as nature is socialized and comes to be recognized through a naturalized code for conduct), Wagner proposes an analogic approach in which he intends to handle both synchronic and diachronic uses of traditional kin criteria. In laying out the features of such an approach, he indicates that it is "of necessity diachronic and sequential," by which he means that it must be "concerned with 'relationship' as the analogic consequence of *contrived differentiation*" (Wagner 1977:626) (emphasis added). It must also operate from the premise that the process of contrived differentiation aims to exhaust "a terminological-relational series through temporal sequence rather than logical systemization" (626). Through such temporal sequences, the process of differentiation obviates "the distinction between 'natural' and 'cultural' kin relationship by subsuming terminology and relationship within a single entity" (626). This entity, as unit of a system, is also a feature of a "universe of apprehended cultural construction (and culturally constructed apprehension) that is contiguous with other realms of conceptualization" (627). Thus, kin relationships are "an integral part of a wholly symbolic conceptualization of things" rather than a "response to a set paradigm of 'natural' contingency" (627). From an analogic standpoint, a universe of social relationships are constructed as "simultaneously conceptual and phenomenal" because such an approach does not incorporate the contrast between 'mental' symbolization and 'physical' fact" (627).

Wagner's willingness to remove from cultural constructions of relatedness the limits of real kin versus mental apparition allows an advance beyond Marshall's conclusions. The move is made possible, however, only by returning us to the critical contribution of Marshall's initial insights: that kin and "created kin" merge over time, making the fact and fiction of substance exchange dialectical, rather than mutually exclusive, constructions of the manner in which nature is socialized; and that socialization comes to be represented as natural. One learns that there is no need for the distinction between "created kinship" and "real kinship" except insofar as one wishes to contrast a dynamic process of social-relations construction to a static model of assumptions about the "proper" relation between the *character* of kinship and a theory of procreation or to debate whether the membership of descent groups on the ground is consistent with a mental model distilled from a descent principle and its marriage rules.

This recognition allows Wagner to turn to the making of intensive social relationships as the invoking of interdicts on the flow of similarity, which, in his view, always begins with a reassessment of this flow's character at the point where a particular form of differentiation can facilitate a particular, and desired, set of social actions. The interdict takes place within the context of the historicity of substance creation, i.e., within a local theory of procreation that defines the nature of maleness and femaleness as forms of socialized biogenetic substance as well as the rules for exchanging and combining it in the production of new humans.

Among Wagner's ethnographic example, the Daribi, it is not a generic male or female who can produce a new human, but rather a type of male and a type of female, the conjoining of which allows each party to recognize that *"the force of the moral obligation is that each party to the interdict shall represent and perceive its own lineal flow as that of male substance,* for its primary concern is the retention and replenishment of this substance" (Wagner 1977:628). In effect, not *all* the shared biogenetic substance of which a human is composed defines the character of the interdict necessary to appropriately direct the flow of relatedness. From the male substance comes some elements and from the female other elements of the total biogenetic substance. While both are needed to make the new body, both do not equally define the interdict on flow. It is as if we took literally the passing comment, "he gets his looks from his mother and his temper from his father," and created rules of exchange intended to maintain and replenish the substance of temper over looks. Consequently, not all of nature is socialized by nurture, nor is all of such nurtured nature equally significant in the formation of the criteria that allow intensive social relationships to move people to resources and resources to people.

While sharing, as a symbol of the flow of relatedness, suffuses the character of kinship, Wagner's contribution, through the Daribi case, is to highlight the dialectical forces that link the sharing of *partible* biogenetic substance to the symbolic underpinnings directing the flow of resources:

> There is a flow of meat, women, and pearlshells just precisely where there is no flow of substantial analogy, because the exchange of these detachable markers in one direction is the means by which substantial flow is emphasized (and hence created) in another. This is why Daribi say "we marry those with whom we do not eat [that is, share] meat." It is a self-contained statement, a model "of" and a model "for." (Wagner 1977:631)

All such interdicts, rather than flowing from a noncritical assessment of unsocialized nature, are products of "appropriate human actions (such as 'sharing') . . . [and] are the subject of great care and discretion" (Wagner 1977:631). In fact, arguing that the interdicts call to mind the food and pollution issues raised by Dumont's analysis (1970) of the Hindu caste system, Wagner states:

> as in Dumont's analysis, it is not necessary to adduce literally constituted "groups" (or even "societies") here: all that is necessary is for people to observe the niceties of the interdict and its concomitant exchanges and prerogatives, and the sociality (and its analogies of substantial flow) will take care of itself. (631)

Which people? At this point we confront the issue of how to treat the content and historicity of the precepts of kin ideology as part of social ideology or of an ideological field containing several competing or complementary ideologies. In order not to privilege kin differentiation in the final analysis, we must not consider kinship either the sole or the reigning social ideology. Such analytic restraint is necessary, although precepts most directly traceable to kinship might be found in other ideologies (or aspects of other ideologies) and in their interconnections to, on the one hand, the creation of certain types of intensive social relationships and, on the other hand, interdiction of relatedness where the rules controlling the analogic flow of kin similarities require no such interdict. To return to pure principle, and to watch the historically and politically unimpeded analogic flow of unsocialized logic, are no less analytically limiting than the drawing of a line between created and real kin or accepting the presumption that facts and fictions stand outside social time and process.

This is especially true in cases where the social order, as an ideological field, is not composed of a single group, as in the Daribi and its lineal divisions. Few, if any, situations remain in which the interdiction of flow is simply among types of kinspersons rather than among *types of humans* as nations, races, or castes, each ideologically assumed to be a self-contained homologue within which analogy can direct the flow. In many of these situations, the moral obligation is to dam (and hence damn) most if not all flows of relatedness across homologues. Consequently, although Wagner's treatment adds to Marshall's love story the possibility of star-crossed matches, the conservation and replenishing of lineality still leaves us well outside the colonized, racial world in which lineality and its Daribi homologue is being produced in Wagner's ethnographic presence (present). While we can imagine a Daribi Romeo and Juliet, missing from this Daribi love story are those precepts linking place and identity in group formations that allow a Damon's display of brotherly love to be made possible by a Pythias capable of longing for one last look at his homeland.

Once we recognize that the diachronic practices out of which intensive social relationships are *made* form part of the processes out of which the substance of nature is *created,* we may then reasonably view kinship ideology as the set of principles or precepts that legitimate particular synchronic deployments of that substance across acceptable homologous boundaries. In addition, we are then positioned to place kinship ideology in the broader frame of a society's social ideology or ideologies, asking how other precepts within that ideology or ideologies inform the production of the interdictions on similarity that make such deployments of substance possible and legitimate. That is to say, if we do not assume the beginning of the social order to be given in the theory of procreation and its culturally constituted consequences, we need not privilege kinship ideology as the prime social motivation ordering the range of ideological precepts or ideologies constituting a particular ideological field. For example, in the Daribi case, we would want to know *why* the Daribi are interested in maintaining and replenishing the male substance for what it tells us about the homologous identity "Daribi" as well as for what it reveals about the internal flow of relatedness across Daribi lineality.

Beyond the fact that everyone cannot be everything to everyone, our analyses must begin without a priori constraints on the specification of the ideological underpinning directing the flow of similarity. Instead we begin our search for these ideological underpinnings in the history of a social formation and the active traces of that history revealed in contemporary practices and social processes. If we do not consider kinship ideology the starting point for other ideologies, then we can ask of what conceptual material kinship ideology has been made. We can inquire into the role this material plays in establishing the character of interdicts on the flow of similarity. In short, socialized nature as sharing becomes an aspect of a code for conduct that does not begin or end with the role it plays in constructing and interdicting the flow of consanguinity and affinity in the domain of kinship.

Thinking about social ideologies and their role in producing types, and the classificatory systems in which these types can be deployed, we then see that Marshall and Wagner interject into the study of social organization efforts to develop time- and process-sensitive theoretical and methodological approaches to social classification. Both essays are concerned with how social orders develop systems of classification capable of handling socialized nature as a dialectic out of which oppositional conceptual categories (nature/ nurture, real kin/fictive, created kin) construct one another. Each aims to demonstrate how the dialectically produced categories then provide the source for criteria presumed to distinguish the categories as features of mutually exclusive symbolic domains in a cultural system. The cultural system becomes, at least in principle or ideologically, the taken-for-granted, "naturally" occurring, moral order.

As Wagner's reference to Dumont suggests, his and Marshall's efforts provided fertile ground on which to begin connecting their propositions and conclusions about the nature of kinship creation and classification to those developed in studies of caste and pollution. Examination of these connections suggests how further analytic links can be drawn between such processes for kin creation and those entailed in identity formation and boundary maintenance as disclosed by discussions of ethnicity, ethnogenesis, and nationalism.

"Extensions" of Caste: The Misallocation of Substance in the Civilizing Process

In the societies that anthropologists study today, theories of procreation have developed in, and adjusted their regulation of the flow of similarity among kinspersons to, the presence of ideologies (or particular precepts of ideologies) that produce and deploy castes, races, nationalities, and ethnic groups in the social space of nation-states. Systems of classification resulting from these adjustments employ a variety of legal and customary marriage rules to divide an absolute homologue (i.e., the social formation) into a presumed order of vertical or hierarchical classifications of homologies (i.e., ordered categoric distinctions). Within and across the politically defined boundaries of social formations, these adjustments have attained differing degrees of legality and moral legitimacy.

What has come to be called the "caste school of race relations," which focused primarily on the United States, is one of the earliest efforts to draw analogies between race-relations practices in complex capitalist societies and the Hindu ideology of caste classification and its deployment of occupations in an economic order. This school has been justifiably criticized for oversimplifying ideology and for a methodology that encouraged simplistic parallels between caste and race. For example, Oliver C. Cox (1987) castigated the school's theorists for ignoring fundamental differences in the moral legitimacy underpinning both the production of group identities and the specification of their legal rights to positions in the occupational structures constituting the economic orders of the two systems. In his view, the caste system was a "bipartite interracial adjustment," which he deemed to be "ancient, provincial, culturally oriented, hierarchical in structure, status conscious, nonconflictive, nonpathological, occupationally limited, lacking in aspiration and progressiveness, hypergamous, endagamous, and static" (37). Production in such a caste system, he argued, was based on hereditary monopoly, thereby producing no proletariat and, hence, no class struggle.

By sacred texts, castes were morally forbidden to change occupations except in situations where an allocated occupation became unproductive. In such a situation, the caste was allowed to take up a "less respectable" occupation in order to discourage occupation shifting. As a consequence of this tight linkage between caste and occupation, Cox argued, caste was spatially tied to its economic order and lost its significance for individuals and groups when they migrated beyond the confines of that economic structure. In sum, like other kin-producing ideologies, the caste ideology moved people to resources and resources to people, but, unlike some kinship ideologies, it did so only within the confines of a fixed symbiosis of territory and economic space.

By contrast, for Cox, race, racism, and the systems of race relations these concepts make possible, are modern outgrowths of the capitalist mode of production based on competitive opportunism. Races have a legal right to sell their labor in the best market, despite practices that block access to some occupations. Particular races have neither a constitutional nor a religious right to any given occupation, nor is there an accepted plan for the sharing of occupations. According to Cox, the opportunism that marks capitalist society's economic order reverberates throughout its social order and, unlike caste, can be transported from one territorially defined economic space to another. Although both caste and race are ascribed statuses, caste, he contends, is lost in migration because, embedded as it is in the structure of the local economic system, its meaning is indexical.

The openness made possible and necessary by the competitive opportunism of the capitalist economy, Cox suggests, also makes the meanings of phenotype, "blood," the amalgamation of biogenetic substances, and other issues linking marriage rules and social reproduction to racial and caste classifications fundamentally different in the two systems. Unlike castes, races are antagonistic on all these points precisely because the caste "is socially and contentedly locked within its immediate marital circle; [whereas] the race . . . is opportunistic and will intermarry or refuse to do so as its interest or cultural strategy demands" (Cox 1987:46). Thus, interdicts on sharing, and the consequences for the creation of relatedness, have different moral charges in a society divided into races as opposed to one composed of hierarchically arrayed castes. For Cox, in caste systems, biogenetic amalgamation has no meaning because one is either a full member of a caste or one has no caste at all. Racial amalgamations of individuals in a system of races, however, alter both individual identity and group identity, thereby altering, in the long run, the biogenetic substance of the social formation as an absolute homologue. In our terms, these systems socialize nature differently and, therefore, have varied consequences for a naturalization of power differentials.

In racially divided systems, nature is contained in and reproduced by the individual as a token of the type, and hence it is assumed that its flow can be controlled by controlling the flow of individuals. "The mobility which racial antagonism abhors is movement across a color fence which surrounds each race regardless of the social position of the individual. The mobility which the caste system limits is movement from one corporate group into another within an *assimilated* society" (Cox 1987:41). Racial identity is maintained in migration, then, because its meaning is defined in the changing nature of an historically dynamic set of national and international power relations. Cox's reasoning is not clear on this point. Perhaps it is because he views the creation of race and racism as an ideological by-product of the development of a capitalist world economic order. The attitude of individuals toward racial identity is determined, he contends, by "the world position of a race" (Cox 1987:42) rather than by its place in a local system of statuses. In contrast, he concludes that the Hindu who migrates becomes an "East Indian," retaining a concern with racial identity and the group's place in the world order while leaving behind concerns with nonportable caste. Hence, while there are no "half-castes," in his view, the portability of race and the opportunistic nature of interdicts on intermarriage makes possible, and perhaps inevitable, the production of "half-race" individuals as well as group identity formation among them.

The impartability of caste substance and its consequences for rules of hypergamy and endogamy further distinguish the two systems and, for Cox, make vacuous "neology" of the caste school of race relation's analogic approaches. The impartable biogenetic substance of caste, contrasted with the partable and portable substance of race as group identity, overdetermines differences in the implications wrought by interchanges of these substances through marriage. According to Cox,

> hypergamy does not affect the identity of the [caste] group whereas in race, the more frequent the intermarriage the less clear the racial distinctions; castes can only gain a sense of spiritual gratification from the fact that their women participate in a higher *dharma* whereas for people of color the result varies all the way from complete amalgamation to the establishment of a restless mixed-blood people who tend to become a challenge to the pretensions of their fathers' race." (1987:45–46)

For Cox, in class-stratified and racially divided societies, class endogamy is impossible because classes do not "know" their boundaries, and racial endogamy can neither be clearly proscribed nor usefully fixed by prescription. Apart from the pragmatic difficulties of drawing incontestable lines in the murky biology of half-race identities, it is in reference to the "social ideals" that the two types of systems differ. For example, in the discriminatory practices of U.S. race relations, "whites [can] *wrongfully* take the position of excluding groups from participating freely in the common culture, while castes [can] *rightfully* exclude outsiders from participating in their *dharma*" (46).

Overall then, Cox's critique cautions us against facile attempts to assimilate the interdicts that protect and make possible the reproduction of *dharma* as shared caste "substance" to those that protect and make possible the reproduction of racial patrimony as common culture, manifest destiny, or other renderings of the shared substance of a nationality. Critiques of the type Cox provides, however, are weakened by failing to distinguish *varna* from caste (*jati*) and ideology from practice; and by a tendency to reduce Indian society to the Hindu caste system, i.e., to a set of ideological precepts removed from the historical processes of prewestern colonial conquest, absorption, and the incomplete assimilation of non-Hindus to the political and economic order dictated by Hindu sacred scripture. Often these critiques fail, as did Cox's, to consider the potential interpenetration of race and caste ideologies in societies where forms of the two have long coexisted as features of the western colonial process. Caste and race ideologies in these societies are not simply mutually exclusive. Various groupings in capitalist societies, grappling with the contradictions between their social ideals and practices encouraged by the economic order, actively engage the metaphorical entailments of caste to produce ideological justifications for the practices structuring race relations. At the same time, caste ideologies and the status criteria on which their hierarchicalization depend grapple, often involuntarily, with the racialized implications of criteria common to both race and caste ideology, altering the range of interpretations associated with color and other phenotypical features, with "blood," and with other aspects of substances.

The actual nature of transformations wrought by such interpenetrations must be sought in the historical processes of particular social formations. For example, as students of East Indian society in the Caribbean can attest, when viewed as indexical to an economic structure, the *ideology* of caste is not entirely supplanted by an orientation to racial identity, if by that we mean that conceptualizations of "East Indian as a race" is free of the moral interdicts of purity as superiority. The historicity of this ideology retains social force through the new meanings given to knowledge of ancestral caste ranking and the manner in which efforts are made to transform class position into *varna*-like status. Moreover, these are now intricately intertwined with criteria of phenotype, "blood," and other factors that acquire their meanings from race ideologies. Likewise, as students of the ideological aspects of "cultural pluralism" can attest, while no fixed relations exist between occupation and races as status groups, conceptions of historical experience as future "prerogatives" to be jealously guarded have more than gentle moral overtones, despite their lack of constitutional legitimacy.

For these reasons, Dumont's attention to purity and impurity as the principles of caste ideology provides a better starting point for a comparison of how the precepts of these ideologies interpenetrate in the broader social ideologies that produce interdicts on the flow of similarity within and across the homologues of nation-states. Following Dumont's discussion of caste, one may note that first among the elements common to caste and race ideology is the manner in which both merge the oppositions of pure:impure and superior:inferior (Dumont 1970:59). This initial merge allows a second merge of hygiene and civility such that "the etiquette of purity corresponds in one way to what we call culture or civilization. . . . [T]hose who are pure are in one way the equivalent of what we call 'decent' or 'well-born' people" (59). Purity, Dumont suggests, can be said to "occupy a region in our society that derives directly from good and evil, but it introduces a relative rather than an absolute distinction" (60–61). In addition, attention to purity as superior civility under conditions that distinguish *varna* from caste and that treat caste as empirical practice as well as an ideological system reveals other moral underpinnings relevant to a comparison of how the two systems of classifications produce common interdicts on marriage within and across groups composing nation-states.

First among these is the manner in which impurity differentially affects individuals and groups and superiors and inferiors. Temporary impurity, he notes, adheres to individual actors, while permanent impurity leads to a fall or threat to social status. Temporary impurity results in taboos to protect the inferior who comes in contact with the superior, while permanent impurity requires taboos to protect the superior from the inferior. Within a caste system, ideologically, it is a relatively simple matter to generate criteria to manage and hierachicalize these two forms. Empirically, the matter is more problematic. Dumont states, "as corollary it can also be seen that if one supposes that there is a large number of groups to be classified, a considerable linear and unambiguous ordering of n groups $n-1$ criteria of distinction are required" (Dumont 1970:57).

Apart from the requirement for numerous and complex criteria of distinctiveness (because these criteria must all be derived from a single opposition—purity:impurity), the task is accomplished by analogic segmentation of this opposition (Dumont 1970:55). In practice, it remains impossible to order and to hierarchically fix all castes in a geographical area. This results both from the need for a multiplicity of concrete criteria as well as from needing to evaluate these criteria in relation to one another (57). Beyond these complications, both practice and aspects of the internal logic of the ideology are further ordered by the manner in which relations of force shape linkages between practice and ideology. For example, Dumont notes that while a concrete, localized whole is "decisively oriented" by its ideology (37), the sociological significance of relations of force encourage "each group to protect itself from the one below and not . . . from the one above," and to do so with criteria capable of serving the triple function of separating the group from the one below, the one at a corresponding rank, and the one above (60). Consequently, although *varna* are vertically and hierarchically arrayed by the sacred specifications of caste ideology, the issue that shapes interdicts on flow and their moral obligations is that of how such an ideology allows for the production of criteria necessary to define and order the multiplicity of castes that result from an initial flow of substance produced by inter-*varna* unions.

On this point, Tambiah argues that, taken alone, attention to a hierarchical mode of classification is inadequate to disclose how caste ideology produces caste distinctions out of the sacredly defined *varna* categories (1975). Instead, he suggests that the system of caste distinctions, derived from the opposition of pure:impure, combines hierarchical and key modes of classification to define, sort, and distribute the embodied consequences of mixed *varna* substances.

By hierarchical mode of classification, he refers to a systematic framework designed to produce a sequence of classes, each at a different level, wherein all except the lowest class is subdivided into one or more subordinate classes (Tambiah 1975:191). The consequence of such a taxonomic hierarchy is a system of vertically arrayed entities, classed according to nondimensional criteria that place them in nonpermutable hierarchic positions (191). In contrast, he defines a key mode of classification as one that produces a systematic framework containing a sequence of classes "at each level of which more restricted classes are formed by the overlap of two or more classes at the next higher level" (191). The consequence of a key classification is the production of multidimensional criteria of inclusion that may allow a "permutable arrangement of attribute oppositions, which by their hierarchic application help to locate the entities being identified" (191). A taxonomic hierarchy can define and class opposed categories of beings such as, on the one hand, two-toed mammals, and, on the other hand, horned mammals, whereas, through the selective overlap it permits, a key mode of classification can generate and position a class of two-toed, horned mammals. Therefore, the latter mode of classification supplies a means for recognizing and relating the dimensional attributes of criteria necessary to identify hybrid types, whereas the former is focused on arranging pure types.

The significance of the two modes of classification lies less in the differences between them than in the kind of unitary classification system made possible by their combined application. Sociologically, the units made possible are simultaneously fixed and fluid as different dimensions of relevant criteria are employed to relate them to one another and to the functional

motivations underlying particular ranking concerns. In fact, while the opportunistic nature of the system may differ in important ways from Cox's
conception of its character in race-relations societies, Tambiah's analysis
suggest that such a dimension is a critical feature of caste production.
Applying the hierarchy/key mode of classification to caste ideology as
gleaned from sacred texts and secondary analyses of such, Tambiah concludes that the texts and interpretations all agree on certain features of caste
ideology. First, in terms of a hierarchical mode, caste ideology provides an
explicit ranking of the four *varnas,* and, second, it sanctions marriage rules
that approve and disapprove certain types of unions that make possible,
and morally direct, the flow of substance among *varnas* to generate hybrid
categories (castes). These hierarchical specifications serve as the base from
which techniques of the key mode of classification define and rank mixed
types as entities within a single, universal system.

His analysis of caste as a hierarchy/key mode of classification also suggests
how the logic of caste ideology solves three problems raised by Dumont.
One is the problem of how to generate sufficient criteria to distinguish large
numbers of castes. A second is how to evaluate these criteria in relation to
one another for the purpose of hierarchically ordering such castes. A third
concerns how we can view a system as oriented by an ideology yet also
shaped by the relations of force that constrain its praxis. Criteria for the
identification of castes are generated out of approved (*anuloma*), disapproved (*pratiloma*), and secondary marriage rules that provide a built-in
evaluation mechanism for ranking the different products of unions formed
by adherence to or breaches of these rules. Such that, "the beauty of the
total scheme is that because we start with four ranked *varna* categories
(derived on the basis of hierarchical taxonomy) and because the procedures
for mixing are themselves evaluated as approved and disapproved, etc., the
categories progressively generated are themselves automatically ranked"
(Tambiah 1975:207).

Tambiah's analysis is also revealing on another point germane to a treatment of the interpenetration of caste and race ideology. He begins his construction of caste ideology with the Aryan, Dasyu division, which he terms
an "ethnic division," but which could be, as reasonably, designated a racial
division because it is based on assumptions about shared biogenetic substance as opposed to criteria of cultural differentiation.

> There are two basic distinctions which the texts reiterate—that between the
> Aryans and the non-Aryans (e.g., Dasyu), and among Aryans the distinction
> between the twice born Brahmans, Kshatriya and Vaisyas and the once
> born Shudra. The Dasyu are those "tribes" excluded from the community
> of those born from Brahma (i.e., the four *varna*), and they are of that status

irrespective of *whether they speak the language of Mklekkas (barbarians) or that of Aryans.* (Tambiah 1975:197), (emphasis added)

This ethnic or racial division that is also a division of superordinate/ subordinate categories, precedes and provides a meaningful context for the particular aspects of sacred specifications of *varna* distinctions. Note, however, his analysis of textual derivations of the status of products generated of *anuloma* and *pratiloma* unions across the subordinate ethnic divisions as well as among the superordinate *varna* categories further indicates that, from the standpoint of types of divisions, biogenetic substance is viewed as male substance, the quality and virtue of which is either degraded or replenished depending on whether the products are consequences of adherence to or breaches of the interdicts on the flow of Aryan-*varna* substance. In the following example, he outlines the consequences of an assimilation of the "alien ethnic groups" (Tambiah 1975:206) encountered by the Aryans.

> Here is an example of how two such alien ethnic groups—the Andhra of the Deccan and the Meda of S.E. Rajput—are placed on the margins of the classification grid by characterising them as products of sexual unions in "the reverse order of castes." Thus an Andhra is said to be the product of a union between a Vaidehaka male and a Karavara female (i.e., $[(V + k) + ((B + s) + (V + k))]$=Andhra); and a Meda is described as the product of a union between a Vaidehaka male and a Nishada female (i.e., $(V + k) + (B + s)$=Meda). Finally . . . we may include the formula that a Dasyu (i.e., non-Aryan) male unites with an Ayogava female ($S = v$) to produce a Sairandhra who is described as living like a slave and subsisting by sharing animals. (206–207)

The classification does not simply sociologically *assimilate preexisting* ethnic divisions to an otherwise homologous substance; it produces new divisions within and across ideologically defined, but historically constituted, homologies of *varna* and "tribe." Underlying assumptions place the unities of substances in nature and naturalize them in oppositions of civility/barbarism and in the superiority and inferiority that these oppositions imply. As we would expect, the creation of unities of substance, therefore, precedes formulation of rules constituting a code for conduct. Any such code is, under these conditions, already politicized. That is to say, it is part of the naturalization of power differentials. The socialization of a culturally constructed similarity is then made possible through acceptable patterns of nurturance and exchange.

Recalling Wagner's proposition that the initial interdict directs the act of differentiation, we may note that if such were not the case neither would there be a continuous flow of similarity and relatedness for there would be no criteria by which to recognize them. Instead, we note that, when placed in historical time rather than logical structure, Wagner's proposition retains its analytic force only if we reverse the order of invention. First the criterion according to which similarity is recognized must be invented—form of shared substance—then the moral obligation to direct flow can be conceptualized and encoded in rules for conduct. In other words, it returns us to the question raised as we departed the Daribi case: Why the selective replenishment of male substance and not some other form or definition of the targeted substance? We cannot answer this except through an analysis of the historical particulars of Daribi society, which may not be empirically accessible, but we can reasonably hypothesize that the answer is to be found in the political motivations underlying the invention of substance. What was the character of unrecognized homology prior to its division into a Daribi homologue and its lineal division, and what implications did this prior conception of a unity of substance have for the theory of procreation that developed?

On this point Tambiah provides two more useful suggestions that reveal the historicity of practice contained in, constrained by, but not explicable solely in terms of, the logic of textually defined caste ideology. First, the particular character of the relations of force (i.e., naturalization of power differentials) motivates opportunistic, albeit highly regulated, crossbreeding in caste systems. Second, there is a proliferation of degraded impure types and greater attention to the multiplex ways in which such categories can be produced as opposed to the limited range of pure, high status ones and the absence of textual concerns with their production and interrelations.

Tambiah's explanation of this situation and the logical paradoxes it poses for caste ideology places both the ideology and its implementation within two sets of constraints: (1) sociological factors ordering the economic structure (i.e., few positions at the top and a multitude of positions to be filled at the bottom); and (2) the means by which power differentials that economic structure entails are justified (*varna*, in general, and Brahmans, in particular, representing the source and apex of a pyramid of purity and power in relation to which all categories must be situated). Consequently he finds that few of the logically possible permutations of *anuloma* unions among *varna* are represented in the classification system, and the classical texts give little attention to this problem. Instead, classification focuses greater attention on disapproved (*pratiloma*) unions between *varna* and caste and, more specifically, among castes. Attention is given to the multiplicity of categories and the rankings that result from these types of intermixing, he argues, because the economic system is pyramidal, requiring a multitude of diverse occupations at the bottom and few at the top. Yet, given this understanding of why degraded types proliferate and command both moral direction and classificatory attention, he notes an even more puzzling fact with respect to *varna* and caste intermixing: Brahman participation exceeds that of the other twice-born *varnas*. His observation returns us to myths of origin and the fold in social space that these make possible and necessary as we recall that "this mythical charter which the impure use to bolster their claim also implicitly and tacitly reinforces the fact that the Brahmans are—because they are the point of reference—the fountainhead of purity and the apex of the [economic and symbolic] pyramid" (Tambiah 1975: 207).

From Tambiah's insights, we may conclude that the similarity of substance out of which uncontrolled relatedness flows (thereby making necessary criteria for differentiation) is first invented in order that it may be seen as a problem. The invention is synchronic in that it is always in the making, although at any given moment it must *appear* fixed and capable of defining categories and deploying their occupants across social space. Second, we may recognize that the historicity of the invention of similarity and the differentiations it makes possible reveals intricate and inextricable connections between power differentials and the symbolic and ideological practices out of which these are naturalized in substance definitions and categorical deployments in classificatory system. Biogenetic substance is not simply drawn from nature to serve social functions; the criteria that permits its recognition in nature constructs it at the same time it defines which actions are required to socialize what is recognized as nature. Systems of ideology are not autochthonously produced and the world of practice sprung from their loins. Third, and of greatest importance here, products of unions between the source of legitimacy (i.e., the apex of purity) and the lowest derivations resulting from its ideological reckonings (i.e., impurity marking the boundary between civility and barbarism), although deemed repugnant and defiled threats to the moral fabric, are necessary to the conceptual construction of a homology that transcends all categorical divisions if such an homology is to be coterminous with the sociopolitical unit. Otherwise one has more than one social order occupying a single political unit. While the naturalization of power differentials requires divisions into socialized substance, at some level it must be a unitary substance that constitutes and places all types in the social order.

It is on these points rather than on the contradictions of race, opportunistic mating, or the legalities of constitutional rights that U.S. nationalist ideology confronts the limits of the interpenetration of race and caste ideology for reckoning the relationship between race and kinship. Brahma, as homologue for the body politic, was composed of partable substance that could be mixed and hierarchicalized. It could be hierarchicalized precisely because all variants of substance were ultimately thought to derive from or to have been absorbed into a unitary whole; each represented a more or less pure version of the original substance now bounded as a discrete unit of a type of pure impurity. Nature, as biological diversity and environmental variation, although acting on the common concept of *human*, did not provide a unitary whole composed of discrete units of purity. It could be said that each race of humans was made in nature's own image, but the fact that from place to place and from time to time nature's image was *variable* posed a problem for nationalism and nationalist ideologies' efforts to define, bound, and hierarchically arrange the biogenetic "races" of the body politic to set the constraints within which the combined key and hierarchy modes of classification would be applied. This problem was not shared by caste ideology and its employment of Brahma as source for the classification of a unitary, but stratified, social body.

No Love Lost Here: Contrived Differentiation, Damnable Flows of Relatedness, and the Problem of Unitary Substance in U.S. Nationality

In "Kinship, Religion, and Nationality," Schneider aims to demonstrate to a skeptical audience that in U.S. American culture symbols and diacritica generally associated with the domain of kinship are also present and similarly organized in the domains of religion and nationality. These objectives encourage him to identify, for each domain, its key symbols, the order of relations among its symbols, and the distribution and order of relations among symbols common across the boundaries of institutions. Using this procedure, he is able to suggest the presence of a common ideological under-girding for the symbolic content and structure of domains of social life that hitherto had been analyzed separately.

The different symbols of U.S. American kinship are organized either as a "unity of substance" or in terms of the "unity required by the code for conduct" (Schneider 1977:67). The unity of substance is represented by "blood," shorthand for biogenetic substance. According to Schneider, "blood," produced of coitus, becomes the "shared physical substance" that is "an 'objective fact of nature,' a natural phenomenon, a concrete or substantive part of nature" (65). As such it cannot be terminated, it endures. Shared biogenetic substance is a "symbol of love which links conjugal and cognatic love together and relates them both to and through the symbols of sexual intercourse" (66). Sexual intercourse is both a "natural" act and a symbol of unity.

Under these conditions, Schneider argues, marriage has the opposite distinctive features and, thus, creates an opposing kind of relatedness such that whereas "blood is a natural material, marriage is not; where blood endures, marriage is terminable; and since there is no such 'thing' as blood of which marriage consists, and since there is no such material which exists free in nature, persons related by marriage are not related 'in nature' " (65). Consequently, a "blood relationship is a relationship of identity, and those who share a blood relationship share a common identity" (65). Relatives by law, however, become recognizable as relatives not simply because of the legal tie but through practice, which he refers to as the enactment of a "code for conduct" that provides the identity necessary for a kin-tie specification.

The dichotomy (unity of substance vs unity required by the code for conduct) is integrated into a higher level conceptual dichotomy that he identifies as *the natural order* and the *order of law*. The first order produces relationships created through blood/coitus, and the second creates relationships through a combination of legal stipulations and enacted social code. All relatives in U.S. American culture can be derived from these two orders because, as is typical of structural mediations of dichotomies, features of the two orders are combined to create three categories: in nature, in law, by blood. Hence, he suggests that "what we have heretofore regarded as the single domain of kinship is really made up of two distinct domains: the distinctive features of kinship on the one hand and the kinsman as a person on the other" (Schneider 1977:64). Kinship as a domain is then seen to be constituted of a set of "aspects which distinguish kinship from any other domain of American culture—the domain of kinship as distinct from commerce, politics, friendship, etc, [and another that distinguishes] kinship from other domains" (64).

After establishing the coordinates of the kinship domain through an analogic description, Schneider presents the shared diacritica of kinship, religion, and nationality. For nationality, his analogic procedure is limited to outlining how the "citizen" is defined in U.S. American culture and what role responsibilities follow for the "national" as citizen.

> In American culture, one is "an American" either by birth or through a process which is called, appropriately enough, "naturalization." In precisely the same terms as kinship, there are the same two "kinds of citizens," those by birth and those by law. And indeed it would not be hard to show that the same three categories are derived from these two elements as three categories of kinsmen are derived from those elements. There is the person who is by birth an American but who has taken the citizenship of another country; there is the person who is American by naturalization but not by birth; and there is the person who by birth and law is American. (Schneider 1977:68)

And:

> What is the role of a national? To love his country, his father- or motherland. Loyalty and support for his nation and all those who belong to it. Patriotism in the extreme of "My Country Right or Wrong" is one statement of it. But even where it does not take that particular form, loyalty to and

love for one's country is the most generalized expression of diffuse, enduring solidarity (68).

Whereas he provides a diachronic view of the features of citizens and nationality, when he turns to religion he finds it necessary to discuss the historical derivation of interconnections between the two predominant forms of U.S. American religion—Judaism and Christianity. He notes that "there is a special problem . . . in that there is a historical continuity to the relationship between the Jewish and Christian traditions. At the same time both co-exist in America and their co-existence as well as their historical relations pose problems" (Schneider 1977:69).

Unfortunately, he drops these problems on the ground that they are not problems in Christianity precisely because, "as is well known, the criterion for membership shifted from birth to volition. . . . [O]ne is Christian by an act of faith and an act of birth, and correspondingly conversion to the Faith becomes a very different matter and a real possibility since it takes only an act of will to effect" (Schneider 1977:69). Nonetheless, with respect to this issue of birth and will, he is careful to point out that Christianity and Judaism actually only appear to be very different. In Judaism, he argues, appropriate birth is a necessary condition, but without the enactment of a code for conduct it is not a sufficient claim to Jewish identity. The apparent shift away from identity through particulars of biogenetic substance he takes to be a realignment that allows the substantive element of identity to be redefined as a spiritual element. Thereby, the spirit triumphs over matter, and the spiritual aspect of love is given a prominent place in the creation of identity (70). To the extent that kinship, religion, and nationality are ideologically undergirded by the same symbols and order of relations among them, all may also be said to be about a unity of substance and a unity required for the code for conduct (67).

Without disagreeing with Schneider's general conclusions, we must note that both the order of nature and the order of law are products of the historical processes out of which forms of substance have socialized nature in conjunction with naturalizations of power differentials. Neither analyses of these symbols within distinctive domains nor the careful detailing of commonalities of content and structure across institutional domains of culture are complete without reference to the historicity of ideological elements that link them back to European-derived nationalist ideologies and their transformations and augmentations during different historical junctures in the creation of U.S. American nationality. The kinship universe of American culture is part and parcel of the definition of this nationality that both makes possible and necessary the relativized and hierarchicalized notions of citizen that Schneider describes.

Given Schneider's objective, it is not surprising that his treatment of substance in kinship, nationality, and religion is not an analysis of the *production* of that substance. Whereas he states that blood is produced through acts of social intercourse, in fact we may recognize that what he really describes is how such acts *distribute* bloods produced by "races." Yet, whereas he notes that a systematic analysis of the symbolic interrelations of these domains of U.S. American culture ultimately requires a treatment of race and racism, his discussion does not include attention to these factors. As a result, precepts defining and ordering the production of the "substance" or "substances" constituting the two kinds of U.S. citizens are also omitted. Despite the mention of birth as a one factor in the production process, his discussion of what constitutes a citizen and a national is defined in terms of the role expectations—the unity required by a code for conduct—but not in terms of either the substance that qualifies a person for these roles or how that substance is created.

In the formation of nationalist ideologies, the concept of race has served as a reigning image of socialized nature. Race, whether fashioned of the embodiment of climatic diversity or of variations in God-given character, has represented the homologous substance—an undifferentiated similarity—presumed both to represent human forms of nature and to be transmittable across generations in a manner that reproduces the diversity of nature. History, not sexual intercourse, makes distinctive bloods as the races, which then reproduce and distribute their substance through appropriate acts of sexual intercourse. Consistent with Cox's view of race, racial ideologies, whether based in scientific notions of gene pools or lay conceptions of "blood," see amalgamation as the destruction of nature's ability to reproduce its range of types. Although conceptions of race in U.S. nationalist ideology have no attached legal rights, the "wrongful" application of racial prerogative within and across socially recognized races establishes the ideological constraints within which we must analyze the socialization of nature and the naturalization of power in the interpenetration of kinship and nationality in U.S. social ideology. Despite the lack of constitutional legitimacy for both the criteria and the rank order it aims to fix, the classification of U.S. races is ideologically hierarchic. Ideologically, to mix races, although constitutionally sanctioned and legally recognized, is to commit a *wrongful* act against nature.

The same precepts that make possible the creation of kinship also make possible the creation of races within the nation, and represent the embodied historicity of the system of classification within which additional interdicts take place. Lacking a sacred fountainhead, nationalist ideologies, in effect, reverse the process of caste production in Hindu ideology. Unlike the unity of substance that is Brahma, the nature of western-derived precepts produces views of nature that are diverse in character and that conceptualize the consequences of interactions with it in a variety of ways. Ideas about the logical possibilities for the production and reproduction of racially defined substances shape the means by which nature gets into persons as tokens of types (e.g., races, nations, ethnics) through reckonings of shared historical events, both adverse and triumphant. From the standpoint of racial ideology, varied patterns of interaction with nature as climate, with forms of social adversity and of triumph socialize conceptions of the natural out of which groups as races produce the biogenetic substance of nationality. The flow of this substance is then directed by a code for conduct required to replenish and maintain the unity of substance.

The different symbols of U.S. American kinship that are also contained in U.S nationalist ideology represent aspects of the ideological field concerned with unity as it defines the boundaries of unnatural and inappropriate difference. Until 1967, when the Supreme Court struck down the last of the miscegenation laws, ideologically and legally, the unity of those appropriately related by blood and those who could be appropriately joined in love belonged to the same hierarchically produced categories. Through the order of substance and the order of law they formed a singular category, a race, which was subject to further divisions made possible by an application of key techniques.[3] For example, Yanagisako (1985) shows that the Japanese American Nisei, a historically produced product of hierarchic classification, used a variety of criteria based in locality, behavior, and approved and disapproved cultural "exchanges" with high (Caucasian) and low (Negroid) racial categories to define and assess the rank and feasibility of marriage among persons residing in different communities and states but belonging to the same ethnoracial class. Their processes of classification are historically consistent with patterns described for the production of Whiteness as a unity of substance (i.e., a U.S. racial class) out of the international racial category, Caucasian. This lower-order class of the racial category is made from the historically dynamic shifts in the interdicts that directed constructions of endogamous categories and that defined, at any given time, what constituted hypergamous and hypogamous unions within these categories. For example, Spickard provides the following (native) description of the classification procedure:

> There was a time when most Americans who thought about ethnicity would divide the human population conceptually first into race: red, yellow, black, brown, and white on the North American continent. Ethnic groups, according to such thinking, were simply subdivisions of these larger phenotypic categories. Thus, a person whose ancestors came from Bavaria belonged to the German ethnic group and the Caucasian race, while a person from Kyoto was seen as a member of the Japanese ethnic group and the Mongolian race. . . . In the increasingly egalitarian and polyglot atmosphere that has emerged in last three decades, however, the number

of categories has multiplied and the mechanical distinction between a large category called "race" and a subsidiary division called "ethnic" has blurred. . . . [T]he issues at work between what have been called races have a common basis with the issues at work between what have been called ethnic or nationality groups. (1989:9–10)

There is a multitude of scholarly and lay views of these divisions and their subdivisions, and the objective here is not to state the final case for an order of classification but rather to exemplify a process of classification that suggests that where kinship is made in and of the biogenetic substance of race and its subdivision, nationalist ideology promotes moral obligations that direct one to pick one's kin within these particular naturalized forms of socialized nature. Within the "opportunistic" structures," capitalist society uses the hierarchic mode of classification to define the forms of similarity (i.e., races and their ethnic groups) within which these interdicts on flow should apply. This has been a dynamic process, at one time combining lower-order divisions of an earlier era into a larger pool of similarity at another point in time. The synchronic character of these processes of classification has served both to produce interdicts on intermarriage within and across racial categories and their ethnic subdivisions, and to link the act of classification to the production of divisions or the amalgamation of previous subdivisions. Thus, "where in the 1920s the union of a Norwegian American man and a Swedish American woman might have caused a scandal in Minnesota, by the 1980s almost no one would have noticed any ethnic difference between them at all" (Spickard 1989:5–6). However, rules of racial hypodescent directed and limited the production of amalgamated substances such that what was nationally possible for variations among Caucasians was both informally disapproved of and locally difficult to accomplish in practice (as the Yanagisako case suggests) among subordinated racial categories. Between the superordinate racial category and subordinated categories, amalgamation was not simply disapproved ideologically, locally, and nationally, but also evaluated according to a rule of hypodescent. Root (1992) notes the rule of hypodescent served to link the hierarchic/key mode of classification to the naturalization of power:

The mechanisms that have historically evolved to suppress multiple heritage identification have largely benefited White society. The rule of hypodescent enlists simplistic, dichotomous rules of classification (e.g., White versus non-White) and has been obviously employed in our historical amnesia. These strategies have fueled the oppression of America's people of color . . . and definitely that of the multiracial people of our country. In fact, attempts of racially mixed persons to move back and forth between color lines have been viewed pejoratively rather than as creative strategies in a multiracial reality. (6–7)

Marriage interdictions on the exchange of substance constitute an obvious problem for a racially ordered classification system. The act of differentiation, however, must be prior to the problem of intermarriage because it must define which features of solicitude inappropriately direct the flow of relatedness. Because conjugal love, ideologically speaking, begins in spiritual love and its representations of diffuse, enduring solidarity, friendship constitutes the danger zone wherein interdictions of relatedness begins. Under these conditions, one cannot pick one's friends, if friends be defined by their willingness to share *all* forms of substance. In this danger zone, historically, rites of passage have marked the point at which the act of contrived differentiation recognizes and defines the form of similarity in nature on which interdicts will focus. Numerous are the memoirs of Blacks and Whites who make poignant commentary on the age and social event when first they discovered that the familiarity of interaction in friendships they, to that point, had taken for granted became highly problematic, if not impossible. Making a point about what he calls the "present-past," Du Bois (1969) plays with this rite of passage. He notes the chagrin of a southern White gentleman who' while inveighing against northern ignorance of the flow of affection and friendship between Blacks and Whites in the South, waxes nostalgic about a Black childhood companion from whom he was inseparable, only to become quite unsettled when he noticed a Negro, whom he had earlier stumbled over in the hallway, seated next to him in the theater orchestra. Today, efforts to maintain friendships that go against the flow of appropriate sociality call for justifications in human identity: "I do not see color/race, I only see a human being."

Thus, whereas we may agree with Schneider (1977) that ideologies are based within culturally constructed persons, when attention is directed to the formations of ideologies and their interpenetration, viewed dialectically and synchronically, culturally constructed persons *embody* the historicity of prior ideological formations. For nationalist ideologies, this means beginning with the proposition that nation, as homologue for a social order, has no singular fountainhead for the classificatory criteria out of which a unity of substance can be recognized. Nonetheless, a major objective of nationalist ideology has been to invent a unitary substance and to link that substance to a sociopolitical unit and its economic structure.[4] Nationalist ideologies, therefore, cannot be reduced to constitutionality or the laws that develop to protect rights associated with it. At best, constitutions and laws can be deemed the positively sanctioned aspects of a social ideology or ideologies. No constitution or legal system sanctions, either negatively or positively, all the precepts of a single ideology or all those of the multiplex interpenetrations wrought of their coexistence in a single social order composed of a variety of ideologies. The absence of formality cannot be grounds for eliminating such conceptions from an analysis of the social ideology or ideologies out of which classification systems are dialectically produced. In stating that "it is not nationality as it applies to what makes a person a resident of a country for purposes of meeting the relief requirements" (Schneider 1977:68) that is at issue, blood and its purity in the construction of group, nation, and place in the social order are reduced to analogs that obfuscate the cultural politics out of which the boundary between the order of nature and the order of law are created and maintained.

When practice is neither reduced to a mirror image of ideology nor treated as a simple, unsanctioned, contradiction of its precepts, we can recognize that, as Dumont proposed, ideologies orient systems, while relations of force shape their diachronic implementation in practice and their synchronic formulation of additional ideological precepts. Systems of classification generated in conjunction with relations of force and the naturalization of power need not be limited to one mode and its technique. Instead, as Tambiah demonstrates, motivations underlying the naturalization of power and its socialization of nature direct the selective combination of techniques from different modes of classification.

Which motivations and which strata of a population are most implicated in linking them to naturalizations of power, are, of course, to be located through analyses of the historical particulars of a social formation. These particulars further shape conceptions of shared substance and determine the character of the interdicts that produce persons properly embodied and positioned to engage in specific forms of solicitude. Systems of classification, however, that lack the legitimacy of a sacred source or completed transformation of socialized nature (i.e., a unity of substance based on sacred texts and their interdicts) into the constitutionality of an order of law (i.e., a unity required for a code for conduct) also lack the wherewithal to uniformly implement the system of classification produced. This does not mean that ideologically there is no system or that practices are not systemic in their illegitimacy.

If we but briefly examine the issue of mixed unions in U.S. nationalist ideology, we may suggest some of the analogic connections between illegitimate racial classifications, wrought of constitutionally "wrongful" interdicts, and the incomplete systems of classification, wrought of wrongful ethnic conceptions of occupational prerogatives, in ideologies of cultural pluralism. For both we may note the role of the hierarchic mode of classification in defining the characteristics of nature (shared social adversity or environmental conditions, etc.) out of which the groups' biogenetic substance is made. This process we can then relate to how diverse/impure biogenetic substance becomes the homologue of similarity. Acts of differentiation begin with the proposition that the distribution and reproduction of substance in the creation of intragroup kinship is a natural act between culturally constituted appropriate beings, whereas when performed by those from inappropriate categories of the family/nation as unit for the (pro)creation of citizens, as opposed to that for the continuity of races of citizens, the act of intercourse is deemed "unnatural."

These issues suggest another view of Schneider's conclusion that all the types of unity expressed in these bounds can be distilled as the *unity of substance,* now seen as race, and the *unity required by the code for conduct,* now viewed as modes of discrimination/interdiction on ethnicized versions of U.S. nationality (Schneider 1977:67). In the latter situation, reproductive acts made possible by sexual intercourse do not replenish and distribute blood. They become productive acts that create polluted bloods from which, at worst, spring "monsters" or sick and weakly degenerates or, at best, come embodiments of substances that pose classificatory problems beyond the capability of a hierarchic mode of classification operating in a nationalist context—bloods that are both dimorphic and biracial. This they share with castes descended from *varna.* By the fact that these products are outside the hierarchic classification grid, they share a position with "tribals" assimilated neither to the margins of that grid nor integrated into a system of classification made possible by a combined hierarchy/key mode. Yet, as the myths of origins with which we began proclaim, these problematic productions are not beyond the pale. Instead, they (or, more accurately, their structural illegitimacy) are evidence of the source of the socialized nature that legitimates the unity of a social order and directs the flow of relatedness across a classificatory grid that arranges contrived differentiation of sameness. From kinship to race, from tribe to caste, the love in enduring solidarity is made in the fold of degraded social space. There ain't no love lost here.

Notes

Thanks are due Drexel G. Woodson for his very helpful comments on an earlier draft of this essay, and to Catherine Benoit and Peter Redfield for their critical comments when I presented several ideas now contained in this essay during a discussion group at University of California, Berkeley. All errors of fact and interpretation are my responsibility.

1. I have selected Cox because he represents the most systematic effort to reject the utility or comparability of the caste/race analogy applied to U.S. American race relations. In this choice I also follow conclusions reached on this point by Dumont (1977) and McKee (1993).

2. I borrow this expression from Drexel G. Woodson (1990:49) as a reference to the relation between abstract ideas and the manner in which these ideas are increasingly particularized in actions across different settings as individuals attempt to adjust their general meanings to interpretations of appropriate and inappropriate conduct.

3. On this point, Dumont (1977) links the problems of substance production, inheritance, and status evaluation to the Christian tradition and its emphasis on the individual soul as repository of character under conditions that insisted on the *identity* of human substance as "man" as body. This identity of embodied substance (i.e., all men are created equal)

removed from egalitarian ideologies produced under Christian doctrine the ability to attribute the character of individuals to groups as cultural entities. Thus he notes,

> once equality and identity bear on the individual *souls,* distinction could only be effected with regard to *bodies.* What is more, discrimination is collective; it is as if only physical characteristics were essentially collective where everything mental tends to be primarily individual. . . . [T]he proclamation of equality burst asunder a mode of distinction centered upon the social, but in which physical, cultural, and social characteristics were indiscriminately mixed. To reaffirm equality, the underlying dualism demanded that physical characteristics be brought to the fore. While in India heredity is an attribute of status, the racist attributes status to race. (84–85)

However, to Dumont's conclusion we must add that the racist makes the attribution within the context of a nationalist production of substance as race qua heredity that determines what is taken to be a race within the hierarchic distribution of human substance as identity. In this ideological context, cultural groups (i.e., ethnic groups as races) are reinvented as the source of differences in mental attributes essentialized in physical forms. This move is consistent with Dumont's overall conclusion about the place of hierarchy in U.S. American egalitarianism: "the relation is inverted: equality contains inequalities instead of being contained in hierarchy. . . . [A] whole series of transformations happen which can perhaps be summarized by saying that hierarchy is repressed, made nonconscious: it is replaced by a manifold network of inequalities, matters of fact instead of right, of quantity and gradualness instead of quality and discontinuity" (86).

4. See George Mosse (1985) for a discussion of how nationalist ideologies assimilated nature to the project of constructing race and utilized both in oppositional constructions of "respectability" as the code for conduct required by the unity of substance.

References

Alexander, Jack. 1977. "The Culture of Race in Middle-Class Kingston, Jamaica." *American Ethnologist* 4(3):413–35.

Cox, Oliver C. 1987. *Race, Class, and the World System: The Sociology of Oliver C. Cox,* edited by Herbert H. Hunter and Sameer Y Abraham. New York: Monthly Review.

Du Bois, W. E. B. 1969. *The Souls of Black Folks.* New York: New American Library.

Dumont, Louis. 1970. *Homo Hierarchicus: The Caste System and Its Implications.* Translated from the French by Mark Sainsbury. Chicago: Univ. of Chicago Press. Originally published as *Homo Hierarchicus: Un Essai Sur le Système decastes* (Paris: Gallimard, 1966).

———. 1977. "Caste, Racism, and 'Stratification': Reflections of a Social Anthropologist." In *Symbolic Anthropology,* edited by J. Dolgin, D. Kemnitzer, and D. Schneider, 72–88. New York: Columbia Univ. Press.

Huggins, Nathan Irvin. 1990. *Black Odyssey: The African American Ordeal in Slavery.* Rev. ed. New York: Vintage Books.

Keyes, Charles. 1981. "The Dialectic of Ethnic Change." In *Ethnic Change,* edited by S. Giner and M. Archer, 124–71. London: Routledge & Kegan Paul.

Marshall, Mac. 1977. "The Nature of Nurture." *American Ethnologist* 4(4): 623–42.

McKee, James B. 1993. *Sociology and the Race Problem: The Failure of a Perspective*. Chicago: Univ. of Illinois Press.

Mosse, George. 1985. *Nationalism and Sexuality*. New York: Howard Fertig.

Root, Maria P. P., ed. 1992. *Racially Mixed People in America*. Newbury Park, CA: Sage.

Schneider, David. 1968. *American Kinship a Cultural Account*. Chicago Univ. of Chicago Press.

———. 1977. "Kinship, Nationality, and Religion in American Culture: Toward a Definition of Kinship." In *Symbolic Anthropology*, edited by J. Dolgin, D. Kemnitzer, and D. Schneider, 63–71. New York: Columbia Univ. Press.

Smith, Raymond. 1988. *Kinship and Class in the West Indies: A Genealogical Study of Jamaica and Guyana*. Cambridge, UK: Cambridge Univ. Press.

Spickard, Paul R. 1989. *Mixed Bloods: Intermarriage and Ethnic Identity in Twentieth-Century America*. Wisconsin, London: Univ. of Wisconsin Press.

Tambiah, S. J. 1975. "From Varna to Caste through Mixed Unions." In *The Character of Kinship*, edited by Jack Goody, 191–230. Cambridge: Cambridge University Press.

Wagner, Roy. 1977. "Analogic Kinship: A Daribi Example." *American Ethnologist* 4(4):643–62.

Woodson, Drexel G. 1990. "Tout Mounn sé Mounn, men Tout Mounn pa Menm: Microlevel Sociocultural Aspects of Land Tenure in a Northern Haitian Locality." Ph.D diss., University of Chicago.

Yanagisako, Sylvia J. 1985. *Transforming the Past: Traditions and Kinship among Japanese Americans*. Stanford: Stanford Univ. Press.

The American Dream:
Gender, Class and Ethnicity

9

"The Self-Made Woman": Gender and the Success Story in Greek-American Family Histories

Phyllis Pease Chock

"Naturalization" is the provocative word that Americans use for the transformation of immigrants into citizens. It refers to a legal change of status that is overseen by an agency of the state, the Immigration and Naturalization Service. But the word evokes more than the law. It suggests, for example, that it also has to do with "nature." As David Schneider (1969:120) pointed out, nature and law may define both kinship and nationality in American culture.[1] Feminist scholars have pointed out similar, infrequently noticed connections between definitions of gender and of nationality.[2] This is because "naturalization" is accomplished not just through legal processes but also through such cultural practices as talking about, telling and retelling, gender-inflected immigrant success stories. These stories are told widely in settings that Americans call "family" or "community," where they comprise "family history"; they also are told in scholarly works, in curricula, in mass media, in legislatures, and elsewhere. Immigrant success stories reiterate national mythic themes of rebirth, of opportunity, and of nationality. In general, telling these stories transforms social identities, reflexively reinvents the storytellers' own family histories, and confirms their authority to do so. Telling them also reproduces, but sometimes transforms, problematic gender hierarchies.

I pay special attention in this essay to the latter, namely, to how gender makes a difference in this "naturalization" storytelling. Although the narratives are ostensibly unmarked for gender, they construct an immigrant/citizen who is male in that they use the theme of effective activity in the world. The narratives are about a heroic male immigrant who is an active protagonist who transforms himself into an American and a success. An immigrant success story depicts the link between the gender of the protagonist and his becoming a success and an American as one that is given, unnoted, and unproblematic. The gender of the immigrant/citizen is thus "naturalized." Telling the story reproduces gender differences and implies, by women's virtual absence as protagonists, that women are less assuredly successes and American.

That this reproduction of differences occurs is supported by the contrast in the ease with which people talk about men as opposed to women immigrants in their families. Storytellers readily speak of male immigrants. In interviews with me, for example, people told their fathers' stories first and with relative ease. Immigrant fathers were portrayed in these stories as having worked hard and overcome obstacles with little or no assistance from anyone in order to make their way in America. Accounts of immigrant women would follow these stories as auxiliaries to the main narrative, in which women appeared as fathers' sisters or as wives and mothers. As sisters, women were signs of men's obligations to other men and of obstacles that men had to overcome to transform themselves from immigrants to citizens. Sisters, for example, needed brothers to find them dowries and husbands, things that women could not do themselves. As wives and mothers, women were also less actors than objects brought by men to the new land. A man had to find a wife, sometimes by returning to the homeland or hometown to seek her out. Thus in men's stories, women signified something passive but problematic for men.

But when people tried to talk to me about immigrant women in their families as actors, the success story's markedness for gender presented them with difficulties. The possibility of active women confounded the immigrant success story's connections between gender and citizenship. There were no terms in which people could speak about women as actors. In particular, women storytellers glimpsed that markedness when they tried to tell these stories, and their storytelling was shaped as much by their anger, bemusement, resentment, or bewilderment as by the form of the story.

My thesis is that what women storytellers in particular faced when they told their stories about their mothers and themselves were not just conceptual dilemmas of how to relate gender and nationality. The cultural work that people did when they told family stories challenged and moved toward transforming the naturalized connections between gender and citizenship. The terms of the American success story did not suffice for these storytellers, but there was no alternative to which they could turn. They had to find a language in which to speak about these things. In that respect, the affect of the storytelling analytically resembled what Raymond Williams (1977) called a "structure of feeling." Affect replaced the "self-made man" myth's silence about women. Affect pointed to the myth's unstated depiction of male success and nationality as nature. In effect, then, the women's stories suggested the possibility of regendering and denaturalizing the terms both of nationality and family history.

My data are mainly from middle-class Greek-American women who were the daughters of immigrant mothers, but some data are also from men who were sons of immigrant mothers. Many of the women were "housewives" in the 1960s (when they told me these stories) at a time when their husbands and brothers were white-collar employees.[3] What these women in particular produced culturally was not confined to family and household, nor did it merely reproduce categories of family and household. In stories, women's work was often depicted as crossing boundaries. In the routines of everyday life women moved between family business and home; between home and children's schools; between religions, languages, nationalities, and customary practices as they sorted out, revised, or created links where there were none before. These were activities that were commonly left out of more formal accounts of immigrant and ethnic "communities" that were conceived in institutional terms. So while men were depicted as building businesses, churches, newspapers, and political and civic organizations (see, for example, Moskos 1989), women were nearly invisible because they were in between.[4]

In indigenous models, the first American-born Greek Americans lived in "two worlds"—"Greek" and "American." My focus here is how women produced terms for the reconstructing of those "worlds."[5] The process, I will argue, involved more than just sorting ideas and customs into what was "American" and what was "Greek," that is, puzzle solving, but rather involved a reconstitution of those terms. In the stories of their immigrant mothers and themselves, women were depicted as they discussed, argued, gave up, revised, and invented anew, practices that ranged from domestic division of labor, to religious belief and ritual practice, to designs and aspirations for the future.

Silence and Resentment

Women who were daughters of immigrants focused much of their attention on the cultural forms through which immigrants and now the American-born connected themselves to life in the United States. In the American myth of success, the "self-made" man reordered and transformed his "old" self into a "new man"; but one of the conceptual dilemmas that the myth created was captured in a much quoted account by an anonymous Greek-American woman:

> To be born a woman and intelligent is definitely risky. But to be born a sensitive, intelligent woman and to be born Greek—that is little short of calamity. Because to Greek Americans the concept of the equality of the sexes is so completely demoralizing that the superior woman is beaten before she begins! . . . I spent my childhood and adolescence in constant inner and often outward rebellion at the deference accorded to the male members of my family, even when they were patently in the wrong.

Again and again I was told, "You must give in. You are a girl." But no one ever took time to explain *why* the woman must give in. ("Forgotten Generation" 1950:22)

This passage, from an article written for a Greek-American cultural magazine in the 1950s, has been quoted in three scholarly works on Greek-Americans (Moskos 1980:91; Moskos 1989:91; Scourby 1984:121–22). It is in fact a rare first-person account by a woman (or in a woman's "voice") in these studies of Greek-Americans.[6]

In her article, the anonymous woman juxtaposed two cultural myths: a Greek myth of honor that irreparably separated the sexes ("the much vaunted sense of honor [of] men of Greek extraction depended only upon the degree of repression of the decent Greek-American girl" ["Forgotten Generation" 1950:23]); and a version of the American myth of success ("The woman . . . having tasted the sweet fruit of economic independence, hesitates to marry just for the sake of acquiring the MRS." [23]). The "independent female" of her story was a "self-made woman," after the model of the successful, "naturalized," "self-made [American] man." But this self-made woman was like a trickster in that she confounded both the ethnic and the American myths. She was not dependent, as the ethnic myth required of a "Greek"/"ethnic" woman; and she was not male, as the American success myth required of an active, "American" protagonist. Her story brought together contradictory possibilities in a self-made woman—that is, she was active/not dependent and female/not male, instead of the myths' expected dependent/not active, female/not male. The gender entailments of the two myths contributed the inconsistencies in this new version of an immigrant success story, which left unanswered the questions, Was she not truly female? not truly a success? not truly American?

Her story also evinced a "structure of feeling" (Williams 1977) in that her anger and resentment,[7] rather than the available myth, rearticulated domains of family, nationality, and gender. Beyond bringing out the disjunctions and inconsistencies of the myths, the structure of feeling moved toward denaturalizing them. Her anger and resentment pointed to the constructedness of "naturalization"; it was possible, if not sayable, that the gender (male) of immigrant/ethnic American success was an artifact of culture and not a "fact of nature." Affect raised the possibility of another story, of a woman's story that could not be told for mothers, wives, and sisters.

This story, despite the author's claim that the younger among the American-born escaped the full force of its contradictions, reveals cultural dilemmas that also configured some of the stories that Greek-American women told about themselves a decade later in the 1960s. One such story was told me by an American-born woman;[8] she inverted the American/immigrant success story that was told about men in many families and claimed it, like the anonymous author had, for women. In the canonical masculine version, an immigrant husband/father, for the most part alone and unaided, by his own hard work overcomes tremendous obstacles of custom (having to provide sisters' dowries is a prominent one) and poverty to achieve success and make a mark for himself as an American. But in the inverted form this woman told, the success story, having been shifted to the next generation, was taken away from sons and awarded to daughters:

> W1: The male's role generally is superior to the female's. In my generation. They're boys—they can do no wrong because they're boys, whatever they do can be hidden. . . . That's why Greek girls in this country have turned out much better than boys. They've been more successful. . . . I think they've turned out to be better citizens, to be better human beings, because the boys were spoiled. And it didn't do them any good.

Women, she said, were actually more successful than their brothers: there is another scale, she was saying, on which to judge success—as "citizens" and "human beings." The protagonist in the dominant version of the success story transforms obstacles into money, career, or status; but here the worth of a "person" was the outcome. She was trying new gender coordinates for the self-made man's success by changing the definition of success.

Besides the one anonymous story, little mention has been made by scholars and others of its "structure of feeling"; it has generally been understood as women's contented domesticity (e.g., Moskos 1977), their long suffering (Petrakis 1963, a novel), or their utter silence (Saloutos 1973).[9] Silence about gender was not confined to scholarship. Not infrequently stories about immigrant mothers stymied the people I talked with; what, they wondered, could they say about a woman's arranged marriage, a woman's not having learned English, or her being marginal to her husband and children.[10] Some made little comment, for example, noting differences between their generation and their parents' and stating, "They [the parents] were matched for marriage." One man told me more, namely that his immigrant mother, a widow, had been "forced" by her family to remarry: "They arranged the marriage for her through some friend of my cousin's, and my mother became introduced to my stepfather."

Their mothers' arranged marriages were for some of the American-born a scandalous social fact that could not be translated into the American mythic idiom of individual success. In the myth's terms, no one could envision reasons for a woman's inability to choose a partner for herself. Because "choosing" made the American-born generation's accounts of itself possible, because for them "choosing" entailed an individual who was self-made by choices, people could be rendered speechless by the anomaly of a person without choices.

In an exchange between another couple I was interviewing, the husband reversed a family story he had told me earlier in which his mother was peripheral to his father's success, and averred, "Mom was a little stronger person, in a sense, than Pop was." Then he retracted this new claim and, in the story below, admitted she may have been "a little bit like a slave." But his wife in the end, in a flash of annoyance, challenged his trying to make his mother's story like his father's:

> H: Mom was, you know, a little bit like a slave almost. When she was married, she didn't know who she was going to marry. Her father told her to get on the boat and gave her a ticket, and marry somebody on the other side. That kind of thing. I think that was accepted back in those days. She was hoping her father knew enough and wouldn't lead her astray. So she had confidence in that system. . . .
> W2: It was acceptance rather than confidence, wasn't it?
> H: I think that was part of it. Of course, you had to accept. But if you didn't want to, you had other avenues open to you. . . .
> W2: What?
> H: You could always run away. . . .
> W2: Run away?!
> H: And hustle!
> W2: That's what I mean. There's practically nothing you could do! I think you're glossing it over a little bit. (Chock 1989:173)

Both husband and wife were embroiled in a dilemma in telling the American success story when they found that it resisted being revised for women. The success story's male heroes control their destinies ("have confidence," never "give in"), work toward goals ("success"), never get closed out of options ("other avenues"), and are resourceful ("hustle").[11] It was impossible for them to recount the man's mother's strength in these terms. Her arranged marriage contradicted for them their wish to speak of her as an active, "strong" person. His wife having pointed out that he was "glossing it over a little bit," the man conceded both that his mother had been "a little bit like a slave" and that imputing "confidence in that system" to her was absurd. So the immigrant success myth (for example, "hustle"[12]) was unavailable to them if they wanted to talk about this immigrant woman. After this impasse, neither tried again during the interview to tell me about her.

Others tried further to analyze their mothers' experiences. The man I quoted earlier, who had said that his mother had been forced by her family to remarry, had thought a great deal about "family roles" in his professional capacity:

> H: I think if you keep a woman down, if you keep a Negro down, if you keep a minority group down, they're going to get you. . . . Our fathers

were authoritarian—or claimed they were. . . . When a man says he's the boss, he may be outwardly the boss, but the woman is boss underground.

He and his wife, who was also participating in the interview, had obviously already discussed "sex roles" (his professional term)[13] among themselves, an examination that hinged on their stipulating that there were differences between their parents' generation and theirs.[14] His strategy had been to create a distance between generations. Their immigrant parents, he implied, were different. Their fathers, he suspected, might have been regularly suborned by mothers, who implicated their children in their ruses to maintain hierarchy:

> H: In spite of that fact that the male, the father, was dominant, "quote," or thought he was, the Greek mother seems to undermine the dominance. She would tell the children, "Don't tell your father." . . . My mother forced me to lie. But nevertheless she didn't want me to lie.

His wife's response to this posing of the dilemma as a generational one (even if possibly based on a man's self-delusion) was to turn to her own predicament: that they had two young children and that she was "staying home" with them:

> W2: I was teaching . . . until my marriage and I became pregnant, and right after that we had our second child, so I took a maternity leave—a second one. And we felt it would be too much work, so I turned in my resignation, and I have two more years of resignation time left. . . .

Her culturally unquestionable "nature," that is, her pregnancies and then her children, was what made "too much work" by scrambling the terms for her life. She conceptualized the problem concretely, and was bewildered by it.

Ironically, the structure of anger and bewilderment and such inverted but masculine stories appeared with some regularity in family stories, as well as in silences about women in Greek-American life.[15] The conceptual dilemmas they created were sometimes displaced onto another culture ("European custom") or onto the past (by the use of past tense), though not consistently so, as the laughter that cues the structure of resentment in following examples shows:

> I: Why is it that just men's namedays are observed?
> W2: It's true, the male children are much more highly revered and we're just nothing! (She laughs)
> H: It's a European custom—the male dominance showing through.

W3: You must understand that the boy in the family is different from the girl—girls aren't expected to make money, and neither did they expect them to get educated.

W4: [On dating] We [girls] weren't permitted to do anything. (Husband laughs)

But when talking family history, people had access to other narrative possibilities and to memories that allowed them to speak, sometimes, of other things in other forms, such as in the following story in which women tried to configure their situations as middle-class women in the 1960s:

W5: Here, a woman is expected to do more [than in Greece]. I think it's the American way of life. She's expected to keep house, to bear children, [to have a son to carry on the family name].

This woman never specified to me what the "more" that was expected of her was. She could describe to me what she did, for example, to keep her children in Greek Orthodox circles and her reasons for doing so—in effect describing to me her deliberations on what was "Greek" and what "American," on "family" and on modernity, that is, on what connected or distanced her generation from her parents'; but there was nothing she could point to that would register as the something "more."

Women's Stories

But other people tried other tacks.[16] The long story that follows was told to me by a young suburban housewife in 1967. It was a story about her mother's struggle in adversity, and what is significant about it is that it was told mainly in a woman's voice.[17]

[I was raised in] a typically Greek family. My father was a restaurant man; my mother was a housewife. She was an interesting person too. She was twelve years old when her mother died. And she was left to raise a forty-day–old baby. . . . Her mother died of what I suppose they called childbed fever at the time. . . . So she had literally no girlhood. She was a mother.

Then [my] Uncle George [MB] came to this country. And when she was twenty—of course she raised them as best she could—she brought [the rest of the children] to this country. She was about eighteen, I think. With the intention of going back to Greece. . . . Uncle George worked very hard—a daytime job and a nighttime job. And he brought them here. . . . And when she got here, they were going to settle the children in school. . . .

But my uncle met my father and there was an arranged marriage. Very much arranged. And my mother took [two of] her brothers to Sioux City[18] with her. . . .

Anyway, she came to Sioux City as a bride. She knew her husband about twenty-four hours before she married him. I remember she said about riding to Sioux City on the train sitting next to her father-in-law, with her husband sitting across the aisle.

The woman's story about her mother began much like the male immigrant success story. It focused first on her father, on her mother (a housewife), and on her "typical" family. But then the story shifted to focus on her mother, who became an actor in her own right. Like the male immigrant success, she initially was faced with adversity; hers was to be left to be a child-mother to her younger siblings. She came to the United States, but the story wavered on whether her activity was her own or the result of her brother's activity—between her being "brought" by her brother, and her bringing the children [and herself?]. She was active in that she had her own intention to return to Greece.

Then the woman who was telling the story abruptly qualified her mother's activity by noting the arranged marriage. The arranged marriage was incomprehensible to her, as it was to others of her generation. For this woman the arranged marriage was, emphatically, "very arranged"; and it paralleled her mother's being left an orphan to raise her siblings: another adversity, a condition about which she also had no choice. Then she set her mother's loneliness and isolation in a narrative frame similar to that of the obstacles that the self-made man transformed into success. She built toward an antiphonal story, in place of "the old story," for her immigrant mother and for herself as a young, isolated, lonely, suburban wife/mother.

Sioux City was a small town where there were maybe two or three other Greek ladies. And she didn't speak any English at all. And so you cling to the people who can speak the same language. The town consisted mainly of men who were in the restaurant business and the shoe business and the grocery store business. Who either married non-Greek women because there weren't any Greek girls around, or went back to Greece, got married, and brought them back. They were all lonely women and they grouped together and they had their little organizations. Sewing circles.

We were born one right after the other. So mother no sooner finished raising one family than she was raising another. Incidentally, my mother was very well educated in Greece. The equivalent of high school and two years of college. That's why she intended to go back and enter the convent and teach. Now, as an adult and as a mother, I feel as though she didn't get to use all her potential. She feels it too, but she doesn't begrudge it, because she still thinks the best thing you can do is raise a family, even though she did it twice. . . .

I got married very late, and had my children late. And I think as a result. I'm a little more content to stay home with the kids. And not pursue a career. Oh, I've missed it. The first year I was married I thought I was going to die. I was terribly lonesome. The old story.

The woman was framing a story for herself as she put together her mother's. They both were well-educated women, for whom raising children had taken precedence over other possibilities. While she was speaking out of her own loneliness as well as her mother's, she began to investigate her mother's accomplishments and prospects for her own:

At first, my mother rarely had [my father] at home. If she wanted to see him she had to go to the restaurant, because he was there most of the time. We would go down there to visit.

The arena of family politics was structured as "the typical Greek family, the mother raised the child while the father worked." The story here explored what a woman was able to do in such an arena. This woman's stories about her father were brief, though respectful and kindly. He worked long hours, she said, because he had to.

But the success story that was prominent in other people's narratives about their fathers was held on the sidelines here and the mother was the protagonist, a "she" who was the actor.

My mother had a good classical education. When we were growing up, there was no Greek school and she was teaching us Greek. . . . She liked America and never wanted to go back. She liked Greece, but she wanted us [just] to go and see things. . . .

She was the one who taught us Greek dancing. And religion. We were brought up in the Episcopal church. . . . But she made sure we did not take communion. Three times a year she would take us to Des Moines or Waterloo or Mason City, where there was a Greek church, and take communion. These visits were a chance for her to get together with other Greek ladies and for her kids to be exposed to other Greek children. I have to say that she was the Greek religion in our home. When we wanted a thing badly, she'd take us in this little room with the icons and we'd say our prayers. It didn't matter whether we got it or not, the point was that we asked for it. Nine times out of ten, we'd forget about something. She had all kinds of motherly tricks. She'd drop candy over the door, and we thought it came from the icons because our heads were bowed. . . .

When my brother, who was the oldest, went to school, he was fluent in Greek. So in kindergarten, there was this foreign language being jammered [*sic*] at him, and do you think he wanted to stay? He'd run home. . . . So she did something that I think is terribly clever of a woman who didn't know what was going on in the American school system. She took a big

box of candy to the teacher. "Before he goes out, give him a piece of candy so he will stay." And out of desperation, my mother went to night school [to learn English]. . . .
My father felt that girls didn't need a college education. I think that's the only argument that I know of between my mother and father. That was about pulling us out of school. But then as we got out, he was so proud that we were all teachers and making money.

The mother's isolation in Sioux City in itself does not account for this singular story. It began with and recursively returned to "the old story" in which women were not actors but were acted upon by circumstances of "nature." But here with the father absent, the mother was depicted as rearranging relations among Greek language, religion, education, gender, and family, as she moved between home, schools, church, and economy. In the course of its telling, her story became, at least provisionally, a heroic narrative.[19] It imputed to the mother the ability by her work not just to transmit culture to her children but also to invent practices, negotiate meanings, and struggle with new coordinates to her life. In the process, she was glimpsed by her daughter as transforming what was "Greek" and what was "American"; at the same time, her story opened up for her daughter the possibility that neither "Greek" nor "American" was naturally male.

The storytelling also included the storyteller's anger that dissolved the terms of "the old story" and framed other possibilities. The anger suggests that the anchor for the story is the woman's own situation at home with her children. She was giving up her career, she was saying, like her mother twice gave up her childhood and her education to raise children. Within this structure, the woman then used her mother's story to configure and transform her own practices as accomplishments—in language, religion, and childrearing—and in relations with kin and with the larger social world. She was engaged in a dialogue with her mother about women's work that was not limited to family, religion, and custom, but that connected and mediated these domains and others. Like the woman's father, her own husband was a bit player. She said her husband agreed that this was her sphere.[20]

The structure of resentment emerged clearly, late in the interview with this woman, when she spontaneously remarked:

I don't want to raise my son like my husband or my brother were raised. My brother got away with murder because my mother was raising him, and not my father, because he was working. Boys should be disciplined too.

She had kept it to the side while she was trying work on another problem, namely, how to construe her mother's active construction and mediation of terms and relationships within the home and family, between home and family on the one hand and church and school and professions on the other, and even across time between the past and the future.

Also significant here were the regret and loss of having given up or having been denied something ardently hoped for. The speaker was trying to transform the constraints in which she had been placed as wife and mother and because of which she had doubts about her ability to create and order her life, that is, about her own ability to act and to transform. She used her mother's accomplishments as a guide to telling me in the interview, for example, about her own "motherly tricks" and also about her judgments as to how to be "Greek" and at the same time modern, female, middle class, suburban, and American.

Women's Cultural Work

The cultural operator called "choosing" made the first American-born generation's accounts of itself possible, because for them "choosing" entailed an individual with reason who was able to choose and who had possibilities to choose among. Marking differences in order to have alternatives to choose from was in one respect a "science of the concrete" (Lévi-Strauss 1966). In the self-made–woman stories, for example, women objectivated practice as customs and practices and turned them into tokens with which to separate the past from the present. By thus operating upon the "domestic," women transformed the connection between the "two worlds" in which the American-born lived, from an unbridgeable gulf (represented, for example, by arranged marriages and by contemporaneous "European customs") to a temporally connected, yet distanced, relation of before and after.

In women's accounts, these customs and practices included performances of family ritual, preparation of food, identifying and using signs of status, and more. As the woman who had told me the long story about her mother said, "Something I will not be Greek about is the superstitions. And I don't hang family pictures all over the house, and have the house filled with furniture and flowers." She had icons in her children's rooms, "but," she said, "I don't like candles. I think of it [sic] as a fire hazard." Styles of mourning, housekeeping, or grooming, for example, counted as signs of separation from the past and of women's modernity; yet these practices also made connections between the old and the new. What was reckoned a fire hazard, or "superstition," or just "old fashioned," marked the difference and conjoined the differences.

Women also sought to mark differences between the old and the new by simultaneously limiting the "old" areas of women's work and contrasting these limited areas with the new areas that entailed the old, plus new, activities. The old was not enough; as the same Greek woman said, "A lot of mothers have part-time jobs or clubs. A young mother now has a fuller life. Then, there was just the family and the house. That's nice, but it gets to be a drag."

Women creating the new and mediating between the old and the new were the "more" that, according to the woman (W5) I quoted earlier, women of her generation had to do, beyond the "fact of nature" of bearing sons. Their struggle to tell stories of "self-made women" was about their own "naturalization," that is, about what made them American, middle class, modern, female, and Greek (-American). As it was reckoned in their daughters' unfinished, reflexive stories, immigrant mothers had reinvented family life. Their cooking and household management, childrearing and kin-keeping, and transmission of religious practices were narrated by their daughters in the same terms as those with which they reimagined and affirmed their own practices.

Far from being limited to the "domestic" or to "sex roles," this cultural work in storytelling was about being American. The daughters viewed themselves as cultivators of middle-class life and as guardians of the production and transmission of values. They were configuring themselves as successes or living "fuller lives" as "better citizens" and "interesting persons." They were also keepers of stories about change and continuity in family life, and stories they could tell about their mothers in particular (and other women kin) were assimilated by them as gauges of their own ethnic identity, class, and modernity. "Naturalization" in the people's own words was the result of "choosing" (Chock 1986; see also Carbaugh 1988). These women assiduously "chose," they hoped, the "best of both worlds." In practice, most of the choosing and sifting depicted in the stories was done on the "Greek" side of the equation, so that some practices were kept in domestic routines or rituals; but more were banished as "superstitious," "old-fashioned," or "not practical."

In the interstices of social life—between generations, in "mixed" marriages, in language shifts, and more—meanings were confounded because myths seemed not to hold. Much of the cultural production in these spaces in between was women's work. Wives, mothers, and sisters were described to me by storytellers as negotiators of large things and small. Some depicted these activities as petty family quarrels, as bizarre behaviors of particular people, or as willful misunderstandings. Other stories disintegrated under the weight of myths that would not work for women. Anger, bewilderment, and resentment marked these stories as sites of cultural invention. Such stories opened narrative spaces for other possibilities for relating gender and "American."

Notes

I thank Jack Alexander, Jon Anderson, Richard Handler, Lawrence Poos, Bonnie Urciuoli, and Sylvia Yanagisako for critical comments on earlier drafts of this paper.

1. Schneider (1969) wrote that he suspected that "nationality" was an American cultural domain constructed out of cultural units similar to those he had found were constitutive of the domain of kinship. He noted that "land" and "birth," as well as "love" and "law," were parts of the American domain of "nationality," and that Americans calling the process of becoming a citizen "naturalization" seemed further to suggest that symbols of "nature" and "law" structured both domains.

2. Scholars who have explored connections across institutions between citizenship and gender in American law and public policy include Nelson (1984), Sapiro (1984), Fraser (1989), and Young (1990). My analysis supplements theirs by examining cultural processes in family history storytelling, through which relations of gender and citizenship are reproduced, contested, and sometimes transformed.

3. My data on immigrant success stories and other family history stories are from my fieldwork notes. Some of these data were analyzed in Chock 1989 and Chock 1991. I conducted interviews in the Chicago metropolitan area in 1967–68 with more than thirty-five individuals and couples. My fieldwork focused on people who were the adult children of people who had emigrated from Greece in the late nineteenth and early twentieth centuries. They included white-collar employees, small-business proprietors, housewives, retirees, and service-sector employees. They lived most of their lives within American institutions and in American English.

4. Yanagisako's analysis of Asian-American studies courses that configure male immigrants as protagonists and that remain nearly silent about women suggests a remarkable similarity between our two cases. Both may be instances of cultural operations of mythic themes of immigrant success.

5. The discursive practice of using women as signs of changing social identities in family stories is examined in Chock 1986. In this essay, I am focusing on women as producers of signs of social identities.

6. There are published accounts of Greek immigrant women, for example, H. Papanikolas's (1987) biographical book about her immigrant parents and S. Coumantaros's (1982) brief chapter on the founding of the Philoptochos Society, the women's service and philanthropic auxiliary of the Greek Orthodox church in the United States. But it is notable that scholars of Greek-American life largely overlook women as historical subjects.

7. Sandra Morgen's (1983) article helped me to confirm my hunch that indigenous spheres of silence and feeling indicated where I might locate sites of cultural invention and political thought/action.

8. She was probably a contemporary of the anonymous author, that is, she was probably born between 1900 and 1910. I interviewed her in 1967.

9. Two arenas of talk—scholarship and family reminiscence—provide different contexts for these and similar remarks. Scholarship on (Greek-American) ethnicity has typically selected and redacted indigenous narratives and mythic themes, so that scholarly versions have been supported and confirmed by their resonances with local idioms of family history. The family stories of the interstitial places where women worked need to be accounted for equally as sites of cultural production. Analytically they may be expected to be rich environments of invention.

10. Women and men had not only to struggle with silences about their mothers, aunts, sisters, and themselves, but also to be able to offer a "better" story than of the "weak." Weakness was also read and feared as a front for subversion and strength a front for weakness. For example, one very articulate woman told me, "[My mother] came from a family of very soft people and not aggressive or domineering, the way my father was. Very gentle. . . .

But if the father isn't very aggressive, then the mother takes over. The way my mother-in-law [in Greece] took over her grandchildren."

Compare novelist Harry Mark Petrakis' portrait of his own immigrant mother, the wife of a Greek Orthodox priest, and her "unwritten articles of dissent" to the community's "adulation" of her husband (Petrakis 1970:44). She carried on, he writes, a life of strength, energy, wry humor, zeal, and a whirl of family and community activities (44–53 passim). His parents' marriage, he writes, was the result of a bishop playing matchmaker (19–21). Presbytera Petrakis herself generously agreed to two interviews with me in 1967. About her experience she explained to me, "At that time the girls marry by somebody helping."

11. I thank Bonnie Urciuoli for helping me to spell out this point. See also Chock (1989).

12. That "hustle" is a double-entendre when used for a woman points to the contradictions wrought by gender upon the success story.

13. Scourby's sociological analysis (1989) is likewise in terms of "sex roles," a frame that naturalizes gender categories.

14. What they had to say had the sound of a rehearsed discussion. The woman, for example, used much the same terms as he, and they coached each other on points of the discussion and examples. One model the husband was using was racial politics: his fear that gender hierarchies, like racial hierarchies, were after all social and not natural and therefore could be (and would be, violently) challenged. Our interview took place in 1968, and in Chicago, as elsewhere, that latter possibility was already being realized.

15. Other stories of resentment focused on particular restrictions on women, such as in family ritual, expectations, and social life.

16. Other "odd" relatives were also grist for unusual stories. The brilliant uncle who didn't want to work for a living is a creature who fascinates, because, like a trickster, he conjoins contradictions. The woman quoted in the following text also related this story:

My grandfather on my father's side is kind of a sketchy thing. We used to hear jokes when we were little, and to this day, I don't know if they were true or not. . . . He was very brilliant and he just couldn't see working for a living. And my father had no time for my grandfather, because he did not work for a living. But my mother was fascinated by him. My father felt that he could do nothing that would earn them something to eat, or a place to live. And the boys went to work. The father sort of reaped the rewards of his children working for him. Whereas he thought he could just amuse the group with his tales and his learning. He just was an unappreciated intellectual, I think.

17. This long story about her mother began to spill out early in the interview, with little interruption from me; it continued in passages of substantial length throughout.

My analysis of this story has benefited from reconceptualizations of domestic politics in patrilineal and other male-dominant systems, such as those Yanagisako (1979:190) reviewed: Collier (1974), Lamphere (1974), and Rogers (1975). They argued that, while domestic politics are marginalized ideologically in such systems, and attributed, for example, to women's penchants for petty disturbances, that women's quarrels, disputes, and the like, should be analyzed as political actions. In a similar vein, I attribute the silence about women's transforming of culture to an ideology-based selection by scholars for institutional scenes in which men were active—for example, civic politics, church, press, fraternal associations—in ethnic culture change.

18. Some details, such as place names, have been changed to protect the identities and privacy of interviewees.

19. The heroic themes of this story resemble the achievement themes that Ginsburg (1989) has analyzed in the "procreation narratives" of the women activists in Fargo, ND's, conflicts over abortion.

20. No special attention is paid here, unlike in other accounts both from my informants and in the literature (e.g., di Leonardo 1987), to women's command of holidays and family celebrations as such.

References

Carbaugh, Donal. 1988. *Talking American: Cultural Discourses on DONAHUE.* Norwood, NJ: Ablex.

Chock, Phyllis Pease. 1986. "The Outsider Wife and the Divided Self: The Genesis of Ethnic Identities." In *Discourse and the Social Life of Meaning,* edited by P. P. Chock and June R. Wyman, 185–204. Washington, DC: Smithsonian Institution Press.

———. 1989. "The Landscape of Enchantment: Redaction in a Theory of Ethnicity." *Cultural Anthropology* 4(2): 163–81.

———. 1991. " 'Illegal Aliens' and 'Opportunity': Myth-making in Congressional Testimony." *American Ethnologist* 18(2): 279–94.

Collier, Jane F. 1974. "Women in Politics." In *Woman, Culture, and Society,* edited by M. Z. Rosaldo and L. Lamphere, 89–96. Stanford, CA: Stanford Univ. Press.

Coumantaros, Stella. 1982. "The Greek Orthodox Ladies Philoptochos Society and the Greek American Community." In *The Greek American Community in Transition,* edited by H. J. Psomiades and A. Scourby, 191–96. New York: Pella.

di Leonardo, Micaela. 1987. "The Female World of Cards and Holidays: Women, Families, and the Work of Kinship." *Signs* 12(3): 440–53.

"Forgotten Generation, The." 1950. *Athene* 10(4): 22–23, 41–42.

Fraser, Nancy. 1989. *Unruly Practices: Power, Discourse, and Gender in Contemporary Social Theory.* Minneapolis: Univ. of Minnesota Press.

Ginsburg, Faye. 1989. *Contested Lives: The Abortion Debate in an American Community.* Berkeley: Univ. of California Press.

Lamphere, Louise. 1974. "Strategies, Cooperation, and Conflict Among Women in Domestic Groups." In *Woman, Culture, and Society,* edited by M. Z. Rosaldo and L. Lamphere, 97–112. Stanford, CA: Stanford Univ. Press.

Lévi-Strauss, Claude. 1966. *The Savage Mind.* Chicago: Univ. of Chicago Press.

Morgen, Sandra. 1983. "Towards a Politics of 'Feelings': Beyond the Dialectic of Thought and Action." *Women's Studies* 10(2): 203–223.

Moskos, Charles C., Jr. 1977. "Growing Up Greek American." *Society* 14(2): 64–71.

———. 1980. *Greek Americans: Struggle and Success.* Englewood Cliffs, NJ: Prentice-Hall.

———. 1989. *Greek Americans: Struggle and Success.* 2d ed. New Brunswick, NJ: Transaction.

Nelson, Barbara J. 1984. "Women's Poverty and Women's Citizenship: Some Political Consequences of Economic Marginality." *Signs* 10(2): 209–231.

Papanikolas, Helen. 1987. "Αιμιλια – Γεωργος: *Emily – George.* Salt Lake City: Univ. of Utah Press.

Petrakis, Harry Mark. 1963. *The Odyssey of Kostas Volakis.* New York: David McKay.

———. 1970. *Stelmark: A Family Recollection.* New York: David McKay.

Rogers, Susan Carol. 1975. "Female Forms of Power and the Myth of Male Dominance: A Model of Female/Male Interaction in Peasant Societies." *American Ethnologist* 2(4): 727–56.

Saloutos, Theodore. 1973. "Growing Up in the Greek Community of Milwaukee." *Historical Messenger* 29(2): 46–60.

Sapiro, Virginia. 1984. "Women, Citizenship, and Nationality: Immigration and Naturalization Policies in the United States." *Politics and Society* 13(1): 1–26.

Schneider, David M. 1969. "Kinship, Nationality, and Religion in American Culture: Toward a Definition of Kinship." In *Forms of Symbolic Action,* edited by R. F. Spencer, 116–33. Seattle: American Ethnological Society.

Scourby, Alice. 1984. *The Greek Americans.* Boston: Twayne.

———. 1989. "The Interweave of Gender and Ethnicity: The Case of Greek-Americans." In *The Ethnic Enigma: The Salience of Ethnicity for European-Origin Groups,* edited by Peter Kivisto, 114–33. Philadelphia: Balch Institute Press.

Williams, Raymond. 1977. *Marxism and Literature.* Oxford: Oxford Univ. Press.

Yanagisako, Sylvia. 1979. "Family and Household: The Analysis of Domestic Groups." *Annual Review of Anthropology* 8: 161–205.

Young, Iris Marian. 1990. *Justice and the Politics of Difference.* Princeton, NJ: Princeton Univ. Press.

10

Ethnography Among the Newark: The Class of '58 of Weequahic High School

Sherry B. Ortner

Counting the cars on the New Jersey Turnpike,
They've all gone to look for America.
—Simon and Garfunkel, "America"

Something unreal. For me, it was a feeling that persisted throughout this
adventure. (How else can I describe this undertaking? It was the daily
experience of *others*, their private hurts, real and fancied, that I was probing.
In lancing an especially obstinate boil, it is not the doctor who experiences
the pain.)
Studs Terkel, *Working*

We have heard a great deal in recent years about the crisis in anthropology,
a crisis of representation. The problem in a nutshell is this: the standard
form of anthropological writing, the ethnography, is now seen as a deeply
problematic medium. Typically portraying the group under study at one
point in time, and emphasizing longstanding traditions, ethnography fails
to grasp and convey the historical dynamism of the society. Attempting to
convey a portrait of the group's "culture," and emphasizing those aspects
of the culture that are shared by the group as a whole, it fails to grasp and
convey the multiple subject positions and contending voices within the
society. Thus, while the concept of culture was originally meant to be radically opposed to natural essence concepts like "race," standard ethnographic
writing ironically inverted its intention: because societies were portrayed as
static and homogeneous, their "culture" took on the quality of a natural
essence. Whatever part of the globe the people lived in, they were—in
Edward Said's (1978) potent term—orientalized, turned into exotic Others.

The specific stylistic device heightening the problem of ethnography as text was the mode of writing James Clifford (1986) dubbed "ethnographic realism"—a bland yet authoritative and seeminging omniscient voice that represented itself as purely descriptive, factual. To subvert ethnographic realism, then, anthropologists were urged to experiment with both authorial style and ethnographic form. My own reaction to all this was initially suspicious. While I recognized the problems of timelessness, homogeneity, and orientalism being raised, it seemed to me that these were theoretical problems, or framework problems, rather than formal or stylistic ones. Yet as I embarked on the American project discussed in this paper, I began to realize that the two were not so easily separable.

The specific difficulty with representing America, as I see it, is that America is overanalyzed and underethnographized. Here I use the term ethnography to signal a kind of knowledge rather than a kind of text. Ethnographic knowledge is knowledge of the lived worlds of real people in real time and space, and while we may be able to do without ethnographies as we have known them, we cannot do without ethnography. And although there is a significant body of ethnographic work on America, much of it quite good, the ratio of knowledge derived from this work to knowledge derived from polling, statistics, media analysis, and journalism is radically out of whack. When a woman at a presidential debate asks the candidates how the national debt has affected them personally, she is saying that they may have the numbers but they don't have the ethnography. But what kind of ethnography, in the textual sense, can be written?

At least two relatively novel forms have emerged in recent years, primarily (though not entirely) in the context of the study of America. The first is what has been called an ethnography of issues (Messerschmidt 1981). The work tends to center on a specific site of contemporary conflict and attempts to illuminate the practices and assumptions underlying that conflict for all the parties involved. Faye D. Ginsburg's *Contested Lives* (1989), a study of the abortion controversy in a midwestern town, and Jonathan Rieder's *Canarsie* (1985), a study of racial conflict in a Brooklyn neighborhood, are excellent examples of this genre.

The other emerging form may be called documentary ethnography. Here the effort is to enter relatively small life-worlds and examine how large-scale social forces work themselves out in everyday life. Judith Stacey's *Brave New Families* (1990), exploring the twin impact of Reaganomics and shifts in norms about "the family" on two kin networks in the Silicon Valley, is a brilliant example. There is an almost cinematic quality to this book, reminding one of the PBS documentary series of some years ago, "An American Family." In that series, the lives of the members of a California family literally unraveled before the camera, as Pat and Jim Loud exploded their marriage and their gay son came out to his parents and several million viewers. It is this genre of documentary ethnography, in somewhat less dramatic form than the Loud family epic, that I am considering adopting for my own ethnography of America and that I will try out in this paper. Before saying more about it, however, let me introduce the project.

The ethnographic population for the study is my own high-school graduating class, the class of '58 of Weequahic High School in Newark, New Jersey. One of the central questions for the project concerns the ways in which social class seems to both exist and not exist in America. As many observers have noted, American discourse lacks a developed vocabulary of class; Eisler's (1983) book about American elites called class "America's last dirty secret." Although a phrase like "middle class" is used in casual conversation all the time, class as a social phenomenon is almost never talked *about*. (The primary exception to this point is during election years, and always with reference to the middle class.) And while class is sporadically the basis of media representations (more in television than in film), the history of these representations is complex to say the least. Even today, when there is far more cinematic portrayal of social difference and social conflict than there was in the past, and despite the now mantra-like status of the race/class/gender triad, class is the least represented form of social difference.

I begin from the position that class in America is real and has major long-term consequences, but it is silenced by this lack of vocabulary and the many ideological cross-currents (see Ortner 1992) that make it hard not only to speak class but to think it. I take class to be real in the standard Marxist sense: classes are objective structural positions within a capitalist economic order. Whatever the transformations of capitalism in the late twentieth century (and they are multiple and important), these positions still exist and will be filled, if not by Americans then by cheap labor elsewhere on the globe. It is the positions that carry the consequences: things like the differential rates of smoking and lung cancer between the middle class and the working class; or the fact that when the state of California has to cut its higher-education budget the community colleges, which have a high percentage of working-class and lower-middle-class students, are the first to go; or even in the impact of natural disasters, as when a hurricane primarily destroys mobile homes, most of them uninsured.

Thus class is real like the squares on a board game, and landing on or staying in these squares has real consequences. But to say this is not to deny the equally fundamental point that class is discursively constructed, that in some sense it is only called into more than statistical being—or not, as the case may be—by the prevailing discursive formations as heard in everyday forms of talk as well as in public representations of all sorts: elementary school textbooks, mass media, rap songs, presidential campaign speeches.

So my research project concerns, among other things, the play of class in people's lives in the context of a culture that gives them an impoverished language for thinking and speaking it. It involves looking for the ways in which class shapes their lives, while listening for the ways in which class pain, privilege, and antagonism are displaced into more culturally elaborated discourses.

The project consists mostly of interviewing my former classmates, and the interviews almost always begin with the informant asking me what the project is about. I always answer this question relatively incoherently—and you will see the many forms of my incoherence—initially because I, like any native, had trouble talking about class clearly, but after a while because I realized that this was a productive strategy. Here is a fieldnote from early in the project about this opening gambit:

> She asked what the project was about. I said it wasn't fully articulated yet—that seems like a better strategy all around, especially since it's true, but also because it seems more open to a wide range of responses. I said there were two general areas, and I'm not sure how they link up: the general question of "success" or lack of same, both in reality and in people's perceptions; and the general question of social divisions and differences—class, race, etc., both in h.s., and later. On the last point I said some people may feel that there weren't many divisions in our class, that it was very homogeneous, and she said, well "in broad sociological terms" it would appear that way, but obviously there were subtle differences. For example, "of course I wouldn't associate with E.U. or J.J."

After some sort of introductory exchange like this, however, I simply ask people to tell me the story of their life. I must say hearing these stories has been an overwhelming experience. For they tell about everything under the sun: success and failure, marriage and divorce, crime and punishment, love and hate, friendship and enmity, religious conversions, affairs, kids, work, politics, nostalgia, death, and more. Moreover, the narrative shapes of people's stories have been equally fascinating: the orderly, year-by-year presentation of an accountant; the obsessive, one-subject interview of a man who just went through a bitter divorce; the funny, sarcastic narrative of a woman who won a custody suit; the large, circular, bubbly talk of someone who had so much to tell she didn't know where to start; the apologetic, defensive talk of someone who didn't go to college and was faced with an overeducated anthropologist; the people who've got a secret and both do and don't want me to know about it; and more, more, more.

I have pondered long and hard about how I want to represent all this, particularly in light of my earlier point that America is in some sense overanalyzed, that the ratio of analysis and interpretation and punditry to actual ethnographic description is too high. Far too little is known about what actually goes on, as we anthropologists like to say, on the ground. This brings me back to the question of genre. I want very much to retain the immediacy, the power, of these stories. While of course I will not be able to resist a good bit of analysis and interpretation myself (though I hope to avoid the punditry), I want to push the raw ethnography to the fore as much as possible. I thus find myself drawn to textual models that include not only the Stacey book and the PBS documentary mentioned earlier but also the documentary films of Frederick Wiseman and Michael Apted and the oral-history books of Studs Terkel. Wiseman's films (e.g., *High School* and *Law and Order*) and Apted's extraordinary *Twenty Eight Up* make your head jerk back from the impact, while Terkel's interviews in *Working* (1974) produce a deeper, but equally powerful, kind of engagement. I was particularly impressed with the capacity of *Working*, which has no narrative structure and is simply one interview after another, to keep me reading from beginning to end. Of course all of these works are highly constructed and implicitly interpreted; it is not as if they present some unmediated view of reality. Nonetheless they provide, in the current jargon, plenty of "voices," strong voices, and I think that's what we need to hear.

So this paper is something of a tryout for this ethnographic endeavor. Although, as I said, the interviews cover just about anything you can think of, and although I plan to write eventually about all of it, I will stick fairly narrowly here to some of the class issues sketched above, simply for the sake of coherence. But I will build the paper as much as possible out of direct quotes from my fieldnotes and from transcripts of some of the eighty interviews that I have completed to date. I want to let the ethnography do the talking.

I should explain why I chose my high-school graduating class as the ethnographic population for the project. The first and most obvious reason was accessibility: there was a high likelihood that people would talk openly to me, and a high likelihood that I would understand what they were talking about. But the group is not unrepresentative of "America," providing we recognize the tricky qualities of the notion of representativeness: it all depends on what you're trying to represent. Are we talking about the race/ethnic demographics of the country as a whole? Then the answer is no: the class of '58 of Weequahic High School was 80 percent Jewish, 13 percent other White ethnics (Italian-Americans, Irish-Americans, etc.), 7 percent persons of color (mostly African-Americans), and 0 percent WASP. But are we talking about certain kinds of urban and suburban neighborhoods— mostly White, mostly middle class—that probably a majority of Americans inhabit (including an increasing number of minorities)? Then we're getting closer. About class composition? Close again: in the high-school era the group was, like America generally, mostly middle and lower-middle class, though those categories of course cover a multitude of sins that it will take the whole project to unravel. About the dominance of the professional-managerial classes in this country today? Close again: the group is now probably about one third PMC. About gender? The class is 50–50. And finally, if we are talking about geography, Newark, New Jersey, seems to me as representative of the urban experience in the second half of the twentieth century as any other city one could name—its closest parallel is probably Detroit.

Moreover, there is a sense in which the status of this group as a community, a set of people who once shared a geographic place but no longer do, reflects the standard mode of community in contemporary America. That is, people for the most part still grow up in "communities" in the traditional sense, in towns or suburbs or neighborhoods where people know one another in overlapping ways. But then they disperse to varying degrees of geographic and social distance and in varying moods of escape or nostalgia. The traditional anthropological practice of settling in to one residential community fails to capture the reality of these patterns of movement, fails to capture the space-time trajectories of people's lives. However, to interview an assortment of grownups wherever they happen to be, as in Robert N. Bellah et. al.'s *Habits of the Heart* (1985), fails to capture the past communities that their lives embody. Studying the class of '58 of Weequahic High School, like studying any cohort of genuine "consociates," (Geertz 1973, adapted from Alfred Schütz), lets me capture both dimensions.

The double aspect of the group—once a group in the on-the-ground sense, now a set of three hundred or so individuals spread around America—also both poses and solves a methodological problem. The study is necessarily interview based, and the critical question for interview-centered research is that of making sense of the interviews. What helps one decipher what people say in the classic fieldwork situation is one's access to their lives outside of what they say to the ethnographer; that is one of the many benefits of participant-observation. Here I do not have that; with some exceptions, and the exceptions are golden, I zip in, do a two-hour interview, then hit the freeway again. In the early stages of the fieldwork, I felt this absence of backstage access acutely. But as the project progressed I discovered that there were significant networks of relationships that had survived and, equally important, networks of gossip that held even those who had completely lost touch with one another within a web of memory, rumor, and mutual fascination. Gossip, rumor, and memory go a long way toward serving the backstage-access function of classic participant-observation. Here is one of my fieldnotes on that (I have made occasional interpolations to clarify certain references):

> So the rumors about K. P. and [his wife] seem quite extraordinary in retrospect—that he had had an affair and tried to break up the marriage but she had threatened suicide and so he stayed. If it's not true, and it doesn't sound like it is, there's a kind of magnitude of exaggeration here

that is awesome. Still, if I weren't wired into these kinds of rumors, this project would be infinitely poorer. First of all some of them are true. And second of all, even if they're false, they provide me with some questions that I would never otherwise ask. And even when I don't ask, as [in an interview with a man whom I had heard had a criminal past; I was hoping he would raise it himself, he never did, and I couldn't get up the courage to pop the question],—even when I don't ask, they provide me with a sense of what is *not* being said, as well as of what is being said. It's what makes the whole thing ethnography, even more than going into physical sites like M.'s [fancy] club, though that helps too—everything helps. It reminds me of how flat [some interviews I did for an earlier Sherpa project] were, just because I didn't have wires criss-crossing through that set of people and their stories.

Now let me ease into the fieldwork itself. The work consists primarily of traveling around the country and interviewing people for a few hours or so, wherever they choose to meet. Some of the interviews are done in people's homes, some in workplaces, and some in restaurants, bars, shopping malls, and the like. For the most part I have been taping the interviews, but some number of them are not recorded for various reasons, and even when I tape, a great deal happens both before and after the tape runs. In fact, I am struck by the number of games that can be played, by both informants and myself, with the presence, absence, and on/off status of the tape recorder. Even this simple instrument of so-called objective data recording can come to embody a large number of meanings, including class anxiety. A note about an evening with an Italian-American woman:

> T. talked non stop. I forgot the tape recorder, forgot the whole work bag, somehow was just thinking of it as a social event. In a way I think it would have been difficult to tape—I never could move her toward anything resembling a formal interview anyway, partly because it was a kind of party, defined as social, partly because of her rambly style, partly because of the class factor in some sense—I had to work to just be an ordinary person, not high status, about which she almost definitely felt insecure, or so I felt/feared. If I had pulled out the tape recorder, she would have gone all formal (she had worked into the conversation very early that she felt bad about not having gone to college), and her husband would have moved into the hostile teasing mode [that I'm familiar with from my Uncle Gerry]. This is all by way of justifying forgetting the tape recorder, though I think maybe I really would have wound up not using it.

I don't think, on that evening, that I ever directly raised the subject of class; as the notes indicate, I was too worried about putting her off. In most interviews, though, I did, and it is certainly the case that *some* people were quite clear on what I meant by class and were eager to talk about it, whether in the mode of snobbishness from above—the woman who kept talking about how some people "weren't very fine"—or in the mode of feeling slighted from below—the man whose parents joined a fancy club where "they made him feel like shit." It was also the case that people whom I would categorize as lower-middle class were more likely to pick up and run with the class category than the middle middles. This is not surprising—privilege rarely recognizes itself. And finally, a handful of people who had experienced downward mobility had a particularly acute sense of the differences between the different squares on the board:

> K. U. immediately got into the class issue—yes indeed there was a big difference between [the two more solidly middle-class grammar schools] on the one hand and the other ones on the other. She moved from [one of the better school districts] when she was small to one of the other districts and was very conscious of the difference. Somebody once saw O.E. going into her house and said, what are you doing here, slumming? She definitely got into this topic. She herself got a B.A. but married a plumber and that was a real problem [in their marriage].

But while some people connect strongly to the class question, the majority of people, regardless of actual class position, simply cannot or will not think with the category. With them, talking class is a genuine struggle, both in the sense of struggling for language, for words, and, in the sense of literal resistance, of informants struggling against my attempts to focus discussion through this category. Here are some examples of outright resistance. The first is from an interview with a Polish-American woman, the daughter of a Teamster:

> I tried to raise the question of class, and she refused the category. When she was saying that her father wouldn't hear of her going to college, she said it was because he had old-world values. And I said do you think it was a factor of class, and she looked slightly disconcerted, so I tried to smooth it over and continued, or just his cultural values, and she pounced on that, and said "just his cultural values."

The next example is from a Jewish woman whose family background I don't have specific information on, but who was probably—judging by a snobbish comment by someone in another interview—working or lower-middle class. This woman had refused to be taped and avoided talk about her past, but was happy to make pronouncements on more impersonal subjects:

> I emphasized that the project was about "class" and "money"—seemed safer than anything more personal or open-ended—and she resisted that this was a major factor in both the cliques in high school and in people's

lives generally. She said she thought the biggest factor in high-school cliques was "intelligence." Also that cliques formed around "different values." Anyway, she said, mildly rebuking my focus, money is such a Jewish value, Jews think that money is the most important thing in life.

And finally, among these examples of resistance, here is a note on a conversation with a middle-class Jewish man:

> D. denied that class or economic differences affected [our group] at all, either in high school, or long term. About long term, I said we'll see. About high school, I said, well what about the people who had to work after school and couldn't participate in all the sports as he did, and committees, and clubs, and so forth, and that finally sank in—he could see the point. He said that as a businessman he tended to see things in dollars and cents, and my point was materialistic enough to make a dent.

By far the most common reaction among informants is to change the subject, sometimes in the strong sense of shifting to some entirely different topic, and sometimes in the weaker sense of translating class into related but subtly different categories. These include first and foremost success and money. For most people, and in most contexts, success and money are interchangeable, though success also has a wider range of uses that will be unpacked in another context. In any event, here are two examples of the easy-lure-of-success discourse, compared to the difficulty of talking class. The first is from a woman who was middle class in high school and now is married to a wealthy man:

> She asked what the project is about. I see that it is critical that I get a good opening line on this. So I said it's about success in America, about what makes people successful or not. [She didn't pick up on the second part, which was meant to elicit ideas of advantage and disadvantage, but instead] launched on a big speech about how incredibly successful our whole class has been. How people have made incredible amounts of money and really succeeded. She said, now you, of course you're successful, uh, uh, in your *field*, but you're not really successful in terms of, uh, uh, like you don't own a movie studio or something, I mean *monetarily*. She said it's just fantastic how well our class has done, even jerks who were nothings in high school have done well, you remember what's his name (I didn't, so I don't now), well he retired at forty. And [somebody else] retired at forty too. She said she loves to hear success stories, she thinks it's just great, she doesn't have an envious bone in her body, it just makes her feel good to hear of other people's success. And when she hears about people who haven't succeeded, she feels really bad because it's so unfortunate, everyone else is making it.

A second example of the power-of-success discourse to preempt questions of structural difference is the following, an excerpt from a transcript of an interview with a Jewish man who is now a very wealthy lawyer. You will hear him change the subject of class twice, once by translation into success discourse, and once by tracking off the subject completely:

SBO: David, let me go back to Weequahic a little bit and . . . the stuff I was talking to you before about these kind of divisions and differences in the high school. How did you perceive the social groupings and the social, I mean, or were you just, I think of you as so much having been on top of the heap.

DP: Well, our group, so to speak, we weren't the, from a financial standpoint, we weren't wealthy. Some of the kids were, my family wasn't, my family was middle class. I had everything I needed or wanted but I got scholarships to go to college because my folks were in that sense not really that affluent. But in all other respects I was so-called at the top of the heap, in the sense that we were, you know how I would look at it? We were the college prep group, we took the college prep curriculum, you know what I'm saying?

SBO: Yeah, it was the success track, right.

DP: Exactly. That's exactly the word, I was just gonna say success track.

SBO: Sorry.

DP: No, that's good!

SBO: I shouldn't be taking the [words out of your mouth].

DP: No, that's good, it means we're thinking the same way. But the point is that I didn't think, when I say the top of the heap, I'm using your term, when I say the top of the heap I don't mean, I didn't feel snobby about the folks that weren't in our group, I really didn't. In fact I was maybe friendlier with them than many of the other people in our group. But the success track is what I mean by the top of the heap. Because we were all, D., Y., K., and all of us, y'know, we were all gonna be success—C.—we were all gonna be hot shots. We were all gonna go to college, we were all in the top whatever of the class, we were all gonna go to university, we were all gonna be doctors, lawyers, or indian chiefs. Y'know, that was our success track, there's no doubt about that. My folks didn't push me, but there was a certain unstated expectation, there's no question about that. I love my parents, they were wonderful to me, compared to other parents. And grandparents! As grandparents they were so wonder—I'm getting off on a little bit of a tangent—

SBO: That's all right.

Both money and success are graduated categories—the idea behind both of them is also the idea behind social stratification theory in general—everybody is the same, everybody has the same opportunities, and some people just do better than others. The major alternative discursive move is to identify class with specific ethnic or racial groups, or rather to implicitly identify specific groups with specific class positions as if the class positions were essences of the groups. While the racial/ethnic coding of class differences may seem in one way to be further removed from the reality of class than "money," I have begun to think on the contrary that it is actually closer to that reality, in the sense that it signals the greater drag of class on identity and on "success" than is normally recognized. In any event, many people, both Jewish and non-Jewish, translate the class question into a question of Jewishness. The following is from a fieldnote summary of a taped interview with a Jewish man from a working- or lower-middle–class background. Notice that class is first shunted into Jewishness, but then brought back into the discourse in classic form: "workers" and "employer."

> After he told me the story of his life (terrible divorce, both parents immigrants, one of eight children, the only one who went to college), I asked what he thought was the most important factor in either propelling him ahead or holding him back in life (this formulation seemed pretty good). I tried to introduce the notion of class, but that never got off the ground, but then he launched into Jewishness and this was clearly the most important thing to him. . . . The main thing was how the Jewish people are disappearing because of all the intermarriage, and how important it was to put one's energy into saving this group, because it is the group that supports one and helps one get ahead. He also did some rap on how workers need to identify with their employers, because we're all in it together, and if businesses fold then there won't be any jobs anyway. This seemed to come out of the blue sky.

The same coding of class as Jewishness is performed by this Italian-American man, the son of a chemical worker:

> I asked H. if he felt sentimental at all about Weequahic High School and he said oh yes, definitely. He said he thinks it really got him started in life, having to overcome being looked down on. I said, did you feel looked down on at Weequahic and he said, well, yeah, coming into a Jewish school like that, of course.

But now let me back off from discussions in which class was actually the subject. I said earlier that, more often than not, class has this fleeting quality, floating through discussions of almost every subject under the sun, rarely focalized, barely textualized. And I want to preserve the integrity of those discussions, even while recognizing the play of class in and through them. Here, for example, is an excerpt of a transcript of an interview with one of the ten African-American men in the class, four of whom are already dead. This man, like a number of other blacks in the class, had come up from the South. What you need to know to understand this conversation is never stated: Barringer High School, where he went his first year up North, was a working-class high school, and the influx of Blacks from the South in the fifties was putting pressure on the White working class. Weequahic, on the other hand, was for the most part securely, or at least subjectively, middle class:

> SBO: So when did you come up here [from the South]? How old were you when you came up?
> FY: I think it was '56. See, my first year of high school in Jersey was in Barringer High School. It was a very bad experience for me, I couldn't believe it. Everything that I heard that was . . . bad in the South was what I saw in Barringer High School, and going to Weequahic was a unique experience, what I was looking for. It turned out to be exactly what I thought integration was supposed to be about.
> SBO: You mean there was a lot of racism at Barringer?
> FY: Oh, my god, I couldn't believe it. I was so glad to get out of there I didn't know what to do. . . .
> SBO: How about the teachers in Weequahic, did you feel that they treated you well, that they . . .
> FY: I was in *love* with Miss T. I thought she was great. I think I was crazy about her because she was *rough*. She didn't take any stuff on her.

Miss T., by the way, was a White Jewish woman and almost certainly very left wing, as I have now come to realize was true of many of the Weequahic teachers at the time. She has been spontaneously mentioned in several interviews as a tremendously inspiring teacher. One woman said she can still see—and she jumped up from her chair—Miss T. pacing the room and teaching them about the glory of—here she flung her arms wide— DEMOCRACY.

And finally, an excerpt from an interview with a middle-class Jewish woman, in which the only subject was her divorce and extended custody battle. It is a story of gender relations and marriage and children and in-laws and financial difficulties and the law; class is not the topic. But class, as you will see, is part of what made it all happen, and as the narrative progresses it sort of rises to the surface, then sinks again.

Her earliest reference to her ex-husband was as "not a success-oriented kind of guy." I pick up the narrative at the point where she begins to contemplate divorce:

> And for three or four years it really wasn't bad. I had this nice little house, I had friends, my kids were ok, I wasn't working, I was busy with the kids, and then I don't know what happened, I don't know if there was a catalyst, but I started having, I was really not happy with the kind of person Ed was. I kept saying to myself, if I wasn't married to him, I wouldn't be his

friend. It got to the point that I wouldn't go out to dinner with him unless we were with other people. If there were other people around, fine, but he and I alone, I had nothing to say to him. His whole family was like, Sherry, my mother-in-law, I remember that she used to say to me, when he was out of a job, I should've sent him to trade school. I kept thinking, you're talking you should've? He should've been a brain surgeon, you should be saying. You should've sent him to trade school? What are you talking about?

The couple got divorced, there was a custody battle, and the father got the older son while she got the younger one. The father turned the older son's mind against her, she believed, and for many years the son would not speak to her. At the time of the divorce the husband had not been working, so no child support had been awarded. Later, when she was broke and he was working, she went back to court to sue for child support, and he countersued for custody of the younger son. She fought and won. After that, the older son agreed to see her again.

DL: He must have been about fourteen or fifteen by the time he decided to meet me for lunch. And I had lunch with him and we talked and it was like, after the second custody thing was over and done with, all the fight went out of him. He had lost the anger, and he was ready to have a relationship with me again. People used to say to me, y' know, you'll see, he'll get older, he'll come back to you, and I said y' know what, Laura, he's killing me now, and I'm not going to let him stomp on my face any more. This is enough, I've had it. He really was. And by the time he was a junior in high school, I had to go with him to his college interviews, he wouldn't, y' know Ed is really a typical blue-collar kind of person, I never met a Jewish person like that, did you ever hear of a Jewish mother talking about sending her son to trade school? That was the kind of thinking that he came from, and he embarrassed Owen, and ultimately Larry [the younger son] too. There are only certain places Larry will go with him. But after that Owen was, I had to go to the orientation tea and everything, he wouldn't let his father go anywhere, and we became very very close, except that they both do have a very fierce loyalty to their father. When Owen comes home from Chicago, he stays at his father's, and he says to me that he doesn't worry about me, they don't worry about me, because I'm the strong one, which I found to be amazing. I never ever thought that I was the strong one in *anything*. Y' know, I'm almost so passive that I don't get up to walk from here to there.

So much could be said about this text. So much could be said, as I reach the end of this paper, about the project more generally. My resolutely ethnographic focus here has intentionally blocked analysis and interpretation, except in passing. I chose this focus for several reasons—partly because, being in the middle of the project, I am not really ready to talk about it, and partly because I wanted to see how far one could get as an anthropologist with the strategies of a Studs Terkel or a Frederick Wiseman. The answer here is probably, "not far enough for most academic audiences."

But if I *were* going to analyze and interpret, here are some of the things I would talk about:

Jews and America. How persuasive is the argument earlier in this paper about this particular group being reasonably representative of "American culture"? Judging by reactions of readers and hearers, not very. There seems to be some sense in which Jews *cannot* be representative of anything but themselves. I would resist this position. The native texts quoted in this paper show that, if anything, Jews articulate hegemonic American discourse very well indeed. If there is any "problem," it is that they articulate it a little too baldly, a little too nakedly, for the taste of others.

The personal is personal. The degree to which informants stick to a very intimate level of conversation is striking. The real world seems hardly to enter their accounts. This is true not only of the texts quoted in this paper but more generally in the eighty or so interviews completed to date. There are many ways to think about what is going on here: the framing of the question ("tell me about your life") may trigger this kind of response for Americans; the fact that my informants and I all know each other from more innocent times, and/or the fact that I am a female interviewer, may also have this effect. But I would pursue a different line of thinking about this, concerning the pervasive apoliticalness of much of middle-class discourse. This seems to me all of a piece with the submersion of class.

"Changing the subject." This phrase has taken on new meanings in the context of poststructuralist and postmodern theorizing. Although I used it earlier with respect to people's inability to "talk class," it can be thought about with respect to questions of selfhood, personhood, agency—the subject—in the context of a discursive formation that hides class and blames the victim. White, middle-class males generally "have" (and see themselves as having) more agency than anybody else; the saleswoman who fought a brilliantly successful custody battle is nonetheless discursively disabled from seeing her own agency: "I never ever thought that I was the strong one in *anything.* . . . I'm almost so passive that I don't get up to walk from here to there." The question of "changing the subject"—of being or not being the author of one's actions, of having or not having agency—should thus be thought of in the context of various forms of inequality, including class (see Ortner 1991; see also Sennett and Cobb 1972).

"Class." Finally, the category of class itself has been undergoing radical rethinking for the past two decades, and this paper (as well as the larger project) embodies much of this rethinking. In particular, we are all faced with the challenge of understanding, following the discursive turn, how class can be culturally constructed and yet continue to be "real." In addition, we

must learn to find class discourse where it lives—in discourses of success and money, of course, but also in discourses of gender, race, and ethnicity. The issues here tie back in part to the "Jewish question": In many ways talking about Jewishness and non-Jewishness is one of the strongest ways these people have of talking class. But when class is couched in terms of Jewishness, what happens to both categories?

This of course is one of the most common discursive patterns of American ethnosociology. Most of our so-called ethnic categories contain a secret class component: the discursive effect for native informants is a blurring of domains, a tendency to slip and shift back and forth between the two categories. The slipping and shifting in turn tend to insure a constant exchange of meanings between the categories, a naturalization of class and an unspoken ranking of ethnicities.

These, then, are some of the things I would talk about more analytically if I had time, and if this were that kind of paper. But it's not. Thus I want the ethnography to have the last word, and I will conclude with a final excerpt from my fieldnotes:

> March 8, 1992. I've been arranging LA interviews. No leisurely housewives out there. All the women (as well as all the men) are working, and it's a lot harder to schedule. E.I. in particular sounds virtually hysterical about her time, and constantly says that she doesn't want "to commit." And she gets terribly edgy and this note of hysteria creeps into her voice at the slightest pressure. Nonetheless with people like her it is clear that I actually—against my "niceness" and agreeability instincts—have to put on some pressure. Otherwise people keep wanting to put me off. Usually I'm in the opposite position, very busy and putting off nuisance callers of various kinds who want a piece of me. And of course with the Sherpas I could just barge in. (I mean, I don't think I was *so* assuming of privilege and entitlement when I was with the Sherpas, but comparatively speaking I feel ashamed of myself. I do think I got better with the Sherpas as time went on.) Anyway, it's healthy to be in this more symmetrical position vis-à-vis my informants. Nobody can accuse me of silencing *them*.

Acknowledgments

This paper was previously published in the *Michigan Quarterly Review* (Summer 1993): 410–29. It was first presented as a lecture at the University of Michigan in October 1992, on the occasion of my assuming the Sylvia L. Thrupp Professorship of Anthropology and Women's Studies. The project as a whole was supported by funds from the John D. and Catherine T. MacArthur Foundation, the Office of the Vice President for Research of the

University of Michigan, the Rackham School of Graduate Studies of the University of Michigan, the LS&A Faculty Assistance Fund of the University of Michigan, and the Wenner-Gren Foundation for Anthropological Research. Special thanks to Judy Rothbard for ongoing research assistance and hospitality, and for helpful feedback on this paper; to Roger Rouse for some very helpful brainstorming sessions; to Carol Delaney, Laurence Goldstein, Tim Taylor, and Sylvia Yanagisako for illuminating comments; and to Tim Taylor for day-to-day solidarity.

References

Books and Articles

Bellah, Robert N., Richard Madsen, William M. Sullivan, Ann Swidler, and Steven M. Tipton. 1985. *Habits of the Heart: Individualism and Commitment in American Life.* Berkeley: Univ. of California Press.

Clifford, James. 1986. *Writing Culture: The Poetics and Politics of Ethnography.* Berkeley: Univ. of California Press.

Eisler, Benita. 1983. *Class Act: America's Last Dirty Secret.* New York: Franklin Watts.

Geertz, Clifford. 1973. "Person, Time, and Conduct in Bali." In *Interpretation of Cultures.* New York: Basic Books.

Ginsburg, Faye D. 1989. *Contested Lives: The Abortion Debate in an American Community.* Berkeley: Univ. of California Press.

Messerschmidt, Donald A., ed. 1981. *Anthropologists at Home in North America: Methods and Issues in the Study of One's Own Society.* Cambridge, UK: Cambridge Univ. Press.

Ortner, Sherry B. 1991. "Narrativity in Culture, History, and Lives." Working Paper #66, Program in the Comparative Study of Social Transformations, University of Michigan.

————. 1992. "Reading America: Preliminary Notes on Class and Culture." In *Recapturing Anthropology: Working in the Present,* edited by Richard G. Fox, 163–90. Santa Fe, NM: School of American Research Press.

Rieder, Jonathan. 1985. *Canarsie: The Jews and Italians of Brooklyn Against Liberalism.* Cambridge, MA: Harvard Univ. Press.

Said, Edward. 1978. *Orientalism.* New York: Pantheon.

Sennett, Richard, and Jonathan Cobb. 1972. *The Hidden Injuries of Class.* New York: Knopf.

Stacey, Judith. 1990. *Brave New Families: Stories of Domestic Upheaval in Late 20th Century America.* New York: Basic Books.

Terkel, Studs. 1974. *Working: People Talk About What They Do All Day and How They Feel About What They Do.* New York: Pantheon.

Films

Apted, Michael. 1985. *Twenty Eight Up*. New York: Real Video. Video recording.

Gilbert, Craig, producer; Raymond, Alan and Susan, filmmakers. 1971. *An American Family*. New York: WNET/13. 12 part Video series.

Wiseman, Frederick. 1969. *High School*. Cambridge, MA: Zipporah Films. 16 mm. Film, 75 min.

———. 1980. *Law and Order*. Cambridge, MA: Zipporah Films. 16 mm. Film. 81 min.

11

Transforming Orientalism: Gender, Nationality, and Class in Asian American Studies

Sylvia Yanagisako

"Asian American" poses the conundrum of how a category of people whose only common experience is that of having been labeled "Oriental" in an "Occidental" nation can forge for themselves a politically empowering ethnic identity. Put another way, "Asian American" raises the question of how people from diverse linguistic, cultural, religious, and national backgrounds who are situated in different class locations can fashion a unifying ethnic identity and at the same time challenge the dualistic model of world cultures that has lumped them together in the first place.

In this essay I analyze a cultural practice through which some Asian Americans have attempted to accomplish this paradoxical goal. The cultural practice is the teaching of "Asian American History" in universities and colleges in the United States.[1] In light of the high rate of college attendance among Asian Americans, what might otherwise appear to be an academic pursuit marginal to the politics of ethnicity is, in this case, central to it. Indeed, college courses on Asian American History offer a particularly appropriate site for studying the ways in which academic and pedagogical practices construct ethnic identity.

This essay also responds to a hypothesis offered more than two decades ago by David Schneider. Following his analysis (1968) of American kinship as a cultural system structured by the symbolic opposition between shared "substance" (The Order of Nature) and shared "code for conduct" (The Order of Law), Schneider (1969) suggested that other cultural domains constituting relations of "diffuse, enduring solidarity" might be similarly structured. As a first step, he argued that we must distinguish "the pure domain of kinship" which "has as its defining element a single symbol, coitus" from the "conglomerate domain of kinship" that is "the system of person-defined statuses" (Schneider 1969:70).

If we consider only the "pure" domain of kinship and treat this as a system of diffuse, enduring solidarity, it seems possible that what is called "nationality" and "religion" are defined and structured in identical terms, namely, in terms of the dual aspects of relationship as natural substance and relationship as code for conduct, and that most if not all of the major diacritical marks which are found in kinship are also found in nationality and religion. (Schneider 1969:70)

If this hypothesis is valid, Schneider proposed that

> ... it might well be that at the level of the "pure" domain, religion, nationality and kinship are all the same thing (culturally), and that their differences arise through the kinds of combinations and permutations they enter into with other "pure" domains, and at the level of the "conglomerate" domain. (Schneider 1969:71)

My musings on this provocative hypothesis have led me to appreciate both its promise and its limitations. Its limitations reside in its unabashed structuralist commitment to the generative power of a pure cultural domain of meaning unaffected by the ways in which people enact historically situated social relations. Its promise lies in its challenge to the conventional model of society as a functioning whole in which different social functions are performed by different institutions, each of which, in turn, is structured by its respective cultural system of meaning.

This essay explores the promise of Schneider's hypothesis about the common structure of meaning underlying kinship, nationality, and religion in our society by tracing the narrative of "Asian American History" to the multiple fields of contested meanings and social relations that have shaped it. Unlike Schneider, my aim is not to identify parallels in the structures of meaning of cultural domains isolated from social action in hopes of discovering the pure domain of culture underlying them all. Rather, I am interested in understanding the historically situated social process through which ideologies of nation, gender, ethnicity, kinship, and social class have generated dilemmas of national allegiance and class alliance for Asian Americans who, in turn, have produced an Asian American historical consciousness.

The Diversity of Asian American Experience

An appreciation of the pedagogical dilemmas entailed in teaching Asian American history courses requires an understanding of what those people generally classified as Asian American do and do not share. Any review of the history of immigration from Asia to the United States in the nineteenth and twentieth centuries reveals the linguistically and culturally diverse backgrounds of Asian Americans and their different historical experiences in the United States.[2]

Roughly speaking, there have been two major periods of Asian immigration to the United States: the period from 1840 to 1930, during which the immigrants came predominantly from China, Japan, and the Philippines;[3] and the period from the late 1960s to the present, during which the immigrants have come mostly from China, Korea, and Southeast Asia (Vietnam, the Philippines, Cambodia, Laos).

In the earlier period, first Chinese and later Japanese and Filipinos were recruited as workers by U.S. capitalists seeking sources of cheap labor for enterprises in Hawaii and on the West Coast. Chinese immigrant men worked initially in the mines and railroads of California as well as on the sugar plantations of Hawaii. When anti-Chinese sentiment and legislation stopped the flow of immigrants from China, Japanese were recruited. For both groups, a general movement out of working-class laboring jobs to service occupations occurred over time, with a significant proportion of the immigrants becoming self-employed, small-scale entrepreneurs—in other words, petty bourgeoisie. After World War II, which was a particularly devastating experience for Japanese Americans who were imprisoned in what were euphemistically called "relocation camps," employment opportunities improved and both Japanese and Chinese Americans experienced considerable occupational mobility. The second, third, and fourth generation descendants of the original immigrants moved into predominantly white-collar, managerial, and professional occupations, with a smaller percentage remaining entrepreneurs. By the mid-1970s, as a group Japanese and Chinese Americans had attained a higher median educational and occupational level than the White population. The Filipino immigrants, who came in the 1930s, were not as socially mobile and instead remained in working-class service jobs.

The second period of Asian immigration to the United States began with the revision of U.S. immigration laws in 1965. Since then, the flow of immigrants from Asian countries has increased; at the same time the Asian American population has become increasingly diverse. Preliminary figures released by the U.S. Census Bureau indicate that the U.S. Asian and Pacific Islander population now numbers over 7.3 million people—a 108 percent increase over the past decade. Although Chinese Americans (23 percent) are still the largest ethnic group among Asian Americans, followed by Filipino Americans (19 percent); Japanese Americans, who thirty years ago constituted 52 percent of the Asian American population, now make up only 11.7 percent of it. According to the *Japanese American National Library Bulletin,* the fastest growing groups are Vietnamese, Indians, and Koreans (1991:4).

As a consequence of this history of immigration, Asian Americans today range from sixth-generation Chinese Americans to recently arrived Vietnamese and Chinese immigrants. The economic and class diversity among Asian Americans is as great as their cultural diversity. The descendants of the earlier immigrants are by now a more homogeneous group characterized by the high educational, occupational, and income levels cited above. The members of the later immigrant group are more heterogeneous; while many are concentrated in unskilled service occupations, others are petty entrepreneurs or professionals. For the most part, however, it is the more recent immigrants who are engaged in the working-class occupations pursued by the immigrant ancestors of today's fifth and sixth generation Asian Americans.[4]

The Emergence of Asian American Studies

In light of their diverse cultural, linguistic, and national backgrounds and their equally diverse current social class positions, it is not surprising that Asian Americans have not formed a unified social movement or political lobby. Some individual ethnic groups of Asian Americans have formed viable and politically effective community organizations.[5] The history of geopolitical relations among China, Japan, Korea, the Philippines, and the United States, however, impeded political alliances among the various Asian American communities until the late 1960s, when the first attempt to forge such an alliance was made. The impetus for this alliance came from the Asian American student movement, which emerged out of the widespread student political activism of the 1960s (the antiwar movement, the Black-power movement) and demographic history (the coming of age of a large group of middle-class, third and later generation Chinese and Japanese American college students).[6] The most tangible result of this movement was the funding of courses on Asian Americans and, eventually, Asian American Studies programs at several universities and colleges on the West Coast, where the bulk of the Asian American population has concentrated.[7]

From its inception, Asian American Studies has been a self-consciously political and pedagogical practice aimed at raising the ethnic consciousness of Asian American college students.[8] Courses on Asian American history have occupied a central place in that practice. By teaching students about their "collective past," the instructors of these courses have created a historical memory that, like all histories, carries with it ideas about the past and the present and their meaningful connection.

It is not surprising that history courses constitute the core of Asian American Studies, as they do in all ethnic studies programs. Blu has argued that the increased emphasis on ethnicity in North American society has brought an increased concern with historical matters. "History, as perceived by both insiders and outsiders is at the core of ethnic identification" (Blu 1980:215). It is not a frill, but rather lies at the "heart of a symbolic structure of ethnicity in the U.S." (215). A wide range of symbols from many domains, including food, music, kinship, language, religion, and even race, can represent ethnic diversity. But all of them are deemed to share a link with a group's past. In other words, people's ideas of how their present experience, social location, and orientation are to be understood in relation to their past and future ones play an important role in shaping identity and politics.

In its most powerful moments, Asian American History courses constitute a resistant cultural practice (Williams 1977) that explicitly challenges the hegemonic narrative of "American History." It points to the omission of Asians, as well as to the history of race and class oppression they have experienced, in the grand narrative Americans are taught about how "we" became to be who "we" are today. Yet, like all histories, Asian American History is itself a selectively constructed narrative through which a collective historical memory is created that renders the present meaningful in terms of the past. The excavation of the "buried past" constructs Asian American historical experience and with it Asian American ethnic consciousness. In short, Asian American History does for an ethnic group what American History does for the nation. Perhaps because Asian American History entails a critique of dominant national ideologies such as the claim of equal opportunity, little attention has been paid to the ways in which ethnic histories themselves render invisible some kinds of experiences and meanings in the name of forging unity out of diversity. But, just as nationalisms "mold diverse realities within their uniform message" (Kapferer 1988:4), so do ethnic identities constituted by ethnic histories.

In the following section, I examine the narrative structure and content of "Asian American History" as it was being taught in the late 1980s in several major universities on the West Coast.[9] I recognize the risk in undertaking a critical analysis of these courses, because it could be misinterpreted (or misused by some) as an attack on Asian American Studies as a legitimate field of scholarship. This is *not* my intention. On the contrary, my hope is to contribute to the strengthening of scholarship and pedagogy in Asian American Studies by sharpening the critical dialogue within the field about the theoretical and political implications of the narrating of Asian American History.

All histories, after all, are incomplete and selective narratives. All are written by people situated within fields of culture and power.[10] Critical analyses of the production of history can give us invaluable insight into the politicocultural issues faced by collectivities of people, whether they constitute themselves as a nation, race, gender, social class, ethnic group, religious group, or diaspora.

Asian American History as Pedagogical Practice

While some variation exists among introductory courses in Asian American History, there is a high degree of uniformity as regards the topics covered, the periodization of time, the linkage between periods and topics, and the core required readings. The usual chronological sequence of topics begins with the mid-nineteenth–century Chinese immigration experience. Students are introduced to the international and domestic political economy that shaped Chinese labor migration and the discriminatory laws passed to control Chinese immigration, prohibit naturalized citizenship and racial intermarriage, and restrict the movement and enterprises of immigrant Chinese. The violent racism of the nineteenth-century anti-Chinese riots, which led to the concentration of Chinese into segregated Chinatowns, is described, as is the symbolic violence committed by that era's virulent racial stereotypes of Chinese.

Courses then move on to Japanese immigration at the end of the nineteenth century. Here again the initial experiences of the first-generation immigrants are presented within the context of the political economy of labor immigration and the discriminatory legislation against Japanese. The early labor history of Japanese Americans as agricultural workers is followed by coverage of their uprooting experience during World War II, when all Americans of Japanese descent on the West Coast were imprisoned in concentration camps. Following this, attention in most courses shifts to the Filipino immigrants who arrived during the depression years and, in particular, to their experiences as migrant workers on the West Coast.

During the post–World War II period, the focus is on the new immigrants (in particular the Southeast Asians), their problems of economic and social adjustment, and their need for social services. Courses commonly include a section on the resurgence of anti-Asian racism in the 1980s, often linking it to resentments spawned by the increased flow of Asian immigration and by the expansionist success of Japanese business.

Between the pre–World War II past of the early immigrants and the post-1960s present of the new ones, occasionally there is sandwiched a brief section on the social-class mobility of third-and later-generation Chinese and Japanese Americans. It is notable that a discussion of the "model minority myth"—which casts Asian Americans as the minority whose success affirms the American myth of equality of opportunity—is generally not incorporated into this section on social-class mobility. Instead, the critique of this myth, which is a distinctive feature of all introductory Asian American history classes, is placed either at the beginning of the course, where it is followed by the harsh history of anti-Chinese racism, or at the end of the course, where it is juxtaposed with the precarious situation of the new immigrants.

The chronology of immigration from different Asian countries provides Asian American History courses with a seemingly logical succession of subjects—from Chinese to Japanese to Filipino to Korean and Southeast Asian. In each historical period, a new group of immigrants is seen struggling against the tide of White racism to gain a foothold in the new land. The exception is World War II, when the imprisonment of first-, second-, and third-generation Japanese Americans yields a different drama of racism and struggle for survival.

A concern with "origins" and "ancestors" endows this pedagogical structure, in which each historical period bears the stamp of a single immigrant group, with a compelling narrative logic. It seems commonsensical to ask what was happening to Chinese Americans in the nineteenth century, to Japanese Americans during World War II, to Filipino Americans in the 1930s, and to Vietnamese Americans in the 1980s. But the flip side of this logic makes it appear reasonable *not* to ask what was happening to Chinese Americans during World War II, to Japanese Americans in the 1930s, and to Filipino Americans in the 1980s. As a consequence, an amazingly uniform succession of historical experience—a collective narrative—is constructed out of the diverse histories of Asian American communities.

Even more striking than the degree of uniformity in course content and structure is the agreement as to the core readings in Asian American history courses. In the late 1980s, a small number of books were used so commonly as to qualify as the canonical texts of Asian American history. The three books that almost invariably appeared as required readings were *America Is in the Heart* by Carlos Bulosan (1973 [1943]), *Longtime Californ'* by Nee and Nee (1986 [1972]), and *Pau Hana: Plantation Life and Labor in Hawaii, 1835–1920* by Ronald Takaki (1982).

The first book, *American Is in the Heart*, is the "autobiographical" account of a Filipino American poet, which is more accurately described as a mythic, collective biography of the Filipino men who came to the United States during the 1930s to work as cannery workers, domestic servants, and migrant field laborers. *Longtime Californ'* is a compilation and interpretation of oral histories collected from inhabitants of San Francisco's Chinatown in the early 1970s. These oral histories are organized into three sections according to the distinct societies the authors found existing in Chinatown: the "bachelor society" of immigrant male laborers that predominated in the nineteenth century, the small-business–centered "family society" that developed later in the early twentieth century, and the new immigrant working-class that began to arrive in 1965. *Pau Hana* chronicles the development of the sugar industry in Hawaii and the plantation labor force into which it inducted an ethnically diverse, but predominantly Asian (Chinese, Japanese, Korean, and Filipino), immigrant population.

Together, these three core texts emphasize the working-class past of Asian Americans. The heroic figures of that past are the working-class men who struggled to survive the lean years of hard labor, racist violence, and class exploitation. Although women are not entirely absent, the laboring past has an unmistakably masculine cast to it. I do not mean to claim that materials by and about Asian American women are entirely excluded from courses on Asian American history: All the courses I reviewed included some materials on Asian American women, although there was nothing close to a "gender balance" in them. The readings on women, however, tend to avoid the issue of sexual inequality *among* Asian Americans. Instead, they either present a "woman's version" of the past[11] or they show how Asian American women have been doubly burdened by the racism and sexism of White society. Noticeably absent from the reading list are books such as Evelyn Nakano Glenn's *Issei, Nisei, War Bride* (1986), which discusses sexual inequality and physical abuse by husbands in Japanese American marriages, and articles like Lucy Cheng Hirata's (1979) on the exploitation of Chinese women as prostitutes in Chinatown.

An implicit functionalist theory of adaptation permeates the celebratory narrative of endurance and survival in which people's actions are explained in terms of their instrumental advantages. The effect is the validation of both past and present cultural practices and institutions in Asian American communities. The limitations of such a teleological functionalist analysis, which can do little to help us understand either the emergence or transformation of cultural practices, are well known and need not be rehearsed here. Instead, I want to consider how in the case of Asian American history the tendency to overlook these theoretical limitations is compounded by dilemmas rooted in the representational politics of Asian American Studies.

Acts of Exclusion and Redundancy in Meaning of Asian American History

The pedagogical practice of privileging a masculine working-class past in Asian American History courses molds a uniform ethnic, gender, and social-class consciousness out of more divergent material realities. In one sweep, the experiences of women, farmers (as opposed to farm laborers), and petty bourgeoisie are pushed to the margins of the collective past. That the occupational past of Asian Americans was much more diverse and dynamic than its representation in these courses is documented in a wide range of articles and books, all of which are accessible to college undergraduates.[12]

Lacking, too, is a discussion of the relationship between Asian American social mobility and their economic and political organizations in the post–World War II era. For example, Takaki's book *Pau Hana*, in which Japanese

Americans are one of the key groups in the Hawaiian plantation labor force, is not followed by an account of how second-generation Japanese Americans (Nisei) came to dominate the Democratic Party and state government in Hawaii after statehood. Nor does it discuss the key role they have played in linking U.S. mainland and overseas capital to local real estate development (Cooper and Daws 1985). Likewise, studies of Japanese American agricultural workers in California do not evolve into studies of Japanese American farms and agribusiness, their ethnic business organizations (such as the Nisei Flower Growers Association), and their labor practices (for example, the latter's conflicts with the United Farm Workers Union).

The privileging of each successive immigrant group's earliest social and class experience produces a redundant ethnic history that drowns out different stories and lessons that might be gleaned from other experiences in other periods.[13] Just as an immigrant group or its children begins to experience significant social mobility, Asian American History courses shift their gaze to more recent immigrants. This practice is mirrored in some of the comprehensive volumes on Asian American History recently published. Takaki's *Strangers from a Different Shore: A History of Asian Americans* best exemplifies this narrative strategy. Not only are the first 400 of the 491 pages of his book devoted to the period up until the end of World War II, but the two chapters concerned with the post-war period are devoted primarily to the second wave of recent Asian immigration—those who Takaki labels the new "Strangers at the Gates Again."[14]

Longtime Californ' (1972) would appear to balance this emphasis on the working-class past by devoting equal sections to the three distinct "societies" that coexisted in San Francisco's Chinatown in the 1970s, including the small-business family society. Yet, even these authors construe the memories of the oldest generation of bachelor laborers as the collective past that "is an organic part of the present" and that ultimately causes much of what is observed in the present (Nee and Nee 1986). They do not consider the possibility that there may be *more than one historical consciousness* in Chinatown shaping different, and perhaps even conflicting, ethnic identities. The book's focus on Chinatown also draws attention away from the middle-class and upper-middle–class Chinese Americans who have moved out the original space of the community.

My point is not simply that Asian American Studies courses suppress the histories of social-class mobility and economic success of Asian Americans, but rather that they deny the constitutive character of these experiences. In other words, the past that constitutes Asian American subjectivity—the collective conscience and sense of being and acting in the world—is deemed a working-class one.

The acts of exclusion and redundancy in meaning of Asian American History courses reflect the issues and dilemmas, at once political and pedagogical, that the instructors of these courses feel compelled to address. Not surprisingly, they move to correct the erroneous but prevalent assumption that all Asian Americans arrived at these shores with slide rulers in hand and surplus capital to invest in business enterprises. Most Americans, including some Asian Americans, after all, are ignorant of the working-class history of many Asian Americans and their struggles against class exploitation and racial discrimination.

The redundant narrative and exclusions of these courses, however, signal the social gaps instructors feel they must bridge to construct a unifying and politically mobilizing ethnic identity. One such gap is that between the early and the recent waves of immigrants. The weight given to the working-class past is an attempt by the descendants of the early immigrants, who comprise the predominantly Japanese American and Chinese American instructors of these courses, to bridge the economic and cultural distance between themselves and the recent immigrants from Vietnam, Cambodia, China, Korea, and the Philippines. It is this latter group, after all, that constitutes the contemporary Asian American working-class. In celebrating the laboring past of their ancestors, the college instructors and students link their ancestral past with the present of the new immigrants and thereby construct a shared and seemingly stable Asian American working-class identity.

The second gap Asian American History courses attempt to bridge is both wider and of greater political significance: it is the gap between Asian Americans and other people of color in the United States. Both in terms of their assigned place in the racist hierarchy of essential, biogenetic difference and on the basis of social class, Asian Americans are precariously perched at the margins of this category. Certainly, ample evidence can be marshalled to debunk any claims of uniformity in Asian American economic success.[15] At the same time, however, it cannot be denied that, as a whole, Asian Americans enjoy significantly higher levels of income, education, and occupational status than do African Americans, Chicanos, and American Indians. Two telling indicators of the economic gap between Asian Americans and African Americans, for example, are rates of infant mortality and college attendance. While the former are comparatively high and the latter are low among African Americans, the reverse is true of Asian Americans.[16] Facts like these make strikingly clear the comparatively favorable socioeconomic position of Asian Americans among people of color in the United States.

The emphasis on the working-class past of hardship, struggle, and resistance is an attempt by instructors, many of whose commitment to Asian American Studies was forged in the Asian American student movement of the late 1960s, to challenge the stereotype of Asian Americans as an accommodating model minority striving for acceptance by White society. What is offered in its place is a collective identity of an oppressed but resistant minority that has more in common with other people of color than with White Americans.

One of the dominant themes guiding Asian American student activism as well as other student movements in the 1960s and 1970s was a critique of U.S. imperialism. Asian American immigration and labor history were located within the context of American imperialism and labor exploitation of third-world peoples, both at home and abroad. According to Nee and Nee, the student activists in the San Francisco community in the early 1970s

> feel that as victims of racism and economic exploitation, American Chinese share a similar experience with blacks and other minority groups in the U.S. as well as third world people in Asia, Africa, and Latin America. They see themselves as standing in solidarity with these people and the international workers' movement in a broadly based political struggle against a common oppressor which they have identified as American imperialism. (1986:356)

Emerging as they did out of this student movement, Asian American History courses became the pedagogical practice through which this analysis was inscribed in the collective historical consciousness of students for whom that past had been lost in more ways than one.

The tension between the desire of the founders of Asian American Studies to stand in solidarity with other people of color and the fact that in socioeconomic terms Asian Americans are more like White Americans than African Americans, Chicanos, and American Indians, helps to explain why the attack on the "model minority myth" is a core theme of Asian American History courses. There are, of course, several good reasons for challenging this myth, the most obvious being to refute the claim embedded in the myth that the success of Asian Americans is proof that equal opportunity exists in the United States for all races and, consequently, that those groups which have not been successful are responsible for their own failure. After all, thinly disguised behind the celebration of Asian American achievement in the myth is both the legitimization of White privilege and the reinforcement of racist beliefs about African American failure.[17]

Above all, however, the critique of the "model minority myth" has become an integral practice of Asian American Studies because the myth calls into question the solidarity of Asian Americans with other people of color in the United States. By casting Asian Americans in the category of the successful and, consequently, the advantaged, the myth raises doubts about whether Asian Americans share the same experience and interests with other people of color and—in the context of the academy—makes for the uneasy coexistence of Asian American Studies with other ethnic studies programs.

Asian American Studies has responded to the challenge of the anomalous status of Asian Americans in both "advantaged" and "oppressed minority" categories by displaying Asian Americans' historical credentials as members of the working class. They have done this most effectively through Asian American History courses and their metanarrative of struggle and survival.

The *masculine* character of that working-class past calls for a different explanation. It might be explained in part by the sexism of instructors and by their tendency to privilege male actors. Certainly, one of the histories submerged by the dominant narrative of Asian American Studies is the history of Asian American sexism. Such a history would undoubtedly compromise the heroic stature of Asian American men by casting them as both oppressed and oppressor. This appears to have been the main reason why Maxine Hong Kingston's book *The Woman Warrior* was so strongly criticized by many Asian American Studies scholars when it was first published. Kingston's epic-mythical tale of the liberation of a young Chinese American girl, who is struggling to throw off the binds of a "tradition" that devalues women, hangs out the "dirty laundry" of Chinese American sexism.[18]

The almost exclusive focus on working-class *men*, it should be noted, cannot be explained by the absence of working-class women in the Asian American past. Asian American women, after all, have labored as farm workers, factory workers, domestic workers (Glenn 1986), and prostitutes (Hirata 1979). No doubt it might be somewhat controversial to identify as the founding "ancestresses" the first working-class Asian women on U.S. soil—namely, the prostitutes; but it would certainly reduce the redundancy of the masculine heroic narrative.

Yet a blanket charge of sexism and chauvinism is both too simple and too general an explanation of the androcentrism of Asian American History courses. I suggest that it is more illuminating to trace the marginalization of women to some key dilemmas of Asian American identity. In the following section, I argue that the "woman problem" of Asian American History is in fact an issue that goes beyond gender and lies at the heart of the dilemmas of Asian American identity.

Dilemmas of Asian American Identity

The first of these dilemmas derives from the fact that the only experience shared by all Asian Americans is that of having been assigned an essential character by what Edward Said (1978) has called "Orientalism." Although his concept refers specifically to French and British discourse on the Middle East, it is also applicable to American (and western European) discourse on the Far East—the region that Americans today are most likely to identify as "the Orient." "Orientalism" refers most broadly to a style of thought based upon an ontological and epistemological distinction between "the Orient" and "the Occident," which is the starting point for elaborate theories, epics, social descriptions, and political accounts of the Orient, its people, customs, and destiny. It is the "corporate institution" for making statements about the Orient, authorizing views of it, describing it, teaching about it, and (above all) ruling over it (Said 1978).

Just as earlier British and French discourses on the "Orient" of the Middle East and South Asia erased the cultural differences between societies as diverse as India and Egypt, lumping them together in moral opposition to the "West," so during the nineteenth and twentieth centuries American discourse on the "Orient"—that is, the Far East—asserted a similar dualism. Like French and British discourses, the American one defined the essential characters of East and West in terms that justified the political and cultural hegemony of the West. Whereas the East was portrayed as mired in traditionalism, the West moved boldly ahead in its modernism; where the East respected the authority of fathers and emperors, the West lauded the independence of sons and rational individuals, thus facilitating both the technological inventiveness and the democratic justice of advanced, western industrial society. Finally, whereas the East languished in an unmistakably feminine passivity, the West struck a decisively masculine pose.[19]

Said's critique of "Orientalism" enables us to see that to be labeled an "Oriental" in the United States is to be identified as having origins in a cultural tradition that is supposedly antithetical to that of the West and inferior to it. It was this system of representations and the power relations inscribed in them that student activists in the late 1960s rejected—along with the label "Oriental"—when they redefined themselves "Asian Americans." Naming oneself was an integral part of reappropriating intellectual authority over one's own historical experiences.

The emphasis on the active agency of men in Asian American history is likewise a conscious attempt to challenge the metonymic equation of Asian with the feminine. To celebrate male ancestors characterized by an "indomitable spirit, fiercely hopeful and resilient" (Takaki 1983:178) is to undermine the symbolic equation that East is to West as female is to male.[20] This celebration of fierce resistance is taken the farthest in Carlos Bulosan's book, which recounts several instances in which he had to be forcibly restrained from killing his White humiliators.

The move to restore the masculine dignity of Asian American men unfortunately relies upon, and thus reproduces, one symbolic opposition inscribed with relations of domination for the sake of challenging another. An Orientalist characterization of Asians as "female" and "passive" in opposition to a "male" and "active" West is challenged; but what remains unquestioned is the equation of active agency with men and passivity with women and the logic of male dominance that flows from it. Nor are the disadvantages of this attempt to restore the masculine honor of Asian American men limited to its reproduction of gender hierarchy. As I will show in the next section, it drowns out other accounts that would enhance our understanding of both the past and the present.

The second issue to which I trace the marginalization of women in Asian American History courses is one generated by the demand for exclusive national allegiance from people whose experiences, families, and commitments have often crossed the borders of a single nation-state. The confinement of Japanese Americans in prison camps during World War II was accompanied by the coercive confinement of their allegiance to a single country. First-generation Japanese Americans (who had only Japanese citizenship because they had been barred by U.S. law from becoming naturalized citizens) and their U.S.-born children (most of whom had only U.S. citizenship) were asked to declare exclusive allegiance to the U.S. government and forswear any allegiance to Japan and its Emperor at the risk of deportation. This precipitated both great distress and intense conflict within families. Many second-generation Japanese Americans found themselves in bitter disagreement with parents; siblings chose opposing sides; and the government's segregation of the "loyal" from the "disloyal" Japanese Americans broke up families, some of which never reunited after the war (see Thomas and Nishimoto 1946; Bloom 1947; Kikuchi 1973; and Yanagisako 1985). Following all too quickly upon the heels of this Japanese-American nightmare was the Chinese-American one of the Cold War and the demonization of Communist China.

The demand that Japanese Americans and Chinese Americans confine their political loyalties within the borders of the nation led to a suppression of relations that crosscut national spaces. Not only did World War II and the Cold War cut off the flow of people, goods, and information across national borders but it also stigmatized and silenced talk about relations with people defined as political enemies. This in turn led to the confinement of historical memory to spaces inside the nation. In addition, in the case of Japanese Americans, the government suppression of Japanese-language schools during World War II resulted in the loss of the linguistic means among the third generation of reestablishing those relations and recovering their histories through Japanese texts even after the end of overt political hostilities.

Women, Petty Capitalism, and Transnational Kinship and Community

In spite of its emergence as a counter-hegemonic practice, Asian American Studies has born the legacy of this demand for exclusive national allegiance by including only those people, relations, communities, and institutions located on U.S. soil in its field of study. The marginalization of women is part and parcel of the suppression of a history of transnational relations that threatens to disrupt the narrative of an ethnic history neatly encompassed within the borders of the nation and the working class. Women disrupt these seemingly exclusive, natural boundaries of class, nation, and ethnic identity by signalling the boundary crossings that have occurred.

Two cases will illustrate how the marginalization of women has impeded our understanding of historical processes central to the formation and development of Asian American communities. My discussion of the two cases is necessarily abbreviated; a more complete analysis would require further research and more space than I can devote here. Nevertheless, the two display the connections among women, petty entrepreneurship, and the transnational character of communities. These links are, in turn, crucial to understanding Asian American social mobility.

Japanese American Women and Family Business

In the earliest "frontier period" of Japanese American history, single working-class men constituted the overwhelming bulk of the population. The arrival of women, who came primarily as wives, marked the shift to a family-business economy. Family businesses, however small and labor intensive, were an attractive alternative to the low-paying service and laboring jobs that Whites offered. Consequently, in urban areas many Japanese Americans invested small amounts of capital they had been able to accumulate or borrow into enterprises like vegetable stands, peddling routes, laundries, restaurants, cheap hotels and apartment houses, barber shops, and small retail stores. In rural areas, they moved from being farm laborers to operating family farms.

It is not just historical coincidence that the movement of Japanese Americans from working class to petty bourgeoisie occurred at the same time that the sex ratio in their communities became more balanced. Rather, the arrival of women was a critical part of that transition. The labor of wives—and later of children—enabled men who had been wage earners to eke profits out of small family enterprises.[21] These family businesses constituted the economic base of pre–World War II Japanese American communities and they helped finance the educational pursuits of the second generation.

Transnational exchanges of capital, labor, services, goods, and children were crucial to the establishment and success of Japanese American small businesses. Young children were commonly sent to be raised by grandparents or other relatives in Japan, both to enable their mothers to devote their labor to family enterprises in the United States and to affirm their parents' commitment to households in Japan. Capital from parental households in Japan—although usually small—was sometimes crucial in launching a small enterprise; and siblings, parents, and children flowed back and forth between Japan and the United States depending on the labor needs of households.

Women are, consequently, both the symbol and the material basis of Japanese Americans' petty bourgeois past. Women, families, and small business are all mutually implicated in an entrepreneurial history that Asian American History courses have muted in their celebration of working-class men. Not only does this deny Japanese American women a central role in the history of their communities, but it also denies students the knowledge they need to understand Japanese American social mobility.

Chinese American Women and Transnational Families

In the Chinese American case, the overwhelming predominance of men in the Chinese immigrant population until the 1960s would appear to justify the centrality of men in any Chinese American historical narrative.[22] Where wives were present, the link between women and entrepreneurship was rather different from the Japanese American case. The few women who were brought in as wives were usually married to merchants (Lyman 1968:325). Hence, among Chinese Americans it was not that wives provided labor crucial to entrepreneurship, but rather that men with capital could afford wives and were allowed to bring them from China.

An attempt to recover ancestresses in early Chinese American history might appear to lead only to the prostitutes who were the complement to the "bachelor society" (see Hirata 1979). Granting prostitutes a central place in the narration of Chinese American history would surely be a useful corrective to current practices, not only because it would bring women into the early history of that group, but also because it would open up important topics of inquiry regarding sexual exploitation, entrepreneurship, social class, and the links between them in Chinese American communities.

A history of Chinese American prostitution, however, would not uncover all the women hidden by the androcentrism of Asian American History courses. Above all, it would miss the wives and mothers in China whose key role in Chinese American history has been rendered invisible by a nationalist mode of historiography that ignores the contributions of people outside the borders of the United States.

Books such as *Strangers From a Different Shore* draw empathetic attention to the "lonely [immigrant Chinese] bachelors stranded in a foreign land" and lament the fact that "for the overwhelming majority of Chinese men, the future would not include the possibility of a family in their new land" (Takaki 1989:126). It is well documented, however, that at least half the Chinese "bachelor" population was married and had wives and children in China.[23] Many of these children, especially the sons, came to the United

States as the next generation of immigrants. Lyman, for one, claims that it was common for an immigrant Chinese man "to return to China periodically, visit his wife, sire a child, hopefully a son, and then to return to America alone. Later, these China-born sons would be brought to America and asked to help out in and eventually take over the father's business" (1968:328–29). In some Chinese American communities, family businesses were handed on from one generation to the next despite the geographical dispersal of conjugal families.[24]

Although it is not clear what percent of Chinese immigrant men returned to China and with what frequency, we know enough to conclude that the wives—as well as, most likely, the mothers and sisters "left behind"—played a crucial role in producing the next generation of immigrants and, in many cases, the labor for their overseas husbands' enterprises. They also provided the "homes" to which immigrant men aspired to return, whether or not they eventually did.

For Lyman and O'Brien, as for Takaki, "family groups" did not exist for Chinese immigrants. Yet, I would argue that Chinese male immigrants—whether married or single—did indeed belong to "family groups." These family groups were transnational ones that cut across national boundaries and pursued coordinated economic strategies in spite of immigration exclusion acts. Only a narrow, ethnocentric definition of "family" as the "natural unit" of the conjugal (nuclear) family composed of husband, wife, and unmarried children who live under the same roof blinds us to the existence of families whose members inhabit not only different houses but different countries.[25]

Conclusion

Asian American Studies has responded to dilemmas of national allegiance and class alliance by confining "Asian American experience"—in other words, the collective experiences that constitute Asian American ethnic subjectivity—to locations within the borders of the nation rather than viewing it as a transnational process involving individuals, families, communities, events, and sociopolitical structures that crosscut these borders. Social class, likewise, has been construed as an exclusive, stable position rather than as a historical process often entailing multiple locations. By confining Asian American History within the narrative space of working-class history, the boundaries of social class are stabilized and naturalized along with those of the nation and the ethnic group.

The recognition that national borders do not constitute social borders would open up Asian American History to include a multitude of people, both female and male, who never set foot in the United States but whose lives and labors were integral to the formation and transformation of Asian American communities. Little research has been undertaken on these people, families, and communities, yet such research would prove extremely useful for amplifying our understanding of the transnational context in which Asian American communities have been forged along with modes of entrepreneurship, political organization, and social mobility. It would also offer an opportunity to break out of the restrictive boundaries of a nationalist Asian American historiography. For the exclusion of those people "left behind" is rooted in a model of culture and society that can only reproduce an ideology of the Nation as a fixed, natural unit, even while it challenges its monoracial representation. Setting aside this nationalist ideology would open up a new transnational dimension to Asian American Studies that would enable us to better understand the ways that flows of people, money, labor, obligations, and goods between nations and continents have shaped Asian American experiences.[26]

While the subject of this essay has been Asian American Studies and Asian American historical consciousness, its implications extend beyond the seemingly natural boundaries of one ethnic group to others in our society. The Asian American case, I suggest, is a particular version of a common process through which people make themselves as ethnic subjects by narrating ethnic histories in which ideologies of kinship, nationality, gender, and social class are deeply implicated. The demand of hegemonic nationalism in the United States, like those of other modern nation-states, for exclusive political allegiance from its citizens is rooted in and constitutive of a concept of the individual as the locus of exclusive and stable commitments of diffuse, enduring solidarity. Like ideologies of unilineal descent and monogenetic theories of procreation (see Delaney in this volume), nationalism suppresses the historical memory of those multiple strands of commitments that stray across sacred boundaries, thereby threatening to reveal the historically constructed and contingent character of all human commitments and collectivities.

Notes

Several people have read drafts of this paper and provided invaluable comments and suggestions at various stages of its production. I thank Harumi Befu, Jacqueline Brown, Carol Delaney, Gaylord J. Ferguson, Estelle Freedman, Donald Moore, Peter Novick, Lisa Rofel, Renato Rosaldo, Roger Rouse, Anna Tsing, Karen Yanagisako, and the members of Stanford University's Asian American Studies Faculty Seminar, 1991.

1. In this paper I use the term Asian American History to refer to what is taught in introductory Asian American studies courses and not to the entire subfield of scholarship on Asian Americans. The boundaries of the latter are too difficult to define and, moreover, there is a significant difference between what is presented in courses on Asian American

history and the corpus of published scholarship on Asian Americans. That very difference is what generated this essay.

2. Recent books on Asian American History all emphasize the diversity of Asian Americans. See for example Takaki (1989), Chan (1991).

3. There were, of course, other immigrant streams in the period before World War II, including those from Korea and India (Takaki 1989; Chan 1991).

4. Two qualifications must be appended to this admittedly crude description of the cultural, linguistic, and social class differences between these two groups of Asian Americans. The first is that there is considerable economic diversity within each of the two groups. Among Vietnamese immigrants, for example, the first wave of refugees were better educated and came from higher socioeconomic groups than the second wave (often referred to as "boat people") and the current wave arriving from refugee camps throughout Southeast Asia. Among recent immigrants from Hong Kong, some are middle class while others are wealthy transnational capitalists (Ong 1992). The second qualification is that, depending upon which group of immigrants or their descendants one focuses, Asian Americans can be described as either doing very well economically or doing rather poorly.

5. There are numerous examples of ways in which Asian American groups have mobilized for effective political action, including labor unions, business associations, and citizen groups. The national Japanese American Redress movement, which successfully sought congressional approval of compensation for the World War II imprisonment, is a recent example.

6. Nee and Nee (1986:355) recount the history of the Asian American student movement as follows:

. . . The Third World Strike at San Francisco State College in 1968 was a pivotal event for American Chinese students in the Bay Area. Those who participated emerged with a new awareness of continuing discrimination against racial minorities in America which gave rise to militant anger and a renewed sense of identification with their ethnic community. The tumult at SF State was followed by the Third World Strike at Berkeley in 1969, and the subsequent rapid growth of an Asian American student movement on campuses throughout California. At the university, Asian American movement focused on continued participation in anti-war efforts and the establishment of Asian American ethnic studies programs. At the same time, motivated by a deepened sense of responsibility to their own ethnic community, increasing numbers of students returned to participate in concrete projects there.

7. Almost 40 percent of the Asian American population resides in California (Japanese American National Library Bulletin 1991:4).

8. According to Endo and Wei, "the first goal [of most programs] was related to the socialization of Asian American students and involved increasing their ethnic consciousness and self-awareness" (1988:7).

9. In this quick survey, I examined the course syllabi and reading lists of nine introductory Asian American history courses taught at four West Coast universities in 1988 and 1989 (University of California at Berkeley, University of California at Los Angeles, University of Washington, and San Francisco State University). Each of these campuses has a well-established Asian American Studies program. A more complete study would have entailed observation of class lectures and discussions, as well as interviews with students and instructors. I note that there are already indications that these courses, as well as Asian

American Studies scholarship in general, have begun undergoing a significant transformation for the first time since their inception twenty years ago.

10. This seems the appropriate place to describe my own location as a cultural critic of Asian American Studies. Two points seem most telling. The first is my academic location as a feminist cultural anthropologist who has conducted research and published on the transformative history of Japanese American kinship. Cultural anthropology has not been one of the disciplines central to the development of Asian American Studies. Indeed, there has been almost no dialogue between Asian American Studies and cultural anthropology. Likewise, although I am familiar with scholarship on Asian Americans, my academic location is decidedly outside the field. The second telling point is my family, class, and regional background. I am a third-generation (Sansei) Japanese American who was born and raised in Hawaii. Like the vast majority of Hawaiian Japanese Americans, my grandparents emigrated from Japan at the turn of the century to work as laborers in the pineapple and sugar plantations there. While my paternal grandparents remained on the pineapple plantation and some of their children also worked there, my maternal grandparents (like a significant proportion of their fellow Issei) moved quickly into small business.

11. See, for example, two of the most commonly used books by and about women in these courses: Uchida (1982) and Uchida (1987).

12. Some examples of excluded books are Miyamoto's (1939) sociological study of the predominantly petty bourgeois Seattle Japanese American community in the 1930s; Embree's (1941) ethnography of Japanese American coffee growers and small merchants on the Kona Coast of Hawaii in the 1930s; Loewen's (1971) study of the Mississippi Chinese who were imported as agricultural laborers but quickly became retail store owners (and who strove successfully to change their racial classification from Black to White); and Bonacich and Modell's (1980) book on small business in the Japanese American community before and after World War II.

13. In this sense, Asian American History courses replicate the redundancy in meaning that characterizes nationalism. According to Kapferer,

> It is a feature of nationalism and its totalitarian ideological form that it is highly redundant in meaning; that is, the meaning with which its logic is imbued and in which the very being of its audience becomes reconstituted can threaten to become the totality of meaning for all contexts. In a way, the gathering tide of redundancy in the meaning of nationalist ontology drowns out a hitherto great diversity of meaning. And thus action in a variety of contexts becomes driven, often destructively, in the force of a nationalist logic which has become the only truth. (1988:19)

14. In his response to L. Ling-Chi Wang's (1990:79) criticism of his failure to adequately cover the post–World War II period in *Strangers from a Different Shore,* Takaki argues that his last two chapters present "an analysis of post–World War II developments" and "represent seventeen percent of the book's text" (1990:118). However, these two chapters are primarily devoted to the post-war experience of the new wave of immigrants. When he is not focused exclusively on recent immigrants, Takaki is more concerned with debunking the myth of the Asian American "model minority" and documenting the recent rise in anti-Asian racism than he is with describing and explaining Asian American social mobility.

15. A good example of such an argument is Takaki's critique (1990:474–78) of the "myth of the 'model minority'. "

16. As regards infant mortality rates, according to a report by the U.S. Department of Health and Human Services entitled "Health United States 1990," Asians and Pacific Islanders of all ages have the lowest death rates among all ethnic groups, including the lowest infant mortality rates. Compared to the overall infant mortality rate in the United States, which dropped to 9.1 deaths per every 1,000 live births in 1990, the rates of deaths per 1000 for Asian American groups were: Japanese Americans: 6; Chinese Americans: 6.9; Filipino Americans: 7.1. The death rate for Asian American children up to 14 years old was 24 per 100,000, nearly half the rate of Blacks, which was the highest of all groups. As for college attendance, in California, Asian high-school graduates are more than twice as likely as their White counterparts to meet the University of California's academic standards based on high-school grades and test scores (Japanese American National Library Bulletin 1991:3–5).

17. The "model minority myth" also homogenizes Asian Americans and obscures the economic and social problems and racist discrimination many continue to face (Lowe 1991:40).

18. Lowe casts the gender wars in Asian American literature and the attacks by Frank Chin, Ben Tong, and others on Maxine Hong Kingston in the following terms:

> While Chin and others have cast this conflict in terms of nationalism and assimilationism, I think it may be more productive to see this debate, as Elaine Kim does in a recent essay . . . as a symptom of the tensions between nationalist and feminist concerns in Asian American discourse. . . . [I]t is a debate in which Chin and others stand at one end insisting upon a fixed masculinist identity, while Kingston, Tan, or feminist literary critics like Shirley Lim and Amy Ling, with their representations of female differences and their critiques of sexism in Chinese culture, repeatedly cast this notion of identity into question. Just as Fanon points out that some forms of nationalism can obscure class, Asian American feminists point out that Asian American nationalism—or the construction of an essentialized, native Asian American subject—obscures gender. . . . The trope that opposes nativism and assimilationism can be itself a colonialist figure used to displace the challenges of heterogeneity, or subalternity, by casting them as assimilationist or anti-ethnic." (Lowe 1991:33–34)

19. For an especially illuminating discussion of the gendered representation of East and West and international politics, see Dorinne Kondo's (1990) discussion of David Hwang's play *M. Butterfly*.

20. Unfortunately, in the case of some Asian American writers such as Frank Chin, the rejection of an emasculated Asian American image of "sissiness" entails the wholesale adoption of a (White) American cowboy image of manly ruggedness or a tough, aggressive "adolescent sexuality and aggression" (Fischer 1986:211) appropriated from a caricature of Black and Chicano working-class males.

21. For a more complete discussion of the link between the arrival of wives and the emergence of family business in urban Japanese American communities, see Bonacich and Modell (1980) and Yanagisako (1985).

22. According to Glenn, "For most of the period from 1860–1920 the ratio of men to women ranged from 13 to 20 males for every female. As late as 1930 there were only 9,742 females aged 10 or over in a population that included 53,650 males of the same age" (1985:92).

23. According to Glenn (1985) and Lyman (1968:324), it is estimated that over half of the men had left wives behind in China or returned to China to marry and then remigrated back to America without their wives.

24. According to O'Brien,

"A third factor aiding the growth of the Chinese community [in the Mississippi Delta region] was the fact that in many instances the stores were passed from father to son or to some other relative. During the early days the men would leave the Delta region for the trip home where they would be married, have children, and then return alone to the United States. After the boys in the family had been reared and educated in China they migrated to the Delta to take over the stores from their fathers. (1941:388)."

25. See Yanagisako (1979) for a critique of the concept of family in social science literature.

26. For a general discussion of the usefulness of a transnational approach to culture and community see Gupta and Ferguson (1992); for an illuminating analysis of Mexican American transnational communities see Rouse (1991).

References

Bloom, Leonard [Leonard Broom]. 1947. "Transitional Adjustments of Japanese-American Families to Relocation." *American Sociological Review* 12:201–209.

Blu, Karen. 1980. *The Lumbee Problem.* New York: Cambridge Univ. Press.

Bonacich, Edna, and John Modell. 1980. *The Economic Basis of Ethnic Solidarity: Small Business in the Japanese American Community.* Berkeley, CA: Univ. of California Press.

Bulosan, Carlos. 1973. *America Is in the Heart: A Personal History.* Seattle: Univ. of Washington Press. (Originally published 1943. New York: Harcourt, Brace.)

Chan, Sucheng. 1991. *Asian Americans: An Interpretive History.* Boston: Twayne.

Chu, Louis. 1961. *Eat a Bowl of Tea.* Seattle: Univ. of Washington Press.

Cooper, George, and Gavan Daws. 1985. *Land and Power in Hawaii: The Democrat Years.* Honolulu: Univ. of Hawaii Press.

Embree, John. 1941. *Acculturation among the Japanese of Kona.* No. 59, American Anthropological Association Memoirs. Washington, DC.

Endo, Russell, and William Wei. 1988. "On the development of Asian American Studies Programs." In *Reflections on Shattered Windows: Promises and Prospects for Asian American Studies,* edited by Gary Okihiro, et al. Pullman: Washington State Univ. Press pp. 5–15.

Fischer, Michael J. 1986. "Ethnicity and the Post-Modern Arts of Memory." In *Writing Culture: The Poetics and Politics of Ethnography,* edited by James Clifford and George E. Marcus, 194–233. Berkeley: Univ. of California Press.

Glenn, Evelyn Nakano. 1985. "Racial Ethnic Women's Labor: The Intersection of Race, Gender and Class Oppression." *Review of Radical Political Economics* 17(3): 86–108.

———. 1986. *Issei, Nisei, War Bride: Three Generations of Japanese American Women in Domestic Service.* Philadelphia: Temple Univ. Press.

Gupta, Akhil, and James Ferguson. 1992. "Beyond 'Culture': Space, Identity, and the Politics of Difference." *Cultural Anthropology* 7(1): 6–23.

Hirata, Lucy Cheng. 1979. "Free, Indentured, Enslaved: Chinese Prostitutes in Nineteenth Century America." *Signs* 5(1): 3–29.

Japanese American National Library Bulletin. 1991. Vol. 2, no. 4. San Francisco: Japanese American Library.

Kapferer, Bruce. 1988. *Legends of People, Myths of State: Violence, Intolerance and Political Culture in Sri Lanka and Australia.* Washington, DC: Smithsonian Institution Press.

Kikuchi, Charles. 1973. *The Kikuchi Diary: Chronicle from an American Concentration Camp.* Edited by John Modell. Urbana, IL: Univ. of Illinois Press.

Kingston, Maxine Hong. 1976. *The Woman Warrior: Memoirs of a Childhood among Ghosts.* New York: Knopf.

Kondo, Dorinne. 1990. " 'M. Butterfly'—Orientalism, Gender, and a Critique of Essentialized Identity." *Cultural Critique* 16(Fall): 5–29.

Loewen, James W. 1971. *The Mississippi Chinese: Between Black and White.* Cambridge, MA: Harvard Univ. Press.

Lowe, Lisa. 1991. "Heterogeneity, Hybridity, Multiplicity: Marking Asian American Differences." *Diaspora* 1(1) 24–44.

Lyman, Stanford M. 1968. "Marriage and the Family among Chinese Immigrants to America." *Phylon* 29(4): 321–30.

Lyotard, Jean-Francois. 1984. *The Postmodern Condition: A Report on Knowledge. Theory and History of Literature,* Vol. 10. Translated from the French by Geoff Bennington and Brian Massumi. Minneapolis: Univ. of Minnesota Press.

Miyamoto, Shotaro Frank. 1939. *Social Solidarity among the Japanese of Seattle.* Seattle: University of Washington Press.

Nee, Victor G., and Brett de Bary Nee. 1986. *Longtime Californ': A Documentary Study of an American Chinatown.* Stanford: Stanford Univ. Press. (Originally published 1972. New York: Pantheon.)

O'Brien, Robert W. 1941. "Status of Chinese in the Mississippi Delta." *Social Forces* 19 (March): 386–90.

Ong, Aihwa. 1992. "Limits to Cultural Accumulation: Chinese Capitalists on the American Pacific Rim." *Annals of the New York Academy of Sciences* 645: 125–43.

Rouse, Roger. 1991. "Mexican Migration and the Social Space of Postmodernism." *Diaspora* 1(1): 8–23.

Said, Edward W. 1978. *Orientalism.* New York: Vintage.

Schneider, David M. 1968. *American Kinship: A Cultural Account.* Englewood Cliffs, NJ: Prentice-Hall.

———. 1969. "Kinship, Nationality and Religion in American Culture: Toward a Definition of Kinship." In *Forms of Symbolic Action,* edited by Victor Turner, 116–25. Washington, DC: American Ethnological Society, pp. 116–25.

Takaki, Ronald. 1983. *Pau Hana: Plantation Life and Labor in Hawaii, 1835–1920.* Honolulu: Univ. of Hawaii Press.

———. 1989. *Strangers from a Different Shore: A History of Asian Americans.* New York: Penguin.

———. 1990. "A Response to Ling-Chi Wang, Elaine Kim, and Sucheng Chan." *Amerasia* 16(2): 113–31.

Thomas, Dorothy Swaine, and Richard S. Nishimoto. 1946. *The Spoilage: Japanese-American Evacuation and Resettlement.* Berkeley: Univ. of California Press.

Uchida, Yoshiko. 1982. *Desert Exile: The Uprooting of a Japanese American Family.* Seattle: Univ. of Washington Press.

———. 1987. *Picture Bride.* Flagstaff, AZ: Northland.

Wang, L. Ling-Chi. 1990. "A Critique of Strangers from a Different Shore." *Amerasia* 16(2): 71–80.

Williams, Raymond. 1977. *Marxism and Literature*. Oxford: Oxford Univ. Press.

Yanagisako, Sylvia Junko. 1979. "Family and Households: The Analysis of Domestic Groups." *Annual Review of Anthropology* 8:161–205. Palo Alto, CA: Annual Reviews.

———. 1985. *Transforming the Past: Tradition and Kinship among Japanese Americans*. Stanford, CA: Stanford Univ. Press.

Contributors

Phyllis Pease Chock is Associate Professor of Anthropology at Catholic University. She is editor, with June Wyman, of *Discourse and the Social Life of Meaning* (1986), and author of "The Irony of Stereotypes" (1987), " 'Illegal Alien' and 'Opportunity': Myth-making in Congressional Testimony" (1991), and "Culturalism: Pluralism, Culture, and Race in the Harvard Encyclopedia of American Ethnic Groups" (forthcoming). Her current research examines constructions of culture, race, class, and gender in policy making and legislative talk about immigration.

Carol Delaney is Assistant Professor in the Department of Anthropology, Stanford University. She holds a Ph.D. from the University of Chicago (1984), and her primary research interests are gender and religion. Her publications include "The Meaning of Paternity and the Virgin Birth Debate" in *Man* (1986) and *The Seed and the Soil: Gender and Cosmology in Turkish Village Society* (1991). She has just completed a manuscript tentatively titled *Abraham's Trial: Essays on Paternity, Power and Patriarchy.*

Janet L. Dolgin, Professor of Law at the Hofstra University School of Law, is an anthropologist and a lawyer. Her present research concerns the law's response to the changing parameters of the family in the western world. Recently, her work has appeared in *Buffalo Law Review, Brooklyn Law Review, Women's Rights Law Reporter, UCLA Law Review, Georgetown Law Journal,* and *Connecticut Law Review.* Her book, *Reproductive Technology and the Law,* is forthcoming from New York University Press.

Susan McKinnon is Associate Professor of Anthropology at the University of Virginia, where she has taught since 1984. Her research in eastern Indonesia resulted in a book entitled *From a Shattered Sun: Hierarchy, Gender, and Alliance in the Tanimbar Islands* (1991). In addition to her work on Indonesia, she is currently exploring the multiple intersections of American ideas concerning kinship and gender, memory and narrative, and science and law.

Sherry B. Ortner is the Sylvia L. Thrupp Professor of Anthropology and Women's Studies at the University of Michigan. She is the author of *Sherpas through their Rituals* (1978) and *High Religion: A Cultural and Political History of Sherpa Buddhism* (1989). She has coedited, with Harriet Whitehead, *Sexual Meanings: The Cultural Construction of Gender and Sexuality* (1981) and, with Nicholas B. Dirks and Geoff Eley, *Culture/Power/History: A Reader in Contemporary Social Theory* (1993). She is currently completing a book on twentieth-century Sherpa history, tentatively entitled *Sex and Death on Mount Everest,* as well as conducting fieldwork with her high school graduating class on the relationship between ethnicity, class, and "American culture."

Rayna Rapp is Professor of Anthropology and Chair of the Graduate Program in Gender Studies and Feminist Theory at the New School for Social Research. She edited *Toward an*

Anthropology of Women (1975) and co-edited (1994) *Promissory Notes: Women and the Transition to Socialism* (1988); *Articulating Hidden Histories* (1994); *and Conceiving the New World Order: The Global Politics of Reproduction* (1995). She also helps to edit the journal *Feminist Studies* and has been active in the reproductive rights movement and the development of women's studies for over twenty years. She is currently compeleting a book on the social impact and cultural meaning of prenatal diagnoses.

Anna Tsing teaches anthropology at the University of California, Santa Cruz. She is co-editor, with Faye Ginsburg, of *Uncertain Terms: Negotiating Gender in American Culture* (1990) and the author of *In the Realm of the Diamond Queen: Marginality in an Out of the Way Place* (1993).

Kath Weston is Associate Professor in the Social and Behavioral Sciences Department at Arizona University West in Phoenix. She is the author of *Families We Choose: Lesbians, Gays, Kinship* (1990), and a coeditor of *The Lesbian Issue: Essays from SIGNS*. Her recent essays include "Do Clothes Make the Woman?: Gender, Performance Theory, and Lesbian Eroticism," "Requiem for a Street Fighter," "Lesbian/Gay Studies in the House of Anthropology," and "Get Thee to a Big City: Sexual Imaginary and the Great Gay Migration." Her new book, *Render Me, Gender Me: Lesbians and the Power of Representation*, is forthcoming from Columbia University Press.

Brackette F. Williams teaches in the Anthropology Department and the African-American Studies Program at the University of Arizona. Her teaching interests include anthropology of North American and Caribbean communities and their relation to African and Indian communities. Her work appears in such journals as *Annual Review of Anthropology, Cultural Critique, International Journal of the Sociology of Language, The Journal of Historical Sociology, Current Anthropology,* and *Visual Anthropology*. She is author of *Stains on My Name and War in My Veins: Guyana and the Politics of Cultural Struggle* (1991). She has recently completed a manuscript entitled *Just Yesterday Talking to Tomorrow: Studies in Guyanese Ritual, Memory, and History,* and has edited the volume *Mannish Women, Retraditionalized Female Gender, and The Nationality of Domesticity*.

Harriet Whitehead received her Ph.D in Anthropology from the University of Chicago in 1975. Her doctoral research on the Church of Scientology is reflected in her book *Renunciation and Reformulation: A Study of Conversion in an American Sect* (1987). Her subsequent work on gender appears in the collection (coedited with Sherry Ortner) *Sexual Meanings: The Cultural Construction of Gender and Sexuality* (1981). She is currently working on a book on the food rules and eating practices of the Seltaman people of Papua New Guinea and is a visiting teacher at Washington State University.

Sylvia Yanagisako is Professor of Anthropology at Stanford University. She is coeditor with Jane Fishburne Collier of the collection *Gender and Kinship: Essays Toward a Unified Analysis* (1987) and author of *Transforming the Past: Kinship and Tradition Among Japanese Americans* (1985). She is currently writing a book on family firms in the silk industry of Como, Italy.

Index